MAKING MEANING

Bad only
at INPUT

Studies in Print Culture and the History of the Book

Making Meaning

"Printers of the Mind" and Other Essays

D. F. McKENZIE

Edited by

Peter D. McDonald

and

Michael F. Suarez, S.J.

University of Massachusetts Press

Amherst   Boston

LC 2001052473
ISBN 1-55849-335-2 (cloth); 336-0 (paper)

Designed by Jack Harrison
Set in Monotype Joanna by Graphic Composition, Inc.
Printed and bound by The Maple-Vail Book Manufacturing Group

Library of Congress Cataloging-in-Publication Data

McKenzie, D. F. (Donald Francis)
    Making meaning : "Printers of the mind" and other essays / D.F. McKenzie ; edited by Peter D.
McDonald and Michael F. Suarez.
    p. cm. — (Studies in print culture and the history of the book)
Includes bibliographical references.
ISBN 1-55849-335-2 (lib. cloth ed. : alk. paper) — ISBN 1-55849-336-0 (pbk. : alk. paper)
    1. Bibliography, Critical—Social aspects. 2. Transmission of texts—Social aspects.
3. Criticism, Textual—Social aspects. 4. Book industries and trade—Social aspects—Europe—History.
I. McDonald, Peter D. II. Suarez, Michael Felix. III. Title. IV. Series.

Z1005 .M325 2002
010'.42—dc21

                                                                                          2001052473

British Library Cataloguing in Publication data are available.

To Philip Gaskell

in friendship and admiration

Contents

Acknowledgments

The editors have received much assistance from friends and colleagues during the production of this book; it is our pleasure to offer our thanks. Paul Wright, of the University of Massachusetts Press, helped bring this collection into being with estimable professionalism. Michael Winship gave useful advice at an early stage in our work. Michael Turner and Jack Flavell helpfully answered difficult queries about particular essays. Isabel Rivers, Anne Goriely, Zoe and Ben Goriely-McDonald, Matt McKenzie, Robert Darnton, Lesley Higgins, Suzanne Aspden, Antonia Forster, Roger Chartier, Bernhard Fabian, John Horden, Trevor Howard-Hill, David Pearson, David Vander Meulen, Walter Brooker, Joseph Viscomi, and the late Michael Treadwell variously provided encouragement or welcome impediments to our progress. Ian Willison, David McKitterick, Hugh Amory, and Michael Winship generously read the manuscript in its entirety and offered many expert suggestions. Christine Ferdinand graciously provided professional copyediting and gave the project her unflagging support.

This book began to take shape when we proposed to Don McKenzie the idea of publishing a selection of his essays so they might reach a wider reading public. In the months that followed, Don helped us to determine the contents of this volume. Regrettably, he died suddenly in March 1999, before we began to write. Our greatest debt of gratitude is to him, not only because the essays that comprise *Making Meaning* are his, but also because it was Don who first instilled in us a fascination with the fields of bibliography and book history. It was he who first enlivened us to the manifold ways in which meaning may be made.

The ten essays republished in this volume originally appeared in the following collections, journals, or limited editions and are reprinted with permission; the texts follow copy exactly as first printed except for the correction of typographical errors: "Printers of the Mind: Some Notes on Bibliographical Theories and Printing-House Practices," *Studies in Bibliography* 22 (1969): 1–75; "'Indenting the Stick' in the First Quarto of *King Lear* (1608)," *Papers of the Bibliographical Society of America*, 67.2 (1973): 125–30; "Stretching a Point: Or, The Case of the Spaced-out Comps," *Studies in Bibliography* 37 (1984): 106–21; "The London Book Trade in 1668," *WORDS: Wai-te-ata Studies in Literature* 4 (1974): 75–92; "The London Book Trade in 1644," in *Bibliographia: Lectures 1975–1988 by Recipients of the Marc Fitch Prize for Bibliography*, ed. John Horden (Oxford: Leopard's Head Press, 1992), 131–51; "Trading Places? England 1689—France 1789," in *The Darnton Debate: Books and*

Revolution in the Eighteenth Century, ed. Haydn T. Mason (Oxford: Voltaire Foundation, 1998), 1–24; "*The Staple of News* and the Late Plays," in *A Celebration of Ben Jonson*, ed. William Blissett et al. (Toronto: University of Toronto Press, 1973), 83–128; "Typography and Meaning: The Case of William Congreve," in *Buch und Buchhandel in Europa im achtzehnten Jahrhundert*, ed. Giles Barber and Bernhard Fabian, vol. 4 of *Wolfenbütteler Schriften zur Geschichte des Buchwesens* (Hamburg: Hauswedell, 1981), 81–125; "Speech—Manuscript—Print," in *New Directions in Textual Studies*, ed. D. Oliphant and R. Bradford (Austin: Harry Ransom Humanities Research Center, 1990), 86–109 (also published as vol. 20, nos. 1/2 of the *Library Chronicle of the University of Texas at Austin*, 1990); "*What's Past Is Prologue*": *The Bibliographical Society and History of the Book*, The Bibliographical Society Centenary Lecture, 14 July 1992 (Munslow: Hearthstone Publications, 1993), 3–[32].

We would like to thank the News International Fund and the Faculty of English Language and Literature at the University of Oxford for generously supporting the publication of this volume.

P. D. McD.
M. F. S.

MAKING MEANING

D. F. McKenzie, Oxford, ca. 1997

Editorial Introduction

I

Most major scholars make important contributions to their chosen fields; a few transform them. Donald F. McKenzie, "the greatest bibliographer of our time," according to the distinguished Princeton historian Robert Darnton, began the central phase of his scholarly career in Cambridge, England, in 1957 as a student of traditional Anglo-American bibliography, and rapidly became one of its virtuoso practitioners.[1] At the time of his death in Oxford in 1999, he was celebrated not only as a brilliant orthodox bibliographer, but also as the pre-eminent advocate of a new, capacious method of bibliographical investigation rooted in what he termed "the sociology of texts." In effect, he led and fostered the intellectual movement that opened traditional textual and historical bibliography to "the history of the book," a reorientation that attracted both high praise and fierce detraction. The aim of this book is to make readily available a diverse body of McKenzie's writings for the first time and to begin charting the evolution and reception of his revisionist thinking. The eleven essays in this collection, selected in consultation with the author, illustrate the range of McKenzie's scholarly concerns, his intellectual energy, and his mastery of particulars—historical, economic, literary, political, and bibliographical—in service of more comprehensive understandings of how meanings are made.

His scholarly beginnings were inauspicious and controversial. When the initial topic for his Ph.D. thesis proved untenable, the bibliographer Philip Gaskell (to whom McKenzie wished to dedicate these selected essays) suggested that he examine the business records of the Cambridge University Press. Having worked as a printer himself, McKenzie soon realized that the archive of accounts, payment vouchers, and official minutes of the Press for the period 1696–1712, unprecedented in its completeness, provided a unique key to understanding the complex working patterns and conditions of an early-eighteenth-century printing house. The resultant thesis, which focused largely on the economics of book production and the sociology of human labor, was a source of contention in the Cambridge English Faculty, then dominated by F. R. Leavis. To some, it seemed

---

[1] Robert Darnton, "How to Read a Book," *New York Review of Books*, 6 June 1996, 52. A native of New Zealand, McKenzie had already taken his M.A. and taught briefly at Victoria University in Wellington, New Zealand. He returned there to teach for a further twenty years on completing his Ph.D. He spent the final decade of his teaching career (1986–96) at Oxford University as Professor of Bibliography and Textual Criticism.

too remote from the textual and aesthetic concerns central to the study of canonical English literature, yet it was judged so successful by others that McKenzie was awarded not only the degree but also a prestigious research fellowship at Corpus Christi College, Cambridge.

This institutional tension left its mark. The problem of how best to relate the history of book production to the considerations of literary studies was to preoccupy McKenzie for the rest of his career. In the late 1950s, however, his immediate concerns were primarily bibliographical. The evidence he had uncovered—typically dismissed by other bibliographers as "collateral" because it was derived, not from analyses of printed books themselves, but from archival documents about book production—called into question the "scientific" aspirations of the then-dominant "new bibliography." In particular, the complex and unpredictable realities of human labor revealed in the Cambridge papers confounded the idealist assumption that compositors and printers worked according to consistent and rational patterns. The working routines and weekly productivity of individual laborers were, McKenzie found, astonishingly variable. He lost no time in making this known. While still a graduate student, he launched his initial challenge in a robust review of Fredson Bowers's *Textual and Literary Criticism* (1959), the most strident manifesto of the positivist school that had been the prevailing orthodoxy since the days of Sir W. W. Greg. The vagaries of actual printing-house practices, McKenzie argued, introduced "too many imponderables and variables" for bibliographers accurately to infer the detailed circumstances of production from the printed page alone.[2] To test their theories against history, they had to recognize the value of the publisher's archive as important bibliographical evidence.

Over the next decade McKenzie refined and developed this argument with remarkable tenacity. He undertook an extraordinarily ambitious program of editing and publishing primary documentation relating to the actual working conditions and habits of English book trade personnel. In 1961 he published the *Stationers' Company Apprentices, 1605–1640*, the first of three volumes minutely recording the entrance into the trade of compositors, printers, booksellers, binders, and stationers. (When the final volume appeared in 1978, he had documented the early careers of almost ten thousand men and women at work between 1605 and 1800.) In 1966 his two-volume history *The Cambridge University Press, 1696–1712: A Bibliographical Study* appeared, winning great acclaim. Based on his thesis, this authoritative work comprised not only a meticulous presentation of the documentary record, but also a thorough analysis of the economic, social, and bibliographical details of book production at a crucial juncture in the history of the oldest press in the English-speaking world. Though his next substantial publication, *A Ledger of Charles*

---

[2] D. F. McKenzie, review of *Textual and Literary Criticism*, by Fredson Bowers, *The Library*, 5th ser., 14, no. 3 (1959): 212.

Ackers, Printer of "The London Magazine" (1968), co-edited with J. C. Ross, provided further primary material for the study of the trade, his Cambridge volumes inevitably attracted the greatest praise and the most intense controversy.

Some critics—John Sutherland, for example—subsequently questioned whether McKenzie's "fanatic reverence for precise notation of the publishing historical fact" did not provoke labors of "Sisyphean inconsequence."[3] Others doubted if his principal conclusion about the unsystematic nature of "concurrent production"—that parts of many different books were typically printed simultaneously on several presses—applied to non-academic printing houses in London. With the publication of "Printers of the Mind" (1969), however, McKenzie unassailably established the broad application of his earlier arguments. Using a wide range of evidence, including the business ledgers of the London printers William Bowyer and his son, he convincingly demonstrated that "concurrent production" and the variability of work habits it necessarily entailed were predominant characteristics of printing-house operations in seventeenth- and eighteenth-century England. Moreover, in answer to those who questioned the value of his "staggering diligence," he showed that "collateral evidence" about printing house practices, when allied to rigorous analysis, could transform the premises of bibliographical inquiry.[4] Once the working habits of actual laborers were revealed, it became clear that most bibliographical arguments tacitly depended on fictive "printers of the mind," imagined constructs that bore no relation to the human agents of history. McKenzie's "reverence" for historical facts, together with his openness to the uncertainties they bred, called positivist theories of bibliographical analysis permanently into question.

II

In the 1970s McKenzie continued to advance his revisionist project by developing new methodologies for studying the history of English book production. In "The London Book Trade in 1668" (1974), he expanded the idea of "concurrent production" to embrace the extant annual output of English printing houses, a synchronic method he went on to use again in subsequent single-year studies (most notably in "The London Book Trade in 1644"). This innovative but highly demanding investigative technique enabled him to rethink established ideas about censorship in the seventeenth century and to demonstrate the usefulness of book-trade history for political studies. At the same time, he began to redirect his scholarly energies. Using his Sandars Lectures, "The London Book Trade in the Later Seventeenth Century," delivered in Cambridge in 1976, he called for "a new concept of 'text'" and "for a fuller acknowledgement of the historical rela-

---

[3] John Sutherland, "Publishing History: A Hole at the Centre of Literary Sociology," *Critical Inquiry* 14 (Spring 1988): 584–85.

[4] Sutherland, "Publishing History," 584.

tionships between trade and text."[5] One reason for this new turn was that a large project—his edition of William Congreve's *Complete Works*—gradually led him to realize that the theoretical precepts of contemporary textual criticism were inadequate to his undertaking. Specifically, the time-honored distinction between textual variants which effect meaning and those which do not (significant "substantives" versus inconsequential "accidentals") ran counter to his insight that the book may best be understood as a comprehensively expressive form in which every textual and material detail contributes to the significance of the work as a whole. McKenzie enlarged on this crucial notion in "Typography and Meaning: The Case of William Congreve" (delivered 1977, published 1981), his first major statement on the relationship between bibliographical forms and meaning. Against reductionist theories of the text, held in different ways by both literary and textual critics, he insisted that "text," as a purely verbal form, does not exist. The reader, critic, or editor can only ever encounter particular, materially embodied, and historically mediated textual *instances* that inevitably bear traces of the complex economic, social, political, aesthetic, and bibliographical circumstances of their making. This principle had, he believed, far-reaching implications, not only for notions of textuality, but also for conceptions of reading, editing, and authorial intention. Accordingly, McKenzie proposed that the meaning of a book is not the product of the author's intentions alone, but of the intentions and actions of all the agents involved in its production and reception.

Once again, McKenzie's radical questioning of established orthodoxies attracted as much criticism as support. While recognizing "how essential a knowledge of typographic and book-trade history is to editors," G. Thomas Tanselle, the leading exponent of the Bowers school of textual criticism, took issue with McKenzie's social conception of intentionality: "In many—no doubt in most—instances," he contended, "one cannot accommodate both the private wishes of the author and the collaborative product of the publishing process simultaneously."[6] Rejecting McKenzie's belief that "current theories of textual criticism" are "quite inadequate to cope" with the book as an expressive form, Tanselle insisted that "actually there is no theoretical problem on this score at all," maintaining that McKenzie "makes no case . . . for the necessity of what he grandiosely calls 'a new and comprehensive sociology of the text.'"[7] For scholars not preoccupied with Anglo-American debates about editorial theory, however, McKenzie's new concept of the text had an immediate and enduring appeal. In 1991 the prominent French cultural historian Roger Chartier declared that

[5] D. F. McKenzie, "The London Book Trade in the Later Seventeenth Century," unpublished typescript of the Sandars Lectures for 1975–76, 54.

[6] G. Thomas Tanselle, "Historicism and Critical Editing," *Studies in Bibliography* 39 (1986): 17. For some of Tanselle's further criticisms of McKenzie, see G. Thomas Tanselle, *Literature and Artifacts* (Charlottesville: Bibliographical Society of the University of Virginia, 1998), esp. 280–84 and 302–5.

[7] Tanselle, "Historicism," 17–18.

"Typography and Meaning" has "become a classic." In his view, it "teaches a number of lessons":

> Against the abstraction of the text, it shows that the status and interpretation of a work depend on material considerations; against the 'death of the author,' it stresses the author's role, at the side of the bookseller-printer, in defining the form given to the work; against the absence of the reader, it recalls that the meaning of a text is always produced in a historical setting and depends on the differing and plural readings that assign meaning to it.[8]

Others, too, recognized that McKenzie's theory of the text had implications far beyond the editing of Congreve. As Robert Darnton had earlier affirmed, McKenzie's "remarkable study" demonstrated that the "design of a book can be crucial to its meaning"; hence, the "history of reading will have to take account of the ways that texts constrain readers as well as the ways that readers take liberties with texts."[9] Indeed, McKenzie's arguments, as appropriated by Darnton and Chartier, were crucial in helping to effect the turn away from quantitative, macrohistorical methods of traditional French book history to a new-style *histoire du livre* of the 1980s and 1990s emphasizing readers, materiality, and meaning.

III

"Academic bibliographers of the 1950s and 1960s . . . generally conceived their rôle to be the creation of authoritative editions as the necessary basis for a literary criticism responsible to an author's words and most likely meaning," McKenzie observed in his programmatic essay, "History of the Book" (1992).[10] While acknowledging that "reporting the bibliographical evidence about [the text's] physical construction and readings remains one highly important function of the discipline," he insisted that bibliography could no longer be considered merely the servant of textual editing. "Since bibliographers have much more to tell from their knowledge of the making and use of books," he suggested, "such a focus now seems too narrow to meet the changed needs of critical enquiry in the academy."[11] McKenzie's reconception of the bibliographical enterprise, grounded in his use of new evidence, his formulation of new questions, and his development of new methods, constituted the basis of what he termed the "sociology of texts," a revisionist concept articulated most fully in two major publications of the mid-1980s: his presidential address to the Bibliographical Society (London), *Oral*

---

[8] Roger Chartier, *On the Edge of the Cliff: History, Language, and Practices*, trans. Lydia G. Cochrane (Baltimore: Johns Hopkins University Press, 1997), 85. Chartier originally made these remarks in his foreword to *La bibliographie et la sociologie des textes* (Paris: Éditions du Cercle de la Librairie, 1991), the French edition of McKenzie's 1985 Panizzi Lectures.

[9] Robert Darnton, *The Kiss of Lamourette* (London: Faber and Faber, 1990), 132, 183.

[10] McKenzie, "History of the Book," in *The Book Encompassed*, ed. Peter Davison (Cambridge: Cambridge University Press, 1992), 299.

[11] Ibid.

Culture, Literacy, and Print in Early New Zealand: The Treaty of Waitangi (1984), and the in-augural Panizzi Lectures, *Bibliography and the Sociology of Texts* (1986).[12]

Although their concerns were widely divergent, both works took the primacy of the material artifact as their starting point. In the Waitangi study, McKenzie re-constructed the history of the treaty, made in February 1840, in which forty-six chiefs of the indigenous Maori people surrendered their lands to the British Crown—or so the colonial authorities believed. Exposing the gulf between an imperial culture, which privileged the written word, and the native oral culture, McKenzie revealed how both parties brought contradictory understandings of writing and its authority to the agreement they signed. For the Maori, who had lived with scribal and printed texts—imposed by the British—for just twenty years, genuinely binding pledges and promises could be made only orally, in ac-cordance with long-established traditions. For the colonizers, however, the act of signing a written document alone conferred legal authority. McKenzie's essen-tially bibliographical argument had profound implications not only for New Zealand's understanding of its national past, but also, more generally, for com-prehending the social, cultural, and political history of colonial encounters. The 1840 treaty, as well as the misunderstandings it engendered, demonstrated that forms of textual transmission strongly determine their varying status and inter-pretations. Bibliography, capaciously imagined and catholic in its interests, could, he showed, cast new light on a decisive episode in the history of colonialism.

Extending the role of bibliography was the dominant preoccupation of the Panizzi Lectures. While again insisting on the indispensability of the material ar-tifact—his first lecture focused on "the book as an expressive form"—McKen-zie used the occasion to reassess the aims and scope of the discipline in accor-dance with changes in late-twentieth-century scholarship. Three developments were, he believed, particularly salient for bibliographers. First, they needed to recognize and address the challenges posed by non-book and even non-verbal texts—including maps, music recordings, films, and computer-processed data. (He considered this last "textual form" more fully in "What's Past Is Prologue" [1992], and the complex interaction of communicative modes in his 1990 study "Speech—Manuscript—Print.") The ideal of comprehensiveness underlying this mandate also informed his attitudes to the acquisition and retention policies of national libraries, as witnessed in his 1988 unpublished consultation paper for the British Library, "Our Textual Definition of the Future." Far from being a source of anxiety, these new media for storing and transmitting texts should, he thought, stimulate creative engagement among bibliographers and librarians alike. Second, pointing to the growing emphasis in the academy on questions of dissemination and reading, McKenzie underscored the importance of historical bibliography—the study of "the social and technical circumstance of text pro-

[12] Both works have recently been reprinted in D. F. McKenzie, *Bibliography and the Sociology of Texts* (Cambridge: Cambridge University Press, 1999). This edition also contains a very useful revised and expanded introduction by McKenzie.

duction"—as a source of cultural history.[13] The bibliographer's task was no longer simply to create scholarly editions in strict accordance with authors' intentions but also to bear witness to the multiplicity of textual forms and the proliferation of their meanings as works are re-edited, re-produced, and re-read. Third, in an effort to foster "a fruitful response to recent developments in critical theory and practice" and most particularly in editorial theory, he gave his fullest expression to the idea that the forms of texts affect their meanings. Although he affirmed that "each version has some claim to be edited in its own right, with a proper respect for its historicity as an artefact," he also recognized that in many cases the "variety of authorised forms has opened up editorial choice in new ways, even to the point of creating, through conflation or more adventurous forms of adaptation, quite new versions" that had never before existed.[14] Once again, the bibliographer was not merely a servant but also a critical and creative agent in the process of textual transmission.

IV

Some scholars police the boundaries between academic disciplines; others redraw them. Whenever he seemed to have reached "the border between bibliography and textual criticism on the one hand and literary criticism and literary history on the other," McKenzie decided that "no such border exists."[15] For many of his critics, this was, at best, an ingenious tactical maneuver or, at worst, irresponsible, wishful thinking. McKenzie's "global conception of sociology," argued the eminent Harvard bibliographer Hugh Amory, "turns bibliography into a game without rules."[16] The highly respected Trevor Howard-Hill forcefully asserted that "the theories and principles which underlie literary, dramatic, musical, etc. criticism are *essentially* not bibliographical and a common implication in texts does not make them so."[17] At the same time, McKenzie's work to help create "the history of the book" and "the sociology of texts" from the foundations of traditional bibliography won many adherents within the tradition of Anglo-American textual studies and in other disciplines as well. Most notably, his understanding of the "book as an expressive form," first articulated in 1977, was endorsed by Jerome J. McGann, whose *Critique of Modern Textual Criticism* (1983) has exercised considerable influence in the United States.[18] As we have discussed, Robert Darnton and Roger Chartier championed McKenzie as part of their own

[13] McKenzie, *Bibliography*, 1.

[14] McKenzie, *Bibliography*, 2.

[15] McKenzie, *Bibliography*, 23.

[16] Hugh Amory, review of *Bibliography and the Sociology of Texts*, by D. F. McKenzie, *Book Collector* 36, no. 3 (1987): 413.

[17] T. H. Howard-Hill, review of *Bibliography and the Sociology of Texts*, by D. F. McKenzie, *The Library*, n.s., 10, no. 2 (1988): 158.

[18] McGann, writing in the persona of a fictional colleague "Anne Mack," later expressed the opinion that McKenzie was "confused in argument" and derided his "politicizing of scholarship." It should be remembered, however, that Mack is merely a fictional interlocutor in a Platonic dialogue and does not

transformation of French *histoire du livre*. Indeed, the new-style "history of the book" that emerged in the 1980s was, in many respects, the result of a multinational convergence of scholarly interests which McKenzie himself did much to initiate and promote. Other scholars have successfully applied his principles in fields as diverse as the Renaissance history of science and nineteenth-century feminist cultural history.[19] In 1989, along with Ian Willison and David McKitterick, McKenzie was instrumental in conceiving and launching the *Cambridge History of the Book in Britain*, a multivolume study inspired by Roger Chartier and Henri Jean Martin's four-volume *Histoire de l'édition française* (1982–86). It is in this project, and in similar enterprises in the United States, Canada, the Republic of Ireland, Australia, and New Zealand, that McKenzie's legacy—both as "the greatest bibliographer of our time" and as a driving force in creating the new discipline of book history—is most clearly visible.[20]

---

represent McGann's own position in propria persona. See Jerome J. McGann, *The Textual Condition* (Princeton: Princeton University Press, 1991), 154.

[19] See, for instance, Adrian Johns, *The Nature of the Book: Print and Knowledge in the Making* (Chicago: University of Chicago Press, 1998), and Laurel Brake, *Subjugated Knowledges: Journalism, Gender, and Literature in the Nineteenth Century* (Basingstoke: Macmillan, 1994). See also Adrian Johns, "Science and the Book in Modern Cultural Historiography," *Studies in History and Philosophy of Science* 29, no. 2 (1998): 167–94.

[20] The first volume of the seven-volume *Cambridge History of the Book in Britain* to appear (vol. 3: 1400–1557) was published in 1999 (Lotte Hellinga and J. B. Trapp, eds. Cambridge University Press).

Part One
BIBLIOGRAPHY

1

Printers of the Mind: Some Notes on Bibliographical Theories and Printing-House Practices

This essay was a response and a provocation. Although McKenzie's magisterial two-volume study *The Cambridge University Press, 1696–1712* (1966) was widely recognized as a pioneering contribution to printing history, many doubted whether his exemplary analysis of the day-to-day workings of a printing house was applicable beyond the local circumstances of a small scholarly press in the early eighteenth century. "The main question is whether the practice of this one house has universal application for the era of hand-printing," opined the eminent bibliographer Paul Morgan (*Modern Language Review* 63 [1968]: 194). Did McKenzie's findings apply to commercial presses? Did they apply to London firms? McKenzie's most immediate aim in 1969 was to extend his argument and analysis beyond Cambridge in response to these questions. When in 1963 David Fleeman discovered a cache of business records belonging to William Bowyer and his son—an extraordinarily comprehensive account of a large London printing house spanning most of the eighteenth century—McKenzie saw his opportunity. The working routines of compositors and pressmen in the large London operation, he proved from the Bowyer papers (and other sources), were even more complex than in Cambridge. The fundamental principle of concurrent production, where compositors and pressmen alike were working simultaneously and in unpredictable patterns on a diverse range of books, applied to virtually all book manufacture.

Even before the reviews of his Cambridge study appeared, however, McKenzie had begun to recognize that the principle of concurrent printing—which he discovered in the Cambridge records was a standard practice—introduced radical uncertainties that undermined many of the methodological and epistemological foundations of analytic bibliography. Convinced that the sustaining "scientific" assumptions of the "New Bibliography" in the 1950s and 1960s bore little relation to the historical realities of printing-house practices, he set about replacing orthodox bibliographers' "printers of the mind" with real pressmen and compositors whose endlessly variable working habits challenged presuppositions about the orderliness necessary for so many significant bibliographical "proofs." This was the provocation. Pseudoscience had to give way to historical fact; analytic bibliography had to open itself to the sociology of human labor. With this, arguably the most influential of his essays, McKenzie established his own "uncertainty principle," which was as far-ranging in its consequences for analytical bibliography as Heisenberg's was for quantum physics.

I

IN RECENT YEARS we have all come to recognize the need for what might be called 'scientific' investigation in bibliography, a phrase which at its best implies, as Professor Bowers has succinctly put it, a strict regard for certain fixed bounds of physical fact and logical probability.[1] The achievements resulting from such a concern are clear and important. In descriptive bibliography we have gained a new, accurate and rational vocabulary, and formulae that are both economic and unambiguous. In analytical bibliography—with which I am principally concerned—we have been taught to use the critical tools of comparison and analysis in a new way; and the importance of establishing press variants by collation, of detecting setting by formes, of distinguishing between compositors by spellings or impressions by press-figures is no longer questioned. Scientific bibliography, complete with its laboratory aids, has become a new orthodoxy.

Yet, as T. S. Eliot puts it, *All our knowledge brings us nearer to our ignorance*. In the very act of opening our eyes to new and exciting possibilities, our discoveries raise fresh problems of understanding and breed an awareness of our limitations. In particular, the detailed relation of analytical bibliography to the editing of seventeenth- and eighteenth-century texts depends upon a number of assumptions about printing-house conditions that are only now beginning to be tested. Indeed, if I were to give this paper an epigraph, it might well be that quoted by Sir Karl Popper from Black's *Lectures on the Elements of Chemistry* published in 1803: "A nice adaptation of conditions will make almost any hypothesis agree with the phenomena. This will please the imagination, but does not advance our knowledge."[2] Our ignorance about printing-house conditions in the 17th and 18th centuries has left us disastrously free to devise them according to need; and we have at times compounded our errors by giving a spurious air of 'scientific' definitiveness to our conclusions.

There has of course been nothing morally reprehensible in this, for 'scientific' in such a use has meant little more than an honesty of method in respect to the physical phenomena available for study.[3] As in the physical and natural sciences,

---

This paper was originally given in a very much shorter form as a lecture at the University of Illinois, the University of Virginia, and the University of California (Los Angeles) in May 1963. In revising it I have tried to take account of more recent work but I am very conscious of the injustices I am doubtless doing to those whom I quote out of context. May I plead lack of space and offer the reflection that although methodological discussion has a way of seeming unfair to those criticised, it's only a form of intellectual house-keeping, dependent upon and tributary to the greater work of others? Mottos for the day might be: "Profound truths are not to be expected of methodology" (Sir Karl Popper) and "Methodology is at best a short-cut for the inexperienced" (R. C. Bald).

[1] *Textual and Literary Criticism* (1959), p. 115.

[2] Quoted at p. 82 of *The Logic of Scientific Discovery* (Harper Torchbook edition, 1965).

[3] Bibliographers' use of the word may be consulted at the following points: W. W. Greg, *Collected Papers*, ed., J. C. Maxwell (1966), pp. 76, 220–3; R. B. McKerrow, *Prolegomena for the Oxford Shakespeare* (1939), pp. vi–viii; R. C. Bald, "Evidence and Inference in Bibliography," reprinted in *A Mirror for Modern Scholars*, ed. Lester A. Beaurline (1966), pp. 2–3; Fredson Bowers, *On Editing Shakespeare* (1955), pp. 41, 95, 99, 124; *Textual and Literary Criticism*, pp. 70, 81, 96, 100–1, 115; *Bibliography and Textual Criticism* (1964), pp. 72, 74, 90; J. Hazel Smith, "The Composition of the Quarto of *Much Ado about Nothing*," SB, XVI (1963), 10.

at least in their more elementary stages of observation and classification, it has, as I have indicated, simply meant placing the stress in the first instance on a finite number of particulars and drawing a conclusion from them. And since bibliographers very rarely have anything to work on but the physical evidence of the books themselves it has seemed only natural that any methodology should work within these limitations and seek its exactitude by describing and relating only the observable facts of the paper and the marks it bears.

Some distinguished bibliographers, it is true, have had their doubts. R. C. Bald remarked that "whatever bibliography may or may not be, it is not an exact science, if one understands by an 'exact' science a branch of study which arrives at its conclusions through experiment and observation and can reproduce the conditions of an experiment so that the results can be repeated and checked at any time" ("Evidence and Inference," pp. 2–3). And R. B. McKerrow, late in life and writing more particularly of textual criticism, made much the same point and added the comment that "Nothing can be gained, and much may be lost, by a pretence of deriving results of scientific accuracy from data which are admittedly uncertain and incomplete" (*Prolegomena*, p. vii). It is this last point which I wish to take up.

The effect of Bald's suggestion that bibliography "cannot claim for its conclusions the same universal validity as belongs to those of the exact sciences" is simply that we should rest content with a very different order of certainty but take the precaution of scrutinizing more frequently than we do the procedures of bibliographical scholarship. McKerrow's comment, however, runs far beyond his intention and offers a radical criticism of the very bases of all knowledge inductively derived. It is not that bibliographical inquiry differs in any essential respect from 'scientific' inquiry as described, but that the method common to both is itself logically unsound. Bibliography, as it happens, is a convenient area in which to demonstrate its unsoundness.

For whatever the short-term advantages, to assume, as we have been asked to do, that analytical bibliography must be empirically based, and to limit our knowledge to that which may be derived by inductive inference from direct observations, is to invite the obvious objection that no finite number of observations can ever justify a generalization. Bertrand Russell remarked that so far as he could see induction was a mere method of making plausible guesses. "It is far from obvious, from a logical point of view," writes Sir Karl Popper, "that we are justified in inferring universal statements from singular ones, no matter how numerous; for any conclusion drawn in this way may always turn out to be false: no matter how many instances of white swans we may have observed, this does not justify the conclusion that *all* swans are white" (*Scientific Discovery*, p. 27). David Hume had made essentially the same point: "Even after the observation of the frequent conjunction of objects, we have no reason to draw any inference of any object beyond those of which we have had experience."[4] And more graphically

---

[4] *Treatise of Human Nature*, Book I, part iii, sec. 12.

the Lilliputians' ignorance is ironically exposed: "Besides, our histories of six thousand moons make no mention of any other regions than the two great empires of Lilliput and Blefescu."

Nor is it simply that there is no logical way of arriving at general truths from the examination of sampled cases. To observe at all is to bestow meaning of some kind on the thing observed; to gather particular pieces of evidence is to seek those relevant to some preconceived notion of their utility.[5] But the main point is that any general laws derived by the inductive method remain highly vulnerable to fresh evidence. Where the known particulars are few, this risk will be greatest.

The inductivist in all subjects may of course freely admit that *incompleteness* is almost invariably a characteristic of his evidence and that his conclusions may therefore be subject to modification when new evidence comes to hand. Looked at in this way the inductive process carries a burden of assumed truth waiting to be converted into proven error: knowledge, that is, comes with the act of disproof. And until that moment arrives we may be offered conclusions that lay claim only to some degree of 'reliability' or 'probability,' based on reasonable assumptions about the comprehensiveness of the evidence used and about the predictability of past or 'normal' examples into the future.[6]

Even such a qualified attitude, however, is still inadequate to the demands of bibliography. For one thing, I doubt that 'normality,' in any serious and extended sense, is a meaningful concept.[7] For another, even granting the inductivists' case, I doubt whether bibliography has yet either the body of documentary evidence or the fund of experimental proof necessary to bring most of its conclusions

---

[5] The point is neatly made by Robert K. Turner, "Reappearing Types as Bibliographical Evidence," SB, XIX (1966), 198: "hypothesis is essential to observation." Professor Hinman has a relevant paragraph: "When I first learned from the indisputable evidence furnished by individual types that the Folio was indeed set throughout by formes rather than by successive pages, I was probably as much surprised as anyone else. But should I have been? To *prove* setting by formes required evidence not adduced before; but not to have suspected it sooner was to have failed to see facts—or at least the probable implications of a complex of related facts—that had long been staring us all in the face, so to speak." The point is made "in order to suggest a not unimportant general principle of bibliographical investigation"—*Printing and Proof-Reading of the Shakespeare First Folio* (1963), I, 50–51.

[6] The difficulties created by limited criteria are indicated by Antonin Hruby in "A Quantitative Solution to the Ambiguity of Three Texts," SB, XVIII (1965), 153–4; and Professor Bowers warns of the inadequacy and dangers of inferential arguments in "Some Relations of Bibliography to Editorial Problems," SB, III (1950), 54, 57. Professor Bowers' most thorough and challenging investigation of the problem is offered in chapter III of *Bibliography and Textual Criticism*. He suggests three orders of certainty, "the demonstrable, the probable, and the possible" (p. 77), and stresses the importance of "the postulate of normality" as a necessary curb on the number of plausible conjectures that human ingenuity might otherwise devise (pp. 64, 70, 72). See also Hinman, "The Prentice Hand in the Tragedies of the Shakespeare First Folio: Compositor E," SB, IX (1957), 3.

[7] Professor Bowers remarks: "No one can argue that we know all about the printing processes of the past, and it is just as obvious from time to time this postulate of normality has fostered incorrect explanations based on imperfect evidence." (*Bibliography and Textual Criticism*, p. 72). The cautionary note is justified, not because the elementary physical actions of setting, transferring, imposing, inking, proofing, printing from, or distributing type differed from century to century, nor even because the kinds of work and sizes of shops differed, but because the amount of work done and the relations between those performing it differed from day to day. "Normality" in one sense is limited, though within its limitations valuable; in the other sense it doesn't exist.

within a usefully narrow range of probabilities. Under present conditions, therefore, we are tempted either to over-stress the few 'proofs' achieved (by restricting further inquiry to a demonstration of their 'normality' and so asking that new conclusions be consistent with it), or conversely (in the greater number of cases where we have little developed knowledge of the causative conditions) to tolerate any number of 'probable' explanations for the same limited range of phenomena. Neither alternative is a particularly happy one. The first protects us from open-ended speculation by a crippling limitation of the subject; the second, although it characterizes the subject as practised, is rarely capable of conclusive demonstrations.[8]

But there is another way of looking at the whole problem; nor does it involve any question-begging distinctions between bibliography and 'science,' for it applies equally to both. It simply consists in recognizing the present situation of multiple 'probabilities' as the desirable one and regarding them as hypotheses to be tested deductively. I am naturally tempted to it because the productive conditions in early printing houses display an incredible variety which, if it is to be reconceived at all, demands an imaginative facility in devising hypotheses;[9] and also because bibliographers, as a matter of fact, are becoming increasingly concerned to trace processes involving complex relationships less susceptible of conclusive demonstration. More seriously, deductive reasoning (by which a general hypothesis dictates particular possibilities or 'predictions' and rules out others) does offer a sound way to knowledge. Like induction, it is open to logical objection, for no amount of positive evidence can ever conclusively confirm an hypothesis; but one piece of negative evidence, one contradictory occurrence, will conclusively falsify it.

These comments are philosophic commonplaces and stated so baldly must seem slightly naive. Yet they do serve to point quite sharply to the two main directions open to bibliographical inquiry. If bibliographers wish to persist as inductivists then they must diligently search out the historical facts which will alone provide a fairly accurate definition of 'normality' and offer these as a corrective to the logical defects inherent in the method. Alternatively they may confess outright the partial and theoretic nature of bibliographical knowledge, proceed deductively, and at the same time practise a new and rigorous scepticism.

---

[8] "The subject as practised": it could be urged that no science is a disembodied activity, but only the activities of its practitioners, and that it is defined less by its body of commonly accepted knowledge than by the dynamics of difference. Robert K. Turner's "The Composition of the *Insatiate Countess* Q2," *SB*, XII (1959), 198–203, for example, does not offer mechanical demonstration and proof from the physical and inexorable evidence of the printing house so much as a proliferation of unrelated, arbitrary hypotheses to explain away inconsistencies.

[9] May I recall what Greg said of Professor Dover Wilson? "He is of imagination all compact. And imagination, I would remind you, is the highest gift in scientific investigation, even if at times it may be the deepest pitfall" (*Collected Papers*, p. 217). I have myself a pleasant recollection of meeting Professor Dover Wilson in May 1958. "I always believe," he said, "that if you have a good idea you should send it out into the world. If it survives, fine. If it doesn't, then at least you *know* it's wrong." The serious implications of that last phrase are only now beginning to dawn on me.

In fact the nature of 'normality' as so far revealed by historical evidence suggests that the 'norm' comprised conditions of such an irrecoverable complexity that we must in any case adopt the latter course. If the 'scientific' proofs offered in some recent bibliographical analyses of older books were seen philosophically for the conjectures they are, we should I think be nearer the true spirit of scientific inquiry and the humility that always accompanies an awareness of the possibility of fresh evidence and therefore of falsification. The subject would not then be circumscribed by the demand for demonstrable proofs; rather it would be expanded in its hospitality to new ideas and in its search for fresh historical evidence in the service of disproof. Such a method would be, in the best sense, scientific.

In the following section I wish to offer some varieties of fresh evidence. Its main implication is that the very fixity of the physical bounds within which we are asked to work is inimical to the development of a sound methodology—first, because if the stress is laid on 'proof' then the small number of paradigms available to us unreasonably restricts the subject; second, because in the present state of our knowledge the finite particulars with which we must work are too few and therefore permit too many alternative generalizations to be induced from them; third, because the conception of 'normality' as a corrective to the undisciplined proliferation of generalizations misrepresents the nature of the printing process; fourth, because induction is necessarily an inconclusive method of inquiry. The evidence is consistent with my belief that we should normally proceed in our inquiries by the hypothetico-deductive method which welcomes conjectures in the positive knowledge that productive conditions were extraordinarily complex and unpredictable, but which also insists that such conjectures be scrutinized with the greatest rigour and, if refuted, rejected.

II

When the University of Cambridge set up its printing house in 1696, nearly all the records relating to the erection of the building, and then subsequently to its operation throughout the next decade, were preserved. The annual press accounts show clearly the kinds of expenditure involved in running a small printing house; and the workmen's vouchers for composition, correction and presswork, together with the joiners', smiths', glaziers', plumbers', typefounders', fellmongers', carriers', and printers'-suppliers' bills, reveal the week-by-week operations of a printing house in a detail which is, I believe, unparalleled. In addition the Minute Book of the curators of the Press provides direct evidence of printing charges and edition sizes over the period.[10] With such a wealth of primary documentary material it has been a simple matter to construct detailed

[10] The primary records are printed in volume II of my *Cambridge University Press, 1696–1712* (1966).

production charts for the books printed, showing their progress sheet by sheet and recording the exact division of work between different compositors, correctors and pressmen. It has been a simple matter also to offer definitive details on the wages earned and the actual amount of work done by compositors and press-crews, and to construct work-flow diagrams illustrating the disposition and organization of work within the printing house as a whole on all books and ephemera in production over any one period. It must suffice for the moment simply to observe that the patterns which emerge seem to me to be of such an unpredictable complexity, even for such a small printing shop, that no amount of inference from what we think of as bibliographical evidence could ever have led to their reconstruction. To this Cambridge evidence we may now add the invaluable record of work done in the Bowyers' printing house over the years 1730–9. The ledger which records this work is in the possession of the Grolier Club of New York and is to be edited for the London Bibliographical Society by Mr Keith Maslen. The details which it gives of compositors' and pressmen's work, sometimes week by week, also permit the accurate reconstruction of working conditions, whether for one book or for the printing house as a whole. As Mr Maslen has remarked, "Work patterns are more complex at the bigger and busier London house, but in broad outline the picture is unchanged."[11]

Let me now look briefly at our ruling assumptions about the amount of work that a compositor and pressman might get through in an hour, day, or week. On these points, however carefully we qualify it, the evidence such as we have leads us to suppose a maximum setting rate of something like 1000 ens or letters an hour by one man and a printing rate of 250 impressions an hour at full press.[12] Taking each of these figures as averages which allow for imposition, proofing, correction, make-ready, washing and distribution, we may then, to estimate daily production, multiply by twelve to get as totals 12,000 ens and 3000 impressions. Finally, for weekly totals, we multiply by six to get figures of 72,000 ens and 18,000 impressions. These totals, we allow, are probably too high, but translating them cautiously into terms of actual book production, we might say that a quarto of five to six sheets, each containing some 10,000 to 12,000 ens and printed in an edition of 1200 to 1500 copies, would take about a week to produce if only one compositor and one full press were at work on it. Given the conditions mentioned, the logic is impeccable. Nor is it, as a method, foolish simply because we cannot know of occasional human aberrations from these norms. Yet I cannot forbear a quotation from George Eliot's *Daniel Deronda*:

[11] *AUMLA* (May, 1967), p. 109. Dr J. D. Fleeman's discovery of the Bowyer ledger was reported in *The Times Literary Supplement*, 19 Dec. 1963, p. 1056, and some of its details were put to use in his note "William Somervile's 'The Chace,' 1735," PBSA, LVIII (1966), 1–7.

[12] Professor Hinman conveniently summarizes the evidence and offers some very careful qualifications of it in *Printing and Proof-Reading* I, 39–47. Although his method and purposes must in fact assume a norm, he is quite clear about the foolishness of trying to pretend that there may not have been considerable variation from it (cf. I, 46).

Men may dream in demonstrations, and cut out an illusory world in the shape of axioms, definitions, and propositions, with a final exclusion of fact signed Q.E.D. No formulas for thinking will save us mortals from mistake in our imperfect apprehension of the matter to be thought about . . . [and] the unemotional intellect may carry us into a mathematical dreamland where nothing is but what is not.

The Cambridge and Bowyer papers (and they are not the only ones) make it quite clear that wages and therefore output, since the men were on piece-rates, varied considerably as between one man and another. It is not just a matter of occasional lapses or minor disparities to be cautiously conceded; it is a fundamental fact that should radically alter our whole conception of 'norms.' Moreover, any one man's income and therefore his actual output might fluctuate greatly week by week. Taking the Cambridge compositors first, one of them (John Délié) averaged 13s.5d. a week over one period of 59 weeks, and only 9s.9d. over a further period of 80 weeks. Yet on 11 May 1700 he was paid at the rate of £1.6s.8d. a week for setting in two weeks eight sheets of a book which required a daily average of 10,240 ens plus marginal notes. William Bertram averaged 10s.8d. over one period of 78 weeks and 10s. over another period of 47 weeks. Clement Knell and John Muckeus were content to average just over 13s. a week for long periods, and William Great 10s.3d. The only compositor to show sustained application at a high level was Thomas Pokins. His average weekly income over a period of two full years was £1.1s.5d. Yet in the five weeks up to 6 June 1702 he set some 318,000 ens, giving a daily average of 10,600, and his reward for this work was just on £1.7s.11d. a week. To reinforce the implications of these comments on the fluctuations in wages earned, we have only to look at the amount of work actually done in ens per day. Pokins's averages throughout 1702 were 6,307 (not 10,000 or 12,000) ens a day or 37,842 (not 72,000) a week. The next best daily averages for any lengthy period were those of Bertram with 5,700 ens and Knell with 5,603. Often the daily totals were well below these figures, and all of them of course are well below even such an elastic hypothetical norm as 10,000 to 12,000 ens a day. A glance at appendix II (d) below will show a similar variation of performance within the Bowyers' shop. The wages for the two-week period range from as much as £3.15s.0d. to as little as 8s.2d. And this personal variation as between compositors may be paralleled by comparable fluctuations in the amount of work done at various periods throughout the year. Strahan's ledgers, although they do not yield the same detail, also show great fluctuations in the total wages he paid out week by week (B. M. Add. MS. 48,801). And the records of the Plantin-Moretus Museum, the Oxford University Press, and even the "Case-Book" of John Wilson, printer in Kilmarnock in 1803, tell the same story.[13]

[13] I must express my gratitude to Dr Léon Voet, Curator of the Plantin-Moretus Museum, for supplying me with photocopies of entries from the *Mémorial des Ouvriers* for the months of Jan.–Mar. 1622. Dr Voet has brought together much valuable information in "The Making of Books in the Renaissance as told by the Archives of the Plantin-Moretus Museum," *PaGA, X*, no. 2 (Dec. 1965), 33–62. The most relevant Oxford document is a "Bill Book" for the years 1769–72 which I cite by courtesy of the Printer to the University.

Turning now to presswork, we have precisely the same situation. One of the better performances at full press in Cambridge was that of Jonathan Cotton and Robert Ponder during the week ending 24 February 1700 when for £1.4s.6d. each they worked off 10,350 sheets on four different books, averaging well over 3,400 impressions a day. But such figures and therefore such high incomes were quite exceptional. Albert Coldenhoff, working by himself at half press, earned on average 13s.3d. a week over a period of 67 weeks, and other average weekly wages earned by various workmen at half press were, in round figures, 11s., 12s., 15s. and 18s. At full press the average receipts show the same kind of range. If instead of wage bills we again look at the actual amount of work done, we can point to Thomas Green's single-handed production of 8,250 impressions one week, and only 4,750 the next; or to the work of Ponder and John Quinny who printed the following numbers of impressions week by week from mid-June to mid-July 1700: 15,200; 13,800; 9,700; 12,700; 10,700; 17,000 and so on. The hypothetical norm, you may recall, was 18,000.

Well, conclusions? Simply that our hypothetical figures are too high? Certainly that seems to be true, but the implications are I think more far-reaching. One is that we have perhaps failed in our historical sense, too readily imputing our own twentieth-century ideas and interests and the assumptions of our own society—especially our economic assumptions—to men whose attitudes to work were quite different from ours. We cannot afford to disregard contemporary social conditions and pre-Industrial Revolution attitudes. One careers adviser pointed out in 1747 that many pressmen played a great part of the time, and Benjamin Franklin took much the same jaundiced view of the British workman. As one economic historian puts it, "the conditions of life and habits of the people were all against the monotony of regular employment;" and again: "Contemporary evidence indicates that few cared to take advantage of their opportunities." The mass of labourers, said Sir William Temple, work only to relieve the present want.[14] Our society today reacts to the stimulus of high wages because modern society can satisfy a wide range of wants. But if wants don't increase, there is little point in working for anything beyond the bare necessities, and good wages will only suggest to a workman "an opportunity to avoid part of his toil."[15] An anony-

---

John Wilson's "Case-Book" was brought to my attention by Miss Frances M. Thomson who is preparing an edition of it. I should also mention Mr Rollo G. Silver's contributions to this journal, especially "Mathew Carey's Printing Equipment," SB, XIX (1966), 85–122, which form a valuable addition to the primary documentation on early printing houses. There is a more general point to be made. Greg, recognizing the level of generality that any respectable discipline must seek, insisted that bibliography comprehend manuscript as well as printed texts. Similarly it might be argued that ancient and modern book production should not be too readily separated. Mr Simon Nowell-Smith has shown in his 1966 Lyell Lectures how more recent books can be usefully (and disturbingly for such concepts as "edition" and "issue") documented from publishers' archives. The growth of such bibliographical work in the modern period will, if the subject is to keep its integrity, enforce a greater realism in discussing the productive conditions for earlier books.

[14] For these references see Cambridge University Press I, 89–92, 139–40.

[15] E. S. Furniss, The Position of the Laborer in a System of Nationalism (1920), p. 234. Furniss remarks that "The English laborer . . . responded, when prices fell or wages rose, so that he could satisfy his wants with di-

mous writer of 1728 makes the point well: "People in low life who work only for their daily bread, if they can get it by three days work in a week, will many of them make holiday the other three *or set their own price on their labour*" (my italics).[16] One of the reasons why Elizabethan printers tried so often to exceed their allowed number of apprentices may have been that apprentices could be commanded to work regularly where journeymen could not.[17] So although we may today think of piece-rates as an incentive, it would seem that in the 17th and 18th centuries they were the employers' best protection from men who had no intention of working any harder than necessary for food and drink. A journeyman's output, that is, was conditioned largely by what he was able or willing to earn. As Moxon revealingly says, "they are by Contract with the Master Printer paid proportionably *for what they undertake to Earn* every working day, be it half a Crown, two Shillings, three Shillings, four Shillings, &c." (my italics). That is, he speaks quite casually of a performance difference of one hundred percent.[18]

The significance of this system of individual contracts—operating as far back as 1631 and even, I would claim, 1591—has I think been overlooked. What it meant in effect was that a workman need work no harder than he had contracted

---

minished effort, by 'keeping holiday the remainder of his time'" (p. 235). The contemporary evidence cited by Furniss is full and detailed. D. C. Coleman, in "Labour in the English Economy of the 17th Century," *Economic History Review*, 2nd ser., VIII (1956), 280–95, points out that modern writers have underrated the recurrent problem of unemployment and comments that half-employment was often the rule. He cites Thomas Manly's note of 1669 that "They work so much fewer days by how much the more they exact in wages;" remarks that this was said of "agricultural workers and of industrial, of urban as well as of rural;" and adds "Irregularity of work . . . was not confined to the working week. The working day at one end of the scale, the working year at the other, were both very different from their counterparts in the modern industrialized community" (p. 291).

[16] *Some Thoughts on the Interest of Money* (1728), cited by Furniss.

[17] Such an argument was in fact used in litigation in 1592 when Benjamin Prince, a journeyman employed by John Legate, said he need only do what he could whereas Parker, an apprentice, had to do as his master bade him. See "Notes on Printing at Cambridge, c. 1590," *Trans. Cambridge Bibliographical Society*, III (1959), 102. The whole question of full or partial employment, however, needs to be related to the evidence we have of journeymen's grievances. It may be that under conditions of widespread unemployment an increase in part-time work is to be expected rather than a severe restriction of the labour force to the few men of highest efficiency.

[18] *Mechanick Exercises*, ed. H. Davis and H. Carter (1958), p. 327; see also p. 328 for the phrase "their Contracted Task." Professor Hinman (*Printing and Proof-Reading*, I, 42–45) considers some of the evidence for daily output at press and case (e.g. the Gay-Purslowe contract of 1631, Moxon, Richardson's figures of 1756, and early 19th-century rates for setting). He clearly considers the figures rather high and suggests that they were not consistently attained. I am sure he is right, notwithstanding abundant evidence elsewhere for high press output—see "Notes on Printing at Cambridge," p. 101 n., where a number of references are collected. Testimonies for 1592 claim 2500 impressions as the normal daily amount worked off for 3s.4d. per press-crew. But it is also stated that under the rules of the London Company a pressman was to have his full contracted wages if on any day, by agreement with the master, fewer sheets were printed. Several 19th-century ones could be added, but Blackwell's estimate of 2500 impressions per day, cited by Mr Rollo G. Silver, is among the most important ("Mathew Carey's Printing Equipment," p. 102). The real point, however, is not that these figures were norms, except perhaps for very large edition quantities, but the accepted maxima. The evidence is consistent with the hypothesis of extreme variability within the limits indicated, but any "norm" derived from the evidence can be repeatedly falsified and its predictive value thereby seriously impaired. It may be noted that Plantin's pressmen and compositors received differential payments, as did those of Crownfield and Bowyer, for formes of varying difficulty, and in 1592 differential rates applied to presswork according to the size of type.

to do, and only if he fell behind his contracted figure and then kept another waiting might he have to make good his colleague's loss of work. It was the master's job to accommodate these variables, not the workmen's. That the master had to make payments and organize production schedules on the assumption that men worked at different speeds is quite consistent with the Cambridge and Bowyer evidence and any other that I have seen; nor is it, so far as I know, inconsistent with any of the classically 'demonstrable' bibliographical proofs. But its consequence—the normality of non-uniformity—is an uncomfortable one for any methodology.

It might be thought that the fluctuations in output which I have noted are—in part at least—to be expected if there were too little material to keep the men working at high capacity week after week, a state of affairs all too likely in a small provincial academic press. Yet, once more, the evidence available shows a similar pattern at other presses. In fact, both the Cambridge and Bowyer records suggest that fluctuations in the volume of work would be reflected more readily in the number of workmen employed than in the actual level of work done by any one man.[19]

Where output varies so markedly from man to man and period to period, any reliance on 'norms' would seem to imply an almost irresponsibly large burden of probable error; polite concessions to occasional departures may serve a while as palliatives but general statements that can be so persistently falsified whenever any concrete evidence appears to test them are poor premises for advanced argument. Moreover, I have for simplicity here dealt mainly in averages; the actual figures are infinitely more varied and any attempt to trace the total complex patterns week by week, even with all the documentary evidence, is like trying to record the changing images of a kaleidoscope in the hands of a wilful child.

So far I have discussed, too, only the most elementary variables, and have left aside all question of edition sizes or the ways in which work was organized. Assumptions about the edition sizes of early books usually take account of the 1587 ordinance of the Stationers' Company which, with one or two exceptions,

---

[19] The point about fluctuations in the number of workmen is admirably made, in the case of Plantin, by the charts in Raymond de Roover's "The Business Organization of the Plantin Press in the Setting of Sixteenth Century Antwerp," *De Gulden Passer*, XXXIV (1956), 104–20. The figures there given show the absolute variations, but in addition the ratios of workmen to presses and of compositors to pressmen may be easily calculated as at January in every year from 1564 to 1589. To take two years: on 4 Jan. 1572 there were 13 presses in use, 23 pressmen, 23 compositors, and 7 other employees; on 2 Jan. 1574 there were 16 presses in use, 32 pressmen, 20 compositors, and 4 other employees. The smaller English shops could not have tolerated this degree of fluctuation, but where the records survive the ratios of compositors to pressmen to presses can be shown to have varied quite markedly. The Cambridge and Bowyer presses illustrate a disturbingly large variance in weekly, monthly and annual levels of production; Strahan's and Charles Ackers' output differed significantly from one year to the next; and the charts given of Oxford printing in F. Madan's *The Oxford University Press: A Brief Account* (1908), although based only on surviving works, are a graphic corrective to an over-reliance on "norms." I know of no direct evidence that obliges us to exempt Elizabethan and Jacobean printers from such fluctuations, although the legal limitation on the number of printers has tempted some to assume continuous output at maximum levels. There is much evidence that some Elizabethan printers constantly lacked work.

forbade the printing of more than 1250 or 1500 copies of any book from the same setting of type, although as McKerrow remarks "we have no certain knowledge of how long or how carefully the rule was observed."[20] And occasionally edition sizes have been related to the bibliographical evidence of skeleton formes, since it is understood "as a general principle that in any book printed on a single press two sets of headlines will appear only if the book was printed in an edition large enough for composition to keep ahead of presswork."[21] For the later 17th century and the 18th century the problem of variability in edition size is acknowledged to be more complex. Yet even in the early 1590's a pressman, Simon Stafford, giving evidence in court, pointed out that the number of sheets printed in any one day might vary considerably, reflecting different edition sizes, since "they had diverse numbers upon Severall bookes and the numbers did alter."[22] At Cambridge in the early 1700's sermons were printed on average in 650 copies, the minimum being 400 and the maximum 1150. But the mean, as distinct from the average, was nearer 500 copies. One book of theological controversy was printed in a first edition of 750; a second edition of 1000; a third edition of 2000; and a fourth edition of 1250. Yet another of the same author's books ran through three editions in the order of 750, 500 and 500; and another was printed in two editions of 1000 copies each. Other figures for edition sizes of books on a fairly wide range of subjects are: 350, 500, 522, 550, 700, 820, 1050, 1150, 1250, 1500 and 3000. Again the Bowyer papers show a similar variation, apparent even in the Voltaire editions cited in appendix II (g). And the same point is made by the edition sizes given in Strahan's and Ackers' ledgers, and more particularly in those I quote both for the part issues of *A New General Collection of Voyages and Travels* and the monthly numbers of *The London Magazine*. Quite apart therefore from these figures invalidating any hypothetical norm (for any particular case, given the degree of variation, would seldom correspond to the assumptions of a guiding hypothesis), the need for a master printer to juggle with such varying totals, as well as the varying abilities of his workmen, reinforces what has been merely hinted at so far about work organization.

Normally in bibliographical analysis we are concerned with a particular book, usually a work to be edited, and that great range of printing which our literary interests have not led us to examine must be largely ignored. This is as it should be for life is short and, as Professor Todd has indicated in a disarmingly amusing note, some books are more valuable than others.[23] But the consequences of such

---

[20] *Introduction to Bibliography* (1928), p. 132.

[21] Hinman, "New Uses for Headlines as Bibliographical Evidence," *English Institute Annual, 1941* (1942), p. 209.

[22] "Notes on Printing at Cambridge," p. 101. See also P. Hernlund, "William Strahan's Ledgers: Standard Charges for Printing, 1738–1785," *SB*, XX (1967), 89–111, esp. p. 104 where the frequencies of certain edition sizes are given. Professor Hinman notes the folly of setting edition sizes to suit bibliographical equations (*Printing and Proof-Reading*, I, 40), but bibliographers sometimes forget that the number printed is a marketing decision which bears no relation whatever to printing conditions, although a master would of course be concerned to apportion all the work on hand in the most economic way.

[23] "The Degressive Principle," *Times Literary Supplement*, 1 Sept. 1966, p. 781.

selectivity cannot be ignored if bibliography, as the study of the transmission of literary documents, is to continue to lay claim to the serious intellectual status that Greg established for it. I shall return to this point. Meantime I wish to look briefly at a very common assumption, though not a universal one, in bibliographical analysis. It is the assumption that even if the whole resources of a house were not directed towards printing the book under examination, at least one compositor and one press-crew would be set to work fairly consistently on it.[24] Under these conditions we might expect five to six sheets a week to be completed.

Again, however, should we not take pause? The occasional prospectus might serve to put us on our guard, for few require printing times of anything like even five sheets a week. And in fact some surviving Cambridge agreements offer delivery times of—as near as matters—one sheet a week. Out of some 36 books of ten or more sheets produced between 1698 and 1705, only 7 were printed at an average rate of more than 2 sheets a week. *Suidas*, the Greek lexicon, was printed at the rate of 3½ sheets a week, and the remainder of this group of 7 books progress on average at a rate of between 2 and 3 sheets a week each. For 14 books the average was between 1 and 2 sheets, and for 15 books it was no higher than a single sheet and often it was less than that. The Cambridge evidence cannot be discounted by noting that some of these books required careful correction, for the evidence from the Bowyer and Ackers ledgers points exactly the same way.[25] Nor does there seem to be any necessarily significant relationship between the total amount of work on hand and the rate of progress for any one book.

The force of these examples is simply that the Cambridge and Bowyer presses, like any other printing house today or any other printing house before them, followed the principle of concurrent production. Obviously the variety of runs gave greater flexibility in the organization of presswork and permitted more economical use of the several sizes of type available; but, however efficiently *total* production was organized, the system inevitably meant that individual books took longer to print than we might have thought likely, just as most books today

[24] I hope it will be agreed without my listing references that such an assumption is widespread. Professor Todd at least agrees, for he once wrote, in iconoclastic vein: "Implicit in most accounts of presswork on hand-printed books is the convenient assumption that, at a given time, the entire resources of the shop are devoted to the production of a single work . . ."—"Concurrent Printing: An Analysis of Dodsley's *Collection of Poems by Several Hands*," *PBSA*, XLVI (1952), 45. Jobbing work may be invoked as a convenient way of explaining apparent delay, but even in Professor Hinman's discussion of the First Folio, which takes some account of other works printed by Jaggard in 1621–3 (see I, 16–24), the fundamental work patterns are traced in isolation from the other work on hand as though the Folio contained in itself all the evidence of its production.

[25] The Bowyer books tabled in appendix II (g) may serve as examples. The several editions of Voltaire were printed quite quickly (nos. 1–4); the 20 sheets of Baxter, a more difficult text, and the 17½ sheets of Spenser, both took 33 weeks (nos. 5 and 6); Lobb's 34 sheets, on the other hand, were finished in only 29 weeks; more direct evidence of the different speeds of work on different books can be seen in appendix II (a)–(f). For Ackers, see *A Ledger of Charles Ackers, Printer of 'The London Magazine'* (1968), p. 19. Few printers, however, were as slow as Nicholas Okes was with one work: in five years he had printed only 6 sheets of a book called *Speculum Animae*—Jackson, *Records of the Court of the Stationers' Company, 1602–1640* (1957), p. 180.

take far longer than the productive capacity of the machinery would lead us to expect.

The important point, however, was made by Professor Todd many years ago. Under conditions of concurrent production, he remarked, "the book is only one of several components in a more extensive enterprise, and thus exhibits only a portion of the information necessary for its analysis. Until the other portions have been located and the various pieces reassembled in the pattern originally devised the puzzle will remain unsolvable" ("Concurrent Printing," pp. 45–6, 56). And again: "in instances of concurrent printing the bibliographer must examine all the books so related before attempting the analysis of any. To do less than this . . . is to learn little or nothing at all." These remarks cannot be repeated too often, but unfortunately Professor Todd's qualifying comments have tended to minimize their application to "the larger establishments of the eighteenth century [where] the facilities were certainly adequate for simultaneous work on several projects, involving, in some instances, independent groups of compositors and pressmen, in others, the same group intermittently employed, first on a few sheets of one book, then on a few of another." And his more immediate concern, the interpretation of press figures, whose "very presence implies unsystematic piecework engaged in conjunction with other miscellaneous endeavours," has also perhaps encouraged the belief that concurrent production may very well have been a feature of large printing houses in the 18th century but not of smaller and earlier ones.[26]

Such a view must be abandoned. No amount of historical quibbling can neutralize the plain facts of the Cambridge documents: an earlier and smaller printing house, never using more than two presses, often one and a half, and occasionally only one, habitually printed several books concurrently. So far as I am aware there is no primary evidence whatever to show that any printing house of the 16th, 17th or 18th centuries did not do likewise.

Our mistake here I think goes back to a misreading of an observation by McKerrow. He remarked that "for a printing house to be carried on economically there must be a definite correspondence between rate of composition and the output of the machine room."[27] Notice how all-inclusive his terms are: printing house, machine room. I should like to offer now two quotations which take their origin in McKerrow, and I should like you to notice how in each case McKerrow's valid general statement is transformed into an invalid particular statement. First, Professor Turner:

> In the Elizabethan printing shops, a cardinal principle of efficient operation was, we suppose, that composition and presswork should proceed at the same rate. If ma-

---

[26] Professor Todd later wrote of concurrent printing as a practice "extraordinary in the seventeenth century" but "commonplace in the eighteenth"—"Bibliography and the Editorial Problem in the Eighteenth Century," SB, IV (1951–2), 46. G. Thomas Tanselle, "Press Figures in America," SB, XIX (1966), 129–30, also writes of the need for fuller information on all books being handled within a shop at one time.

[27] "Edward Allde as a Typical Trade Printer," Library, 4th ser. (1929), 143.

terial could be set into type faster than the press could run it off, compositors had to waste time; conversely, if presswork went faster than composition, the pressmen would stand idle. Given pressmen and compositors of reasonable skill, the chief factor determining the speed of the presswork was the size of the edition . . .

at this point we become involved in a particular statement

. . . and the chief factor determining the speed of composition was the amount and difficulty of the text material to be set into each forme. Ideally one forme ought to be machined in the time required to distribute the immediately preceding forme and to set and impose the next, and in the case of books which got a great deal of text into each forme, as the [Shakespeare] Folio did, this ideal relationship could be approached only if two compositors could set simultaneously.[28]

Professor Hinman asks:

What plan would ensure the most satisfactory ratio between the time necessary to set one forme of the contemplated book into type and the time needed to print off the desired number of copies of such a forme?—for an efficient balance between composition and presswork was one of the prime requirements of successful printing-house operations in the earlier seventeenth century. (*Printing and Proof-Reading*, I, 45n.)

This last is a quite different and seriously distorting assumption: that an economic relationship between composition and presswork is necessary on any one book for the business as a whole to be successful. The position is really so much more complex; indeed the more variables a printer has to juggle—in numbers of compositors and full or half press-crews, in their individual capacities, in edition sizes, in the number of books on hand, and in the demand for ephemera— the more chance he has of making them compatible and therefore of making his business as a whole economically successful.[29]

　　Such a conclusion is not inconsistent with the figures given earlier to demonstrate the variable levels of production achieved by a printing house; they simply reinforce the point that an 'economic' disposition of men and materials could only be achieved complexly—and that the fine considerations of timing implied by many studies devoted to the analysis of a single work may be a world away from the reality. Relax the time scheme ever so slightly, and a whole house of bibliographical cards comes tumbling down. In particular the correlations often traced between edition size, number of compositors, skeleton formes and presses, must look very different if translated to a context of concurrent printing. But I anticipate.

　　If concurrent production was much the most efficient way of running a printing house, as distinct from the most efficient method of producing a single

---

[28] "Analytical Bibliography and Shakespeare's Text," *MP*, LXII (1964), 55.

[29] Stower, *The Printer's Grammar* (1808), p. 376, makes the point: "Compositors and pressmen are at all times dependent on each other; they therefore demand the *constant attention of the overseer* [my italics] in order that nothing may occur to cause a stoppage or standing still to either party." In a smaller office this concern for oversight and disposition of the work on hand would naturally have been the master's.

book, how then, under these conditions, was work apportioned? What kind of range does a compositor's work, for example, show week by week? Although it was by no means rare at Cambridge for a compositor to have a monopoly on any one book, the work was usually shared. Of a sample of 118 Cambridge books, only 50, or 42%, were set by a single compositor; and if we except very short works like sermons, the percentage drops to 24. Moreover it was unusual for a compositor to work for any long period on one book to the exclusion of all others—usually he would be setting type for two or three concurrently. Of the 13 compositors whose work for Bowyer over a two-week period early in 1732 is recorded in appendix II (d), only *one* was engaged on one book alone.

Undoubtedly the main considerations determining the allocation of work were simply a compositor's freedom to do it and the availability of type. If a compositor had no other work on hand he would be transferred to any that might be offering and for which type was available. For normally, even when two or more compositors worked on a book, they did not work together setting sheet and sheet about. What usually happened was that one took over where the other left off and then composed as many sheets as the master found convenient or as other commitments allowed. A quarto edition of Virgil may be cited to make the point. Bertram set sheets A–E, then Crownfield took over and set F–3R, next Michaëlis set 3S–3Z, Bertram then resumed setting, continuing to 4F, Délié was brought in to set 4G, Crownfield took over once more with 4H and finally, after Crownfield had retired at 4O, Bertram set to 4R and finished off the book. Although four compositors were involved, and although Crownfield worked on two sections of the book and Bertram on three, on no occasion were any two men setting simultaneously. Nor incidentally would it be true to say that they were setting alternately. And it would certainly be quite wrong to assume that work was divided so that the book might be printed more quickly. Meantime of course each Cambridge compositor was also concurrently engaged on some other book or books.[30] In appendix II (g) examples 2 and 4, Bowyer's two English editions of Voltaire, show the same pattern of work. Whereas the printing house printed, and individual compositors normally set, several works concurrently, the composition of any one book would therefore usually be a simple matter of progression from sheet to sheet, or from one group of sheets to another, by consecutive compositors. It follows that the compositorial pattern within any such book will rarely offer adequate evidence in itself of the productive conditions but will have been determined by, and will reflect the exigencies of, the general pattern of work in the printing house as a whole over a period of months or even years.

Turning now to the other half of the equation—presswork—we must again affirm that the most efficient disposition of work, given the variables to be rec-

---

[30] See Table 11, *Cambridge University Press*, I, 106–7. For Bowyer, see appendix II (e) where, of 14 compositors listed for the two-week period, only one (C. Knell) worked on a single book.

onciled, could be achieved only by a highly flexible system. As with composition, the actual manner in which work was apportioned to the men would have depended in part on the number of men employed and the amount of work on hand. But regardless of the size of the plant it seems unlikely that a particular press consistently served the compositor or compositors setting a particular book. At Cambridge, it is quite clear, any press-crew might get any sheet of any book to print off, and consequently it was rare for any book of more than two or three sheets to be printed solely at one press. The production tables for books printed at Cambridge show quite conclusively that the use of two press-crews was a perfectly normal procedure and had nothing whatever to do with increasing the speed of production. If a forme was ready for printing, it went to whichever crew was ready to take it, although usually it seems that a sheet would be printed and perfected by the same crew. The position in the Bowyers' shop is much more complex, for it is clear that formes, not just sheets, might be sent to any press which happened to be free and that any sheet might well be printed at one press and perfected at another. Again the Voltaire and Baxter examples in appendix II (g) make it plain that this practice was very common.

In a large shop the distribution of work is likely to be more complex simply because there are more routes open for a book to take; but in both large and small shops there is such strong evidence of fluctuations in the number and strength of press-crews that a pattern of work must very often reflect such changes too. At Cambridge there was considerable variety in the number and composition of the press-crews, ranging from half press only during the first half of 1699, to full press only during the second half of the same year and a good part of 1700, and various combinations of half and full press during other years. Only for a brief period in 1701 were two full presses in operation simultaneously; but we find (unexpectedly, for the usual arrangement we might think would be for the two men to work together at a single press) two half presses at work during 1705, 1706 and part of 1709. There were frequent changes in the composition of the crews during the period from 1699 until early 1702. In later years the normal arrangement—if you will permit the term—was one full press and one half press. But the varying patterns make it extremely difficult to assume a norm. So too in the Bowyers' shop: 3 presses were in use between 24 Dec. 1731 and 15 Jan. 1732; 4 between 17 Jan. and 29 Jan.; 4 (but only 3½ crews) between 31 Jan. and 12 Feb.; 5 between 14 Feb. and 26 Feb.; and 6 (but possibly only 4 full and 2 half crews) between 28 Feb. and 18 Mar. (Just to complicate matters further for the analyst, press no. 7 was in use throughout the whole of this period and the press figure 7 appears on some of the sheets which it printed, but at no time were there as many as seven presses in use.)

So a press-crew, just like a compositor only more so, would usually be working on several books at a time, with "All work to be taken in Turn, as brought to the Press, except in such Work as may require Dispatch, or the Compositor will want

the Letter . . .".[31] The simplest way of using the crews most efficiently was not to
try to maintain a strict relationship between a particular compositor and a particular press—the varying edition sizes and varying output of the men would have
made this very difficult—but, given the presswork which was offering, to apportion it so that each crew always had something to go on with. This was the easiest
way of accommodating the varying runs required for the different books in production at the same time. In thinking otherwise we may also have under-estimated
the flexibility of the common press itself as a machine. Each press had several
friskets, ready cut to common formats. It was a very simple matter to change them
over; and since the sheets were printed wet on a sopping tympan, the type bit deep
into the paper and careful make-ready was unnecessary—certainly it did not need
the care of the modern kiss-impression. Technically there was no reason therefore
why the press should not work to a number of compositors setting several different books, perhaps within one day, certainly within one week.

It is more than time now for us to reunite the two halves of McKerrow's equation—the 'rate of composition' and 'the output of the machine room.' We have
seen that, both at Cambridge and in the Bowyers' shop, books were produced
concurrently. This meant not only that several books were in production at the
same time but that each workman, whether at press or case, was often engaged
on several books more or less at once. If we are correctly to reconstruct the detailed operations of a printing house—even a very small one—or a true account
of the printing of any one book, we must therefore do it in a way that shows the
complete pattern of work in its full complexity.

The diagrams given in appendix I (a) and (b) are an attempt to do this. They
show precisely how all work on hand at Cambridge was allocated between
26 Dec. 1701 and 28 Feb. 1702 and convey some impression of the flow of
work.[32] Again I am tempted to quote George Eliot and say that the sheets seem
to follow only what she calls "the play of inward stimulus that sends one hither
and thither in a network of possible paths." *Suidas*, an exceptional case, demanded
the almost undivided attention of four compositors working in pairs on each
volume; and Crownfield, Bertram and Pokins spread their work over two to three
books each. When we look at the distribution of work to the different press-
crews, we note that with one exception every compositor or pair of compositors
sent work to both presses; and, moreover, that the work composed during these
weeks was in many cases printed by any of four different press-crews. If we take
a single book—*Psyche*, either volume of *Suidas*, or Whiston's *Short View*—the point
to be made is much the same, that the various sheets of any particular book were
likely as not printed at more than one press. The details given for the Bowyer

    [31] Rules of a London chapel in 1734, printed by Ellic Howe, *The London Compositor* (1947), p. 31.
    [32] The two charts may be compared to those given as Table 15 in *The Cambridge University Press*. Taken to-
gether, the five charts show completely different patterns of work at five distinct stages of a continuous
working period of five months, although many of the men and books involved are the same.

shop in appendix II (a) to (e) cover two distinct periods: first, from 26 Dec. 1730 to 6 Feb. 1731, and second, from 31 Jan. to 26 Feb. 1732. Their testimony in witnessing to the disposition of work is consistent with that of the Cambridge records but the relationships revealed between the several productive units, whether compositors or pressmen, are very much more complex. The information given reveals, for example, the number of *pages* set by each compositor, the edition size, and the number of *formes* printed by each press; in the case of appendix II (a) we can also see the peculiar arrangements between presses 1, 3 and 7 for printing and reprinting the *Defence of the Present Administration*. I take this evidence to be quite conclusive. It shows that the essential procedures for the distribution of work were the same for a larger and later shop as they were for an earlier printing house with only two (or more commonly one and a half) active presses. It shows that although we should doubtless be right to assume—allowing for certain social attitudes and conditions we have mentioned—that composition and presswork *as a whole* were fairly economically balanced, it would be quite wrong to conclude that this balance was either necessary or possible for work on any individual book.

III

The more substantial matters discussed in the preceding section—workmen's output, edition sizes, and the relationship between composition and presswork under conditions of concurrent production—must now serve as a prelude to notes on a number of bibliographical procedures that imply quite different productive conditions. If the evidence of part II withstands challenge, it must I think be held to falsify several current hypotheses. It is not easy to summarize these but the ones I have in mind relate particularly to compositors' measures, cast-off copy, skeleton-formes, proof-correction and press figures.

If one assumes that a compositor usually worked on only one book at a time he would have had no need to alter the measure to which he had set his composing stick. Changes in line measurement within any one book might therefore be taken to indicate an abnormal interruption, after which the stick was reset to a slightly different measure, or the presence of a second compositor.[33] Professor Bowers cites, for example, Bellon's *The Mock-Duellist* (1675) in which sheets B–F are set with a 120 mm measure and sheets G–I with a measure of 121 mm. "In such a book the inference is probably that with sheet G another compositor . . .

---

[33] Bowers, "Bibliographical Evidence from the Printer's Measure," SB, II (1949–50), 153–67, esp. pp. 155–6: "The most elementary and easily discerned cases which can be determined by measurement occur when . . . printing of a book is so materially interrupted that when work is resumed a different measure is inadvertently employed." See also "Purposes of Descriptive Bibliography, with Some Remarks on Methods," Library, 5th ser. (1953), p. 18 n., and "Underprinting in Mary Pix, *The Spanish Wives* (1696)," Library, 5th ser. (1954), p. 248. John Smith, *The Printer's Grammar* (1755), pp. 197–8, suggests other reasons why measures, ostensibly the same, might differ. For Moxon, see *Mechanick Exercises*, p. 203.

took over the work. In general, one is likely to conjecture that any interruption of the printing sufficient to cause a single compositor to adjust his stick again after working on some other book would most likely have been sufficient to cause the skeleton-formes to be broken up . . ." ("Bibliographical Evidence," p. 157). These conclusions must, however, seem misplaced if one begins from a different premise. If we assume concurrent production, for example, then the likelihood of measures reflecting the division of work among compositors will be small. In the first place, production times were too long; and in the second place, compositors working on several books at a time, often in quite different sizes of type, would have had to change their measure constantly. As it happens, these propositions are consistent with the Cambridge evidence, whereas analysis of a few of the Cambridge books suggests that it would be impossible to judge how compositorial work was divided on any of them from the evidence of measures. Not only do the widths of type-pages set by the same compositor vary, but different compositors are often found setting to an identical measure, and interruptions are routine. The general practice inferred from limited physical evidence and the underlying assumption about work method remain mutually consistent, but in most cases they are likely to be quite wrong.

One of the more delicate exercises in advanced analytical bibliography is tracing the pattern of skeleton formes as evidenced by running titles in order to determine the order of presswork and, it might be claimed, the number of presses used. This pattern may be related by a time scale to another showing compositorial stints, or it may of itself be taken to imply a certain number of compositors at work on the book. The relationship indicated between composition and presswork may then be employed as an analytical tool in determining such things as nature of copy, methods of setting, edition size and proofing procedures. Implicit in all such analyses is the fundamental assumption that composition and presswork on a particular book would normally seek a condition of balance. This is a difficult area in which to order the work done while being fair to the arguments of those who have used such evidence; nor am I confident that I fully understand the analytical principles used. But the subject is important and even at the risk of misrepresentation demands discussion.

The pioneer study in the use of headlines, as in much else, was written by Professor Bowers over thirty years ago.[34] The association of sets of headlines with skeleton formes is now so well evidenced that it may be taken for granted, and, as Professor Bowers has also remarked, "the basic principles of the printer's use of headlines did not differ markedly in any period when books were printed by hand."[35] Where a single skeleton was used for both formes of a sheet,

[34] "Notes on Running-Titles as Bibliographical Evidence," *Library*, 4th ser. (1938), pp. 318–22. In 1909 A. W. Pollard had drawn attention to the recurrent headlines in Folio 2 *Henry IV* (*Shakespeare Folios and Quartos*, pp. 134–5).

[35] "The Headline in Early Books," *English Institute Annual*, 1941 (1942), p. 187.

the press was idle while the forme just off the press was being washed and stripped and its skeleton was being transferred to the type pages which were next to be printed. . . . Some printers used two skeletons, each with its own set of headlines. Thus while one forme was on the press, the skeleton was being stripped from an already printed forme and imposed about the type pages next to be printed. Since the transfer of this second skeleton could take place while the press was printing the first, there was no delay at all between the time a forme was removed from the press and the time the new one was planked down on the bed (pp. 188–9).

The phrase 'the press was idle' is perhaps misleading since under conditions of concurrent printing the press would not be 'idle' at all but employed on another book. It has however had considerable repercussions and a great many bibliographical arguments have been constructed on the assumption that this inferred idleness could not have been the norm and must have been avoided in order to secure a balanced relationship of composition and presswork. So Professor Turner: "In order to effect the minimum press delay, the formes . . . would have had to go through the press in the following order . . .".[36] ". . . in one-skeleton work the press was forced to stand idle . . .".[37] "There is every reason to believe that press delays were abhorrent to the 17th-century printer" ("*The Maid's Tragedy*," p. 217). ". . . a compositor would not change from setting by formes to *seriatim* setting without risking a press delay unless he was ahead of his press . . .".[38] ". . . the adoption of one-skeleton printing for several formes, and the resultant press delays . . ." ("*Philaster*," p. 28). "If we assume that two skeletons would have been employed in the most efficient manner . . .".[39] ". . . working on the assumption that composition and presswork could stay more-or-less in balance . . .".[40] ". . . two formes . . . would not have been machined concurrently, for had they been, a delay in presswork would have resulted."[41]

Professor Hinman, however, extended the argument by pointing out that if a book were printed in a very small edition, printing would be so well ahead of setting that a second skeleton would be of little use.

The press will inevitably be obliged to stand idle periodically, waiting for the compositor to get new material for it. In such circumstances, of course, there would be

---

[36] "The Composition of *The Insatiate Countess*, Q2," SB, XII (1958), 202.

[37] "The Printing of Beaumont and Fletcher's *The Maid's Tragedy*, Q1 (1619)," SB, XIII (1960), 201; see also pp. 202, 204, 208 for assumptions about timing.

[38] "The Printing of *Philaster* Q1 and Q2," Library, 5th ser. (1960), p. 22.

[39] *Ibid.* In the article from which the last three quotations are drawn, Professor Turner suggests that "the erratic time-relationship" and therefore the imbalance in the relationship of composition and presswork may reflect variable copy, extra help with distribution, or indicate that "typesetting was attended by serious difficulties"—the textual implications of the latter inference are important.

[40] "Printing Methods and Textual Problems in *A Midsummer Night's Dream*, Q1," SB, XV (1962), 46.

[41] "The Printers of the Beaumont and Fletcher Folio of 1647, Section 2," SB, XX (1967), 37. Another point of view on this whole question of delay is that of A. K. McIlwraith: "It seems that printers . . . were sometimes willing to interrupt their work for quite a slight cause. This in turn suggests that time was not at a premium, and casts some doubt on any argument which rests on the assumption that speed was economically important." See "Marginalia on Press-corrections," Library, 5th ser. (1950), p. 244.

no point in accelerating presswork speed further by the use of two skeletons; for although the use of two skeletons can speed up presswork, it cannot increase composition speed: however many skeletons are employed, the same number of impositions will be required ("New Uses for Headlines," p. 209).

Professor Hinman then suggests that if the edition were a very large one, however, the reverse might be true. Printing would take longer than setting and the pressmen might well seek to avoid delays and restore the balance by using two skeletons. Hence Professor Bowers has subsequently stated that "certain assumptions can be made about the rate of compositorial to press speed and thus about the number of copies printed";[42] and Professor Williams has remarked that "in a small edition press time would be briefer than composition time and the compositor would always be concerned lest he fall behind and so delay his press."[43]

Yet another application was indicated by Professor Hinman when he noted that skeleton formes "have an intimate connection with various possible methods of stop-press correction" ("New Uses for Headlines," p. 222). Applying this principle in a re-examination of the proofing of Lear, Professor Bowers wrote:

> With one-skeleton printing there is nothing for the press to work on when the forme is removed for correction. The most obvious thing to do with two skeletons is to plug this gap by putting the second forme on the press and pulling its proofs so that correction in the type can be made at leisure without further halting the press.[44]

At the same time he offered a succinct restatement of the basic position:

> Two-skeleton printing was an extension of one-skeleton, devised to secure relatively continuous presswork by avoiding the major delay at the press which occurred when a new forme was imposed for printing.[45]

The temporal relationship between composition and presswork here assumed is however capable of many permutations. One might start with evidence of presswork and seek signs of, or infer, compensating adjustments in composition; alternatively, one might begin with some knowledge of the speed of composition and then try to trace evidence of presswork to match. In the first case the

[42] "Purposes of Descriptive Bibliography," p. 18 n. Elsewhere Professor Bowers brings together in a single sentence many of the considerations raised here: "On the evidence of spelling, only one compositor set (*) B–D, but with about half a normal edition-sheet, he could not have kept up with the press and therefore would not have imposed with two skeleton-formes."—"The Variant Sheets in John Banks's Cyrus the Great, 1696," SB, IV (1951–2), 179.

[43] "Setting by Formes in Quarto Printing," SB, XI (1958), 49. The compositor was unlikely to have been "concerned" at the imbalance, since the reason for it (edition size) was none of his making. It is also salutary to observe that the words 'his press,' as in Professor Turner's article cited in note 38, show the unconscious hardening of assumption into self-evident truth.

[44] "An Examination of the Method of Proof Correction in Lear," Library, 5th ser. (1947), p. 29.

[45] Ibid., p. 28. In "Elizabethan Proofing," Joseph Quincy Adams Memorial Studies (1948), pp. 571–86, Professor Bowers added "I feel that this was the major delay which was circumvented and that a certain reduction possible in the time for press-correction was only a minor consideration" (p. 574).

evidence of presswork will almost invariably be in the shape of skeleton formes, although their interpretation may not always be straightforward.

Do they, for example, indicate one press or two? Professor Bowers long ago remarked that "the evidence of running-titles to determine the number of presses is often dubious in the extreme and its application hazardous."[46] And Greg expressed some doubt about the equation of skeleton formes with presses.[47] Yet such equations have been made. Professor Price, writing of *Your Five Gallants*, claimed that "in 1607 [Eld] had at least two presses, as the running-titles . . . show." And again, writing of *Michaelmas Term*, "the series of running-titles seem to imply that at least four presses worked on the book."[48] Professor Bowers: "Since regularly alternating two-skeleton formes produce maximum efficiency for one-press work, the staggered appearance of three skeletons . . . suggests the use of two presses." On this assumption, it becomes possible to observe a "mathematical regularity of transfer between the presses according to a fixed and efficient system"; hence "the three-skeleton pattern . . . is *proof* of two-press printing" (my italics).[49] And again: "The analysis of running titles reveals that two presses printed Q2 [*Hamlet*]," each press being served by a different compositor.[50] It is not surprising then to find others writing of "a normal pattern for two-compositor work in which each man serves a different press."[51] And writing of *The Revenger's Tragedy*, Professor Price noted that the four skeletons present suggest two presses, adding that elsewhere "Eld's pressmen clearly revealed their use of two presses by printing on different stocks of paper."[52]

The attractive simplicity of Professor Bowers' initial proposition about skeleton formes is no longer easy to discern. Nevertheless it has been repeatedly put to use in order to determine also the number of compositors engaged on a book. In an article on the printing of *Romeo and Juliet* Q2, for example, we are told that "variant compositorial characteristics suggest the presence of two compositors"

[46] "Notes on Running-Titles," p. 331. In a later note, Professor Bowers states that "running-titles will almost inevitably reveal simultaneous setting and printing of different portions of a book"—*Principles of Bibliographical Description* (1949), p. 125.

[47] *The Variants in the First Quarto of 'King Lear'* (1940), pp. 48–9.

[48] "The First Edition of *Your Five Gallants* and of *Michaelmas Term*," *Library*, 5th ser. (1953), pp. 23, 28. Professor Price believes that *Michaelmas Term* was printed partly by Purfoote and partly by Allde: "In [its] printing, one skeleton was used for gatherings A and B, two for C–I, one press doing the inner, the other the outer, formes; but for gatherings H and I, the presses twice interchanged the formes" (p. 29).

[49] "Underprinting in *The Spanish Wives*," p. 254. Each press is said to have printed and perfected its sheet with the one skeleton forme.

[50] "The Textual Relation of Q2 to Q1 *Hamlet* (I)," *SB*, VIII (1956), 46. See also "The Printing of *Hamlet* Q2," *SB*, VII (1955), 42.

[51] Cantrell and Williams, "Roberts' Compositors in *Titus Andronicus* Q2" *SB*, VIII (1956), 28. They add: "The book was printed throughout with one skeleton-forme, and so necessarily on one press . . .".

[52] "The Authorship and Bibliography of *The Revenger's Tragedy*," *Library*, 5th ser. (1960), p. 273. Quite apart from the question of skeleton formes, the inference from paper might be queried. It is just as simple to assume that the heaps were told out by the warehouseman (or boy) from alternate bundles as required for each successive signature. Otherwise it must be assumed that each press knew in advance precisely what proportion of the edition it would print and had on hand all the white paper it would need to complete that work.

and are assured that "the *mechanical evidence of presswork corroborates* that suggestion" (my italics). The quarto was printed from two skeletons recurring in regular sequence. The writers continue: "This evidence from running titles can be explained only with great difficulty as accompanying the work of one compositor; but a reasonable explanation may be offered by resorting to the hypothesis of a second press, and *thus of a second compositor*" (my italics).[53] Earlier, Professor Bowers had remarked that "printing by two presses must necessarily require the services of two compositors" ("Bibliographical Evidence," p. 166 n. 13). Again that a "general alternation involving the use of four skeleton-formes is inexplicable for printing with one press; yet if we hypothesize two presses it follows that there must have been more than one compositor."[54] In another case, where only one skeleton-forme was used, "the running-title pattern indicates no second workman."[55] Professor Turner has written: "One skeleton ordinarily means one compositor; two may mean two setting simultaneously . . .".[56] But the clearest example of skeleton formes in relation to composition is offered by *Hamlet* Q2, in which "compositor X served one press and imposed his formes for that press, whereas compositor Y served a second press and, correspondingly, imposed his own distinct formes for that press." These observations led Professor Bowers to remark that "when, as in *Hamlet*, the spelling tests for compositors equate so precisely with what one may conjecture to have been their stints from the evidence of running-titles, we may be somewhat more confident in the future about roughing-out two-compositor work in books on this running-title evidence" ("Printing *Hamlet* Q2," pp. 41–42).

There would appear to be enough flexibility in the principle to allow its reverse application, for, as in the case of *Romeo and Juliet*, two skeletons may become two presses if there is some slight evidence of two compositors (and hence "corroborate" the suggestion that there *are* two compositors). But since compositors have left no skeletons they are less easy to detect than headlines, and there are therefore fewer cases of presswork conditions being inferred from the prior evidence of composition.

By now I hope I have, at the very least, made clear by selection and juxtaposi-

---

[53] Cantrell and Williams, "The Printing of the Second Quarto of *Romeo and Juliet* (1599)," SB, IX (1957), 107, 113–4.

[54] "Shakespeare's Text and the Bibliographical Method," SB, VI (1954), 79.

[55] Cantrell and Williams, "Roberts' Compositors in *Titus Andronicus*," p. 28: "The problem of *Titus* Q2 is further complicated by the fact that in the reprint X and Y did not combine to set their material in a normal pattern for two-compositor work in which each man serves a different press. In fact, the peculiar feature of *Titus* is that there should be a second compositor at all. *The running-title pattern indicates no such second workman*" (my italics).

[56] "The Text of Heywood's *The Fair Maid of the West*," Library, 5th ser. (1967), p. 302. In "The Printing of *A King and No King* Q1," SB, XVIII (1965), 258, Professor Turner had assumed that a single skeleton printing sheets A–F implied one compositor, and that a second skeleton introduced at G implied another, and quicker, one—although apart from signings there were otherwise "no means to distinguish the work of the two compositors" (n. 12). See also Hinman, *Printing and Proof-Reading* II, 522 n. 1.

tion the multiple and often confusingly diverse general statements inferred from the number and order of skeleton formes,[57] and laid bare the fundamental assumptions about desirable ratios between compositors and press-crews. It simply remains to ask how reliable such analyses would turn out to be if tested by analogy (a fair enough procedure, since their authors imply extended application by analogy).

Two Cambridge books may serve: Beaumont's *Psyche* (1702), a folio in fours, and Newton's *Principia* (1713), a quarto (*Cambridge University Press*, I, 126–7, 219–21). To take *Psyche* first, and in particular the quires 2E–2Z which can be related to full work-flow charts,[58] we may observe that the edition was 750; that only one compositor worked on it at a time (Bertram set 2E–2F, 2K–2Q1/2, 2T1/2–2Z; Crownfield 2G–2I, 2Q 1/2–2T1/2); that four skeleton formes were in regular use; and that setting and printing of these 19 quires, or 38 sheets, took about 20 weeks in all (from mid September 1701 to 31 Jan. 1702). All I wish to establish now is the futility of attempting to infer any direct correlation of presswork with these conditions from the four skeleton formes. Two quires set by different compositors (2F–2G), and with identical forme patterns, were both printed at the same full press; two quires set by the same compositor (2K–2L), but with utterly different forme patterns, were both printed by the same half press; two quires set by the same compositor (2O–2P), and with identical forme patterns, were both printed at the same half press; all four skeletons appear in quire 2T, one sheet of which was printed at one full press and the other sheet of which was printed at another full press; all four skeletons appear in quire 2U, one sheet of which was printed at full press and the other sheet of which was printed at half press. And yet if this evidence were not available it would be perfectly respectable to infer that this regular use of four skeletons might mean either (a) a large edition; or (b) two compositors, if not three; or (c) at least one full press in continuous operation.

Newton's *Principia* is a little easier to deal with since it is a quarto, and although there are four skeletons in all, only two of these were in use at any one time. The first printed most outer formes in sheets C–2P, the second most inner formes; in 2Q–2V their roles were reversed. New skeletons were constructed for 2X, one printing all inner formes to 3P, the other all outer formes. Under these very straightforward conditions, we might normally infer one of the following:

(a) There was a single compositor, but the press was evidently lagging behind composition; therefore two skeletons were used to save imposition time. We might also infer a fairly large edition.

---

[57] In some cases two skeletons, regardless of edition size or speed of composition, may be evidence not of increased speed of production, but of a *slower* than normal rate of production, simply because it can be a very convenient way of keeping type safely standing whether before or after printing (either to allow of proofing in the sheet, or to defer distribution). Stower, *Printer's Grammar*, p. 474; "Forms will sometimes remain a considerable length of time before they are put to press."

[58] *Ibid.*, Table 15, but continued below in appendix I (a) and (b).

(b) The edition was probably small and presswork regularly ahead of composition—especially since the text was in Latin and cuts had to be accommodated
within it; but nothing would be gained by the use of two skeletons under such
conditions unless, say, two compositors were at work.

(c) The reversal of skeletons at 2Q is probably insignificant, but a serious interruption undoubtedly occurred after the printing of 2V when the first two
skeletons were broken up.

I trust that this example is thought to be no worse for its approximations than
most such arguments, but it seems to me to point up once more the nature of
our guiding assumptions about skeleton formes and the relationship of composition to presswork. In doing so it also indicates the likely error in our general
statements on these matters since their claim to represent the truth can be falsified by contradictory case-studies. If, as for many books, there were no external
evidence to control speculation, any of the explanations given above, suitably sophisticated, could be employed in a publishable account of the printing of the
Principia. The facts of the matter are: the edition was 700; only one compositor at
a time worked on the book (Pokins set B, 2Q–3R, a–d; Délié C–2P); the book
was printed at both full press (49 sheets) and half press (17 sheets) without these
conditions in any way being reflected in the number or order of skeletons; when
there were changes in skeletons, press conditions remained constant; a delay of
some months in 1712 is unmarked by the skeletons; the mere reversal of skeletons at 2Q was preceded by a delay of 11 months; the creation of entirely new
skeletons for 2X may have been related to a delay of about 3 months; the first pair
of skeletons were in use for over 2 years, the second for 1½ years; printing of the
66 sheets in the book extended from October 1709 until May 1713.[59]

I have not examined the skeleton formes in Bowyer books, but the fact that the
sheets in them were often printed at one press and perfected at another must render very complex indeed any analysis seeking to relate compositors, formes and
presses—even with the help of press figures. It cannot be assumed that other and
earlier presses did not do likewise (without the figures); it is just that we happen
to know for certain in some cases what the Bowyers did.

I wish now to broaden the argument a little by adverting to the Shakespeare
First Folio and by offering yet another case-study. When Professor Hinman
writes:

> Long sequences of Folio formes were often set by two compositors setting simulta-
> neously; yet one press regularly printed off these formes as rapidly as they were set.
> Now, unless our estimates are badly at fault, this would not have been possible if the
> edition had consisted of many more than about 1,200 copies. Nor on the other hand
> could two compositors (and no more than two seem ever to have set type for the

---

[59] We might stand to gain clarity if, when discussing changes in the pattern of skeletons, we were to
abandon the term "interruption" with its assumptions about timing and its implications of delay. Normally what we are observing is simply a discontinuity.

Folio at any given time) have kept even one press continuously busy if the edition had been of appreciably less than 1,200 copies . . .[60]

When Professor Hinman makes this point, he is deducing the probable size of the edition from an hypothesis about timing. The tentative nature of this deduction is made very clear and Professor Hinman's scholarship is of such excellence that it is seldom possible to offer views that he has not already entertained. Yet there can be no mistaking the main import of the above passage: two compositors and one press working on the Folio alone yield 1200 edition-sheets a day. Obviously, without full information about all other work on hand, one cannot falsify Professor Hinman's argument or its implication that the printing of the Folio was, by and large, a self-contained operation. Nor, without such evidence, can one prove it. But it may be salutary to consider its status as a general proposition which is likely to be true for other books of the period. For, as Professor Hinman himself says,

> Because the Folio was a book it must have been produced by methods which, in part at least, were followed in the making of other books; and investigative techniques that are of value in the study of the printing of the Folio should be useful in other studies too (*Printing and Proof-Reading*, I, 13).

Now if roughly comparable books show quite different conditions of production, the above hypothesis about timing and the deduction from it about edition size will be weakened. More, its proven inability to predict the other possibilities will severely limit its standing as a statement of general application.

Volume I of the 1705 Cambridge-printed edition of the Greek lexicon *Suidas* is perhaps a book that is "roughly comparable" (*The Cambridge University Press*, I, 224–33). It is a folio in fours, with some 954 pages, about 8,500 ens per forme set double column in English Greek and English Latin with Long Primer footnotes; being started by 1 Nov. 1701 and finished by 4 Sep. 1703, it took some 22 months to print: the edition size was 1500 (150 large-paper copies, 1350 small-paper); it was set throughout by two compositors working simultaneously on each forme; 166½ sheets were printed at full press and 72 at half press. The Shakespeare volume is a folio in sixes, contains just under 900 pages, has about 10,600 ens per forme set double column in Pica English; according to Professor Hinman's table it took about 18½ months to print but if we add the 2½ months given as the possible length of an interruption, the total would be 21 months; and Professor Hinman suggests an edition of about 1200 on the assumption that two compositors and one press were working on it more or less continuously. It would be foolish

---

[60] *Printing and Proof-Reading* I, 46. See also I, 124 where the same point is made and Professor Hinman cites Moxon: "It is also Customary in some Printing Houses that if the Compositer or Press-man make either the other stand still through the neglect of their contracted Task, that then he who neglected, shall pay him that stands still as much as if he had Wrought." Professor Hinman seems to imply that if a forme were machined in appreciably less time than one could be set the press would stand idle and the compositors would have to reimburse the pressmen. But this can hardly have been so. It was the master's job to worry about these things; Moxon is only concerned with 'neglect' of a 'contracted Task.'

to think of these two books as being any more than only very roughly comparable; the Shakespeare Folio is in English, not Greek and Latin, and has 22 fewer sheets than the *Suidas* volume. Yet the Folio has slightly more ens to the sheet and *Suidas* took slightly longer to print, so that in the quantitative matters of bulk, relation of composition to presswork, printing time, and edition size, the two books are not perhaps so very different.

When we discover, however, that throughout exactly the same period as the one in which the first volume of *Suidas* was being printed the identical one-and-a-half presses that printed it also served three to four other compositors, two of them often working simultaneously, to print another 1500 copies of the *second* volume of *Suidas*—yet another Shakespeare Folio as it were—as well as 20 other books whole or in part and at least 23 smaller jobs, then we might be forgiven for thinking that Professor Hinman's estimate is badly at fault. Nevertheless my point is not that his equation (two compositors and one press yield 1200 edition-sheets a day) is wrong—indeed, under some conditions it might well be exact—but that it seriously misrepresents the general conditions of book production.[61]

If I am right, and there is miscalculation somewhere, the reason for it probably lies in an inference drawn from skeleton formes, and its consequences re-

[61] Although I am not really concerned to query Professor Hinman's estimate of the edition size of the Folio, it is possible to offer more precise estimates on costs than either Greg or Willoughby has given. Such a note in itself may be of interest, but my purpose is larger: to show how costing methods current in 1700 can be applied to the 1620's. It so happens that Cantrell Legge the Cambridge printer has left a very detailed "direction to value most Bookes by the charge of the Printer & Stationer, as paper was sould Anno Dni: 1622" (Cambridge University Archives Mss. 33.2.95 and 33.6.8). The Folio contains about 227 sheets. At the highest of Legge's 1622 prices, for paper and printing of the best quality, it would have cost 13s.4d. per ream. For average quality the cost would probably have been nearer, in all, to 10s. or 11s. per ream. At the first of these prices, an edition of 500 copies would have cost £151.6s.8d. to produce; for an edition of 1000 copies the cost would have been £302.13s.4d.; for 1250 copies it would have been £378.6s.8d. Legge indicates that the Stationers' mark-up was usually twice as much again as the prime costs for paper and printing ("So they gaine clearly for euery 12s. laid out 1-5-0. The like proportion you may make of all other english, & forraine bookes"). However many were printed, the unit cost per copy of the Folio, accounting paper and printing at the highest price (13s.4d. per ream printed), would be 6s.0d. A normal mark-up would therefore give a selling price of 18s. (not far off Steevens' £1.0s.0d.). The maximum possible return therefore to the four partners would be £300 for 500 copies selling at 18s. each; £600 for 1000 copies; and £750 for 1250 copies. These figures are crude, but they are not so wrong as to be irrelevant. If 500 copies were printed, given a two-year printing period, the investment would yield roughly 100% per annum, if 1000 copies were printed it would have been 200% per annum. But since a good proportion of the prime costs would not have had to be met until printing was well advanced, nor the balance paid until after printing had finished, a substantial part of the "investment" monies could have been met from the income from sales. Even the lowest of these returns (on an edition of 500) would have justified the venture.

It may also be noted that the amount regularly allowed to retailers was 3s. in the £. ("Notes on Printing at Cambridge," p. 103).

It is possible to refine the figures further. Legge priced the best paper at 5s.6d. per ream; printing would therefore have cost 7s.10d. per ream. Gay's contract with Purslowe allowed 8s. per week for 3000 impressions per day; this meant, for a full press, 16s. per week for 18,000 impressions (or 18 reams perfected); this gives a price of roughly 10 ½d. per ream. Presswork on the Folio might therefore be set at 11d. per ream. Now, applying methods customary in 1700, allowing for correction at one-sixth the rate for composition, and adding the "printer's thirds" for over-heads, the detailed costs of printing may be outlined as follows:

turn us to the subject of concurrent printing. For the purity of Professor Hinman's argument virtually commits him to the view that the Folio was printed on
one press, "the Folio press." Apart from 18 quires near the beginning, the Folio
is a one-skeleton and therefore, it is claimed, a one-press book: ". . . throughout
most of the book, indeed, two-press work was manifestly impossible, the same
skeleton having been used in successive formes . . .".[62] Professor Hinman here
means that two presses cannot have been in simultaneous use, but as he says at
another point:

> Only one press *at a time* can possibly have been used, and it is but reasonable to sup-
> pose that the successive Folio formes, once set, were ordinarily delivered to the
> same pressmen and printed at the same "Folio" press.[63]

Moreover, two compositors working together and serving this one press are
thought to represent an ideally self-sufficient relationship for an edition of about
1200 copies, and since apparently this is the condition more frequently found,

> it seems clear that the printing of the Shakespeare collection was planned as a self-
> contained operation, one that could be economically conducted altogether apart
> from the other printing tasks with which the establishment was concerned. Yet the
> plan was by no means inflexible. It allowed for the concurrent production of other
> *occasional* work. First of all, however, it provided for the independent printing of
> Shakespeare's plays (I, 75).

Professor Hinman's main stress here, and his concession, are the crux of
the matter. At times of course most analytical bibliographers working in this
field have to confess an *imbalance* of composition and presswork on a book, either

Presswork	11d.
Composition	3s. 8d.
Correction	8d.
	5s. 3d.
Add for overheads	2s. 7d.
Cost of printing per ream	7s. 10d.
Add cost of paper	5s. 6d.
Total price for paper and printing per ream	13s. 4d.

[62] *Printing and Proof-Reading* II, 438. Two skeletons were used in quires F–X, a–b. See also I, 125–6: "One
of the most striking facts about the Folio is that only one set of rules appears throughout most of the book;
and the continuous use of the same rules can be satisfactorily accounted for only if presswork could keep continuously abreast of composition without difficulty. [A footnote adds: "Otherwise two sets of rules—two
'skeletons'—would almost certainly have been used."] Evidence from rules alone therefore establishes the
very strong likelihood that the Folio press regularly worked off one forme as fast as the immediately suc-
ceeding forme was set."

[63] *Ibid.*, I, 123. At this point Professor Hinman also writes: "Each successive forme [in 'o'] had been
printed off and was ready for distribution by the time compositorial work for the next forme but one was
undertaken." The distribution pattern shows that this was so, but I fail to see its relevance to *speed* of presswork; it simply means that setting did not go forward until the last forme but one was distributed. Professor Hinman mentions the possibility that composition was quite regularly interrupted on the completion of each new forme "to allow the press to catch up" but rejects the idea with the words "of such a
practice there is neither evidence *nor any shadow of likelihood*" (my italics). The same *sequence* may be followed
at variable *speeds*.

implicitly by failing to pursue the point or explicitly by marking breaks in an otherwise apparently consistent pattern. When this happens, some odd jobbing at case or press is a likely and convenient suggestion to restore the ratio and avoid idleness. This opportunistic resort to a theory of concurrent printing need not be documented at length but it is important to note its circumstantial origins. For much of the Shakespeare Folio, set by one man, there is persistent evidence that the economic considerations behind the plan (at least in the form suggested) did not apply; and to explain the apparent imbalance Professor Hinman allows that 'the Folio press' must have engaged in some concurrent printing:

> It would be rash to suggest that, if only one compositor at a time set type for the Folio, the Folio press (as for convenience we may call it) must always have stood idle half the time. It could have been used to print other, non-Folio matter—if only this other matter were available. And doubtless it sometimes was; but not always, not regularly (I, 74).

And again:

> Fairly often, therefore, though rarely for long, the rate at which composition for the Folio normally progressed was halved, and accordingly the full-time services of the press were not required for Folio printing. But we need not suppose that press time was therefore wasted. It is in the highest degree probable that, on at least most of these occasions, both the Folio press and one of the Folio compositors were used to produce other work—presumably job work . . .[64]

If I now seem to labour a point it is simply because Professor Hinman's account of the printing process reflects and therefore lends massive authority to the erroneous assumption that a book was normally put into production as an independent unit. The single skeleton forme, its association with 'the Folio press,' the suggested edition size, the 'economic' balance between compositors and press-crew, all combine to reinforce this view. What is offered as exceptional—occasional concurrent printing—other evidence would suggest to be normal; what is offered as normal—a self-contained operation—is elsewhere exceedingly rare. Neither the Cambridge nor Bowyer papers would permit such inferences to be drawn from skeleton formes; neither would permit such assumptions to be made about the operations of a single press; neither would be consistent with the general economic argument put forward. Nor is it, I think, a matter of proven historical difference, as though the early 17th century were doing something that the 18th century no longer found necessary. For no differences have been constated that cannot be seriously questioned by exposing the primary assumptions. Noting at one point that most of the Folio was printed by a single press, Professor Hinman revealingly adds:

---

[64] Ibid., I, 75. At I, 153 we find: "Whether one or two skeletons were used in such a book probably depended upon the composition-presswork relationship." See also I, 28 n.1, 49, 364; II, 490–1, 524.

Or, conceivably, by two presses working alternately on different formes; but this, for all practical purposes, would amount to the same thing.[65]

With all respect, one is obliged to say that 'for all *practical* purposes' it would not. The moment we admit the possibility of two presses we halve the work of one of them on the Folio and concede that each is concurrently printing other books as well. The problems of calculating the ratio between compositors and press-crews are doubled, for the ratio must be assessed for each crew and the assessment must take full account of all other work on hand. The pattern of work becomes far more complex as the various edition-sheets for different books are printed off one with another at the two presses. For some limited *theoretic* purposes the ratios abstracted by Professor Hinman may be sound, but his evidence, as he concedes, is consistent with normal conditions of concurrent printing at press, and much of the time with concurrent work at case.

The implications of assumptions which seem to be so much at odds with usual printing conditions do not end here:

> It is demonstrable, that a single press could (and did) print off a Folio forme at least as fast as *two* compositors working simultaneously, one on each of its two pages, could set such a forme. Hence there can be no doubt that composition by one compositor ordinarily took at least twice as long as the machining of the forme.[66]

Under the latter conditions 'there would be a gross imbalance between composition and presswork,' under the former 'a highly efficient ratio.' Professor Hinman makes much of the economic reasons for simultaneous setting, and hence setting by formes:

> With some emphasis let it be said, for the point is vital, that casting off copy would make possible *the simultaneous setting of different Folio pages by different compositors.* Hence Jaggard might well have undertaken it even if his supplies of type had been unlimited (I, 74).

Again, an economic ratio of composition and presswork for the Folio

> could be effected, and effected economically, if two compositors worked simultaneously on its various formes—and Jaggard probably cast off the copy for it with precisely this end in view (I, 75).

By displacing type-shortage as the primary reason for casting off copy, and substituting an economic relationship dependent on assumptions about timing, Professor Hinman not only diminishes the classical status of his own major

---

[65] *Ibid.*, I, 123. See also I, 49: ". . . one compositor (and hence, it may be added, two or more compositors setting alternately; for this would amount to much the same thing) . . .". One should add that even without prejudice to the main thesis of balanced work on the Folio alone, Professor Hinman's masterly account of the work done on the Folio concurrently with other books makes it quite clear that a 'norm' of concurrent printing, as shown for the 1700's or 1730's, also applied to the 1620's.

[66] *Ibid.*, I, 74 n.2. The demonstration referred to is, I think, that given at I, 123–4; see note 63 above.

demonstration but starts a bibliographical hare. The constant factor throughout the Folio is shortage of type because of the method of quiring, and Professor Hinman himself makes it clear that this "may have made it more or less mandatory to set the Folio by formes." His attempt to give an extended generality to his brilliant particular and practical proof from type-shortages misrepresents the general conditions of work, not only in Jaggard's shop but in the period as a whole.

For this again is my immediate concern: the encouragement given to the view that even where there is no conclusive evidence of type-shortages, revealed by the presence of identical sorts in both formes of a sheet or in the first half of a quire, we may have setting by formes. In such cases reliance is usually placed on a 'pattern of distribution'—evidence which is used with most admirable insight and control by Professor Hinman but which, in lesser hands, and in quarto printing, may prove very tricky indeed. In a folio of course the major production unit was the quire and (now that Professor Hinman has pointed it out) it is obvious enough why in a folio in sixes type should be inadequate for normal page-by-page setting. In a quarto, however, the reasons are far from clear, and despite Professor Turner's assurance that "it begins to appear that [Elizabethan play quartos] were *more often than not* composed by formes" (my italics) ("Printing *King and No King*," p. 255), a certain scepticism ought perhaps still to be exercised. Professor Williams, for example, arguing that the quarto *Epicedium* (1594) was so composed, implied considerable concern on the compositor's part at setting vv for w, an assessment by the compositor of the number of w's required for the work, a count of those available to him in the case, and a decision to set by formes for this one reason despite attendant complications. In another case "Random mixing of roman and italic forms of 'k,' 'K,' 'S' and 'Q' . . . are common in the quarto and are without significance. The shortage of lower-case 'w,' on the other hand, discloses a pattern throughout the quarto."[67] But one may fairly ask whether it is safe to prove a case by accepting only such limited 'patterned' evidence. The idea that a 'pattern' must be significant because it appears to indicate a regular method of work is one of the most perniciously seductive presuppositions of current bibliographical analysis. The conflicting evidence of 'k' is disregarded in part because it "violates the order of imposition and printing as disclosed by the running-title evidence." For "evidence from running titles indicates that outer B preceded inner through the press." This of course is merely a further assumption given the status of proof (and then applied as such) because the skeleton formes *can*, but arbitrarily, be ordered in a pattern.

In the Shakespeare Folio, Professor Hinman noted, "As a rule . . . no forme has types in common with either the forme immediately preceding or that immediately following it" (*Printing and Proof-Reading*, I, p. 81); and the sequential relation

---

[67] "Setting by Formes in Quarto Printing," p. 42. The second quarto referred to is *The First Part of The Contention* (1594).

of setting, printing, and distribution here implied has been adapted for the quartos. Professor Turner had earlier given it shape when, writing of *Philaster*, he observed

> that types which originally appear in B (o) reappear through sheet C; whereas types which originally appear in B (i) do not reappear in sheet C but do reappear in sheet D. Therefore, B (i) must have been distributed after B (o) and doubtless followed it through the press.[68]

Mr John Hazel Smith, discussing *Much Ado*, offers a similar argument: "The precedence of A (i) is proved by three italic types (B$_1$, B$_2$, d$_1$) from that forme which are then divided between the formes of B." And again:

> That *Much Ado* is composed by formes will be abundantly clear later. It is already indicated by the types (B$_1$, B$_2$, d$_1$) which appear in two adjacent sheets: under seriatim composition it would be very rare to find, as we find several times in this quarto, on the first or second page of a second sheet a type from either forme of a first sheet (p. 11).

And Professor Turner's subsequent formulation gives the principle a usefully definitive form:

> in a quarto set by formes, type from the first forme of each sheet normally reappears in both formes of the succeeding sheet, but type from the second forme only in the second forme of the succeeding sheet.[69]

Mr Smith's study is probably the least fortunate example of an attempt to prove setting by formes in a quarto by "applying scientific bibliographical methods," for Professor Hinman has since pronounced it wrong.[70] But the irony is that the methods used by Mr Smith *were* those "illustrated by the work of Charlton Hinman on the Shakespeare First Folio and by George W. Williams and Robert K. Turner, Jr, on other Renaissance quartos" ("Compositor of *Much Ado*," p. 10). And some of these methods are not, inherently, very reliable.[71]

The comment called for here can only be a very general and cautionary one. Neither the Cambridge nor Bowyer records offer much positive evidence of

---

[68] "The Printing of *Philaster*," p. 22. See also "Printing Methods in *A Midsummer Night's Dream*" where Professor Turner argues that if type from B (o) is found in both formes of sheet C, and type from B (i) is found only in part of C (i), and if type from C (o) is found in both formes of D, and type from C (i) is found only in D (i), then, "when type reappears in this manner, composition cannot have been *seriatim*" (p. 36). The following remarks make it clear what Professor Turner means cannot have been *seriatim* "without press delays." The fundamental argument is not bibliographical in the sense that Professor Hinman's is.

[69] "The Printing of *A King and No King*," p. 258. See also, in "Printing Methods in *A Midsummer Night's Dream*," Professor Turner's suggestion that "It seems likely that the compositor, working on the assumption that composition and presswork could stay more or less in balance, originally intended to follow the conventional procedure for setting by formes—to compose two formes, distribute the first, set the third, distribute the second, [set the fourth] and so on." (p. 46).

[70] "Shakespeare's Texts—Then, Now and Tomorrow," SS, XVIII (1965), 31. It is also pointed out there that, before *Richard II*, "no first quarto has hitherto yielded such entirely conclusive evidence of setting by formes as the Folio does throughout" (p. 28).

[71] See Turner, "Printing Methods in *A Midsummer Night's Dream*," p. 39: "By itself the testimony of shortage is, I believe, less reliable than any other bibliographical technique."

setting by formes; although their combined testimony does demonstrate the rarity of such a practice for books other than page-for-page reprints and must therefore give us pause. We must recall too that neither Moxon, Stower, nor any other early grammar mentions casting off as a means of enabling work to be set by formes. In every case it is, as Stower puts it in his index, a "manner of calculating in order to ascertain the number of sheets a manuscript will make, the size of the letter being fixed on"[72]—that is, a device for costing, and for determining the paper required, not for organizing work. Nowadays we call it estimating. As Professor Hinman observes, actual casting off for setting would not have been undertaken without good reason, although it is true that the difficulties may have been overestimated for verse plays as distinct from full prose works (*Printing and Proof-Reading*, I, 73). But if, as is claimed, "the practice was by no means uncommon" and "is to be seen in first quartos that issued from many different printing houses, over a wide stretch of years" ("Shakespeare's Texts," p. 31), it is to be hoped that firmer controls will be applied in its demonstration than have hitherto been evident. In particular, arguments heavily reliant on time-schemes will rarely command that ready assent which was given to Professor Hinman's initial proof that the Folio must have been set by formes.[73] On the face of it, the most important reason for setting by formes in quarto is unlikely to have been urgency, nor even an unusually small fount, but a fount *depleted* because of concurrent printing—for if work overlapped on two or more books using the same fount of type, setting by formes would offer a method of making some progress with all. Professor Hinman has again led the way in showing how, in Jaggard's shop, concurrent setting of other books, reduced the supply of type for the Folio.

If copy is cast off for a quarto text, there is no compelling reason why any sheet should not be printed in any order—say, H, F, A, C, D, B, E, G. One might expect and assume a straightforward progression through the book, but there is no compelling reason for it. But *order* of formes through the press is an important ingredient in much bibliographical work. Where there is detectable damage in the course of printing (whether to types, headlines, rules or ornaments) it may be quite possible to prove order, and in some cases a precedent forme, at least within the same sheet, may be determined by using the Martin-Povey lamp. I am not sure whether it is evidence of this kind that led Professor Turner to write that "information about presswork, specifically the order of the formes through the press, is relatively easy to obtain and is based on evidence that is the least controvertible" ("Beaumont and Fletcher Folio," p. 36), but, so far as I can tell, order has usually been determined, not according to such evidence, but according to a *pattern* of headline recurrences. "Evidence from running titles indicates that

[72] *Printer's Grammar*, index. See also Moxon, *Mechanick Exercises*, p. 239: "Counting or Casting off Copy . . . is to examine and find how much either of *Printed Copy* will *Come-in* into any intended number of *Sheets* of a different *Body* or *Measure* from the *Copy*; or how much *Written Copy* will make an intended number of *Sheets* of any assigned *Body* and *Measure*."

[73] "Cast-off Copy for the First Folio of Shakespeare," *SQ*, VI (1953), 259–73.

outer B preceded inner through the press" (Williams, "Setting by Formes," p. 43) is a familiar form of wording; or "on the evidence of running titles, it is clear that B (o) was machined before B (i)." I confess that I have never understood what was meant when I have read such a phrase, and again I suspect that priority is based on assumptions about timing, and inferences drawn from variants, from a pattern of alternating skeletons, or from reappearing types which permit a hypothesis about distribution. In any case, whatever the internal patterns which some physical features may take within a book, there is little reason to elucidate them by constructing a time-scheme or by supposing the successive printing of all formes of the same book. I know of no evidence that obliges us to think of one sheet (or forme) being followed immediately on the press by another of the same book. There is some case for it when perfecting, none between sheets. There is too much evidence in the Cambridge books of perfectly regular patterns sustained under the most diverse conditions of concurrent printing. It is not always easy to tell when an apparently general statement is really only a singular one made of a particular book, but if it is generally true, as Professor Turner says, that "to prove the order of printing is usually to prove the order of composition of the formes" ("Beaumont and Fletcher Folio," p. 37), important textual consequences may follow from the initial assumptions.[74]

It is perhaps worth looking briefly at one Cambridge book, Bennet's *Answer to the Dissenters Pleas* (2nd ed., 1700). Its testimony is not all that important, since it is a page-for-page reprint, yet it does show quite vividly that, once copy is cast off, any sequence of setting and printing might be followed. The sheets were composed as follows: Bertram set E, K by 13 Jan. 1700; B, H, S by 20 Jan.; Knell set C by 26 Jan.; Bertram D, L, U and X/* by 10 Feb.; Knell completed F, G1/2 between 20 Jan. and 17 Feb.; G1/2, I by 24 Feb.; Bertram P, Q, R by 24 Feb.; N, O, T by 2 Mar.; Knell A, M by 9 Mar. The order of printing appears to have been: E, H, K, B, L, S, U, C, D, F, X/*, G, I, R, Q, N, O, P, A, M, T (*Cambridge University Press*, I, 192–3).

The Cambridge papers, if not those of the Bowyers, provide very clear evidence of regular proof-correction of all books printed. Such a practice may have been slightly unusual as many of the books were classical texts and the press prided itself on its accuracy, yet I think not, for London houses in the 18th century, like Cambridge, regularly set as their price for proofing one-sixth of the rate of composition.[75] There is considerable doubt, however, about the validity of applying 18th-century evidence to Elizabethan books; even Moxon's testimony

---

[74] Another theory that one should like to have some external evidence for is that which closely associates a compositor with a particular set of type cases. Professor Hinman offers a very fine discussion of the question and has much contributory evidence for identifying compositors from type-groupings where distinctive spellings are lacking. See also Turner, "Reappearing Types," pp. 200–3. I have not examined Cambridge or Bowyer books for evidence of this kind.

[75] So Richardson, advising Oxford to do "as the London Printers do, reckon at the rate of 2d in the shilling for the Press Correctors, of what is paid the Compositors"—quoted by I. G. Philip, *Blackstone and the Reform of the Oxford University Press* (1957), p. 40.

from the later 17th century has been rejected as irrelevant to the earlier period. If this is so, then the 'norms' used to introduce some measure of probability into analytical accounts of the proofing and printing of earlier books will themselves be only inferential. Moxon, we may recall, notes that:

> The Press-man is to make a Proof so oft as occasion requires . . . The Compositer having brought the Form to the Press, lays it down on the Press-stone, and the Press-man . . . Pulls the Proof-sheet . . . carries the Form again to the Correcting-stone and lays it down: And the Proof he carries to the Compositers Case [pp. 302–3].
>
> And the Compositer gives the Correcter the Proof and his Copy to Correct it by: which being Corrected, the Correcter gives it again to the Compositer to Correct the Form by [p. 233].

Having corrected it, the compositor

> carries the Form to the Press, and lays it on the Stone for a Second Proof, and sometimes for a Third Proof; which having Corrected, he at last brings the Form to the Press, and again lays it on the Stone . . . After all this Correcting a Revise is made, and if any Faults are found in any Quarter of it, or in all the Quarters, he calls to the Press-man to Unlock that Quarter, or the whole Form, that he may Correct those Faults . . . [pp. 238–9].

And before continuing printing, the pressman will check

> 4thly, That no Letters or Spaces lye in the White-lines of the Form; which may happen if the Compositer have Corrected any thing since the Form was laid on the Press, and the Compositer through oversight pickt them not all up [p. 269].

Professor Bowers has remarked, however, that

> Moxon describes a method of pulling proofs that interrupted the printing whenever a forme to be proofed was prepared. The delay would not be equally serious, but on the evidence this does not seem to have been the usual Elizabethan practice (Bibliography and Textual Criticism, p. 103 n. 1).

To make this point is to stress again the primary importance of continuous printing at press. Professor Hinman would doubtless agree, for he says that

> The proof-correction practices spoken of by Moxon may have been common in his day, but they were certainly not so in the 1620's (Printing and Proof-Reading, I, 228 n. 1).

But Professor Hinman's basic reason for rejecting Moxon's account as in any way relevant to the 1620's has little to do with timing. It is rather the many self-evident errors that survive in the printed text. Discussing—and dismissing— in a footnote the idea that regular proofing may have preceded that established by a collation of the variants he has observed, Professor Hinman notes:

> there are far too many obvious errors of all kinds in far too many Folio pages to allow us to think that any such preliminary reading as may have been done for this book, whether with or without benefit of some kind of printed proof, and whether by compositor or by an official 'corrector of the press,' ever amounted to much (I, 228 n. 2).

It is a view that in general Professor Bowers would probably—and recipro-cally—endorse, since he has observed that

> The automatic assumption is surely wrong that every forme of cheap commercial printing was necessarily proof-read. Any editor of Elizabethan play quartos is fa-miliar with some formes in which the typographical errors are so gross as to make it seem impossible to suppose that these formes had been read (*Bibliography and Tex-tual Criticism*, p. 126).

It may seem singularly fool-hardy not to follow such authority, but I am con-strained to persist in a certain incredulity. Professor Hinman's failure to list the 'many obvious errors of all kinds' at least makes one's task of qualification a little easier since he has not, in this case, sufficiently illustrated, let alone proved, his point. If Moxon, and proofing practices so well evidenced elsewhere in the cen-tury and beyond it, are to be displaced as the 'norm,' the question would seem to demand rather fuller discussion than I have yet seen devoted to it.

The view that Professor Hinman is concerned to question is, essentially, Greg's—that in the Folio "the printer was not indifferent to the accuracy of his text."[76] And it may well be that if we *were* "once possessed of a full record of the press variants in the First Folio" (*Printing and Proof-Reading*, I, 227), such a view might have to be altered. Professor Hinman's labours of collation leave him in no doubt that now "there is in fact considerably more evidence that the printer *was* largely indifferent to the accuracy of his text" (I, 227). Yet such a conclusion is scarcely judicious; there is a great difference between the truth and the whole truth, between "a full record of the press variants" and a full record of the *surviv-ing* press variants.[77]

This is not just a quibble. Traditionally the stages of proof-correction have been at least three: galley (whether page- or slip-), revises, and, as a last resort, stop-press. And let us not forget that the manuscript copy precedes all three. Now it is incontestable that these several stages can be found in increasing fre-quency as one moves from manuscript (how much of that survives?), to page-proofs (very few of these), to revises (slightly more of these—if some of our sur-viving 'proof' sheets can be so considered), to stop-press (hundreds of these). Each successive stage supersedes the previous one; once the unique copy has been set and checked, it can be disposed of, once the single galley proof has been read and checked, it can be disposed of, once the revise has been read and checked, it can be disposed of, but once printing has started, the multiple copies are preserved and of course they are available for consultation in those portions of the edition still extant. It only remains to note that the principle of increasing frequency persists even here, for, as Professor Hinman has observed in the case

---

[76] *The Shakespeare First Folio* (1955), p. 464.

[77] All the statement means is that some evidence of correction has survived; it leaves quite open the pos-sibility that invariant formes already embody corrections, and that even where formes are variant the 'un-corrected' states may be intermediate ones.

of the Folio, the earlier 'uncorrected' state is likely to be preserved in about ten per cent of copies, and the later and latest, press-corrected, states in ninety per cent of surviving copies; these last therefore will be the ones most frequently observed. We must of course work from what we have to what we have not, but our chances of going the full distance and thereby establishing 'a full record of the press variants'—if these are taken to include all stages of proofing—are very remote indeed. When such evidence (of its very nature) demanded to be discarded, it is difficult to see why one should assume that it never existed.[78]

But one may consider the point in another way: it is easy after repeated and intense scrutiny to discover 'obvious' misprints, and it is also very easy to miss them. Each year I put some four or five senior and intelligent students through the rudiments of type-setting and when they come to correct their work they almost invariably have to do it in two or three stages because these latter-day John Leasons have failed to correct all the 'obvious' errors the first time through. Yet there *was* a first time (see *Printing and Proof-Reading*, I, 233). It is true that the more experienced students make fewer mistakes, but it is again remarkable how many of these mistakes my latter-day John Shakespeares overlook in their first attempt at correction. Much the same point is made of course by Professor Hinman when speaking of sections of plays set by Compositor E, sections "which were subjected to much *more* proof-reading than others—yet only to very *careless* proof-reading, since a great many errors nonetheless escaped uncorrected in these plays" (I, 233). Errors, that is, persist through one or more stages of proof-reading; the much-proofed page from *Antony and Cleopatra* leaves errors uncorrected.[79] The existence of some formes in three or more states indicates that at one or more stages of correction errors were missed which were later thought serious enough to alter. Greg's list of misprints in Q1 *Lear*, based on the corrected state of the sheets and therefore taking no account of the original errors that were subsequently altered, is most revealing in this connection (*Variants*, pp. 63–79). Professor Hinman's new evidence from variants introduced at a relatively late stage of the Folio's production does not dispose of Greg's judgement. The 'obvious errors' have been there since 1623 and Greg, who had as good an eye for them as anyone, still thought that "the printer was not indifferent to the accuracy of his text", and that "he took what were thought in his day to be reasonable precautions, and went to some trouble, to reach a moderate standard in the execution of what may not have been at all times an easy task" (*Shakespeare First Folio*, p. 464).

---

[78] Instances of an 'uncorrected' state surviving in a single copy point to the dangers we run if we too readily equate invariant formes with uncorrected ones. The 'uncorrected' states, being earlier, are likely to be fewer and in most cases may have disappeared completely. In "A Proof-sheet in *An Humorous Day's Mirth* (1599) printed by Valentine Sims," *Library*, 5th ser. (1966), pp. 155–7, A. Yamada notes that "out of fifteen copies examined, the Bute copy alone retains the uncorrected readings on the outer forme of G, and all the other copies have the forme in the corrected state" (p. 155). Of twenty copies of Tailor's *The Hogge hath lost his Pearle* (1614), only one has inner and outer E in their 'uncorrected' states.

[79] Stower said that it should be "an invariable rule" to demand a *second* revise, "particularly with foul compositors, as no sort of dependence can be placed on them" (*Printer's Grammar*, p. 382).

There is of course another way of looking at the problem—and I must repeat that I am really only concerned with questions of method and that like Troubleall I merely wish to ask 'by what warrant' certain inferences are given the standing of general statements. So, *a priori*, one might ask whether it is likely that the essentially trivial corrections noted by Professor Hinman would have been made at all if the printer were indifferent to the accuracy of his text? Or, to put it yet another way, is it likely that a printer who put up with so many bibliographically serious delays at press in order to correct minor blemishes would fail to observe routine correction procedures in order to avoid major infidelities and the prospect of really serious delays in the last stages of production? Which brings us back to Moxon.

It is not I hope gratuitously irresponsible to suggest that none of the evidence presented from the Folio demonstrates conclusively that the procedures which Moxon describes were 'essentially different' from those of the 1620's. At the very least, the "*Proofe, and Reuiewes*" pulled by Jaggard for Brooke's *Catalogue* testify to the currency of Moxon's terms at this time, and in Jaggard's shop (McKerrow, *Introduction*, p. 207). We must grant that the copy for the Folio has disappeared; we must grant that the foul proofs have disappeared; but what does remain in evidence corresponds exactly to that which we should expect to find at the later stages of correction as outlined by Moxon. And it is precisely at these stages of correction that copy is *not* consulted. That phase is well behind, and even if some errors have persisted it is not to be expected that substantive matters will *now* command 'painstaking' attention. But it *is* to be expected that typographical infelicities—the things that catch (and for long curiously avoid) a pressman's eye through the repeated pullings—will be picked up from time to time. Turned letters, lifting spaces, uneven inking, badly defective letters—these are precisely the things which at this stage the beater, who "peruses the *Heap*" (*Mechanick Exercises*, p. 292), was deputed to look for. He takes care

> to see if no accidents have befallen the *Form*, viz. that no *Letters, Quadrats* or *Furniture* &c.
> Rise, that no *Letters* are *Batter'd* . . . that no *Pick* be got into the *Form*, or any other accident that may deface the beauty of the Work . . . (p. 303)

Rising letters, quadrats and furniture, and probably loose spacing, are fixed by the pressman, who has a bodkin for the purpose; but if letters are to be replaced, "he *Unlocks* the *Quarter* they are in, and desires the *Compositer* to put in others in their room" (p. 304). None of this is inconsistent with what we find in the Folio; indeed Professor Hinman's variants are clear evidence that Jaggard's beater was doing exactly what Moxon demands—turning out a book that was not marred by too many purely typographical blemishes.

Let us now recall too what Moxon says of revises and of correction at press: the forme, being now on the bed of the press, is *left there*, "and if any *Faults* are found in any *Quarter* of it [the Compositor] calls to the *Press-man* to *Unlock* that *Quarter* . . . that he may *Correct* those *Faults*" (pp. 238–9). There are several points

here: the kind of corrections documented for the Folio are unlikely to have required removal of the forme from the press. At this stage, even after as many as
three proofs, a revise is pulled—but now the forme is virtually ready for printing and the likelihood is great that printing will begin while the revise is being
looked at. The single copy of the revise is likely to be a pull of the full forme; in
the case of the white-paper forme its chances of being preserved are negligible,
but in the case of the perfecting forme this single marked sheet has a greater
chance of being placed on the heap and eventually bound. Although the revise
will be of the full forme, Moxon suggests that it might be attended to in sections,
or quarters, so that the pressman might unlock only so much of the forme as is
necessary, perhaps only a page in the case of the Folio. In many cases in the Folio both pages must have been unlocked and corrected together, yet Moxon's
wording does hint that the revise itself might be read in sections. I find it most
interesting therefore that Professor Hinman should write: "Four actual proof-
sheets for the Folio have survived—although . . . they ought perhaps rather to be
called proof *pages*"; and "the essential proof-reading unit, so to speak, was rather
the single page than the complete forme" (*Printing and Proof-Reading*, I, 233, 234). I
wonder, however, whether these four proof pages should not perhaps be referred
to as revises to distinguish them from the first and substantial stage of correction
as well as from the last and accidental one.

   In any case, however cursory we may think the Folio by our own standards and
in the absence of author-correction, it would seem premature to conclude that
what so closely corresponds to revises and stop-press correction as described by
Moxon was not preceded by the routine proofing procedures which he also out-
lines. These may have been deficient in execution, but I cannot think that Professor Hinman's inferences justify the view that "the method of printing and
proofing adopted," whether in the Folio or beyond it in the earlier 17th century,
"was essentially different . . . from the method described by Moxon some sixty
years later" (I, 228).

   Professor Hinman, in another context, also discounts the testimony of Ashley's translation of Le Roy (1594), "since Le Roy was not a professional printer"
(I, 41). Ashley writes of the pressman who is pulling:

> taking the barre in his hand, he pulleth as hard as he can vntill the leafe be imprinted
> on one side, on which they bestowe halfe the day; and the other halfe, on the other
> side; yelding in a day twelue hundred and fiftie sheetes, or thirteen hundred im-
> printed. But before they do this, they make two or three proofes, which are re-
> uiewed: and on this correction continew the rest.[80]

The late Mr Kenneth Povey found reason to believe that Ashley had expert help in
making his translation; and it may be further noted that Jaggard's precise use of
the word "*Reuiewes*," both as a noun and as a verb in the phrase "viewed, reuiewed,
directed, corrected," suggests that Ashley's use of the word "reuiewed" was not

---

[80] Quoted by K. Povey, "Variant Formes in Elizabethan Printing," *Library*, 5th ser. (1955), p. 42.

idle. Ashley is at one with both Jaggard and Moxon in suggesting that, first, there might be two or three proofs and, next, a 'reuiew' or revise. Even the phrase "continew the rest" could relate to a process of continuous printing, stopped to make the late changes found in the revise, and then resumed. Mr Povey used Allde's 1624 edition of Massinger's *The Bond-man* as a test case, and found all the variants reconcilable with an orderly routine of proof-correcting and perfecting described by Moxon. He suggested, moreover, that

> since Ashley's concise account is fully confirmed by Moxon, it might well be adopted as the credo of students of Elizabethan printing-methods in preference to any modern construction (p. 43).

Nowhere perhaps so much as in the consideration of skeleton formes and proof-correction procedures are modern constructions so crippled by the absence of primary evidence and so vulnerable therefore to the general objections that may be made to all inductive methods. One recalls Black: "a nice adaptation of conditions will make almost any hypothesis agree with the phenomena." It is doubly a pity, however, when writers adapt conditions to suit their theories and then find themselves obliged to discount the testimony of such an excellent palmer as Moxon.

But much the same may be said of many studies of 18th-century printing which have been conducted on the assumption that conditions then were essentially different from those of the preceding century. My own major argument in this paper is of course that productive conditions were constantly changing, not just from century to century in different houses, but from day to day in the same house, simply because concurrent printing has been the universal practice for the last 400 years. If I am right, this fundamental fact poses more problems for analytical bibliography than any minor period differences. These there certainly were, and they must be carefully charted, but we must beware of that ostensibly sophisticated historical relativism which insists on making fine distinctions between periods when virtually nothing certain is known about either element of the comparison. When, for example, Professor Todd writes that

> whenever books contain press figures their very presence implies unsystematic piecework engaged in conjunction with other miscellaneous endeavours. For labour which is predetermined, controlled, and properly recorded by the overseer . . . the figures become superfluous and accordingly disappear ("Concurrent Printing," p. 56)

the implication is that we are here dealing with quite distinctive conditions; but this, as the song says, ain't necessarily so. Whatever the variables, labour was always predetermined, controlled, and properly recorded, whether on piece rates or not. Crownfield's disposition of work, usually without figures, was no different from the Bowyers' with figures, and Stower's "Plan of a Book for checking Compositors' and Pressmen's Bills" assumes exactly the same conditions a hundred years later when press figures are on their way out (*Printer's Grammar*, p. 435).

The procedures have always been the same—only the methods of recording them have differed.

I cannot here attempt to describe the thick web of theory spun around press figures.[81] In their incredible and perplexing variety they are eloquent witnesses to the customary conditions of presswork in any printing house, and perhaps only an imagination as fertile as Professor Todd's, and a mind as subtle, could have penetrated their mysteries. On their usefulness, let him speak:

> Contrary to McKerrow's prediction that [press figures] would prove to be of little importance, recent investigation has shown that they may be interpreted as signs of cancellation, variant states, half- or full-press operation (indicating the employment of one or two men at the machine), type pages arranged within the forme in some irregular pattern, sheets impressed in some abnormal order, an impression of the formes for each sheet by one man working both formes in succession, or two men working both simultaneously, impressions interrupted for one reason or another, reimpressions or resettings of the book, in whole or in part, copy distributed among several shops, overprints involving an increase in the number of sheets machined for certain gatherings in order to meet an unanticipated demand for copies, and underprints consisting of a decrease in the number of sheets in order to reduce the issue and speed its publication ("Editorial Problem in the Eighteenth Century," p. 47).

Much bibliographical writing, like that in any new subject, has a strong proselytizing strain which is apt to show itself in a slight tendency to rhetorical overstatement and the premature elevation of particular observations to the status of general truths. One or two pieces of information that have become available since Professor Todd wrote the above account do call for its qualification; I present them now only to carry forward my general argument that the 'empirical' method, with its reliance on 'direct observation,'[82] might lead us wildly astray. Press figures, as Professor Todd has indubitably shown, are of enormous value in revealing conditions normally concealed, but they still need theories to make them work and the theories so far applied have been largely without benefit of primary evidence from the printing house itself.

As I have indicated elsewhere, Cambridge pressmen in the early 18th century did not normally use press figures, and the first two volumes of *Suidas* are the only two books of the period in which they appear (*Cambridge University Press*, I, 128–32). This exception is wholly due to the employment of John Terrill who came up from London towards the end of November 1701 and who left Cambridge again on 15 May 1703. Terrill's bills for presswork match the figures exactly and make it perfectly clear that, in this case, the figures represent a man, specifically Terrill, not a press. Terrill did not always use a figure, nor keep to the same one; and it is certain that here in the Cambridge house his use of a figure was a purely personal and optional matter. His main reason for using one at all would seem

[81] A useful reference list is given in Tanselle, "Press Figures in America," p. 126 notes 10 and 11.
[82] See Todd, "Observations on . . . Press Figures," SB, III (1950–51), 173.

to have been that the first two volumes of *Suidas* were being printed concurrently and as they were independently signed 'Suidas the quire G' or 'Suidas G1' might refer to either or both volumes. So Terrill played safe by marking the sheets that he printed, although he thought it necessary to figure only one forme in each sheet. In this, his practice was consistent with that recommended by Savage in 1841 but not with that followed by the Bowyers in the 1730's.[83] Terrill's main concern seems to have been merely to use some idiosyncratic mark, and once the work had been paid for any other might serve as well. It is not surprising therefore to discover that Terrill used two different figures (* and ‡) in both volumes. The first (*) was used between the end of November 1701 and 28 Feb. 1702; during this period Terrill worked under markedly different conditions at different times—first with Brown at full press and then alone at half press—yet he used the same figure throughout. From 28 Feb. until 2 May 1702 he worked with Ponder without a figure. Thereafter, until his departure on 15 May 1703, Terrill used the second figure (‡), again in both volumes, to mark almost every sheet on which he worked. When he left, the figure disappeared.

Clearly the consistent use of one figure in one part of a book and of another figure in another part has in this case nothing whatever to do with simultaneous—or even successive—printing of each portion at different presses. Nor has the incidence of variously figured and unfigured sheets anything whatever to do with printing at full or at half press. If, even occasionally, a pressman was personally responsible for his choice of figure, as here, this would go far to account for the many idiosyncratic numbers or marks adopted in some books and their apparently haphazard arrangement. And if, even occasionally, a figure represents a man rather than a press, it is formally possible to argue that a sheet which shows varying figures in copy to copy simply reflects changes in the press-crew part-way through a single impression and not distinct impressions.

Indeed, whether a figure indicates a pressman or a press, such variation is in any case to be expected in books printed in very large editions. *The London Magazine*, for example, was printed for a time in 8000 copies. Since it comprised three and a half sheets, its printing would have kept three full presses wholly engaged for more than a week. Over such a time span—longer if the presses were required to do other work too, as Ackers' were—it is highly probable that changes would occur in the conditions under which the single impression would be completed. Changes of men, as well as changes of press, partway through printing might well be reflected by new figures yet none of them be bibliographically significant—or at least no more bibliographically significant than the daily discontinuities incident to all printing in large editions. Naturally such evidence would rarely be left to stand alone; at the very least it would set one searching for new skeletons, partial re-settings, advertisements and so on; my point is the quite simple one that the relationship between variant states and distinct impressions

---

[83] Savage, *Dictionary of the Art of Printing* (1841), p. 814.

must be very carefully assessed if the general conditions of work are not to be misrepresented.

But, as Dr Fleeman has already shown, there is quite conclusive evidence in the Bowyer ledger to associate press figures with a *press* not a man, evidence which can be corroborated by reference to the printed books themselves.[84] Bowyer numbered his presses and his accounts usually show, by their numbers and crews, the presses at which work was done. If a press-crew had a press of its own at which it regularly worked—and there is some evidence that this was so in Cambridge in 1740—then the distinction between men and machines would virtually disappear;[85] but the Bowyer papers offer us no such simple resolution. In the examples of Bowyer books listed in appendix II (g), the figures and/or presses and/or crews can be lined up with a certitude unparalleled in any purely inferential construction. Yet it is most important to note, first, how many discrepancies there are between the records and the printed figures (especially in No. 5); second, the difficulty of assuming continuity of press-crews for any one figure; third, the irrelevance of the highest figure printed, although it designates a press, to the actual number of presses in use; fourth, that the occasional failures to figure a forme are in fact oversights and do not represent work done at a notionally blank press. It is another example of the by now familiar paradox: primary evidence definitely restricts the generality of many statements hitherto made about the interpretation of press figures; yet it reveals such diversity of conditions in their use that almost any answer might well be true for any particular book. It is another warning that, as Professor Todd has put it, "any theory envisaging a uniform procedure in an unorganized, *laissez-faire* handicraft must be regarded with suspicion" ("Observations on Press Figures," p. 173). When therefore the writer of a review article in the *Times Literary Supplement* took Mrs Russell to task for not adequately listing press figures in her bibliography of Cowper, and suggested that the printers of certain editions might be identified by the pattern of press figures, or that because the figures 3 and 6 recur in Bensley's editions of Cowper these editions were always placed in the care of the same pressmen, the arguments may be much less 'advanced' than they seem.[86] In the light of complexities discovered by *any* primary documentation so far unearthed, such an ostensibly direct frontal assault turns out to be no more than a rear-guard action in defence of a much too simplistic and now obsolescent bibliographical method.

IV

I should not wish to deny that significant changes occurred in printing and publishing between the years 1500 and 1800; but on two counts I wish to offer some

---

[84] "William Somervile's 'The Chace,' 1735," loc. cit.

[85] *Cambridge University Press*, I, 125, but see also I, 131. n. 1, and Tanselle, "Press Figures in America," p. 127 n.13.

[86] "Of Text and Type," *Times Literary Supplement*, 24 Feb. 1966, pp. 233–5.

resistance to the evasive tactics of those who would for their part deny the relevance of conditions in any one period to those in another. Of course 1586 is not 1623, nor 1683, 1695, 1701, 1731, nor 1790. Yet just as Greg has argued that bibliography, as the study of the transmission of literary texts, comprehends manuscripts as well as printed books, so I wish to argue that the integrity of the subject can best be preserved and a sound methodology evolved only if we stress the similarity of conditions in all periods. Then fine distinctions may be entertained, not as period differences but as the inevitable result of variables which will differ from day to day and house to house. My second reason for resisting the too ready rejection of analogy is that very little fundamental research has been done on the history of printing. History is never so gross as when it's being formulated to serve a theory; and bibliographers with their eyes closest to the internal physical evidence have, on the whole, seen least of what lies beyond it.

The familiar picture of 'Elizabethan' printers, restricted in number, presses, edition quantities, and apprentices, and therefore constantly under pressure, and operating an essentially uncomplicated, balanced production schedule, is attractive in its simplicity. But in its generalized form such a picture is also apt to be dangerously misleading. Simpson, discussing the limitation of presses, once wrote that "When a printer with at most two presses had a book on the stocks, he could do nothing else until he had printed it off."[87] Such a view, so stated, now seems extremely naive, although something like it is implied in many studies even today. The documentation that exists for a shop of comparable size in 1700, printing books in editions no larger than those permitted in 1587, makes it clear that productive conditions of enormous complexity involving as many as ten or a dozen jobs at any one time were normal in a small two-press house.

But even the *size* of 'Elizabethan' shops has perhaps been a little too readily set at one or two presses, and the 'strict limitation' on their numbers over-stressed. The evidence would appear to be straightforward, but is it? Were there really too few printers and presses for the work available, or too many? In 1582, at a time of complaints from journeymen about lack of work, Christopher Barker said that the number of printing houses then in London (22) could be more than halved and the needs of the whole kingdom still met.[88] In 1583 the complaint of the 'poor men' of the Company was that they had too little work, and Commissioners appointed to look into the trade recommended that some privileged books be released to the poor for printing, a practice continued by the several Stocks of the Stationers' Company throughout the 17th century to assist printers who were short of work (Greg, *Companion*, pp. 21, 128). In May 1583 there were 23 master printers, possessing in all 53 presses: Barker had 5, Wolf 5, Day and Denham 4 each, and six others 3 apiece.[89] Although the Commissioners of 1583 recom-

---

[87] *Proof-Reading in the Sixteenth, Seventeenth and Eighteenth Centuries* (1935), p. 46.

[88] Greg, *A Companion to Arber* (1967), p. 26. I shall normally cite Greg's calendar instead of the originals.

[89] Arber, *Transcript of the Registers of the Stationers' Company*, I, 248.

mended that no more presses be set up without license, their recommendation in respect of the existing presses was simply

> That euerie printer keping presses be restrained to a reasonable nomber of presses according to his qualitie and store of worke, as for example the Quenes printer hauing but .v. presses, and the lawe printer but twoo, we think it not reason that Wolf haue .v. but to restraine him and such other to one or two by discretion till his stoare of worke shall require moe (Greg, *Companion*, p. 131).

Could anything more permissive be desired? The Star Chamber decree of 1586 forbade the erection of new presses "tyll the excessive multytude of Prynters havinge presses already sett up, be abated" (Greg, *Companion*, p. 41). A statement of the position the following month shows that the number of printers had risen to 25 and that Barker had increased the number of his presses to 6 (Arber, *Transcript*, V, lii). Apart from isolated cases of surreptitious printing punished by seizure of equipment, and apart from the normal licensing of those who succeeded to the select company of master printers, there is nothing to show how this positive abatement in the number of presses was procured. For the next twenty-nine years, there is little primary evidence at all to show in what measure the conditions of 1586 had ceased to apply. Indeed, apart from the recurrent fuss over privileges, there is evidence of a general relaxation.

When in 1613–15 the unemployed journeymen again complained about their inability to set up presses, they saw that a necessary condition of such a freedom would be access to privileged copies—otherwise there would be little work.[90] The master printers for their part were worried, or made a pretence of being so, at the "multitude of Presses that are erected among them" and by a self-denying ordinance agreed that, the King's Printer apart, fourteen of them should have 2 presses each and five of them 1.[91] Since the number of printers was 20 in all, such a rule can only mean that many of them had retained from a much earlier period, or set up over the last few years, far more presses than the numbers now set down. And since the number of printers did remain fairly constant, the agreement can only have been designed to secure a slightly more equitable distribution of work among these very printers; it implied, therefore, considerable under-production in the smaller shops.

Are we to take it that this decision by the Court of Assistants was immediately enforced? There is no evidence of it. *Eight years later, on 5 July 1623,*

---

[90] Greg, *Companion*, pp. 52–3. This point is made time and again. Wood's petition of 1621 makes it clear that even of those with presses some were rich and some were poor: "the rich men of the Company by the power of their ordinances, dispose of all things in priuilege to their owne perticular benefits for the most part, and the poore Masters, and Iourney-men Printers haue little, and some of them no worke at all from the Company . . ." (Greg, *Companion*, p. 170). Lownes, Purfoote, Jaggard and Beale—"those foure rich Printers"—are most complained against for the privileges they hold and the punitive actions they can take against offenders, empowered as they are both by ordinance and their high position in the Company.

[91] Jackson, *Records of the Court of the Stationers' Company*, p. 75.

Whereas the m^r printers of this Company, according to a former order haue re-formed themselues for the number of presses that eueryone is to haue and accord-ingly haue brought in their barres to shewe their Conformitie there-vnto . . . (Jack-son, p. 158)

again it is set down that, the King's Printer excluded, fourteen printers should have only 2 presses each and five of them 1. Augustine Matthews was one of these five, but it is clear from another entry that he had more than one press (Jackson, p. 159). By September the following year the order had still not been put into effect and an inspectorial party was authorized to dismantle any excess presses.[92] By 7 Feb. 1625 the Court was prepared to give up:

It is ordered that if the m^r Printers doe not Conforme themselues to the number of presses as hath ben agreed of by former orders and bring in their barres before o^r ladye day next, *Then those that are already brought in to be deliu'ed backe againe* [my italics] (Jackson, p. 173).

In 1637, after being restricted to one press ever since 1586, the Cambridge printer was graciously allowed a second. When in 1632 Roger Daniel had moved in he took over:

Six printing presses, five copper plates, six bankes, seven great stones, one muller, thirteen frames to set cases on . . . six and fifty paire and an halfe of cases for letters made of mettle and one case for wooden letters, five and twenty chases, twenty gal-lies, fifty paper and letter bords, . . . (Roberts, p. 50).

The Star Chamber decree of 1637, reporting that of 1586 as defective in some particulars so that divers abuses had arisen to the prejudice of the public, at-tempted to keep the number of master printers down to 20 (there were 22), but the number of presses, always more difficult to restrict, was allowed to rise (Greg, *Companion*, p. 105). By 1649 there were apparently some 60 printers in London and by 1660 the number had increased to 70, though it is doubtful whether there were so many printing houses. The Licensing Act of 1662 pro-vided that no more printers be licensed until the number had fallen again to 20, but nothing was done to enforce the ruling and for the next thirty years it was openly ignored.[93] In 1668, after the great fire, there were 65 presses in 26 houses, the King's Printer having 6, two others 5 each, another 4, seven had 3, nine had 2, and six had 1.[94] Negus in 1724 listed 75 London houses and 28 in the provinces. Mr Ellic Howe comments: "There was, therefore, no great ex-pansion in the trade compared with its state seventy years previously" (*London Compositor*, p. 33). By 1785 there were 124 printers; in 1808 "not more than

---

[92] Jackson, p. 169. The search uncovered a press operated by George Woods; it was dismantled. Woods of course had no right to a press at all.

[93] Plant, *The English Book Trade* (1939), p. 84; Howe, *London Compositor*, p. 33.

[94] Plomer, *A Short History of English Printing*, 1476–1900 (1915), pp. 185–8; Howe (p. 33) gives the figure as 35.

130," although Stower in the same year listed 216; by 1818 the total in London was 233.[95]

All I wish to ask now is whether there is much conclusive evidence that 'Elizabethan' conditions in any one printing house were utterly distinctive from those common in the 18th century? Expansion of the trade there undoubtedly was but except in a very few cases (Watts in the 1720's, Bowyer, Richardson and Strahan mid-century—a half dozen at most out of upwards of a hundred?) what we get in the 18th century is proliferation, multiple establishments, not an exceptional growth in any one. The fundamental conditions of work in each remain unchanged. Or again, if it is urged that the multi-press shops of the 18th century have few parallels in the early 17th century, one is entitled to ask quite directly how Ackers' and the Bowyers' three-, four-, and five-press shops of the 1730's differ from those of Barker, Wolf, Day, Denham, all of whom had more than three presses, and the other six printers who in 1583 had three presses each. Or one might ask how significantly, in terms of size, either group differs from those listed in 1668 (eleven of whom had three or more presses). And even if it is conceded that none of the printers limited to two presses in 1615 and 1623 would have grossly exceeded this number, a certain scepticism is still permissible since there is no evidence at all that they conformed to the ruling and much that they refused to. Or take the question the other way round: grant for the moment that most Elizabethan shops were two-press or one-press houses; it may then be asked what the distribution of presses was within 18th-century houses. How many had two, how many had only one? In the second week of October 1732 even Bowyer had only two (see appendix II (f)). For the rest, no one knows, and even press figures may not tell us.

Is the problem any simpler if we look at edition quantities? It is true that these were limited by regulation in Elizabethan-Jacobean times and not in the 18th century. Yet two points must be kept in mind. First, very few books printed in the 18th century, apart from some newspapers and periodicals about which some firm figures are at last available, ever in fact exceeded the limits for editions laid down in 1587 and liberalized in 1637. Neither the Cambridge, Bowyer, Woodfall, nor Strahan documents suggest that for any one edition, however many impressions it might comprehend, there is any very gross disparity between Elizabethan and 18th-century conditions in this matter. Out of some 514 books printed by Strahan between 1738 and 1785, only 43 were printed in 2000 copies or more, and of these only 15 were in editions of 3000 or more (Hernlund, "Strahan's Ledgers," p. 104). The edition quantities I cite for Dyche's *Guide to the English Tongue* may be more in keeping with some statements I have seen about expansion of the trade in the 18th century—and with others implying

---

[95] Ibid., pp. 132–3. Professor Todd states that "By the end of the eighteenth century the personnel of the trade numbered no less than 2815" ("Observations on . . . Press Figures," p. 179). But this figure relates to 1818, not to the previous century, and its user implies that the number of master printers had virtually doubled in the previous 10 years—see Howe, p. 132.

trade restriction and small editions in the 17th century. In any case it leads me to my second point: the prodigious numbers of certain books that were produced in the earlier period. Professor Todd once remarked that "a certain discretion common to most authorities, including bibliographers, moves us to view the unknown as unmentionable." And the loss of much ephemera of the 16th and 17th centuries (almanacks, school texts, and many other books required in multiple editions by the several Stocks of the Stationers' Company) has perhaps made us unmindful of the volume of such work. The late Cyprian Blagden's analysis of the distribution of almanacks in the second half of the 17th century, only one aspect of such printing, is a useful corrective.[96] For the earlier period odd cases reveal substantial printings: the 4000 copies of the Psalms in metre, for example, printed by Frank and Hill in 1585; the 10,000 copies of the ABC and Little Catechism printed the same year by Dunn and Robinson (Greg, *Companion*, p. 37). In three years, during the early 1630's the Cambridge printers provided for the London Company 18,000 *Pueriles Sententiae*, 12,000 Aesop's *Fables*, 6000 *Pueriles Confabulationes*, 6000 copies of Mantuan, and at least seven other books in 3000 copies or more (Roberts, p. 51). But the major evidence of large editions, far in excess presumably of the limits set, is the complaints from journeymen. The Company regulations of 1587, designed for the benefit of the journeymen, sought to provide further work by restricting the use of standing formes and by limiting impressions to 1500 copies of some books and 3000 of others (Greg, *Companion*, p. 43). These were of course Company regulations enforced, if at all, by those least likely to gain from them. The workmen are further complaining in 1614, and in 1635 an organized protest is made about the extraordinary number of books printed at one impression and the abuse of standing formes. The alleviation of the journeymen's distress may have been procured by the restriction of standing formes to the Psalter, Grammar and Accidence, Almanacks and Prognostications, but one doubts it.[97] The 1635 provision that no nonpareil books exceed 5000 copies, no brevier exceed 3000 (6000 in some cases), and that all others be kept to editions of 1500 or 2000 (3000 with permission), suggests that multiple impressions and large editions were hardly the prerogative of the 18th century (Greg, *Companion*, p. 95).

Professor Todd has probably done most to set the general attitude towards 18th-century printing and thereby also to imply that conditions in the earlier periods were considerably different. He writes:

> [Eighteenth-century books] are the products of conditions of greater complexity than those which apply to earlier periods, and therefore occasionally require

---

[96] "The Distribution of Almanacks in the Second Half of the Seventeenth Century," *SB*, XI (1958), 107–16.

[97] The articles of 1635 (Greg, *Companion*, pp. 94–5) were still being ignored in 1637 (*Ibid.*, p. 102). The trouble was partly that their enforcement was left to the men whose interests they were least calculated to advance. So one finds the journeymen continuing to complain that the orders of 1586–7 and those of 1635 had not been fulfilled and pleading that they be recorded in some court of justice so that they could be sued upon before a competent judge (*Ibid.*, p. 326). The complaints come to a head again in 1645.

supplemental techniques for their analysis. It has not been sufficiently realized that printing, in this century, has progressed beyond the era of the simple handicraft and now represents one of mass production, where not a few but hundreds of pages of type may be retained and repeatedly returned to press, where not one or two individuals but batteries of pressmen and compositors may produce, in a matter of hours, editions running into thousands of copies, where not one but several books may be put to press concurrently by the same personnel. These practices, though extraordinary in the seventeenth century have become commonplace in the eighteenth . . . ("Editorial Problem in the Eighteenth Century," p. 46).

And elsewhere:

Before the expiration of the Licensing Act in 1695 the process of book-making was undoubtedly less confused than afterwards: only thirty-five master printers were authorized to practise the trade, and most of these, we may be sure, conformed to the regulation limiting the number of presses and apprentices for each shop. . . . After 1695, though, the conditions for disorder increase in approximately the same ratio as the means for detecting it disappear ("Observations on Press Figures," p. 179).

Professor Todd is undoubtedly right that *some* 18th-century books are the products of conditions of greater complexity: any increase in size will increase the number of variables. Undoubtedly too in the largest houses a good deal of type was kept standing, although it would be interesting to go into the economics of such a practice. For the rest, the case for any really radical difference between the centuries would seem to have been over-stated. Perhaps a fine historical exactitude will be possible when more primary documentation has been published and some serious thought given to its economic implications.

V

Plus ça change, plus c'est la même chose. It's the only way I can explain the central paradox of this paper: that all printing houses were alike in being different. Despite my misgivings about 'norms' I have tried to suggest that all printing houses were more alike over the years than many bibliographers are prepared to allow: in size of plant, variability of work force, edition quantities printed, use of standing formes, proofing procedures, and most important of all in printing several jobs concurrently. I have stressed the supreme importance of primary evidence and I have tried to use it to expose and curb what I take to be erroneous inferences. In doing so, I have also tried to demonstrate more generally some weaknesses inherent in the inductive method. When the standing of general statements is damaged by contrary examples, the inductivist usually seeks a safe retreat in some form of historical relativism; I have tried to show how naive this can be. I am sure that Professor Hinman is right, though my sense pursues not his, when he stresses the importance of the new knowledge which will come "in the light of information about printing-house personnel and printing-house methods that is only now becoming known" ("Shakespeare's Texts," p. 26).

Bright lights will cast deep shadows, and I <u>must confess to a feeling of mild</u> <u>despondency about the prospects for analytical bibliography</u>: limited demonstrations there may certainly be, although they may require a life-time's devotion to make them; wherever full primary evidence has become available it has revealed a geometry of such complexity that even an expert in cybernetics, primed with all the facts, would have little chance of discerning it. But, as Nestor says, "In the reproof of Chance lies the true proof of men." Bibliography will simply have to prove itself adequate to conditions of far greater complexity than it has hitherto entertained. To do so, it will inevitably be obliged to use multiple and ingenious hypotheses, to move from induction to deduction, simply because a narrow range of theories is less likely to embrace the complex possibilities of organization within even a quite small printing house. A cynic might observe that the subject is already characterized by multiple and ingenious hypotheses, but too many of these have been allowed to harden into 'truth.' A franker acceptance of deductive procedures would bring a healthy critical spirit into the subject by insisting on the rigorous testing of hypotheses, and the prime method of falsification—adducing contrary particulars—would impose a sound curb on premature generalizations. It may be little pleasure "to observe how much paper is wasted in confutation," but bibliography might grow the more securely if we retained a stronger assurance of its hypothetical nature.

There is, however, a final paradox. Bibliography has nothing to do with bibliographies, and I only hope that new knowledge about productive conditions will prove disturbing enough to widen the gap between the two. The essential task of the bibliographer is to establish the facts of transmission for a particular text, and he will use *all* relevant evidence to determine the bibliographical truth. Author and subject bibliographies have a completely different function and it would be preposterous now to demand of them any great bibliographical sophistication. This would appear to be an argument in favour of degressive bibliography. Not at all; the phrase is meaningless. Book-listing may be as degressive as it wishes, bibliography never. Greg made the point so clearly that it's surprising to find that there is still any fuss about it; if any notice had been taken, we should have less half-baked bibliography and cheaper book-lists.[98]

But finally, if our basic premise is that bibliography should serve literature or the criticism of literature, it may be thought to do this best, not by disappearing into its own minutiae, but by pursuing the study of printing history to the point where analysis can usefully begin, or by returning—and this is the paradox—to the more directly useful, if less sophisticated, activity of enumerative 'bibliography.' This it is which gave us the Pollard and Redgrave and Wing S.T.C.s, both of which have been of inestimable service to the study of history, life, thought— and bibliography—in the 16th and 17th centuries. It will be a pity if history, life,

---

[98] *Collected Papers*, pp. 76–77, 222–3, 240. The arguments from expediency given in *The Times Literary Supplement* during August–September 1966 seem to me to be beside the point.

thought—and bibliography—in the 18th century are long deprived of a comparable service.

Note to the appendices: The information offered in the following appendices is intended merely to provide supporting evidence for the argument of this paper. It is not offered as a contribution to the detailed bibliographical study of either the books or the printing houses mentioned in it. The original documents referring to the Cambridge University Press are printed in my *Cambridge University Press, 1696–1712: A Bibliographical Study* (1966): the two charts printed here continue those given as Table 15 in that book. The details of the Bowyer printing house are taken from the Bowyers' record of composition and presswork over the years 1730 to 1739; the volume in which this work is recorded is in the possession of The Grolier Club and is being edited for publication by Mr Keith Maslen. An edition of the ledger of Charles Ackers, printer of *The London Magazine,* was recently published by the Oxford Bibliographical Society. The appendices are long, but I have deliberately multiplied the examples to illustrate fully the variety of conditions under which the books mentioned came to be made, by different men, at different periods, and in different places.

APPENDIX I (A)

Cambridge University Press: Work done by Compositors and Pressmen
26 December 1701–31 January 1702

	Already Set	Set in Period	Printed in Period	Printed Later	Printed in Period	Printed Later	Printed Later
Crownfield			Coldenhoff & Ponder		Terrill		Coldenhoff
Propertius	3T–3U						
		2X					
		2Y–3A					
Terence	3S						
Bertram							
Beaumont, Psyche	2U½						
(in quires)	2U½–2X						
		2Y–2Z½					
		2Z½a3A½					
Combination Paper	*						
Great & Muckeus							
Suidas, Vol. I	O½						
(in quires)	O½						
		P–R					
		S½					
		S½					
Terence		2D½					
		2E½					
Délié & Knell							
Suidas, Vol. II	L½						
(in quires)	L½M						
		N½					
		N½					
		O					
Bennet, Discourse		D–G					
		H					
		I					
Pokins							
Bennet, Discourse	B–C						
Milner, Animadversions		B					
		C					
		D					
Whiston, Short View		3Q–3S					
		3T					

APPENDIX I (B)

Cambridge University Press: Work done by Compositors and Pressmen
1–28 February 1702

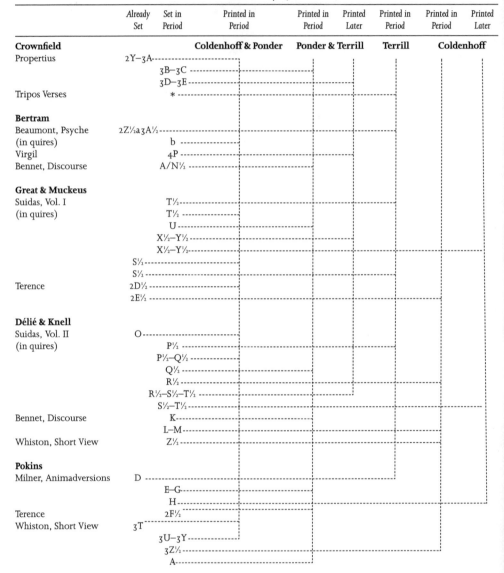

	Already Set	Set in Period	Printed in Period	Printed in Period	Printed Later	Printed in Period	Printed in Period	Printed Later
Crownfield			**Coldenhoff & Ponder**	**Ponder & Terrill**		**Terrill**	**Coldenhoff**	
Propertius	2Y–3A							
		3B–3C						
		3D–3E						
Tripos Verses		*						
Bertram								
Beaumont, Psyche	2Z½a3A½							
(in quires)		b						
Virgil		4P						
Bennet, Discourse		A/N½						
Great & Muckeus								
Suidas, Vol. I		T½						
(in quires)		T½						
		U						
		X½–Y½						
		X½–Y½						
	S½							
	S½							
Terence		2D½						
		2E½						
Délié & Knell								
Suidas, Vol. II	O							
(in quires)		P½						
		P½–Q½						
		Q½						
		R½						
		R½–S½–T½						
		S½–T½						
Bennet, Discourse		K						
		L–M						
Whiston, Short View		Z½						
Pokins								
Milner, Animadversions	D							
		E–G						
		H						
Terence		2F½						
Whiston, Short View	3T							
		3U–3Y						
		3Z½						
		A						

APPENDIX II (A)

William Bowyer's Press: Work done by Compositors and Pressmen
26 December 1730–16 January 1731

Books and Compositors	Edition Size	Press I W. Diggle J. Mazemore	Press 3 R. Collyer R. Franklin	Press 7 J. Clarke S. Peacock
1. Baxter, *Winter Evening Tales* [Already set]	750		A2	
2. Clarke, *Sermons* J. Nutt: P10, Q10, R10, S10, B12, C8 B4, I5, K6 P. James: P6, Q6, R6, S6	1500	S1		S1, P2, Q2 R1
3. *Defence of Present Admin.* J. Hart: A½, B½ C. Micklewright: C½, D½ J. Nutt: Reimposing 6 formes	1st ed. 2500 2nd ed. 500	1st edition A, B 500 + 500 C, D 500 A, C 1500	1st edition B, D 1500 C, D 500 2nd edition A, C 500	2nd edition B, D 500
4. Distilling J. Hart: A4 J. Nutt: I13, K10, A12 P. James: I5, K6	1000	I2, K1	H2, K1	
5. *Foedera vol.. XVIII* C. Micklewright: 12O	500	12L2, 12M2	12N2	
6. Friend, *Hippocrates* D. Redmaine: 3I – 3M	500 +80	3F1, 3G1, 3H1	3F1, 3G1, 3H1	
7. *Greek Grammar* D. Redmaine: 2A½	1500		X1	
8. Gyles, *Catalogue* R. Bell: π (folio page)	100 (½ sheets)		π	
9. *Marmora Oxonia* J. Hart: 7K2, 7L4, 7M2	300 +6	7K1, 3I1	7I2, 7K1	
10. Marshall, *Proposals* [Already set?]	1500		π	
11. Marshall, *Receipts* J. Nutt: 2 Great Primer	1000		π	
12. Peyton, *Catastrophe* R. Bell: G ½ – K½	750	G1	E1, F1	H1, I1, K1, A1
13. *Philosophical Transactions* R. Holmes) 4G – 4T T. Hart)	750	4H2, 4I1, 4L1 4M1, 4N2, 4O2	4G2, 4I1, 4L1, 4M1, 4P2, 4Q2	4K2

APPENDIX II (A)　(continued)

Books and Compositors	Edition Size	Press I W. Diggle J. Mazemore	Press 3 R. Collyer R. Franklin	Press 7 J. Clarke S. Peacock
14. Rapin de Thoyras, *History* 　J. Hart: [No. 53] H6, I6, K6, 　L6, M6, N6 　　　　[No. 47] 2 sheets 　　　　　　4 pages 　R. Bell: [No. 53] H6, I6, K6, 　L6, M6, N6	750		Covers 250 (½ sheet)	
15. Regnault, *Phil. Conversations* 　D. Gaylord: B, C, D, E7, F 　G, H 　C. Micklewright: E9	1000	B1, C1, D1	B1, C1, D1 E2	
16. St. George's Chapel, *Hymns* 　J. Nutt: π [printed later]	500			
17. Wade, *Horace* 　R. Holmes) 　T. Hart　) Title ½ sheet 　J. Nutt: Reimposing 3 　castrated sheets in 4*	250 +24	A½ A2 (4*)	X½ H X2 (4*)	cancelled leaf
18. Wake, *Catechism* 　D. Redmaine: Index ½ 　J. Hart: Index ½ 　D. Gaylord: Index 4 pages	3000		O2	

Note: As Clarke and Peacock received only one weeks' copy money, press 7 was presumably in use for only one of the three weeks. During this three-week period, compositors' and pressmen's earnings were: (a) Compositors: Bell £1.9.7.; Gaylord £1.18.10.; J. Hart £2. 9. 7.; T. Hart and R. Holmes £4.15.0.; James (unrecorded: James was still an apprentice); Micklewright £1.13.7.; Nutt (unrecorded: Nutt was still an apprentice); Redmaine £1.17.3.; (b) Pressmen: Diggle and Mazemore £2.18. 3.; Collyer and Franklin £3.19. 5.; Clarke and Peacock £1.10. 1. (In this and the following tables fractions of a penny have been disregarded.)

APPENDIX II (B)

William Bowyer's Press: Work done by Compositors and Pressmen
18–30 Janury 1731

Books and Compositors	Edition Size	Press 1 [W. Diggle J. Mazemore]	Press 2 T. Farmer P. Wardman	Press 3 R. Collyer R. Franklin	Press 5 [unnamed]	Press 7 J. Clarke S. Peacock
1. *Address* C. Micklewright (4 settings)	8000	1250	3750	2000		1000
2. *Advice to Poultney* [= Poem in Defense of a Walpole?] J. Nutt: Great Primer ½ sheet	100 +12		π ½			
3. *Clarke, Sermons* P. James: C8, D4, E4, F6, G10, H6, I4 J. Nutt, D12, E12, F10, G6, H10, I12	1500		C2, F1, G1, H1	R1, E1	B2, G1	D2, E1, F1
4. *Du Pin, Proposals* D. Redmaine: 4 pages	500	π				
5. *Du Pin, Receipts* J. Nutt: 2 Great Primer	500	π				
6. *Ellen Foord's Case* C. Micklewright: [printed later]	712					
7. *Freind, Hippocrates* [Already set]	500 +80	3K1	3I1, 3K1			3I1
8. *Greek Grammar* D. Redmaine: 2B	1500			Y1		
9. *Lobb, Treatise of Small Pox* D. Redmaine: B [printed later]	750					
10. *Marmora Oxonia* J. Hart: 7M2, 7N2	300 +6			7L1	7M1	7L1, 7M1
11. *Marshall, Sermons* C. Micklewright: E11, G3, H5, I6, K8, L7 J. Lewis: E5, F16, G13, H12, I10, K8, L9	800	F1, H1	C1, F1, G1	B1, C1, G1, I1	H1	B1, D2, E2, I1
12. *Parliamentary Votes* D. Redmaine: 1 and 2 R. Bell: 3	1000 +1250	B1, D½, E½, F½, G½, H½, I½		A1	A1	B1

APPENDIX II (B) (continued)

Books and Compositors	Edition Size	Press 1 [W. Diggle J. Mazemore]	Press 2 T. Farmer P. Wardman	Press 3 R. Collyer R. Franklin	Press 5 [unnamed]	Press 7 J. Clarke S. Peacock
13. *Philosophical Transactions* 　T. Hart　) 　R. Holmes) 4U–5G	750	5A1	4R1, 4S1, 4T1, 4X1, 4Y1, 4Z1, 5C1	4Y1, 5B1, 5C1	4U1, 4X1, 4Z1, 5B1, 5D1, 5E1	4R1, 4S1, 4T1, 4U1, 5A1, 5D1, 5E1
14. Rapin de Thoyras, *History* 　R. Bell: [No. 47] O4, Y4, Z4 　　　　　Wrappers 2 pages 　J. Hart: [No. 47] O6, Y6, 　　　　　Wrappers 2 pages 　L. Grainger: H4, I4, K4, L4, 　M4, N4, O6, Y6, Z8, 2A8	750	M1	H1, L1, M1, N1	H1, I1, N1	I1, K1, L1	N1
15. Regnault, *Phil. Conversations* 　D. Gaylord: K8, L–O, P8 　I. Grainger: I, K8	1000	K1	I1, K1	F1, G1, H2, I1, L1		F1, G1, L1
16. St. George's Chapel, *Hymns* 　[Already set]	500					π
17. Skerret, *Sermon* 　D. Redmaine: 4 pages	250	Title				
18. *State of National Debt* 　R. Bell: A–D, Broadside	750		Broadside		A1, B1, C1, D1	
19. *Warrington's Case* 　J. Hart; [printed later]	800 +50					

Note: Diggle and Mazemore also claimed for '19 Rm Malt Rules @2s.8d. per Rm, Altering 10 shts. Sign. at 4d.' and '18 Rm. 5 qrs. of Gr. Malt. Bv @ 3s. per sht. & Altering 28 signatures @ 2d. each.'. During this two-week period, compositors' and pressmen's earnings were: (a) Compositors: Bell £2.19. 2.; Gaylord £1.10. 2.; Grainger £2. 0. 0.; J. Hart £1. 6.11.; T. Hart and R. Holmes £2.12.4.; James (unrecorded); Lewis £1. 2. 8.; Micklewright £1.10. 4.; Nutt (unrecorded); Redmaine £1.18. 2.; (b) Pressmen: Diggle and Mazemore £4.15. 5.[?]; Farmer and Wardman £2. 4. 3.; Collyer and Franklin £2. 7.11.; Press 5 (unnamed) £1.16. 6.; Clarke and Peacock £2.13. 0.

APPENDIX II (C)

William Bowyer's Press: Work done by Compositors and Pressmen
1–6 February 1731

Books and Compositors	Edition Size	[Press 1 unnamed]	[Press 2 unnamed]	[Press 3 unnamed]	[Press 7 unnamed]
1. Clarke, Sermons T. Hart) R. Holmes) M6, N7, O7 P. James: I2, K8, L5, M4, N3, O3 J. Nutt: K8, L11, M6, N6, O6	1500	H1, K1, L1, M1	I1, K1, M1, N1	I1, L1, N1	
2. Distilling [Already set]	1000		A2		
3. Ellen Foord's Case [Already set]	100 +12 +400 +100 +100	π			
4. Islington Lodgers' Bills J. Nutt	500				π
5. Letter from the West D. Gaylord: A½, B½, C½ [printed later]	6				
6. Lobb, Treatise of Small Pox [Already set]	750		B1		B1
7. Marshall, Sermons J. Lewis: M13, N7, O7, P10 C. Micklewright: M3, N9, O9, P6	800		K1, M1	L1 300 Titles	K1, L1, M1, N2
8. Moss, Sermons J. Hart: B [printed later]	1000				
9. Newcome, Evidence of Christian Religion T. Hart) B [Specimen only? R. Holmes) Presswork unrecorded]	?				
10. Parliamentary Votes J. Hart: 10–14	1250 1000	K½, L½, M½, N½, O½			
11. Parsons, Bills J. Nutt: [printed later]	1000				
12. Pension Bills J. Hart; 1 sheet English	750		1 forme		1 forme
13. Philosophical Transactions T. Hart) R. Holmes) 3H, 5I, 3I, 3K1	750	5F1, 5H1	5H1	5G1	5F1, 5G1

APPENDIX II (C) (continued)

Books and Compositors	Edition Size	[Press 1 unnamed]	[Press 2 unnamed]	[Press 3 unnamed]	[Press 7 unnamed]
14. Rapin de Thoyras, *History* R. Bell: 2A8, 2B8	750		Z1	Y2, Z1, 2A1	O2
15. Regnault, *Phil. Conversations* D. Gaylord: P8, Q	1000	M1		N1	M1, N1
16. *Swedish Dictionary Proposals* Compositor unrecorded: ½ sheet	50 +6		1 forme		
17. *Warrington's Case* [Already set]	800 +50		1 forme		1 forme
18. Wesley, *Prolegomena* J. Hart: B [Specimen only? Presswork unrecorded]	?				

Note: During this one week period, compositors' and pressmen's earnings were: (a) Compositors: Bell 9s.7d.; Gaylord 15s.10d.; J. Hart £2.1.11.; T. Hart and R. Holmes £1.13.11.; James 7s.9d.; Lewis 11s.7d.; Micklewright 8s.6d.; Nutt 11s.6d. [?]; (b) Pressmen: Press 1 £2.1.3.; Press 2£1.9.1.; Press 3 £1. 2. 9.; Press 7 £1.6.10.

APPENDIX II (D)

William Bowyer's Printing House: Composition and Presswork
31 January–12 February 1732

1. Composition

	Work Done	Earnings
I. Lance	Evidence of Christian Religion O, P, Q, R and making up three formes	13. 8.
R. Dennett	Bill for Sugar Colonies 2 sheets Remarks on Lives of the Saints B, C, D, E, F, G, H4 Life of Cleveland, vol. I Title	£3. 0. 7.
B. Baddam	Cocks's Catalogue M1, N8 Charitable Corporations D Hymns for St Dunstan's Sacrament A, B, C, E, F4	£1. 6.11.
B. Tarrott	Charles XII F4 Letter to Member of Parliament 2 sheets Sacrament D half sheet	14. 8.
D. Gaylord	Calmet's Dictionary 3Z, 4A, 4B, 4C Articles of Limerick A, B, and over-running several times Charles XII M, N, O4	£2. 6.11.
G. Grantham	Gyles's Catalogue Voyages 6O2, Q2, R2, U4, Y2, A4	8. 2.
G. Hills	Charitable Corporations A, B4, [C6] Charles XII F4 Tully's Offices L12, M12	£1.11. 8.
C. Micklelwright	Votes 18, 19, 20, 21, 22 Tully's Offices L12, M12, N12	£2.12. 6.
J. Morgan	Charles XII C5, D8, E5, F8, G8, H4 Hutchinson B Gentleman Farrier	£1. 7. 8.
R. Holmes	Scripture Vindicated D6, E, F, G, H, I, K, L Proposals for Hippocrates	£1.10. 4.
T. Hart	Votes 14, 15, 16, 17 Memoria Technica M, N, O Wesley's Job Y, Z and correcting Y	£2.10. 8.
T. Allestree	Gyles's Catalogue A4 Voyages 6O2, 6P4, 6S2, 6X2, 6Z2, 7B4, 7C2	£1. 7. 2.
J. Nutt	Moss's Sermons B, C, D, E, F Charles XII B, C11, D8, E11, F8, G8, H12, I Scheme to Pay Natonal Debt 2 pages ditto imposing 3 half sheets Hymns for St George ye Martyr Greek quarto page of Mr Dwight An English folio page	[£3.15. 0.]

APPENDIX II (D) (continued)

2. Presswork

No.	Job	Press 1 S. Peacock H. Perry	Press 2 [unnamed]	Press 3 R. Franklin T. Reynolds	Press 7 J. Flower
500	Receipts for Lysias	π			
350) 24)	Voyages	$6C_1$, $6H_2$, $6D_1$, $6F_1$, $6E_1$, $6G_1$, $6I_1$, $6O_1$, $6N_1$, $6P_1$, $6S_1$, $6Q_1$	$6C_1$, $6F_1$, $6G_1$, $6K_2$, $6L_2$, $6O_1$, $6R_2$, $6T_1$, $6Q_1$	$6D_1$, $6E_1$, $6T_1$, $6M_1$, $6N_1$, $6P_1$	
500	Cocks's Catalogue	I	K_1	L_1, M_1, N_1	Y
500	Scripture Vindicated		D_1	C, E, F, H	
500	Remarks on Lives of the Saints	B_1	C_2, D_1	B_1, D_1, E_1	
500	Proposals for Hippocrates		One forme		
400) 100)	Wesley's Job	Y_1			
400) 100)	Proposals for Lysias			π	
750	Gyles's Catalogue	¼ sheet	S_1	T_1, U_1	
750	Sacrament	A_1			B
750	Remarks on Scandal	A, B	C_1, D_1		[A]
750	Cock and Bull	B			
700) 64)	Spenser	G_1			
1000	Bill for Sugar Colonies	A_2	B_1	[B_1]	
1000	Moss's Sermons	A_1, E_2, G_1, H_1, L_1	F_1	A_1, G_1, H_1	I_1
1000	Memoria Technica		K, L		
1000	Charles XII	L_1, M_1, O¼	M_1, N_1	N_1	
1000	Charitable Corporations	A_1, B_1, C_1	A_1, C_1, D_1	B_1	
1000	Chirurg. Instit.	A_1, $2C_1$	A_1, R a page	$2C_1$	
1000	Calmet		B_1, C_1	B_1, C_1	
1500	Greek Grmmar		A_1		
1500	Hymns for St Dunstan's			π	
1500	Tully's Offices	I_1		I_1	L_1, M_1
1500	Life of Cleveland	Titles			
2000	Votes	O, Q_1, T, X_1	P_1, R_1, U_1, Y_1	O_1, S_1, X_1, Y_1	
Earnings:		£3.19. 5.	£3.10. 3.	£3. 2. 2.	14. 0.

APPENDIX II (E)

Willia Bowyer's Printing House: Composition and Presswork
14–26 February 1732

1. Composition

	Work Done	Earnings
D. Redmaine	Bankrupts' Bill A, B Votes 28, 29, 30, 31, 32 Spenser H, I, K Injured Innocence G8, H4	£3. 5. 4.
R. Dennett	Remarks on Lives of the Saints H4, I, K Injured Innocence I2, K8 Voyages 7O, 7P2	£1. 11. 8.
B. Baddam } B. Tarrott }	Sacrament F4, G8, H8, I8, K8 Letter to Archbishop 7 half-sheets Gentlemen Farrier C, D, E, F	£2. 7. 2.
G. Hills } C. Micklewright }	Tully's Offices N12, O Ditto Brevier Index P12 Bankrupts' Bill C, D, E, F Life of Cecil A, B	£3. 9. 0.
R. Holmes	Scripture Vindicated, Part II M, N, O, P, Q, R, S Evidence of Christian Religion S, T, U¼, Title ¼	£1. 11. 1.
G. Grantham	Voyages 7E1, 7G3, 7H2, 7K2, 7L4, 7M3, 7Q2, 7R3, 7T2, 7U2 Injured Innocence H4, I6	£1. 18. 2.
D. Gaylord	Calmet's Dictionary 4D, 4E, 4F, 4G, 4H Charles XII F8, Correcting N	£1. 15. 2.
C. Knell	Voyages 6S2, 6T2, 6Z2, 7C2, 7D4, 7E1, 7H2, 7I1, 7M1, 7N4, 7R1, 7S4, 7T1	£1. 17. 1.
G. Karver	Cocks's Catalogue M7 Chiselden's Syllabus Cock and Bull 3 half-sheets Hutchinson C8	£1. 13. 9.
W. Diggle	Voyages 6B2, 6T2, 6X2, 6Y2, 7E2, 7F1, 7G1, 7I3, 7K2, 7P2, 7Q2 Nelson quarter-sheet	£1. 12. 2.
T. Hart	Votes 23, 24, 25 Wesley's Job 2A, 2B, 2C2 Correcting Z, 2A Mr. Chishull's half-sheet Memoria Technica P Bill for Parton Pier	£3. 0. 8.
J. Nutt	Moss's Sermons A, a, G, H, I ditto 2F half-sheet, vol. I Chiselden one page Two Great Primer receipts	£1. 12. 6.

APPENDIX II (E) (continued)

2. Presswork

No.	Job	Press 1 S. Peacock H. Perry	Press 2 H. Davis J. Mazemore	Press 3 R. Franklin T. Reynolds	Press 5 E. Vicaris W. King	Press 7 R. Collyer
400	Vie de Thou					π
250	Owen				Title	
300	Hutchinson	B1, E1, G1	B1, C1, D1, E1, F1, G1	C1, E1		D1, F1, G1
300	Wooton		¼ sheet			
500	Lives of Saints	G1				
350 } 24 }	Voyages	6Z2, 7C1, 7E1, 7G1, 7H1, 7I1, 7L1	6U2, 7A1, 7F1, 7K2, 7L1	6X1, 6Y1, 7A1, 7D2	6S1, 6T1, 6X1, 7B2, 7C1	7F1, 7H1
450 } 50 }	Job	Z1	Z1, 2A1	2A1		
500	Evidence of Christian Religion	R	P1	O1, T1	Q, S	
500	Scripture Vindicated	O	G1, I1, K1	L1, P1		M, N
500	Remarks on Lives of the Saints			C1, F2	E1, H2	G
500	Receipts for Hippocrates	π				
750	Cock and Bull	C, D	Title			
750	Sacrament	H, K		G1, I1	B1, C1, E1, F1	
750	Letter to Archbishop			B1, C1, D1		
700 } 64 }	Spenser	H1			B1, C1, E1, F1	
1500	Greek Grammar	2N				
1000	Calmet's Dictionary		D1, E1	D1, E1		
1000	Moss's Sermons	a2, I1, L1	L1		K1	K1, 2F
1000	Gentleman Farrier					A1
1000	Memoria Technica	M	N1, O			
1250	Bankrupts Bill	A1, B1, C1, D1, E1	A1, C1, E1, F1	F1, D1		[B1]
1500	Tully's Offices		N1	K1, M1	K1	N1
2000	Injured Innocence	K	G1, H1	I1		
2000	Votes	Z1, 2A1, 2B1, 2E1, 2H1	Z1, 2C1, 2D1, 2F1, 2H1	2A1, 2C1, 2E1, 2G1, [2F1]		
4250	Nelson	¼ sheet				
	Earnings:	£4. 1. 8.	£3.14. 9.	£3. 5. 8.	£1. 9. 6.	£1. 2. 4.

APPENDIX II (F)

William Bowyer's Printing House: Composition and Presswork
8–14 October 1732

1. Composition

	Work Done	Earnings
P. Grantham	Bacon's Letters X, Y	9. 1.
M. Newsted	Clifton's State of Physick A, a, b	18. 1.
O. Nelson	Rosalinda D, E, F	18. 1.
R. Holmes	Fryar Bacon 3G, 3H, 3I, 3K, 3L, 3M 1 page	£1. 1. 5.
T. Clark	Essay on Colonies B, C, D, E	£1. 0. 1.
D. Gaylord	Thuanus Part VI 6A, 6B, C 2 pages	£1. 0. 1.

2. Presswork

		[Press 1]	[Press 2]
6000	Latin Testament	L	
300	Chiselden's Tables	XXV, XXVI	
1500	Swift's Miscellany	B1	B1
100	Middleton's Sermon	Titles	
750 150 5 }	Thuanus	6A2	3R2, 3S2
1000	Rosalinda		B2
220 30 }	Fryar Bacon		3D2, 3F2, 3G2
500 25 }	Clifton's State of Physick		M2, N2
200 25 }	Bacon's Letters		S2
	Receipts for Duke of Somerset		π
Earnings:		£1.15. 8.	£1.12. 6.

Note: Neither the names of the crews nor the numbers of the presses used are given, but payments of copy-money show that two full crews were employed. Each man at press 1 therefore received 17s. 10d. and each man at press 2 received 16s. 3d.

APPENDIX II (G)

Books Printed by William Bowyer: Some Case-Histories

---

1. Voltaire, *Histoire de Charles XII*. [London, 1731.]

12°: A–P⁶ (all printed by Bowyer)   Copy: BM. 10761.df.14.

Production: 7½ sheets; edition 750; composition 5s.3d. per half sheet; presswork 1s.9d. per half sheet; price per sheet 24s.; finished by 13 Jan. 1732; volume I only printed by Bowyer. On this and the next three items, see the article by K.I.D. Maslen, *The Library*, 5th ser. XIV (1959), 287–93. (The date of completion, 13 Jan., is derived from the Bowyer Paper Stock Ledger. Bowyer's account of work done covers the entire period from 26 Dec. 1731–29 Jan. 1732, hence the later date given below.)

Composition: A–P, T. Hart 29 Jan.

Presswork: A, 1 (Diggle/Peacock) 29 Jan.; B, C, 3 (Franklin/Reynolds) 29 Jan.; D, 1 (Diggle/Peacock) 29 Jan.; E, F, 3 (Franklin/Reynolds) 29 Jan.; G-M. 1 (Diggle/Peacock) 29 Jan.; N, O, 2 (unnamed) 29 Jan.; P, 3 (Franklin/Reynolds) 29 Jan.

Figures: 1–A4, D3v, G6v, H6v, I3v, K6, L3v, M4v
2–N6v, O3v
3–B6v, F6v, P4v
Note: Franklin's and Reynolds' failure to figure C and E.

---

2. Voltaire, *History of Charles XII*. London 1732.

8°: A1 B–N⁸ O1 (all printed by Bowyer)   Copy: BM. 153. p. 23.

Production: 12 ¼ sheets; edition 1000; composition 6s.; presswork 4s.; price per sheet 18s.; begun by 29 Jan. 1732; finished by 26 Feb. 1732; first 12 ¼ sheets only printed by Bowyer.

Composition: K, L, Lane 29 Jan.; B, C11, Nutt 12 Feb.; C5, D8, Morgan 12 Feb.; D8, E11, Nutt 12 Feb; E5, F8, Morgan 12 Feb.: F8, G8, Nutt 12 Feb.; G8, H4, Morgan 12 Feb.; H12, 1, Nutt 12 Feb.; M, N, O4, Gaylord 12 Feb.; correcting in N, Gaylord 26 Feb.

Note: F may have been set twice. In addition to the claims listed above, the following are recorded: F4, Hills 12 Feb.; F4, Tarrott 12 Feb.; F8, Gaylord 26 Feb.

Presswork: Bi, Bo, 2 (unnamed) 29 Jan.; Ci, Co, 1 (Diggle/Peacock) 29 Jan.; Di, 2 (unnamed) 29 Jan.; Do, Eo, 3 (Franklin/Reynolds) 29 Jan.; Ei, 1 (Diggle/Peacock) 29 Jan.; Fi, 2 (unnamed) 29 Jan.; Fo, 7 (Franklin/Reynolds) 29 Jan.; Gi, 1 (Diggle/Peacock) 29 Jan.; Go, Ho, 2 (unnamed) 29 Jan.; Ko, 2 (unnamed) 29 Jan.; Ki, Li, 7 (Jones/Perry) 29 Jan.; Lo, Mi, 1 (Peacock/Perry) 12 Feb.; Mo, Ni, 2 (unnamed) 12 Feb.; No, 3 (Franklin/Reynolds) 12 Feb.; A/O, 1 (Peacock/Perry) 12 Feb.

Figures: 1–C1v, C8v, E7v, G1v, L6v, M7v
2–B7, B8, D1v, F8, H2v, K7, M7, N8
3–D7, E7, G7, I8, I8v, N8v
7–F8v, H5v, K5v, L5v

Note: Go claimed by 2 but figured 3; the changes of crew for presses 1 and 7; the same crew worked both presses 3 and 7 within the same period, so that both cannot have been in use at once.

APPENDIX II (G) (continued)

3. Voltaire, *Histoire de Charles XII* ('Seconde Edition, révùe corrigée / par l'Auteur'). [London, 1732.]
8°: A–K⁸L⁴ (all printed by Bowyer)   Copy: BM. 611.c.12 (1).

Production: 10½ sheets; edition 1000; composition 8s.; presswork 4s.; price per sheet 21s.; begun by
              18 Mar. 1732; finished by 8 April 1702; first 10½ sheets only printed by Bowyer.

Composition: A–H, Dennett 18 Mar.; I, K, Dennett/Tarrott 25 Mar.; L½, T. Hart 25 Mar.

Presswork: (None of the crews is named) Ai, Ao, 7–18 Mar.; Bi, 5–18 Mar.; Bo, Ci, 3–18 Mar.; Co,
              1–18 Mar.; Do, 3–18 Mar.; Di, 7–18 Mar.; Ei, 4–18 Mar.; Eo, 1–18 Mar.; Fi, 3–18 Mar.; Fo,
              7–8 Apr.; Gi, 3–8 Apr.; Go, Ho, 7–8 Apr.; Hi, 2–8 Apr.; Ii, 3–8 Apr.; Io, 7–8 Apr.; Ko, 4–8
              Apr.; Ki, L, 2–8 Apr.

Figures: 1–C7, E7
              2–H8, K1v, L3v
              3–B7, C8, F8, G8, I7v
              4–E6, K2v
              5–B8
              7–A2v, A3v, D1v, F2v, G2v, H7, I5

              Note: Fo was also claimed by press 2 on 18 Mar.; Do (press 3) unfigured.

4. Voltaire, *History of Charles XII* ('The Second Edition, Corrected.'). London 1732.
8°: A⁶B–N⁸ (all printed by Bowyer)   Copy: BM. 10761.bb.39.

Production: 12 sheets; edition 2000; composition 6s.; presswork 8s., price per sheet 28s.; finished by
              18 Mar. 1732 (as all claims are dated 18 Mar., dates are omitted from the tables of
              composition and presswork given below); sheets B–N only printed by Bowyer.

Composition: B16, C4, Grantham; C6, Knell; C6, D2, Allestree; D11, Grantham; D3, E6, Knell; E6,
              Allestree; E4, F7, Grantham; F5, Knell; F4, G4, Allestree; G8, Grantham; G4, H4,
              Allestree; H4, Knell; H8, I10, Grantham; I2, Allestree; I4, K4, Knell; K8, Grantham; K4,
              L3, Allestree; L7, Knell; L6, M6, Grantham; M8, Allestree; M1, Nutt; M1, N4, Knell; N8,
              Grantham; N4, T. Hart.

Presswork: (None of the crews is named) Bo, 4; Bi, 2; Co, 3; Ci, Do, 7; Di, Eo, 1; Ei, Fi, 2; Fo, Go, 3;
              Gi, 4; Hi, 3; Ho, 2; Ii, 1; Io, Ki, 7; Ko, Lo, 3; Li, 1; Mi, 7; Mo, Ni, 2; No, 1.

Figures: 1–D7v, E7, L8, N8v
              2–B8, E1v, F5v, H2v, M2v, N1v
              3–C8v, F7, G8v, H7v, L7
              4–B2v, G1v
              7–C1v, D7, I2v, K1v, M1v

              Note: Ii (press 1) and Ko (press 3) are unfigured.

APPENDIX II (G) (continued)

5. Baxter, *Glossarium Antiquitatum Britannicarum*. London, 1733.

8°: A⁴a⁸B–T⁸ U⁴ Copy: BM. 7708.b.5.

Production: 20 sheets; edition 500; composition 10s.; presswork 2s.4d.; price per sheet 22s.; begun by 10 Oct. 1732; finished by 2 June 1733.

Composition: (Thomas Hart set the text unaided except as noted for the 8 pages of C) B, 7 Oct.; C8, Hart/Micklewright 11 Nov.; C8, D, 25 Nov.; E, F8, 2 Dec.; F8, G, 9 Dec; H8, 20 Jan.; H8, I8, 27 Jan.; I8, K, L8, 24 Feb.; L8, 3 Mar.; M8, 10 Mar.; M8, N8, 17 Mar.; N8, O, 24 Mar.; P, Q, R, 14 Apr.; S, T8, 28 Apr.; T8, 5 May; U8, 12 May; A, a, 26 May.

Presswork: Bo, 2 (Mazemore/Peacock) 11 Nov.; Bi, 1 (Classon/Diggle) 11 Nov.; Co, 3 (Bradley/Vicaris) 2 Dec.; Ci, Di, Do, 1 (Classon/Diggle) 2 Dec.; Eo, 2 (Mazemore/Peacock) 9 Dec.; Ei, 1 (Classon/Diggle) 9 Dec.; Fi, Fo, 2 (Mazemore/Peacock) 23 Dec.; Gi, 3 (Dennis/Duff); Go, Hi, Ho, 2 (Mazemore/Peacock) 27 Jan.; Ii, Io, 2 (unnamed) 24 Feb.; Ki, Ko, 1 (Diggle/Reynolds) 3 Mar.; Li, 3 (Dennis/Duff) 24 Mar.; Ni, 2 (Clarke/Mazemore) 24 Mar.; No, 7 (Jones/Needham) 24 Mar.; Oi, 7 (Jones/Needham) 14 Apr.; Oo, 3 (Duff/Mazemore) 14 Apr.; Pi, 2 (Clarke/Dennis) 14 Apr.; Po, Qi, 1 (Milburne/Renolds) 14 Apr.; Qo, 3 (Duff/Mazemore) 14 Apr.; Ri, Ro, 2 (Clarke/Jones) 28 Apr.; Si, 1 (Classon alone) 28 Apr.; So, 3 (Duff/Mazemore) 28 Apr.; T (unrecorded); A/Ui, 1 (unnamed) 26 May; A/Uo, 2 (unnamed) 26 May; ai, ao, 7 (Brooker/Clarke) 2 June.

Figures: 1–A3v, C1v, D3v, E7v, K8, K8v
               2–a5, a6, B8v, F7, F8, G4v, H1v, H7, I7, I8, L2v, P7v, R7v, U3v
               3–C8v, L7v, M7v, M8v, O8v, Q7, S6v, T7v, T8v
               5–G5v
               7–N7, O7v

Note: Press 1 failed to figure Bi, Po, Qi, Si; Press 2 failed to figure Eo, Ni, Ro; Press 3 printed Gi but the forme is figured 5; both ai and ao were printed by Press 2 but both are figured 7; the changing composition of the crews at each press:

Press 1: (a) Classon/Diggle (b) Diggle/Reynolds (c) Milburne/Reynolds (d) Classon alone (e) unnamed

Press 2: (a) Mazemore/Peacock (b) unnamed (c) Clarke/Mazemore (d) Clarke/Dennis (e) Clarke/Jones (f) unnamed

Press 3: (a) Bradley/Vicaris (b) Dennis/Duff (c) Duff/Mazemore

Press 7: (a) Jones/Needham (b) Brooker/Clarke

6. Spenser, *The Shepherd's Calendar*, ed. J. Ball. London, 1732.

8°: A⁸a1 B–Q⁸ R⁶ (–R6)   Copy: BM. 11607.f.7.

Production: 17½ sheets; edition 700 Demy, 60 Royal, 4 Writing Royal; composition 5s.6d.; presswork 2s.6d.; price per sheet 20s.; begun by 27 nov. 1731; finished by 10 June 1732.

Composition: (Daniel Redmaine set the whole text except probably for P, A, a) B8, 27 Nov.; B8, C, D, 24 Dec.; E–G, 29 Jan.; H–K, 26 Feb.; L–O, 18 Mar.; P (unrecorded unless it be George Karver's claim below); Q, 25 Mar.; R, 8 Apr.; 1 sheet [=P?], 6 pages, Karver 27 May; 4 pages, Grantham, 10 June.

Presswork: Bi, 2 (Davies/Mazemore) 24 Dec.; Bo, Ci, 1 (Diggle/Peacock) 24 Dec.; Co, 3 (Diggle/Peacock) 24 Dec.; Do, 2 (unnamed) 29 Jan.; Di, Eo, 1 (Diggle/Peacock) 29 Jan.; Ei, Fo, 2 (unnamed) 29 Jan.; Fi, 3 (Franklin/Reynolds) 29 Jan.; Gi, 1 (Peacock/Perry) 12 Feb.; Go (unrecorded, but figured 7); Ho (unrecorded, but figured 5); Hi, 1 (Peacock/Perry) 26 Feb.; Io, Ii, 2 (unnamed) 18 Mar.; Ki, 3 (unnamed) 18 Mar.; Ko, Li, Lo, 1 (unnamed) 18 Mar.; Mo, 2 (unnamed) 18 Mar.; Mi, No, 4 (unnamed) 18 Mar.; Ni, 1 (unnamed) 18 Mar.; Oo, 7 (unnamed) 25 Mar.; Oi, Po, 4 (unnamed) 25 Mar.; Pi, Qi, Qo, 1 (unnamed) 25 Mar.; Ri, 2 (unnamed) 25 Mar.; Ro, 7 (unnamed) 25 Mar.; Ai, 7 (Jones/Perry) 10 June; Ao, a, 2 (Hardicke/Mazemore) 10 June.

APPENDIX II (G) (continued)

Figures: 1–B2v, C7v, D6, E2v, G7v, H1v, K2v, L4v, L5v, P2v, Q7
2–A7, D2v, E1v, F2v, I2v, I8, Q3v, R4
3–C7, K8
4–M8, O3v, P6
5–H2v
7–A7v, B6, G8v, O2v

Note: Bi claimed by 2 (Davies/Mazemore) but figured 7; Franklin's and Reynolds' failure to figure Fi;
the failure of press 2 to figure Mo; the failure of presses 1 and 4 to figure Ni and No; Qi claimed by
1 but figured 2; the failure of press 7 to figure Ro; Diggle and Peacock worked both presses 1 and 3
within the same period.

7. T. Lobb, *A Treatise of the Small Pox*. London, 1731
8°: A⁴ a–c⁸ B–2H⁸ 2I⁶ (–2I6)   Copy: BM. 1174.h.4

Production: 34 sheets; edition 750; composition 8s.; presswork 3s.6d.; price per sheet 18s.; begun by
30 Jan. 1731; finished by 14 Aug. 1731.

Composition: B, Redmaine 30 Jan.; C, D, E8, H8, correcting C, Redmaine 20 Feb.; E8, F, G, Hart/
Holmes 20 Feb.; H8, I, K8, Hart 6 Mar.; L–O, Hart/Holmes 20 Mar.; P-S, Hart/Holmes 3
Apr.; T-Y, Z4, Hart/Holmes 17 Apr.; X12 [sic = Z12?], Morgan 17 Apr.; 2A, 2B, 2C8,
Hart/Holmes 1 May; 2C8, Hart/Holmes 15 May; 2D8, Hart 29 May; 2D8, Holmes 29
May; 2E12, Holmes 5 June; 2E4, 2F-2H, 2I4, Holmes 26 June; a, b, Imperfection B, 2I4,
Holmes 17 July; 2I4, A, c, Holmes 31 July.

Presswork: Bi, 7 (unnamed) 6 Feb.; Bo, 2 (unnamed) 6 Feb.; Ci (no record); Co, 7 (unnamed) 20
Feb.; Di, 2 (unnamed) 20 Feb.; Do, 3 (unnamed) 6 Mar.; Ei, 7 (unnamed) 20 Feb.; Eo, 1
(unnamed) 20 Feb.; Fi, Fo, 7 (unnamed) 20 Feb.; Gi, 1 (unnamed) 6 Mar.; Go, 3
(unnamed) 6 Mar.; Hi, 3 (unnamed) 6 Mar.; Ho, 7 (unnamed) 6 Mar.; Ii, 3 (unnamed)
6 Mar.; Io, Ki, 2 (Clarke/Ward) 20 Mar.; Ko, 3 (Collyer/Franklin) 20 Mar.; Lo, 2 (Clarke/
Ward) 20 Mar.; Li, Mi, Mo, 1 (Diggle/Mazemore) 20 Mar.; Ni, 7 (Farmer/Peacock) 20
Mar.; No. 3 (Collyer/Franklin) 20 Mar.; Oi, 7 (unnamed) 3 Apr.; Oo, 3 (unnamed) 3
Apr.; Pi, 2 (unnamed) 3 Apr.; Po, Qi, 3 (unnamed) 3 Apr.; Qo, Ro, 2 (unnamed) 3 Apr.;
Ri, 1 (unnamed) 3 Apr.; Si, 1 (Diggle/Mazemore) 17 Apr.; So, Ti, 3 (Franklin/Reynolds)
17 Apr.; To, 7 (Farmer/Peacock) 17 Apr.; Ui, 1 (Diggle/Mazemore) 17 Apr.; Uo, Xo, 2
(Clarke/Ward) 17 Apr.; Xi, 3 (Franklin/Reynolds) 17 Apr.; Yi, 1 (Diggle/Mazemore), 1
May; Yo, 3 (Franklin/Reynolds) 1 May; Zo, 2 (Clarke/Ward) 1 May; Zi, 2Ai, 2Ao, 7
(Farmer/Peacock) 1 May; 2B (no record); 2Co, 3 (Franklin/Reynolds) 5 June; 2Ci, 2Do,
7 (Farmer/Peacock) 5 June; 2Di, 2 (Clarke) 5 June; 2Ei, 2Eo, 2Fo, 7 (Farmer/Peacock)
26 June; 2Fi, 2Gi, 3 (Franklin/Reynolds) 26 June; 2Go, 7 (Farmer/Peacock) 26 June;
2Hi, 2Ho, 1 (Clarke/Diggle) 17 July; 2I (not recorded); ai, 7 (Farmer/Peacock) 31 July;
A, ao, bi, bo, 1 (Clarke/Diggle) 31 July; co, 3 (Franklin/Reynolds) 31 July; 1000 loose
titles, 2 (Clarke/Davies) 14 Aug.

Figures: 1–a8v, b2v, c8, E7, G8, I2v, L8, M4v, M5v, R7v, S1v, U8, 2H7v
2–B7, K8, L7, P7v, Q8v, U5, X8v, Z7, 2D7v
3–c7, D7, G7, H7v, K7, O2v, P7, Q7v, S7, T8, Y7, 2F7v, 2G7v
7–a5v, B8, C7, E8, F6v, F7v, H8v, N3v, O8, T5, 2A8, 2B1v, 2B7, 2C7v, 2E2v, 2F4v, 2H6v,
2I4

APPENDIX II (G)   (continued)

8. *A Defence of the Present Administration.* **London, 1731**
[8°: A–D⁴]   Copy: not located

Production: 2 sheets; edition 3000; composition 5s.6d. per sheet; presswork 1s.2d. per 500, 3s. per 1500; price per sheet 16s. for the first 1000 and 5s. per ream for the rest; finished by 16 Jan. 1731.

Composition: A, B, J. Hart 16 Jan.; C, D, Micklewright 16 Jan.

Presswork: 'first edition':
                 Press 1   (Diggle/Mazemore) A, B, D, 500; A, C, 1500; A, B, C 500
                 Press 3   (Collyer/Franklin) C, 500; B, D, 1500; D 500
                 'second edition':
                 Press 3   (Collyer/Franklin) A, C 500
                 Press 7   (Clarke/Peacock) B, D 500

9. E. Peyton, *Catastrophe of the Stuarts.* **London, 1731**
8°: A²B–I⁴ K²   Copy: BM. 110.e.23

Production: 4½ sheets; edition 750; composition 8s. per sheet; presswork 3s. per sheet; price per sheet 18s.; begun by 24 Dec. 1730; finished by 16 Jan. 1731.

Composition: B–F, Grainger 24 Dec.; G–K, Bell 16 Jan.

Presswork: B, C, 1 (Diggle/Mazemore) 24 Dec.; D, 3 (Collyer/Franklin) 24 Dec.; E, F, 3 (Collyer/Franklin) 16 Jan.; G, 1 (Diggle/Mazemore) 16 Jan.; H–K/A, 7 (Clarke/Peacock) 16 Jan.

Figures: 1–B4, C2v, G1v
                 2–F4
                 7–H4v, I3v, K1v

Note: The evidence that Bowyer printed this pamphlet is of more than passing interest, for on Wednesday 27 Jan. 1731 its printer and publisher were taken into custody for publishing a libel. The bookseller, Charles Davis, was bound in a recognizance to appear at the King's Bench, which recognizance was continued for a period of 12 months, when he was discharged without penalty (*Whitehall Evening Post*, No. 1921, 28–30 Jan. 1731). Bowyer debits Davis with the printing costs, but the imprint reads 'Printed for T. Warner'.

APPENDIX II (G) (continued)

10. Regnault, *Philosophical Conversations*. 3 vols. London, 1731
vol. 1–8°: A⁸(–A8) B–2C⁸ 2D⁸(–2D⁸)

Copy: BM. 536.h.6–7

vol. 2–8°: A². . . Q–2D⁸ (all printed by Bowyer)

Production: vol. 1–26 sheets; vol. 2–12 sheets; 38 sheets in all; edition 1000; composition 6s.; presswork 4s.; price per sheet 22s.; begun by 16 Jan. 1731; finished by 26 June 1731; in vol. 2 sheets A and Q–2D only printed by Bowyer.

Composition: vol. 1: B–D, Gaylord 16 Jan.; E9, Micklewright 16 Jan.; E7, F–H, Gaylord 16 Jan.; I, K8, Grainger 30 Jan.; K8, L–O, P8, Gaylord 30 Jan.; P8, Q, Gaylord 6 Feb.; R–X, Y8, Gaylord 20 Feb.; Y8, Gaylord 6 Mar.; Z, 2A, 2B, Gaylord 20 Mar.; 2C, 2D8, Bell/Gaylord 1 May; A8, Gaylord 29 May.

    vol. 2: Q, Bell 3 Apr.; R–X, Bell/Gaylord 1 May; Y–2D, Bell/Gaylord 15 May; 16 pages Long Primer, Bell 29 May; two titles, Bell 26 June.

Presswork: vol. 1: Bi, 3 (Collyer/Franklin) 16 Jan.; Bo, Co, 1 (Diggle/Mazemore) 16 Jan.; Ci, Do, 3 (Collyer/Franklin) 16 Jan.; Di, 1 (Diggle/Mazemore) 16 Jan.; Ei, Eo, 3 (Collyer/ Franklin) 16 Jan.; Fo, 3 (Collyer/Franklin) 30 Jan.; Fi, Gi, 7 Clarke/Peacock) 30 Jan.; Hi, Ho, Ii, 3 (Collyer/Franklin) 30 Jan.; Io, Ki, 2 (Farmer/Wardman) 30 Jan.; Ko, 1 (Diggle/Mazemore) 30 Jan.; Li, 3 (Collyer/Franklin) 30 Jan.; Lo, 7 (Clarke/Peacock) 30 Jan.; Mi, 1 (unnamed) 6 Feb.; Mo, Ni, 7 (unnamed) 6 Feb.; No, 3 (unnamed) 6 Feb.; Oi, 1 (unnamed) 20 Feb.; Oo, Po, 2 (unnamed) 20 Feb.; Pi, Qi, 7 (unnamed) 20 Feb.; Qo, 3 (unnamed) 6 Mar.; Ri, 2 (unnamed) 6 Mar.; Ro, Si, 7 (unnamed) 6 Mar.; So, To, 3 (unnamed) 6 Mar.; Ti, 2 (unnamed) 6 Mar.; Ui, Uo, 1 (Diggle/Mazemore) 20 Mar.; Xi, 3 (Collyer/Franklin) 20 Mar.; Xo, 7 (Farmer/Peacock) 20 Mar.; Yo, 2 (unnamed) 3 Apr.; Yi, Zi, 7 (unnamed) 3 Apr.; Zo, 3 (unnamed) 3 Apr.; 2Ai, 7 (Farmer/Peacock) 17 Apr.; 2Ao, 3 (Franklin/Reynolds) 17 Apr.; 2Bo, 3 (Franklin/Reynolds) 1 May; 2Bi, 2Ci, 7 (Farmer/Peacock) 1 May; 2D, A (unrecorded).

    vol. 2: Qi, 1 (Diggle/Mazemore) 1 May; Qo, Ri, 3 (Franklin/Reynolds) 1 May; Ro, 1 (Diggle/Mazemore) 1 May; So, Ti, 3 (unnamed) 15 May; To, 1 (unnamed) 15 May; Uo, 3 (unnamed) 15 May; Ui, Xi, Yi, Zi, 7 (unnamed) 15 May; Xo, Yo, Zo, 7 (unnamed) 29 May; 2Ai, 2 (unnamed) 29 May 2Ao, 3 (Franklin/Reynolds) 29 May; 2B (unrecorded); 2Co, 1 (unnamed) 29 May; 2Ci, 2 (unnamed) 29 May; 2Di, 3 (Franklin/Reynolds) 26 June; 2Do, 7 (Farmer/Peacock) 26 June; 'A3' and titles to vols 1, 2 and 3 also claimed by Diggle alone at press 1.

Figures: vol. 1: 1–A7, B7, C7, D8, K7, L8v, M1v, N2v, R7, T1v, U6, U7
        2–C7v, I6v, 7S5v, O8v, R8, X7v, Y8v
        3–F7, G7, H7, I8, O8, Q7, S5, Z8v, 2A7
        7–F5v, G5v, L7v, M5, N7v, P2v, Q8, S5v, T7, X8v, Y8, Z3v, 2A7v, 2B1v, 2C7v

    vol. 2: 1–Q1v, R2v, T2v, Z1v, 2C8v
        2–U7v, Y7v, 2A6, 2C6
        3–U7, 2D5v
        7–S3v, X3v, Y5, 2B1v, 2B2v

APPENDIX III

(a) Edition Sizes of Part Issues of
Astley's *A New General Collection of Voyages and Travels* (1743–47)
(Printed by Charles Ackers)

Volume	Part Nos.		Edition		Reprints			Total Edition
I	1	sig. B	1750	+	350	+	1000	3100
		sig. C	2000	+	1100			3100
		sig. D	2000	+	1100			3100
	2		2000	+	1000			3000
	3		2000	+	1000			3000
	4–33							2500
II	34–79							2250
III	80–85							2250
	86–103							1750
	104–117							1500
IV	118–164							1500

Note: Ackers also printed 35,000 Proposals for this Collection.

(b) Edition Sizes of *The London Magazine* 1732–1747
(Printed by Charles Ackers)

Monthly Numbers	1st Edition	Reprint	Total
Apr. 1732–Dec. 1732	[2500]	1500	[4000]
Jan. 1733–May 1733	4000	1250	5250
Jun. 1733–Jul. 1733	4000	1500	5500
Aug. 1733	4500	1250	5750
Sep. 1733–Oct. 1733	5000	1250	6250
Nov. 1733	5000	1000	6000
Dec. 1733–May 1734	6000		6000
Jun. 1734–Dec. 1734	6250		6250
Jan. 1735–Dec. 1736	7000		7000
Jan. 1737–May 1737	6000		6000
Jun. 1737–Jul. 1737	6000	1000	7000
Aug. 1737	6000		6000
Sep. 1737	6500		6500
Oct. 1737–Jul. 1739	7000		7000
Aug. 1739–Dec. 1740	8000		8000
Jan. 1741–Dec. 1741	7500		7500
Jan. 1742	7000	1000	8000
Feb. 1742–Jul. 1743	8000		8000
Aug. 1743–Dec. 1743	7500		7500
Jan. 1744–Jan. 1747	7000		7000
Feb. 1747–Dec. 1747	7500		7500

APPENDIX III

(c) Edition Sizes of T. Dyche's *A Guide to the English Tongue*
(Printed by Charles Ackers)

4 Dec. 1733	19th ed.	10,000
4 Nov. 1734	20th ed.	10,000
5 May 1735	21st ed.	10,000
11 Oct. 1735	22nd ed.	10,000
23 Sep. 1736	23rd ed.	10,000
11 May 1737	24th ed.	10,000
28 Jan. 1738	24th ed. [sic]	15,000
19 Jul. 1738	'a new Edition'	10,000
26 Jan. 1739	'a new Edition'	10,000
17 Jul. 1739	'a new Edition'	5,000
25 Oct. 1739	'a new Edition'	10,000
3 Oct. 1740	'a new Edition'	20,000
17 Jun. 1741	'a new Edition'	20,000
3 May 1742	'a new Edition'	20,000
14 May 1743	'a new Edition'	5,000
18 Aug. 1743	'a new Edition'	10,000
6 Jan. 1744	'a new Edition'	5,000
12 May 1744	30th ed.	5,000
9 Aug. 1744	'a new Edition'	5,000
23 Oct. 1744	'a new Edit'	5,000
10 Jan. 1745	'a new Edition'	5,000
16 Mar. 1745	'a new Edition'	5,000
7 Jun. 1745	'a new Edit.'	5,000
10 Sep. 1745	'a new Edit.'	5,000
14 Dec. 1745	'a new Edition'	5,000
12 Apr. 1746	'a new Edit.'	5,000
4 Jul. 1746	'a new Edit.'	5,000
13 Oct. 1746	'a new Edit.'	10,000
13 Feb. 1747	35th ed.	5,000
27 Apr. 1747	'a new Edition'	5,000
29 Jul. 1747	'a new Edition'	5,000
2 Nov. 1747	'a new Edition'	5,000
1 Feb. 1748	'a new Edition'	5,000

2

"Indenting the Stick" in the First Quarto of *King Lear* (1608)

PBSA, 67 (1973), 125–30.

The envy of many "New Bibliographers" for the way in which it accounts for a vexing textual anomaly in *King Lear* (Q1), this essay demonstrates McKenzie's mastery of the technical aspects of analytic bibliography. Yet, as he modestly points out in his final footnote, it also calls into question the dominant style of bibliographical analysis—he cites Bowers, Williams, and Greg—that restricts itself to "inferences from the printed page." Characteristically integrating textual evidence, historical information, and his own experience as a printer, McKenzie proposes a solution that, however simple, was never self-evident: the compositor, rather than complicating matters for himself by using two composing sticks of different measures for poetry and prose, used a single long stick that he "indented" with large lead blanks, technically known as "em quads," as the need arose. This finding not only put in doubt a central premise of several established studies but also demonstrated in "the most literal and mechanical way possible" that bibliographers must necessarily attend to the practical realities of human labor—McKenzie surmises that the compositor, Okes, "was short of pica quads." In an exemplary fashion McKenzie insists that textual variations, the bibliographer's key to understanding the process of transmission, are consequences of the actual working conditions and habits of living human agents, not of theoretical postulates.

ANYONE WHO LOOKS at a copy of the first quarto of *King Lear* or even a facsimile of it cannot help noticing that two distinct measures appear to have been used, frequently on the same page. The most obvious explanation is that the compositor switched from a short measure of 80–81 mm for verse to a longer one of 93–94 mm for prose. The longer is self-evident, but the shorter one is also easily discerned from the evidence of turn-ups or turn-unders, ampersands and tildes, tight spacing or shortened spellings.

If one looks closer it is also possible to see that on many pages the type which over-runs the short measure is out of alignment. In at least one important case (the omission of the phrase "and appointed guard," at V.iii.46 on sig. K4ᵛ) the difference in measure led to a serious error which was detected only in proofing.

But were there really *two* measures? Why trouble to use both on the same page? And why do words up and down the right-hand edge of so many text pages in this quarto appear to be slightly out of alignment?

Despite appearances, the answer is that only *one* measure was used, the longer one. It is important to understand why this was so, and in the most literal and mechanical way possible. Otherwise we misrepresent the actual working procedures, introduce complexities which do not exist, and account inaccurately for certain kinds of textual variant.

We would do well to recall that giving the length of a compositor's measure in mm tells us nothing of the process of setting it. In fact, if adjustable, it is set, quite literally, to a number of ems of the text type to be used, and a phrase like "23-em measure" applies just as well to sixteenth- and seventeenth-century printers as to those of today.[1] If, as in King Lear, a compositor wished to set to a 23-em measure, he would actually set twenty-three m's or their precise equivalent in em-quads in his stick and then lock it up with just the right tension to allow the line of type to be lifted from it. To check the number of ems in his measure, we have simply to count vertically the number of lines set solid which it is equivalent to. In King Lear, for example, the shorter length of 80–81 mm corresponds exactly to twenty lines of type, the second of 93–94 mm to twenty-three lines. The two line lengths to which the text type was justified in King Lear are therefore 20-ems and 23-ems.

But it is a nuisance to change measures to this extent within the same book, let alone the same sheet, forme, or page, although sometimes it is unavoidable. For one thing it makes imposition awkward. If there is a regular alternation of uniform type areas, it is sometimes possible to add spacing material when tying up the page, in the page galley, or on the stone, to make its width uniform. But this does not happen in King Lear, where many isolated long lines overflow the shorter measure. Simply removing the shorter lines from the stick and resetting the measure as the longer ones occur is to be avoided at all costs, for the inevitable inequalities make side-locking of the page difficult and the risk of loose type dropping from slightly short lines is intolerable. Nor is there any joy to be had in handling the longer lines in a galley or on the stone when they are not an integral part of a properly justified type area.

Quite simply, Okes was short of pica quads. A measure that is unnecessarily wide wastes spacing material, especially quads of the same body size as the text needed for spacing out short verse lines. The readiest answer to the problem, and one which I have often been forced to adopt in hand-setting books of poems, is to leave the composing stick set to the wider measure, using it as necessary for long lines, but indenting it wherever possible by adding large quads at one end.

[1] A setting-rule is an aid to setting, giving a smooth face to work to, not a standard measure, although it is sometimes used as such and may result in a measure which is not of a regular em-length. The use of m's (the square of the body) or em-quads is the only sure way of getting an exact measure, especially in the period before founders standardized their type sizes and sticks were marked in standard 12-point ems. Moxon merely says that a compositor must adjust his stick "till he have exactly fitted his given Measure," without saying precisely how he does so (unless it is a line-for-line reprint): Mechanick Exercises on the Whole Art of Printing, ed. H. Davis and H. Carter (Oxford 1958), pp. 203–04. Smith is more helpful: "For making of Measures we have the best method here in England, where we use m's, laid the flat way." He says that a compositor should first be directed "how many m's wide, and how many lines long he is to make a page of it" and notes "it is common to make our measure by m's of the Letter on which the work is to be done." (The Printer's Grammar (1755), pp. 196–98).

Thus, if the stick were set to 23-ems, but a poem lower on the same page required no more than 20-ems, the stick need not be altered at all. The measure
can be reduced effectively by adding a 3-em quad at the far right-hand side of
the stick and the line can then be justified within the remaining distance. In such
a case, if the text were 12-point, one might add a 36 × 24, 36, 48 or even 72-
point quad (i.e. 3-ems × 2-ems, 3-ems, 4-ems or 6-ems), depending on the
number of short lines remaining. The only thing one has to watch is that, when
the occasional long line comes up and runs to the full measure, the last large
quad set sits flush with the preceding line. This stratagem spares 12-point quads
for filling out verse lines, preserves regularity of page size, and permits accommodation of long lines as they occur in a perfectly safe and methodical manner.
The difference between the two line lengths in King Lear is regularly 3-ems and it
results, not from a change of measure, but from the compositor's indenting his
stick by using a quad which, running up the head of the stick, served to indent
two, three, or four text lines at a time.

That this was the explanation of these features in Q1 King Lear occurred to me
some years ago when I was actually facing an identical situation in setting poetry
and needed to conserve 12-point quads. But Moxon comes close to describing
the practice when he discusses how to set the opening lines of a chapter which
begins with a "Great-letter" to which the text has to be justified. And if it is a great
wooden letter, the compositor "Justifies his Stick-full just to the breadth of the
Wooden Letter with Quadrats or Quotations, and Sets on between those Quadrats or Quotations and the Head of his Stick. . . ."[2]

A similar procedure for indenting the stick (these are Moxon's terms) was followed when setting indented notes. It permitted the notes to be set and justified
separately and then substituted for the stand-in quads. Shoulder-notes offer the
one clear example of material added to a text page during imposition. They
would normally be set in a different size of type and need not align perfectly with
the body of a text line. Hence they could be set separately as an independent column and, "being cloathed with the Furniture," more safely added during imposition than in the galley. When imposing the page, and before setting the marginal notes, the compositor would set a row of "Quotations" down the length of
the page. This kept the page size uniform during imposition and the edge of the
page regular (in particular it kept the end-letters upright). When he adds the
notes, says Moxon, the compositor simply displaces the appropriate quadrats
and then "Justifies them up."[3]

Moxon makes it clear that type founders supplied spacing material to meet all
these needs: "It is generally observed by Work-men as a Rule, That when they Cast
Quadrats they Cast them exactly to the Thickness of a set Number of m's or Body, viz.
two m's thick, three m's thick, four m's thick, &c." And when he writes of the

[2] Mechanick Exercises, p. 215.
[3] Ibid., pp. 218, 228–29.

need to cast quadrats carefully his explanation neatly confirms the point I have tried to make: "The reason is, that when the *Compositer* Indents any Number of Lines, he may have *Quadrats* so exactly *Cast* that he shall not need to *Justifie* them either with *Spaces* or other helps."[4]

The effects of indenting in Q1 *King Lear* are easy to see. Some are exactly of the kind we should expect within tightly set lines (the spelling "daugter." on E3^v or the omitted article in "a womans feruices" on H3^v). But there is this difference: knowing that he can juggle the indenting quads breeds a confidence in the compositor that can lead to oversights not likely if the measure were fixed to the shorter length and the extra words just had to be fitted in there and then. The most notable example is the one already cited, the omission of the phrase "and appointed guard," on K4^v. In the uncorrected forme the long line ends exactly 3-ems short of the full measure and so (as often happens) justified itself nicely within the 20-ems. With his stick already indented for the next line or two, the compositor failed to alter the quads to take in the extra words. Another example is the uncorrected state of K1^r where the compositor failed to add the words "*A letter.*" as he should have done, within the 3-em space to the right. (They were later added within the shorter line-length, probably in place of a 3-em pica quad to which they are exactly equivalent as set, and without disturbing a larger, indenting quad.) A few lines above, however, he had correctly set the direction "*He dies.*" in exactly this position. Two other examples are the "Exit." directions on G1^r.[5]

Another consequence of such a method of setting is that it creates in effect a long, vertical and virtually independent column of type up the right-hand side of the page, aligned but not always interlocked with the type area set within the reduced line length. If the indenting quads are not quite regular or the page locked up squarely, the column may easily move slightly out of alignment. Such misalignment can be seen in Q1 *Lear* most clearly on B3^r, F4^v, I1^v, K3^v, and L1^r but many other pages show small signs of it too.

Finally, there are in *King Lear* three directions set outside the full 23-em measure: "*Enter Edgar*" set in the left-hand margin of both C2^v and D3^v, and "*Enter Glo*" in the right-hand margin of F3^r. All three are marginal notes proper, doubtless set in the way described above by Moxon.

So far I have not offered any verification of the theory outlined here. The best evidence of all would be inadvertent printing from a raised and/or inadequately masked indenting quad. Indeed, in Q1 *Richard II* (1597) and Q1 *Troilus and Cressida*

---

[4] Ibid., pp. 171–72, and p. 349 under "*Quotation Quadrats.*" Quadrats were cast to lengths which enabled them to be used as word spaces in a font of larger body size: see the quad areas reproduced at p. 34 of Philip Gaskell, *A New Introduction to Bibliography* (Oxford 1972). A quadrat 3-picas × 3-picas would be exactly equivalent to a 1½-em quad of (French) canon: see Philip Gaskell's "Type Sizes in the Eighteenth Century," *SB*, 5 (1952), 147–51, and *New Introduction*, p. 15.

[5] Matthew Gwinne's *Vertumnus*, printed by Okes in 1607, offers a nice example of a stage direction inserted and only roughly aligned within the indented area ("abit cum fuis" on F3^v). One of the marginal notes bears witness to Okes's belated concern for accuracy in the form of a slip-cancel bearing the one word "*Duncan*" pasted over the original reading "*Donald*" on H3^r in British Museum copy 636.d.4. (2.).

(1609) printing from pica quads aligned with the text proves that their compositors did not need to indent the verse lines in the way I have described. In King Lear, however, although it may be a case of interpreting the evidence to fit the theory, I think we can show the contrary. On G1^r in the British Museum copy C.34.k.18 there are five thin vertical lines, slightly out of alignment, right at the end of the 23-em measure. These I take to be printed from the ragged outer edge of a large indenting quad, although I have to say that they might also have been made by a raised piece of scabbord.[6] There is a further mark on B3^v; it is uninformative about the size of the quad or quads responsible but it does tell us the order in which the formes were printed.[7]

One last speculation. There is enough evidence of variation in measures unaccompanied by the obvious signs of indenting to confirm that printers were using adjustable sticks long before Moxon. Dr. Gaskell, however, has pointed out that the addition of spacing in the way I have described was the customary method of adapting fixed wooden sticks to a shorter measure.[8] Were these commoner than we had thought? Was Okes not only short of pica quads but here, early in his career, using wooden sticks made to 23 pica ems?

I hope that readers will agree with me that "indenting the stick," resetting it to a shorter measure, or even using two distinct sticks do not in fact amount to quite the same thing and that it is worth drawing the distinction. Bibliography can do the history of printing a disservice if it is not accurate in these matters and at some point may damage its own understanding of the processes of transmission which are its proper study.[9]

[6] Q2 Romeo and Juliet (1599), printed by Creede, shows similar features to Q1 King Lear, with turn-unders, tildes, and ampersands in verse lines of uniform length on pages with longer lines set to the full measure. On G1^v one edge of a large quad appears to have printed and on H4^v the final 3-ems of a long line are dislodged just at the point where the indented measure ends.

[7] If carefully distinguished from set-off and show-through, such marks are a useful physical test of the order in which the formes were printed. In King Lear outer B was printed first and the type was deeply impressed. When the inner forme was printed and the sheet perfected, a quad in B3^v of the inner forme touched the raised impression of the word "Foure" printed on B3^r. Professor Hinman has remarked that the outer formes of Q1 Richard II were printed first. Spacing material which printed on B4^r and H2^r offers independent proof that the outer formes were printed first. See Richard the Second 1597, eds. W. W. Greg and Charlton Hinman, Shakespeare Quarto Facsimiles no. 13 (Oxford 1966), p. xi.

[8] W. Craig Ferguson, "A Note on Compositors' Measures," SB xv (1962), 242–43; and Philip Gaskell, New Introduction, p. 47, citing Plantin's use of wooden sticks only forty years before 1608, a date nearer to Oke's than Moxon's.

[9] See also Fredson Bowers, "Bibliographical Evidence from the Printer's Measure," SB, 2 (1949–50), 153–67, esp. pp. 154–55; G. W. Williams, "A Note on King Lear III.ii.1–3," ibid., 175–82, esp. p. 180; and W. W. Greg, "King Lear—Mislineation and Stenography," The Library 4th ser., 17 (1936), 172–83, esp. pp. 181–82. Greg and Williams suppose that the two measures in Lear reflect the use of two distinct composing sticks, and Williams says that the necessary quads would be added in the page galley. These are fair inferences from the printed page, but they are at odds with Moxon and import nonexistent complexities into the following stages of transmission. John Feather, in "Some Notes on the Setting of Quarto Plays," The Library 5th ser., 27 (1972), 237–44, usefully illustrates these features in several other play quartos and correctly refers to the use of quotation quadrats when setting marginal notes, but fails to account for the practice of "indenting the stick." He further supposes the use of an adjustable stick reset as required to two distinct measures, the use of "furniture" to fill the space to the right of indented verse lines, and that where a catchword is set to the full measure on indented pages it "was set in a specially made opening in the furniture."

FROM—

DEPT.—

BLDG.—

CAMPUS—

TO—

DEPARTMENT—

BUILDING—

CAMPUS—

RM—

Local Hall 1:45

Airport 3:45

4:45 — A+A
— Depart
Arrive

7:12

PL: Plane

INDIANA UNIVERSITY

INTERDEPARTMENTAL COMMUNICATION

To:

Dept.

Subj.

From:

Dept.

Date

Telephone

FOLD AND FASTEN - - - - NO ENVELOPE NEEDED

3

Stretching a Point: Or, The Case of the Spaced-out Comps

SB, 37 (1984), 106 – 21

This essay is a lesson in the virtues of doubt and uncertainty, an attempt to "give some philosophical dignity to disbelief." Uneasy with the commonly accepted proposition that individual compositors may be distinguished by their characteristic habits of placing spaces before and/or after punctuation marks, McKenzie tests this notion by considering some 13,777 commas in the second edition of Beaumont's *Psyche* (Cambridge, 1702). Relying on inferences from an analysis of the physical evidence alone, he constructs an entirely plausible explanation—complete with "scientific" statistical data—convincingly attributing particular compositorial stints to named individuals, only to reveal that this account bears no relation to the actual work patterns as recorded in the Cambridge University Press archives. Again, the weaknesses of a positivistic analytical bibliography are exposed. He then offers a number of alternative explanations only to disprove each one in turn, leaving the reader in a state of suspended ignorance.

Yet, the point of this elaborate exercise is not simply to instruct us in the vagaries of compositorial practices. Rather, it is to use a particular historical case to challenge some of the most important epistemological assumptions that underlie the investigatory methods of bibliography. The problems, at the level of methodological principle, encompass the legitimacy of quantifiable evidence, the rigorous testing of hypotheses, and the relationship between formal analysis and the diversity of human labor practices. Most important, however, McKenzie insists that both what we view as "objective" bibliographical evidence and how we view it are conditioned by our prior assumptions. This playful, antipositivist critique asks its readers serious questions about methodological principles and also raises vital moral issues about the purposes and directions of scholarly practice.

IT IS ALWAYS DISTURBING when logic outruns judgement. We feel obliged to accept an argument but remain, inexplicably and therefore silently, unconvinced by it, troubled by a gentle but patently unfair scepticism based on no more than a conviction, bred of our own imperfect and mixed experience, that things can't have been quite like that.

Take, for example, these two propositions: first, one compositor may be distinguished from another by his manner of spacing punctuation; second, a compositor will, more often than not, set type from the same pair of cases, so that recurring types may be used to plot his work. Since the propositions are simple, and the evidence adduced to exemplify them wholly inferential, it is not difficult to achieve a logical formulation. When there are parallel structures conceived to

91

the same end they will, syncretically as it were but not logically, reinforce one another. So the identification of compositors by spelling, or the division of work between compositors according to a pattern of skeleton-formes, may extend the series of tests and, where they match up, convert correspondence into truth.

Because such tests are only syncretically or accretively, but not logically, related, it is no great loss to the argument if any one of them fails. One merely shifts ground. Were they logically dependent upon one another, since they are directed to the same end ('There were three men at work; here, there and there; namely Tom, Dick and Harry'), the failure of any one test might be thought, if not to refute, at least to bring seriously into question the validity of the others.

Well aware that Gertrude thought the study of empty space a sure sign of madness, and an eye bent to that purpose a deformity in Nature, I nevertheless thought it might be of some service to ask: can the first proposition above be tested? Has it the reliable status we expect of theories which have preoccupied so many editorial projectors, commanded so many hours of scholarly time, transmuted so much vacancy into learned articles?[1] Thinking that one solitary but incontrovertible instance would give some philosophical dignity to disbelief, I found that I could test a comparable method on a book of some substance in which the compositorial stints and press-work were well-documented. But before I report the results, a few words on the spacing of punctuation as a compositorial practice may not be out of place.

The great merit of spaced punctuation as evidence is its purely typographic, if not wholly arbitrary, nature. It is largely independent of copy-influence and indifferent to chronology, of a frequency high enough to imply developed habits, and it appears in texts of several languages, set by compositors of any European nationality. Justification, and a medial or terminal position, may affect frequency, but these are discernible and so discountable influences on the statistics. There are of course various ways in which marks of punctuation may be spaced: the spaces may be placed before or after the mark and may vary in thickness. But such variation merely strengthens the basic assumption that the variety observed indicates the idiosyncratic practices of the men who transferred those palpable, leaden spaces from case to stick.

---

[1] T. H. Howard-Hill, in *Compositors B and E in the Shakespeare First Folio and Some Recent Studies* (Columbia, S.C., 1976) and in "The Compositors of Shakespeare's Folio Comedies," *Studies in Bibliography*, 26 (1973), 61–106, used evidence of "compositors' various habits of spacing after commas in short lines, and at the end of lines." He had earlier applied such a test in "Ralph Crane and five Shakespearian First Folio comedies," D.Phil. thesis, Oxford University, 1970. Gary Taylor, "The Shrinking Compositor A of the Shakespeare First Folio," *SB*, 34 (1981), 96–117, describes terminal spaced commas as a 'near-infallible indicator' of compositor C at one point. MacD. P. Jackson, "Two Shakespeare Quartos: *Richard III* (1597) and 1 *Henry IV* (1598)," *SB*, 35 (1982), 173–190, also uses their evidence. I must in fairness to those writers absolve them at once from any imputation of having reduced their own practice to tests as simple and unsupported as my formulation of the two propositions might suggest.

Without committing them in any way to my general argument, I should like to record my gratitude to several friends from whom I sought informed comment on historical aspects of the present article. I think particularly of Nicolas Barker, Peter Blayney, Philip Gaskell, Lotte Hellinga, Mervyn Jannetta, David McKitterick, James Mosley and David Shaw.

Those who have recently used such evidence have not, I think, offered any 'rationale' for the spacing of punctuation marks; and indeed that does seem a singularly inappropriate demand of a practice so apparently personal, insubstantive and 'accidental.' And yet experience prompts. 'Should I put a space before a comma?', every new student asks. What did an old hand say to apprentices in those early habit-forming days of their youth? 'Lard out your line, lad; fat formes fill fast'? Or 'Tight-setting, son, sees the job soon done'? Moxon must have assumed some such gnomic instruction at case for he has nothing comparable to Fertel's discussion, 'Des Espaces, & de leur usage', at pp. 16–18 of La Science Pratique de l'Imprimerie (Saint Omer, 1723):

> Pour la separation des ponctuations on doit toujours, autant qu'il se peut, mettre une espace devant la virgule, & le point-virgule, & deux aprés; ou une fine devant et une grosse aprés, c'est-a-dire plus d'espace aprés la virgule qu'on en aura mis devant. Mais si on étoit fort géné, soit pour mettre quel-ques lettres qu'on auroit oubliées en composant, ou qu'un Auteur changeroit quelques mots dans son épreuve, de sorte qu'on serait obligé de serrer les mots de la ligne, pour faire entrer la correction; pour lors on pourrait ôter les espaces qui seroient devant les virgules de la ligne; mais pour le point-virgule, on doit autant qu'il se peut faire, laisser une fine espace devant & aprés.

> [For the separation of punctuation, one must always, as far as possible, put a space in front of the comma, & the semicolon, & two after; or a small space before and a large one after, that is to say, more space after the comma than what one would have put before. But if one has an embarrassing problem, either because one wants to add some letters one might have forgotten while composing, or because an Author has changed a few words in his proof, in such a way that one would be forced to squeeze the words on the line, in order to enter the correction; in this case one could remove the spaces in front of the commas on the line; but for the semicolon, one must, as far as possible, leave a small space before & after.—Ed.]

So Fertel says, in effect, that there are rules and he hints that they have a purpose. There is a good practical reason for keeping a line easy and open (apprentices take note), and that in turn implies at least one cause of variation in a pattern—later adjustment to take in corrections.[2]

For a sophisticated formulation of the rules, however, it would be hard to go beyond that of Bertrand-Quinquet whose own book, printed by his own firm, also exemplifies them. His Traité de l'Imprimerie (Paris, An VII = 1799), pp. 126–128, specifies seven marks of punctuation and the 'manière de les placer dans la composition' [ways of placing them during typesetting]. I cite only his comments on the comma and full point:

---

[2] J. D. Fleeman examined printers' widows for signs of correction in a not unrelated way: see "Concealed Proofs and the Editor," Studies in the Eighteenth Century, ed. R. F. Brissenden and J. C. Eade (Canberra, 1979), 207–221. A Dutch printing manual of the late eighteenth century, David Wardenaar's, Beschrijving der Boekdrukkunst, also refers to the spacing of punctuation and its advantages when correcting: see Zetten en Drukken in De Achttiende Eeuw, ed. Frans A. Janssen (Haarlem, 1982), pp. 323, 378–379.

Comma:
LES Anglais, les Allemands et les Suisses la placent toujours immédiatement après la lettre, sans espace. Les Italiens et les Espagnols, la mettent entre deux espaces égales; les Français entre deux espaces inégales, dont celle qui précède la virgule est moins forte que celle qui la suit.

Full point:
LES Français sont dans l'usage de le placer immédiatement après la lettre, sans espaces, et de le faire suivre d'espaces plus fortes que celles qui se trouvent entre les mots, afin de mieux désigner la terminaison complette de la phrase.

[Comma:
The English, the Germans and the Swiss always place it immediately after the letter, without space. The Italians and Spanish put it between two equal spaces; the French between two unequal spaces, the one before the comma being less pronounced than the one following it.

Full stop:
The French usually place it immediately after the letter, without spaces, and follow it with wider spaces than those used between words, in order to emphasise the completion of the sentence.—Ed.]

The extension of the principle from one compositor to a whole nation of compositors has its own theoretical interest, for it is, in form, precisely that—an extension of the same fundamental assumption that compositors, the wordiest of men, may paradoxically give themselves away in, to coin a Pascalian phrase, 'le silence infernal de ces espaces finies' [the infernal silence of these finite spaces]:

LES différentes manières de placer les signes de la ponctuation désignent à l'observateur attentif le lieu où ont été faites les éditions. C'est à leur manière de ponctuer que les contrefacteurs se font plus facilement reconnaitre; c'est par-là qu'ordinairement ils se trahissent et se décèlent. Pour la plupart ils ne connaissent pas ces petites différences, ils suivent aveuglément leurs anciennes habitudes; ceux mêmes qui les connaissent, ont beau y faire attention, il est bien difficile que, dans un ouvrage de longue haleine, rien ne leur échappe; et alors celui dont on vole la propriété, sûr de son fait, peut poursuivre le voleur, sinon devant la loi, au moins le signaler à l'opinion publique.

[The different ways of placing punctuation marks show to the careful observer the place where editorial changes have been made. Counterfeiters can most easily be recognised by the way they punctuate; it is in this way that they usually betray and reveal themselves. Most of them do not grasp these little differences, they blindly follow their old habits; even those who do understand them, despite being careful, would be unlikely not to let something escape them during a long piece of work; and then the one whose property has been stolen, sure of his facts, can pursue the thief, if not before the law, then at least before public opinion.—Ed.]

Logically of course, Bertrand-Quinquet's proposition may offer difficulties. For example, distinct national patterns within the same text could be taken to attest division of work between countries as well as between compositors;

conversely, it could be taken to evidence a cosmopolitan compositorial companionship in the same shop. Lest either of those extensions of the argument be thought frivolous, one need only recall the invaluable work of R. A. Sayce along similar lines, the complexities of clandestine printing on the Continent, and the high proportion of Continental workmen in the English printing trades in the sixteenth and seventeenth centuries.[3]

We need not, however, rely wholly upon French manuals in search of a 'rationale.' John Smith's *The Printer's Grammar* (1755) is the first in English to be explicit, suggesting an en-quadrat after a comma, semicolon, etc., and an emquadrat after a full point. He calls such practice a 'rule' but quickly adds 'it is no law neither' (p. 113) and offers some golden advice on the relation between the spacing of punctuation and the troublesome business of justification: 'putting nothing at all after a Comma, Semicolon, or even after a Full-point, in composing, shews more readily [towards the close of a line] how much more or less may be taken in; and what space may be allowed after a Point or Points in a line' (p. 114). The thought may be fanciful, but that remark rings true and suggests to me a trick of the trade of proven worth and real antiquity. Normally of course a line would be regularly spaced until it was almost full, and then modified to fit. The practice Smith describes would make the spacing more contingent. Writing of word-spacing, he says that 'most Compositors chuse to put a thick Space, called *The Composing Space*, after a word' but adds that this practice makes the lines less easy to justify: '. . . therefore those who put Spaces as they come up, have a better chance to justify the contents of their lines to equal distances.'[4]

Justification is one concern, correction (as Fertel implies) another. Smith ingeniously suggests a way of making both problems easier: if all punctuation were cast to a uniform thickness, it could be changed without rejustifying the line. It would also save spaces, for punctuation cast centrally on bodies of uniform size would, when printed, appear to be spaced. He goes on:

> Even the Comma (we presume) is not under the necessity to clinge to the Matter so close as it always does, in England; considering that all other Printing Nations make it a law to put at least a thin Space before it, lest it should seem that the Comma is govern'd by particular words; whereas its proper function is, to inform the Reader, that a Stop, Rest, or Pause of the shortest duration is to be observed between word and word where the Comma shews itself. That this is the tenor of this observation with the French, appears from their putting as much space before as after a Comma; and in very open lines they put a thin Space even before a Full point. (p. 101).

---

[3] See R. A. Sayce, *Compositorial Practices and the Localization of Printed Books 1530–1800*. Occasional Publications No. 13 (Oxford Bibliographical Society, 1979); and Robert Darnton's work on surreptitious printing and publishing in "Un commerce de livres 'sous le manteau' en Province à la fin de l'Ancien Régime," *Revue française de l'histoire du livre*, n.s. 9 (1975), 5–29; "L'imprimerie de Pancoucke en l'An II," ibid., n.s. 23 (1979), 359–369; as well as in *The Business of Enlightenment: A Publishing History of the 'Encyclopédie,' 1775–1800* (1979).

[4] 'Spaces as they come up': see Philip Gaskell, *A New Introduction to Bibliography* (rev. ed., 1979), p. 46: 'nowhere during the hand-press period were spaces of different widths kept apart in separate boxes of the case.'

Smith's mid-century suggestion, we might note, together with Fertel's and Bertrand-Quinquet's explicit directions, indicate that spaces before and after punctuation marks must have been separately set, not cast on the body. This was certainly so in type set in the seventeenth and eighteenth centuries and still standing at the Plantin-Moretus Museum in Antwerp.[5]

Thus documented, the trade's attitudes to the spacing of punctuation are seen to be related to several different practical concerns. Bertrand-Quinquet's authority supports and extends the general theory that compositors may be distinguished from one another by the ways in which they space such marks; both Fertel and Smith offer sound advice (though in different forms) about setting and using space on either side of punctuation marks to justify or correct a line more easily. They do not, however, offer a 'rationale.' Bertrand-Quinquet shows a faith perhaps too touching in the efficacy of education, forgivable though that might be in Year Seven of a new dispensation. Fertel and Smith complicate matters a little by recommending practices which would obscure a presumed pattern. In sum, however, their comments reinforce the idea that any one compositor should and would have a practice of his own, and his companions perhaps different ones, and that in a book where the practices seemed to differ from one another, those compositors might be separated out. The status of our inferences, if they are not to derive only from a simple juxtaposition of the extremities of the evidence, depends crucially of course upon which of several possible motivations and methods we select to make sense of our analysis, and also upon the extent to which we can define the limits of identity and discount correspondence.

Unfortunately, the theory by definition functions only where the distinctions are in fact extreme, and it collapses into complete inutility at mid-point, where the evidence of distinction declines into spasmodic eccentricity or disappears altogether. Nor is that inutility simply a regrettable inadequacy: it is profoundly subversive of the whole theory. For a theory can hardly be thought sound which predicts one way (division) but not the other (integrity). So, if it anywhere fails to predict (that is, confirm the hunch . . .) that work was or was not divided; or if it fails to accord with the facts as soundly established by other evidence; then, logically at least, even the statistically impressive figures of difference cannot be trusted either. They appear significant only by virtue of the simple assumptions we bring to them, and they appear deceptively attractive because we find it easier to divide than unify.

Such a preamble presupposes a case which proves (i.e. tests) the rule, and disproves (i.e. falsifies) it. The one I offer has involved, in a very literal sense, much soul-searching, for the book is the second, revised edition of Joseph Beaumont's Psyche, a folio in fours printed at the Cambridge University Press in 1701–2. The

---

[5] Howard-Hill, "The Compositors of Shakespeare's Folio Comedies," p. 66, notes: "If there were reason to doubt this [i.e. that a space did or did not follow a comma], perhaps on the ground that different sorts were irregularly centered on the body of the type, the instances of inked spaces and quads . . . would confirm that internal spacing in short lines is a real and not an imaginary phenomenon."

work is a long one in 24 cantos, set in Pica roman, double column, with eighteen stanzas per page. Semicolons, colons, question and exclamation marks almost invariably have a space before them (see Fertel's comment above on 'le
point-virgule'), but the practice with commas, of which the illustrations below
are typical examples, varies in statistically significant numbers. Such features can
be readily seen in other books also set in Pica roman and printed at the Press in
1701–2: Thomas Bennet's *A Confutation of Popery*; the second, reset edition of the
same work; and the second, reset edition of his *Answer to the Dissenters Pleas*. In each,
spaced commas appear throughout the text. William Whiston's *A Short View of the
Chronology of the Old Testament* (1702), also set in Pica, has none; but in *The Harmony
of the Four Evangelists* included with it, spaced commas appear in the extensive sections set in Long Primer. In all cases, the compositors and pressmen are reliably
known from their personal claims for payment, claims which specify the work
units (half-forme, forme, sheet, quire). The function, variety, dating, and range
of men involved, inhibit the entertainment of any conspiracy theory, whether to
defraud the Press or mislead future scholars, and their evidence is still extant and
examinable in the Cambridge University Archives.

Drawing inferences of the kind which mark the use of spaced commas to track
compositors in Shakespearian texts (though the assumptions underlying such
inferences have not I think been made clear), one would come up with wholly
respectable results. For the 224 pages in the quires examined (A–2E), there are,
plus or minus perhaps 2 percent, 13,777 commas, or an average of 61.5 commas
per page. A glance at the appended table will show an unmistakable and *statistically acceptable* distinction between pages in which the ratio of unspaced to spaced
commas varies between 120:0 and 64:14 (say 4.6:1), and those in which spaced
commas equal or outnumber the others in ratios varying from 27:27 (or 1:1 to
8:60 (or 1:7.5). As the text is in verse, justification is not often a factor; as it is a

---

282.
Into the land of *Uzz* They made thee trudge ,
And poure the bottom of thy worst despight
Upon the best of Men , if *Heav'n* can judge
Of pure celestial Sanctity aright.
 More beautiful was *Job* in *Heav'n*'s esteem
 Than thou to Earth didst make him horrid seem.

283.
He heap'd this Scale as full of *Virtue*, as
Fell *Herod* has replenish'd it with *Vice:*
That other , which mounts up so lightly , was
His score of Slips , his empty Vanities,
 Thin as the Air , which though sometimes it be
 Dusky with clouds, regains its purity.

286.
Then to her gloomy Chariot she went,
A Chariot framed of a pois'nous Steam :
Her Speed was headlong , so was her Intent,
And soon to *Herod*'s royal Den she came ,
 By no slowpaced Coursers thether drawn,
 But by a pestilential Tempest blown.

287.
Unseen she came, and with such cunning guided
Her stealing Chariot's silent wheels, that she
Quite down the Tyrant's throat as slyly glided
As do's his unsuspected Breath , which he
 Lets in to fan his heart : and thus , alas ,
 He swallow'd what his own Devourer was.

Four stanzas from Q1ʳ of Beaumont's *Psyche* (1702) showing some of the 50 commas on that page
which have spaces before them. They may be contrasted with the comma in the first line of Stanza
287 which has a space after it but none before. The illustration also shows that the spaces between
a word and the comma which follows it may vary in thickness. (Original reduced by approximately
one-third.)

revised reprint of the 1648 edition which has no such pre-spaced commas, copy-
influence can be discounted. The theory, cautiously applied, might then support
either of two propositions: (a) that two men were involved, one who scarcely
ever set a space before a comma, and another who did so more often than not;
(b) that two groups of compositors were involved, one of which could not be
further divided by this test. A third proposition, however, will doubtless occur
to those who accept the second: (c) that while the common habits of one group
disguise their separate identities, the second group might certainly be further
sub-divided (within statistically reliable limits) by gradations in the incidence of
spaced commas (the statistics tolerating distinctions within the seven-fold difference between $1:1$ and $1:7.5$). In the latter case, some fine distinctions would undoubtedly remain to be made at border-line points, but the success which has
attended the resolution of such problems in the Shakespeare First Folio gives excellent grounds for thinking they could be resolved here too. Some sixty years
ago Thomas Satchell settled for A and B; by a simple but exacting process of subdivision, they have now been splintered into no fewer than nine different men.
With little fear that we run counter to current assumptions and scholarly practice, we may however settle for proposition (a) while conceding, with a proper
openness to fresh evidence, that the compositor who set spaces before commas
might yet turn out to be one of twins or triplets. With that proviso then we may
reasonably infer that the same compositor set the following pages, but no others, in this book:

D1, D3v, D4	I1–I4v, I2v–I3	U3, U4
E1, E3v, E4	K2v–K3, K4v	X2, X3
F2v–F3, F4	L1, L2v–L3	Y2, Y4
G2, G3, G4v	P1, P1v, P2	Z1, Z3v
H2v–H3, H4	Q1, Q1v	2A2

The pattern is itself seductively attractive: three pages in each of nine consecutive formes (with a hiccup in I), then a decline into two pages only in the last
few before the compositor takes leave of the entire book with one page only in
2A. It must be conceded, however, that the inclusion of certain pages in the above
list is questionable: E4, U3, X2, X3, Z3v, 2A2, for example, have only between
16 and 19 spaced commas each (exact figures are given in the appendix). Nevertheless, as a clear case of a slightly imbalanced composition : presswork ratio
it will certainly support a complementary theory of concurrent printing to keep
our less productive man occupied. Bennet's three books could be claimed to
show the same compositor at work on those texts, and quite independent proof
that one of them was indeed in exactly concurrent production sustains the
inference.
    One other element in our analysis may lead us to complicate the theory. I re-
fer to the concurrent use, through the quires examined, of four skeleton-formes.

These are often evidenced to buttress a theory of divided work, on the further theory that, if work was divided, the press-crew would need to save as much time as possible to keep up with the increased rate of setting. Or, were there not such clear evidence of two men, we might posit a larger edition than normal as another explanation of this time-saving practice of using several skeletons. In this case, however, we have independent proof that the edition numbered only 750, a figure which happily reinforces our inference from skeleton-formes that the setting must have been shared. It is rare of course to be able to establish so easily and indubitably the exactly concurrent printing of another book with matching features and a firm figure for the press-run. It would have been too much perhaps to hope for an exact correlation between a particular skeleton-forme and a particular compositor. A recurrent skeleton might then have allowed us to corroborate the theory that, under certain circumstances, a skeleton might substantiate the man; but the subordinate role of the one who spaced his commas in *Psyche* (one-and-a-half formes per quire) really—and reasonably—rules that out. At best, we might explore the significance of his setting both pages of the same forme in F2(i), H2(i), I1(o), I2(i), K2(i) and L2(i), but the other 27 pages give strong evidence of shared setting as the norm in each forme when a second compositor was involved.

I leave it to the appended details to collapse this house of cards. Here I need only observe that the pattern of spaced commas has no significant relation to division of work among the compositors. Six different men worked on the book and they rarely shared a quire, let alone a forme. Four of them (Bertram, Crownfield, Délié and Michaëlis: English, Dutch, French-via-Oxford, German?), each set some pages with very high, and other pages with very low, ratios of unspaced to spaced commas. The statistics are impeccable; the assumptions, and therefore the inferences, are nonsense. As a question of logic, it matters not that compositors in 1600 or 1623 did or did not set spaces after commas instead of before them. Nor can this challenge to the theory be respectably met merely by affirming that 1701 is not 1623 or that Cambridge is not London. The case for the efficacy of a modified theory, reliable for London shops in 1600 or 1623, positing different conditions, motivations and methods, must be rigorously argued as a matter of history and meet the appropriate standards of historical scholarship.

The point was made some years ago but it is probably worth stressing once again: there is no relationship of an easily statable kind between compositors, skeleton-formes and press-crews. The formes for *Psyche* as a whole were printed by six different pressmen in eight different combinations including, on three separate occasions, work at half-press.

For all that, I must strongly and explicitly affirm the importance of such theories—and affirm also the most exhaustive testing of them as an essential complement to their entertainment. Our scholarship is deficient, not in the formulation of interesting hypotheses, but in our failure to test them rigorously, and in the superimposition of one fragile theory upon another, as if two crutches gave us healthy legs.

In that spirit, therefore, let me before I close propose another theory. It is this: notwithstanding the date of Smith's comments on a uniform size of body for punctuation marks, or Fertel's and Bertrand-Quinquet's earlier and later assumptions of compositorial free will, the Cambridge University Press (unusually for 1701–2) might have had a fount of Pica roman which contained a high proportion of punctuation with cast-on spaces. We see it travelling from quire to quire as it was set, distributed, and reset. This theory accounts for its recurrences, its successive use by four different men in the same book, and its concurrent use in others. Taken no further that theory might well salvage some of the others.

In testing it, however, we have at once to confront the absence of historical evidence for such a practice at such a date. The Plantin exhibits show independent spacing before commas, although the Cambridge type, it is true, came from Amsterdam. A new and therefore perhaps distinctive fount of type did reach Cambridge from London on 28 March 1701 and Clement Knell was paid for papering and filling two pair of Pica cases on 17 May 1701, a date which neatly coincides with the start of work on *Psyche*. Yet more evidence, however, shows that it would be wrong to conclude that this new fount contained spaced commas. In the first place, they are extremely rare in *Psyche* before quire D (claimed on 21 July 1701); in the second place, such new types would not have been discarded as early as quire 2A (set by 30 August 1701). Finally and conclusively, such spaced commas had already appeared in two books set in Pica roman and printed the year before.

So let's try another theory: the fount containing spaced commas was an old one and was discarded once the new fount had been brought into effective use. Whiston's *A Short Chronology* may be invoked to support this line of argument, for there are no spaced commas in the main text of this later book which is set in Pica roman. But since external evidence proves that the fount thought to contain spaced commas was no more than two or three years old and had had little use, we must abandon that explanation too.

Perhaps then only the spaced commas were discarded—although they survive in the Long Primer of Whiston's *Harmony* set in 1702. If that were so, the new theory of punctuation with cast-on spaces might be saved and a contribution offered to the history of typefounding (Moxon, for example, has no mention of the practice in his section on typecasting). Let's pursue this form of the theory a little further. It assumes (a) that pre-spaced commas were cast as such; (b) that they formed a distinctive element in at least one pair of cases; (c) that their presence in the text proper was in fact anomalous; (d) that they had a different typographic function which we have still to explain; (e) that after quire P they were gradually segregated and removed from the fount until, by quire 2B, it was wholly cleansed of them. We have now to specify a function: the spaced commas, let us say, were so cast specifically for use with small caps but had been dissed into one lower case, either mistakenly or to make good a deficiency. Fertel's discussion of the spacing of caps and small caps is suggestive:

> Quand [le compositeur] se rencontre des mots de lettres capitales dans la matiere de l'ouvrage, comme J E S U S , M A R I A , ou autres semblables noms, qu'un Auteur souhaite de distinguer, on doit mettre une grosse ou fine espace entre chaque lettre, & cela a beaucoup plus d'agrément; pour les petites Capitales, il n'est point néces-saire d'y en mettre *lors qu'elles portent leur blanc, par l'épaisseur du corps;* c'est ce qui arrive souvent à plusieurs fontes. (p. 17; my italics)

> [When [the composer] encounters words in capitals in the material of the text, like J E S U S , M A R I A , or other similar names, that an author wishes to distinguish, one must put a large or small space in between each letter, & this is much more agreeable; for the small capitals, it is not necessary to put any *because they have their own blank space given the thickness of their body;* this is what often happens with many fonts.]

But before we can accept that Fertel has led us at last to an incontrovertible the-ory, we must in all honesty note that the passage just cited makes no mention at all of punctuation, and that bills of fount treat caps, small caps, lower case, punc-tuation, and figures as discrete categories. More seriously, we must note further that the spacing of the pre-spaced commas is not uniform as we should expect it to be if it had in fact been pre-cast. That objection might, of course, be met by compounding a theory of distinctive types with one of compositorial practice: the cast-on space was a fine one and might be variously expanded by the addi-tion of others as need arose in justifying, correcting, or merely as the mood took each of Bertram, Crownfield, Délié or Michaëlis.

But now Whitehead's admonition, so respected by Greg, bursts through: 'seek simplicity—and distrust it.' The theory of cast-on spacing cannot be quite trusted, and *any* theory of compositorial practice (given the four compositors and the extreme variations within the work of each) returns us to the initial problem—why such distinctive groupings in such a regularly recurrent pattern? Which is also to say that we are indeed back where we started: in a cleft stick. Lest it lead me into self-parody then, let me formally abandon even my own the-ory of commas with cast-on spaces. It is possibly unhistorical, and in any case it would have been seriously damaging to proposition two: if such distinctive types from the same pair of cases recurred with such well-defined regularity, it would have been reasonable—or at least orthodox—to suppose that they had been set by the same compositor from 'his' cases; and that, demonstrably, was not so.

I was tempted to call this paper 'Amoebic Scholarship: Or, The Counsels of Duessa?' because I believe that there is a question of deeper principle to be faced, and perhaps also a moral issue in how best we should spend our bibliographical time and space. The deeper principle relates of course to our use of division as a function of analysis. Evidence of difference is observable and countable; by con-trast, what is common or coherent is thought to be inert and uninformative. The computer, which is becoming indispensable in the service of such analyses, is the child—indeed, the supreme expression—of the binary system. Its virtue lies in the separation of sheep from goats, of chalk from cheese. If it finds it harder to tell the difference between scholarship and pseudo-scholarship, that deficiency we must attribute to our own inability to teach it.[6] Is it then altogether surprising that the same two 'compositors' should have been divided into three, then five, then six, then nine? Or that a refined eye for linguistic distinctions, and a superior technical facility to store and report them, should now lead to a revival of disintegrationalist theories of divided authorship? Or that observed differences between two substantive texts should, within the parameters of each, be offered as evidence of inviolably distinct structures whose division into two their conflation would destroy? Or, where the structures seem inconveniently interlocked, that the 'text' should be divided yet again by the ingenious invocation of an intermediate (but lost) manuscript to create a third (or fourth, or fifth . . .) structural unit into which one might syphon off inconsistent evidence? The formalities of such analyses, but especially the limited assumptions that underlie them, are quite inadequate to the diversity of the human behaviour which created the 'evidence.' Yet the paucity of reliable historical evidence makes it difficult to improve them. More ominously, however, such procedures threaten to redefine bibliography as an essentially disjunctive tool and to distract us from the greater challenge to discern the unity in human variability. ('Two Distincts, Division none'—Shakespeare's own succinct statement of one of Love's mysteries—is not without a certain admonitory force here.)

Having used that phrase 'human variability' I must add that I should be sorry if it became a license for relaxing the rules of evidence in bibliography, any more than it might in a court of law. The pressure to prove our theories (again, that is, to test them rigorously) by what is historically knowable must in no way slacken. A theory which collapses from book to book, like a chain with broken links, is nowhere sound. In the present instance, the forms of two theories (rarely I confess so nakedly exposed) have been stripped and shown as impotent to explain what actually happened in printing just one book used to test them: spacing as a compositorial practice, and founts as a compositorial trace. Even their skeletons are uninformative. Statistics merely compound the errors. And, most damning of all, it is perfectly clear as a matter of fact and of logic that, far from one

---

[6] The comments of two distinguished computer scientists are not impertinent. See John Von Neumann, 'Can We Survive Technology?', *Fortune*, June 1955. One point made by Von Neumann is that computer technology is prodigiously generative: instead of performing the same tasks in less time, we now perform more in the same time. Computer output therefore rapidly pre-empts space; a wrong programme (i.e. a mistaken assumption in the programme) will, with a mad logic, be more prodigal of error; and that prodigality crowds out the more severely disciplined evidence of other kinds of analysis. Massed statistics might therefore be seen as an ominous symptom. One is reminded of the story of the Staff Officer who, when promised another man for his unit, replied: 'Send me one who is brilliant and energetic. If you can't do that, send me one who is brilliant and lazy. If you can't do that, send me one who is stupid and lazy. But for God's sake don't send me one who is stupid and energetic.' Joseph Weizenbaum's *Computer Power and Human Reason* (1976), is also highly relevant here.

theory assisting the other where either is weak, the two theories in this case are mutually exclusive.

My anatomy of Beaumont's *Psyche* is now concluded. I assure the reader that 'no levell'd malice Infects one comma in the course I hold.' But since it takes courage to make a fool of oneself by counting 13,777 commas in public, I can only hope that this example may serve as at least a caution to others doing likewise in their pious efforts to discover how many comps can dance on the point of a bodkin.

APPENDIX

Beaumont's *Psyche* (1702): A Case-Study

> Loves mysteries in soules doe grow,
> But yet the body is his booke.

Psyche, or Love's Mystery, in XXIV. Cantos: Displaying the Intercourse Betwixt Christ, and the Soul. . . . By Joseph Beaumont, D. D. . . . The Second Edition, With Corrections throughout, and Four New Cantos, never before Printed. Cambridge, Printed at the University Press, for Tho. Bennet, at the Half Moon in St. Paul's Church Yard, London, M.DCCII. Collation: 2^0: a–b⁴ A–2Z⁴ 3A².

For a detailed description and production tables, see *The Cambridge University Press 1696–1712: A Bibliographical Study*. 2 vols. Cambridge: at the University Press, 1966, i. 219–221. The compositors' and pressmen's claims are reproduced *in extenso* (and indexed) in vol. ii. Briefly, as the collation shows, the book is a folio in fours comprising 101 sheets. With a text of 6-line verse stanzas in Pica roman fitting 18 to a page, double column, it would have been easy to cast off and set by formes. Composition was shared serially by six men. The sheets were printed off by six different men working in eight different combinations. The book was about 40 weeks printing—from May 1701 to February 1702. The edition was 750 copies.

Composition

When work was occasionally divided within a quire, the records do not specify precisely which pages or formes were set by which compositor. Michaëlis left the Press sometime after 19 July 1701, the date of his last claim: it is probable that he set N–O and Q½ before departing. Quire D was claimed by both Bertram and Crownfield: it is here given to Bertram. Otherwise the composition was shared as follows:

Crownfield:	A¼, C½, G½–I, P–Q½, X, 2D, 2G–2I, 2Q½–2T½
Bertram:	A¼, B–C½, D–G½, T–U, Y–Z, 2E–2F, 2K–2Q½, 2T½–3A, a–b
Knell:	A½
Délié:	R–S, 2A–2B
Michaëlis:	K–M, [N–O, Q½]
Muckeus:	2C

Presswork

The earliest presswork voucher is datable as 26 June 1701, the last is dated 28 February 1702. See *The Cambridge University Press*, i. 126 n. 3 and 127 for an analysis and discussion of the skeleton-formes and the validity of inferring compositorial stints, or the number of presses used, from the number or pattern of skeleton-formes. It is probable that there were three actual printing presses in alternate and/or concurrent use during the printing of *Psyche*; a fourth was put into working order in January 1702. The only doubtful claim relates to 2S½ which was claimed both by Coldenhoff and Ponder and by Brown and Terrill. As Terrill was not using a press-figure in this book it is impossible to confirm his claim. It is here presumed to be a slip by Coldenhoff and Ponder for 2T½, otherwise unclaimed.

Ponder alone:	A
Isburn)	B–Q½, R–T½, U¾–2B
Ponder)	
Coldenhoff alone:	Q½, T½–U¼
Pokins)	2C–2H½
Ponder)	
Coldenhoff)	2H½, 2I¾, 2M½, 2R½, [2T½], 2U½, b½
Brown alone:	2I¼, 2K–2L, 2M½–2Q½
Brown)	2R½–2T½
Terrill)	
Terrill alone:	2U½, 2X–3A, a–b½

Skeleton-formes used to impose pages with high ratios of spaced: unspaced commas may be indicated briefly here:

Skeleton 1: D3^v, E3^v, F2^v–F3, G2, I1–I4^v, I2^v–I3, K4^v, L1, P1, Q1, U3, X2, Y2, Z1
Skeleton 2: D1, E1, K2^v–K3, L2^v–L3, P2
Skeleton 3: D4, E4, F4, G4^v, H4, P1^v, Q1^v, U4, Y4
Skeleton 4: G3, H2^v–H3, X3, Z3^v, 2A2^v

Unspaced : Spaced Commas

The count is limited to the first 27 quires as spaced commas virtually disappear altogether from the book after quire 2A. Unless there is no doubt at all, commas after 'w' and 'y,' sometimes after 'f' and 'r' and certain italic letters, have been conservatively classified as unspaced since they naturally appear to stand apart from the face (if not the body) of the previous letter. The counts have been spot-checked and found accurate to within about 2 percent. The table is followed by another showing which compositors set which pages containing a high ratio of spaced to unspaced commas. For the other pages, see the table of composition above. Figures for unspaced commas are given first.

A1	43– 0	B1	58– 0	C1	69– 1	*D1	35–23
A1v	65– 0	B1v	54– 1	C1v	53– 2	D1v	65– 1
A2	65– 0	B2	64– 0	C2	67– 0	D2	63– 1
A2v	56– 0	B2v	62– 0	C2v	57– 1	D2v	46– 0
A3	59– 0	B3	71– 0	C3	81– 0	D3	58– 0
A3v	61– 0	B3v	61– 0	C3v	55– 3	*D3v	27–29
A4	63– 0	B4	40– 0	C4	55– 1	*D4	30–42
A4v	51– 1	B4v	66– 0	C4v	65– 0	D4v	61– 1

*E1	19–29	F1	45– 0	G1	120– 0	H1	57– 0
E1v	53– 3	F1v	76– 0	G1v	63– 1	H1v	52– 3
E2	64–14	F2	57– 1	*G2	31–35	H2	61– 0
E2v	60– 0	*F2v	38–30	G2v	61– 1	*H2v	14–41
E3	49– 1	*F3	20–34	*G3	18–30	*H3	22–25
*E3v	34–24	F3v	75– 0	G3v	53– 2	H3v	59– 0
*E4	37–19	*F4	26–34	G4	43– 0	*H4	19–41
E4v	62– 0	F4v	61– 2	*G4v	20–29	H4v	65– 1
*I1	19–51	K1	40– 1	*L1	43–38	M1	36– 1
I1v	103– 0	K1v	43– 2	L1v	46– 7	M1v	48– 1
I2	68– 0	K2	68– 1	L2	55– 2	M2	66– 0
*I2v	27–43	*K2v	19–45	*L2v	17–40	M2v	47– 0
*I3	27–35	*K3	27–27	*L3	20–31	M3	54– 0
I3v	45– 1	K3v	46– 1	L3v	58– 0	M3v	40– 1
I4	71– 0	K4	95– 3	L4	53– 0	M4	50– 0
*I4v	15–48	*K4v	23–36	L4v	46– 0	M4v	48– 0
N1	49– 0	O1	64– 0	*P1	7–36	*Q1	8–60
N1v	46– 0	O1v	53– 0	*P1v	9–32	*Q1v	4–50
N2	46– 0	O2	55– 0	*P2	17–40	Q2	51– 0
N2v	52– 0	O2v	64– 1	P2v	53– 1	Q2v	31– 0
N3	51– 0	O3	61– 1	P3	55– 0	Q3	51– 0
N3v	36– 0	O3v	56– 0	P3v	69– 0	Q3v	42– 2
N4	48– 0	O4	68– 0	P4	60– 1	Q4	57– 3
N4v	52– 0	O4v	75– 0	P4v	63– 0	Q4v	62– 0
R1	55– 0	S1	70– 0	T1	70– 0	U1	75– 0
R1v	52– 0	S1v	54– 0	T1v	69– 2	U1v	64– 1
R2	69– 0	S2	51– 1	T2	71– 0	U2	74– 1
R2v	55– 0	S2v	42– 0	T2v	53– 1	U2v	72– 0
R3	53– 2	S3	64– 0	T3	43– 0	*U3	53–17
R3v	52– 2	S3v	66– 0	T3v	59– 0	U3v	45– 0
R4	62– 0	S4	76– 0	T4	57– 1	*U4	52–22
R4v	68– 0	S4v	63– 0	T4v	63– 0	U4v	59– 0
X1	37– 9	Y1	54– 1	*Z1	39–27	2A1	41– 9
X1v	87– 0	Y1v	57– 0	Z1v	58– 0	2A1v	75– 0
*X2	52–16	*Y2	30–49	Z2	60–12	*2A2	37–19
X2v	40– 0	Y2v	63– 0	Z2v	40– 0	2A2v	51– 0
*X3	43–16	Y3	54– 1	Z3	33– 0	2A3	65– 0
X3v	67– 1	Y3v	60– 6	*Z3v	48–19	2A3v	54– 0
X4	68– 0	*Y4	30–28	Z4	45– 9	2A4	52– 0
X4v	69– 2	Y4v	55– 5	Z4v	41– 0	2A4v	54– 0
2B1	42– 0	2C1	53– 0	2D1	58– 0	2E1	60– 0
2B1v	40– 0	2C1v	50– 1	2D1v	49– 0	2E1v	49– 3
2B2	65– 0	2C2	64– 0	2D2	49– 0	2E2	69– 0
2B2v	48– 0	2C2v	69– 0	2D2v	53– 0	2E2v	59– 0
2B3	57– 0	2C3	70– 0	2D3	71– 0	2E3	50– 0
2B3v	69– 0	2C3v	62– 0	2D3v	57– 0	2E3v	72– 0
2B4	72– 0	2C4	80– 0	2D4	63– 1	2E4	50– 0
2B4v	74– 0	2C4v	53– 0	2D4v	52– 0	2E4v	49– 0

The compositors involved in setting pages with a high ratio of spaced to unspaced commas were:

Bertram:	D1, D3v, D4, E1, E3v, E4, F2v, F3, F4, U3, U4, X2, X3, Y2, Y4, Z1, Z3v
Crownfield:	H2v, H3, H4, I1, I2v, I3, I4v, P1, P1v, P2
Délié:	2A2
Michaëlis:	K2v, K3, K4v, L1, L2v, L3

Bertram)
and/or) G2, G3, G4v
Crownfield)
Michaëlis)
and/or) Q1, Q1v
Crownfield)

All of those compositors are also found setting adjacent pages containing few spaced commas or none at all.

Part Two
THE BOOK TRADE

4

The London Book Trade in 1668

This essay first appeared in the New Zealand journal *WORDS: Wai-te-ata Studies in Literature*, edited by McKenzie and printed at the Wai-te-ata Press, which he founded in 1962. In this first experiment in a new synchronic methodology for historical bibliography, McKenzie sets out to examine all the extant texts produced by all the London printers in a single year, 1668. Uncomfortable with the "great disparity between what analytic bibliography might infer, and what we can establish," his immediate object was to build on the comprehensiveness of enumerative bibliography, while testing and extending its investigatory methods and powers. In particular, he sought to free the discipline from its naïvely "innocent assumption that the locus of bibliography as a subject was the book—any book—as a physical object." What he offers, then, is neither the detailed analysis of a single book, nor of an individual printing house, but an ambitious study of the year's total output. Examining 458 books in libraries and private collections throughout the world, he reveals a spectrum of political, literary, economic, legal, and social factors influencing the "generative capacity" of the book trade. This investigation reveals both the complexity of determinants conditioning book production and the centrality of "non-political commercial interest" as the principal motivation directing book trade practices. Moreover, a comparative reflection on the total annual production enables McKenzie to show how the bibliographical forms of certain exceptional books display innovations transcending contemporary conventions to embody literary meaning in new and powerful ways. The comprehensive methodology he develops in this study is an important first step toward his redefining the role of bibliography in literary, cultural, and political history—and in establishing their mutually informing relations.

I

THAT WE think of bibliography as closely linked with English studies is little more than an historical accident, reflecting the personal interests of Greg and McKerrow and the particular need there was, with the growth of English as an academic discipline, to establish the literary tradition in formal terms.

Its primary interest in textual authority—one thinks of Greg's definition: bibliography is the science of the transmission of literary documents[1]—gave it natural affinities with biblical and classical textual scholarship, and its concern for verbal accuracy may be seen in part as an attempt to dignify the word, whether as the medium of divine revelation or the embodiment of human creativity.

---

[1] W. W. Greg, 'Bibliography—an Apologia.' In *The Collected Papers of Sir Walter W. Greg*, ed. J. C. Maxwell (Oxford, 1966), p. 241. Greg's paper was delivered in 1932.

Its efflorescence in a late-Romantic cultural climate reinforced this concern in two ways. First, the development of systematic philology, itself a product of a Romantic interest in the past, reinforced the concern with language and made historical relativism respectable. At its simplest, we see the principle at work in any old-spelling edition of a literary text. Second, and more important, the Romantic view of the artist as genius who did not so much mirror the world as express himself required a different emphasis in scholarship. It is seen in the shift from an overt concern to adapt the past to the present, as in the earlier 18th century, to the unquestioning endorsement of specific, historically authorial intention as the common referent of critical debate and textual scholarship, at least until quite recently.

The philosophy of science which informs Greg's definition and characterises the inductive procedures of analytical bibliography likewise reflects his age in its optimistic sense of discovery, and its belief in the objective nature of the inquiry and the definitive form of its results.

Our progress, however, is not absolute, but only relative to these conditions which have determined its course. This may explain the slight critical discomfort we sense when discussing, say, the accidentals of an Elizabethan dramatic text, where our assumptions about authorial intention conflict with the broad social determinants of the older printing houses; when preparing a modernised edition, where questions of immediate social utility distort the purer concerns of historical scholarship; when dealing with collaborative works, where 'intention' fails of that unity which the divine analogy so compellingly directs us to find; or when seeking to articulate accurately, and therefore completely, by merely verbal means a dramatic experience whose language is gesture, a musical experience whose language is sound, a visual experience whose language is light. Authorial revision upsets our aesthetic assumption of a 'true' text, yet conflation offends our sense of the historical moment; and speculative inquiry so betrays the popular model of a scientific discipline that critical choice, we think, must bow to limited, mechanical demonstration.

But there was another strand to bibliography, not specifically concerned with textual authority although serving that end along with many others. Partly by analogy with the natural sciences, where the instinct to collect served an end more sophisticated than mere pride of possession, partly as an aspect of an antiquarian spirit strong in the 18th and 19th centuries, but most significantly as an attempt to give institutional embodiment—in National Libraries—to the main records of national cultures, collectors and librarians created enumerative bibliography. Collection, and classification according to principles of description which served to identify but not to analyse, supplied enumerative bibliography, together with the profession of librarianship, with a fine social *raison d'être*, but it also gave the subject a great diversity.

Paradoxically, this diversity was both a strength and a weakness. The strength lay in its comprehensive responsibility to classify not merely literary documents but all books, to develop techniques for studying the elements common to them, particularly type and paper, and to foster the study of regional printing and publishing as an essential means of determining the origin and date of the individual editions. The weakness lay in the innocent assumption that the locus of bibliography as a subject was *the book*—any book—as a physical object. For this assumption has had two consequences. First, it accounts for our current failure to accept into the discipline artifacts which are not books but which serve a comparable function. I mean any message-bearing document. Manuscripts may qualify, although Greg felt obliged to argue the case; printed music is acceptable, if not quite central; prints and drawings, if not photographs, have been given a home; but magnetic sound and video tapes, gramophone records, films, and much archival material, are still perhaps regarded as embarrassingly extraneous. Second, any collector of books and almost any subject dealt with in books could legitimately participate in the discipline. Paradoxically therefore, the emergence of bibliography as a coherent subject has been inhibited, not promoted, by its restriction to books, and by the very diversity of motive and interest which books serve.

Despite an agreeable sense of mutual dependence, the relationship between bibliography in Greg's sense and that of institutional and subject bibliographers is another of those points of slight critical discomfort, reflecting, divisively, the different social concerns from which they grew, just as the current limitations of each are implicit in the cultural presupposition of a society some three to four generations older than our own. Hence, although defective types may be useful clues in textual bibliography, typography as such is still thought to be largely irrelevant; decorative material may help to identify a printer, but beyond that it is in the realm of art history; watermarks may assist in the detection of cancels or in distinguishing impressions, but paper sizes and quality are rarely related to questions of authorial intention; an author's works may be printed in three volumes, but each is 'bibliographically' complete in itself. Only recently perhaps has it become evident that the analysis of the printing of any one literary text cannot be pursued very far without taking into account also the other works in production at the same time, works which enumerative bibliography has unquestioningly accepted into the discipline.

These reflections are ways of approaching the main question that I wish to ask: is there any way in which we can look at bibliography in order to see it in its integrity as a subject? If there is, we must account for both its contemporary and its historical applications; indeed the value we place on it as a way of completing and perfecting our view of the past becomes a compelling argument for its application in the present. One might go even further and say that if it signally fails to tell us in large measure what we think we need to know of the past, then such a conclusion must be faced quite honestly, and the kinds of uses to which we *can* put it be pursued instead.

If, as I have suggested, the development of one form of bibliography reflects not so much any absolute view of truth as the presuppositions of a scholarship itself formed by the age, we can accept that it will soon cease to follow paths no longer thought useful and move, under new social and intellectual pressures, in quite new directions. The ideal of definitiveness in analytical bibliography, for example, may well be weakened by the failure of its logic simply for want of evidence, or because the information is too laborious to recover, or because it is trivial when ultimately unveiled. Enumerative bibliography may take on more of its functions and so bring us to an acceptable middle ground where less purist, but also less dogmatic, standards of accuracy combine with the fullest account of accessibility to all the printed records of our society. The need for the discipline to assume this degree of social utility for artifacts other than printed books will occasion its extension, belatedly but inevitably, to film and sound archives. Conflation may become more respectable as an editorial procedure; mixed media forms and those involving chance will inevitably require more complex theories of copy-text and a more abstract concept of ideal copy as a statement, not of the infinitely repeatable form, but of an information-set through which any of several forms might be realised. And for all these projections of bibliography, Greg's definition, albeit with extended meanings for each of its terms, will still serve admirably: the science of the transmission of literary documents.

II

I must now end my induction and turn to the past. In doing so, I have to explain that, from one point of view, there is no reason at all why, of all years, I should choose 1668. Its very arbitrariness is—almost—the point. I say this because my concerns are not at all narrowly historical or textual but broadly so; and just as, I believe, the working model of a small academic and provincial printing house in 1700 could be moved up and down a two- to three-hundred year time scale, and used to illustrate in miniature the basic procedures of houses far larger than itself, so I wanted to ask if it was at all possible to build a comparable working model of the trade as a whole at any one time. The question is probably too ambitious, if we aspire to a complete account. That of course is an important finding in itself. Even to ask the question and to venture upon a construction that attempts to explore the trade in all its diversity at one place, London, and in one year, 1668, reveals the limitations of evidence (the degree of ignorance) that must in turn limit the accuracy, and therefore the usefulness, of some forms of bibliographical inquiry.

Nevertheless, the model which I have been trying to build, however defective still for want of time and evidence to complete it, is far from uninformative, and in several respects indeed it fulfills its prime function as a comparative tool by means of which we can trace developments in the trade. As I shall try to show, an awareness of these developments may in turn have textual consequences of a kind not I think hitherto described.

I have said that 1668 was—almost—an arbitrary choice. But just as the fortuitous survival of printing-house records for 1700 dictated the period of a similar though more limited study, so the existence of Roger L'Estrange's Survey of
the printing houses on 29 July 1668 dictated the choice of this year.[2] His list gives
us the only information we have about the productive capacity of the London
printing trade at any point in the 17th century. At the very simplest therefore we
can match the total workforce, or that in any of twenty-six printing houses, with
their products; and however deficient our information about employment in
those houses before or after 29 July 1668, however inadequate our record of the
books actually printed in that year, and however imprecise our allocation of
work, dated and undated, to 1668, when much would have been completed earlier and some perhaps later, it is embarrassingly true that at no other time can
bibliography command even this amount of evidence.

To begin with the enumerative detail: there are 496 items attributed to 1668
in Wing's *Short-title Catalogue*.[3] If we omit 28 instances of misprints, reissues or
double entries, we are left with 468. To these we need to add 23 not in Wing, accounting periodicals like the *London Gazette*, the *Transactions* of the Royal Society,
the weekly bills of mortality, and so on, as one item each. This gives a total of 491
titles, of which I have seen 458.

Ideally every one of the full total should have been described in such a way
that the following information was systematically listed: binding; paper size,
watermark, quality; type design, type size, lines and em-width per text page;
reprint information; imprint information comprehending the printer, the bookseller for whom the book was printed, those by whom it was sold, their addresses; anonymity; engravings, artists, devices, decorative head- and tail-
pieces, decorative initials, factotums, flowers; format, collation, methods of
signing and paginating, finis notes, nature of prelims, presence of half-titles, vertical titles; blank leaves; imprimatur, licenser, date of licensing, dates to authorial dedications or addresses; rubrication; advertisements, errata lists; division
into parts or volumes; price. Some of this information could be refined by reference to the Stationer's Register, the *Term Catalogues*, and listings in other books.

Up to this point the details are almost physically determinable. Like police estimates of undetected crimes, they are limited only by our ignorance about items
of which no record survives. The next stage—at which we attempt to define
total production—requires assumptions. Two are quite fundamental. First, we
have to assume that work begun in 1667 but dated 1668 is comparable in volume
to that begun in 1668 but dated 1669. Second, whereas the amount of type-
setting and the number of signatures are self-evident, we have to assume some
standard edition quantity. Except for almanacks and one or two other pieces, for
which the quantities are known, I have assumed an edition of 1000 copies for

---

[2] Public Records Office, London. State Papers Domestic, *Car.* ii. 29/243 (126).
[3] D. G. Wing, *Short-title Catalogue of books printed in England, Scotland, Ireland, Wales, and British America and of English books printed in other countries 1641–1700.* 3 vols. (New York, 1945–51).

each item. On these twin bases, we can calculate the total production of the London printing trade for the year. Information about the additional labour required to sustain this work—that of typefounders, engravers, rolling-press operators, paper factors, press-joiners and smiths—is only partially recoverable.

The book trade at large is another matter again. Its generative capacity is measured in part by the number of items published, in part by the size of any one; but it is not wholly dependent upon the London printing trade. Any estimate of its total responsibilities and of the city's requirements in books is limited by inadequate evidence about the precise functions of the booksellers, the sources of their stocks, the extent and the means of their distribution. Their functions extend from wholesaling to the retailing of general stationery and quack medicines; their subject specialties, as publishers and/or retailers, range widely, and the more specialised their subject, the more extensive their sources; their dealings in manuscripts and second-hand books, their trade in books abroad, as exports or imports, their connections with provincial booksellers, the spread of their investments—all these are determinants of a turn-over which it is impossible to quantify although directly related to the more familiar cost ingredients of copy acquisition, editing, paper, printing, warehousing, advertising and transport.

There are considerations of an even more general kind, political, religious and economic. For our period, the second Dutch war of 1665–7 and the triple alliance of 1668 affected paper supplies. The Licensing Act of 1662, Roger L'Estrange's appointment as Surveyor of the Press in 1663, and the effects of the Clarendon code, created political-religious pressures; they were opposed by men like Darby, Chapman, Brewster, Calvert and Francis Smith. L'Estrange's own rights in the newsbooks and his income from licensing, the operation of the several printing patents, especially the Company's stocks, the dominance of the book-sellers and the restriction of printers, created at least four main lines of economic pressure. These contradictions account for the fitful coalescence and divergence of official policy on the one hand and commercial interest on the other.

Plague, fire and imprisonment, intake into the trade by apprenticeship, the incidence of foreigners and aliens in printing houses, the Company's control of printing at Oxford and Cambridge and the relationship of work done there to that of the London trade, piracy at home and competition from the illegal importation of English books printed abroad, the functions of hawkers and mercury sellers at one level, of combinations of booksellers within and beyond London at another—these are each complicating determinants of what printers and booksellers did, collectively and individually, to serve a very diversely motivated, therefore constantly fluctuating, readership. The diversity of that readership and the forms by which it was reached (the relationship, that is, between text and trade) are fully explicable only if we have some such larger view of what is implied by bibliographical inquiry. At the very simplest level, the incidence of

anonymous authorship, printing and publishing, like the shift from direct political criticism to obscene satire, was determined in part by the censorship; surreptitious printing and restricted labour supply imposed obvious constraints on
the quality of paper, typesetting and presswork; the need for quick, inexpensive,
unofficial distribution partly determined the choice of format; religious principle, not unrelated to plainness of utterance, accepted the book unadorned;
commercial interest perpetuated without thought a mediocrity of book design
and execution; private sponsorship, and judicious estimates of the demands of a
new cultural élite, revived a richer concept of the book as a speaking picture.
These simpler clusters of interest and the colouration given to them by external
pressures, by the resources available, and indeed by the partiality of our own inquiries, may be complicated further: first, by content analysis of the books produced; second, by delineating more finely the connections between authors,
promoters, printers, distributors and retailers.

Taken together with our knowledge of the printing houses in 1668 our image
of the trade in that year begins to assume a rough outline. At too many points,
it's true, it lacks definition, but at a great many others the Company records, State
Papers Domestic, the books themselves, bring it into surprisingly sharp focus. It
is sharp enough to create a set of distinctive criteria by which to define what is
common to the trade along an extended time-scale, what is new in the forty-odd
years following 1668, how specific contradictions implicit in its conduct in that
year are later resolved, and with what consequences for such questions as the
history of our public liberties, the expansion of trade, the growth of literacy, the
rise of the publisher's hack, the development of author's copyright, the emergence of the share-book system, the study of book format, binding styles, type
designs, graphic display, subscription ventures, serial publication, and textual
bibliography.

At this point, the arbitrary choice of 1668—apart from the information in
L'Estrange's survey—assumes a quite positive stress, for it suggests that as much
or more might be learned from the printed and manuscript records of any year,
and that in turn implies the possibility and the value of establishing a comparative model for the period following the settlement of 1668 or the lapse of the
Licensing Act in 1695.

Now I must be specific. I deal first with production and face the uncomfortable fact that—full as our information is—the model is quite inadequate to the
acknowledged needs of analytical bibliography. First, there is the high incidence
of anonymous proclamations, almanacks, bills of mortality, and so on. Second,
the incidence of anonymous printing is over 54%: 268 of the items extant for the
year bear no indication of the printer's name. Third, our records of type and decorative materials, their origins and the extent of their duplication, do not permit
us to attribute much anonymous work to particular houses.

These observations enforce another: that any model we create is not an image
of the actual historical situation but only a projection of what we happen to

know of it. What it indicates in this instance is the great disparity between what analytical bibliography might infer, and what we can establish.

To take six printing houses of medium size from the 26 listed by L'Estrange, calculating the amount of type-setting per book in ens and multiplying the number of sheets in each by an edition quantity of 1000, (1) Sarah Griffin, the acknowledged printer of 5 books, would have required one compositor quarter-time and one pressman half-time to complete the work. She had two presses, one apprentice, and six workmen. (2) Anne Maxwell, the acknowledged printer of 12 books, would have required one compositor and 1½ press crews. Indeed, she had 2 presses and 3 pressmen, which meets the hypothetical need for presswork, but she also had one apprentice—unrecorded by L'Estrange—and 3 compositors. The paradox is that our figures about composition are more reliably inferred than those about presswork. (3) John Redmaine, the acknowledged printer of 12 books, would have required 2 compositors and 1 pressman. He had 2 presses, 2 pressmen, one apprentice and 4 compositors. (4) Robert White, the acknowledged printer of 6 books, would have required 2 compositors and 2 pressmen, 4 men in all. He had 3 presses, 3 apprentices, and 7 journeymen. (5) Ellen Cotes, the acknowledged printer of 13 books, would have required 1 compositor and 2 pressmen. She had 3 presses, 2 apprentices, and 9 journeymen. (6) Finally, Thomas Ratcliffe, the acknowledged printer of 12 books, would have required 1 full-time and 1 half-time compositor and 1½ press crews, 5 men in all. He had 2 presses, 2 apprentices, and 7 journeymen.

Were we to ask about the composition of the workforce, its characteristics in terms of training, age, mobility, all questions relevant to some kinds of textual inquiry, we should again be impressed I think by the diversity of answers which the model shows. Of those in Sarah Griffin's shop, one man worked for Felix Kingston in the 1620's, another for him in the 1640's; two others were made free, by different printers, in 1663 and 1664; but apart from one apprentice in his sixth year of service none had been bound to her or her husband. Two had never been bound at all. Ratcliffe's house shows a different complex again. He had himself been bound to Stansby, but his partner was Thomas Daniel who had served with Francis Leach. This explains his binding of Daniel's younger brother, Robert, as it does his employment of Leach's son, Francis, and two others who had served their time with Leach. But it was far from being a closed shop. Of Ratcliffe's other men, one was still formally apprenticed to Fawcett, another to Elizabeth Mascall, primer binder, another to John Sweeting, one was a free journeyman and one was never bound nor made free. As a further indication of mobility, we might note that Ratcliffe's two apprentices freed in 1666 are no longer with him. Ellen Cotes on the other hand, commanded more loyalty. One man bound to her husband in 1644 and another bound to her in 1657 are still with her; but, of the other 9, 2 are otherwise unknown, 1 was still technically apprenticed to Macocke, 2 were never bound although subsequently made free, 1 was free of the Cutlers' Company, 2 were free journeymen, and 1 was the young Benjamin

Motte who that month began his career as a printer. In other words, only 5 of
the 11 were employed according to the rules.

Three different points might now be made. Anne Maxwell's presswork, as evidenced by Margaret Cavendish's book, is exceptionally good. We can see why
when we note that two of her pressmen had long experience: Grantham was
bound to Griffin in 1638 and Harris to Flesher in 1641. My second point relates
to Redmaine. For 5 of his 7 men we have no other record. Further, the list of his
workmen does not include Thomas Leach who in December 1668 was described
as 'a printer who works journey work with Mr Redman'. Leach's circumstances
may have changed after July when he had a press of his own and a newly bound
apprentice, but one suspects a contractual relation with Redmaine and part-
printing of his books. Third, L'Estrange's lists duplicate some names: Francis
Leach, for example, works for both Ratcliffe and Godbid, Roger Vaughan works
at press for the King's Printer as well as for John Streater. The evidence, that is,
combines complexly factors of an historic depth which affect choice of workmen and quality of work, and of a contemporary breadth which affect the stability of the work-force and the regulation of admission to it. Beyond that, and
within a different analytical dimension again, we might note the striking differences in the ratios of compositors to pressmen, where these details are given, or
those of total workforce to presses in each house.

Similarly one should relate evidence about press-correction to particular
houses, checking errata lists for the range and kind of error revealed and relating them to the workmen employed. Lists of errata occur in 65 books, and, the
important point is the pervasive concern they show for substantive accuracy. Occasionally, as in one of Vincent's books, rushed out in reply to William Penn's
Sandy Foundation Shaken, speed was a legitimate excuse for error. 'The speeding of
the sheets off the Presses, hath caused too many both literal Errata's and in the
sence too, the chiefest found out in a hasty review you have as follows . . .'. Lest
we jump to a generalisation on that evidence, Robert Brown's *Jerubaal* offers the
opposite excuse of delay, for its errata were 'occasioned through the difficulty of
Printing, which also occasioned its retardation until now, though intended for
thee some months since.' There are glib evasions like Thomas Mall's 'In the first
two sheets of this Treatise, the Author hath not found any faults . . . ; and he
trusts thou wilt find none in the rest, but what thine ingenuity will correct or
pardon.' Dryden was lax about correcting the first edition of *The Indian Emperor*, 'it
being too full of faults which had escaped the Printer.' The second he therefore
overlooked 'with more care' so that 'the Press is freed from some gross errours
which it had to answer to before.' Its biggest error, however, the only printing of
the *Defence of the Essay of Dramatick Poesie*, had to be expunged by cancellation. Castlemaine, as a Catholic apologist, faced greater problems: 'the Printer not only Ital-
icised where he should not, and omitted where he should, but also left out some
words, and changed others, as if there had been a private correspondency,
betweene my Adversary and him . . .'. The comments are not surprising for

Castlemaine was sensitive to these details. His book shows the only intelligent use of rubrication in the period where to make his polemical point he lists in red the names of Catholics who suffered for the King. Most of the evidence though points to regular correction, even of hastily printed, unlicensed books like *Nehushtan* which, although it lists errata, the author corrected, sheet by sheet, at press. The norm is described by Burnett: 'Notwithstanding the *Corrector's* care, through the carelessness of the Compositor, some faults have escaped . . .'.

I should have liked at this point to say something about the range of types and decorative material held by each printer, not simply to attribute anonymous work and refine the figures, but to assess this form of attribution. My evidence, however, is still incomplete and the test depends absolutely on completeness.

Some inquiry ought now to be directed at the booksellers, by starting, for example, with an estimate of total production and then calculating the extent of their responsibility for it. The 458 items run to 8127 signature sheets. On this basis, Herringman's 26 titles account for 6% of production, a figure which we can for quick comparison set beside one of 4.5% for George Sawbridge. But whereas Herringman ventured alone, Sawbridge also shared in two large enterprises involving a further 616 signature-sheets, so that the scale of his operations was not far short of Herringman's. More surprising perhaps is the proportion of work printed for the author. There are 21 items, but they account for 1228 sheets, which is 15% of production. These figures include the books of the Duchess of Newcastle, Margaret Cavendish, but exclude all other work not specifically stated to have been printed for the author. Most of them, carrying the bare imprint 'Printed in the Year 1668,' would have been at the author's charge, putting the percentage of total production higher still. One such book, Muggleton's *A Looking-glass for George Fox*, makes the point explicitly.

Or, developing this last observation, we may ask about the innovative interests and commercial risks borne by booksellers as reflected, negatively, in their dependence upon reprints. Excluding almanacks, and reissues, whose selling potential is only marginally different from that of any older stock, there were 117 reprints. All but three (which I've still to see) account (in signature-sheets) for over 32% of production. This conservatism in the trade must highlight the originality of a man like Ogilby on the one hand and the expansive, liberating effects of essentially non-commercial controversial literature on the other. Both kinds of printing were informed by ideals of which the trade was ignorant.

The effects of the Licensing Act are only partly reflected in the imprimaturs and Stationers' Register. Only 52 books bear some form of licence; there are only 79 entries for the year in the Register. But these figures are not easy to handle. The more important points are probably that licensing could be safely neglected for non-controversial books; and that it *had* to be evaded for controversial ones. But both licensing and registration are also a function of size. Hobbes disputes cuts with the censor because large books involved large investment and it was better to play safe; pamphlets cost less, were more easily dispersed, and their au-

thors and printers were harder to detect. But the same principle applies to registration of copyright. Pamphlets were coming to be regarded as a distinct branch
of the trade for which retailing booksellers might not even bother to keep par-
ticularised accounts, and their copyright was rarely worth registering. Very few
were entered. Unlicensed books of controversy of course couldn't be registered,
but as commercial gain was not the motive for publication there was no cause to
safeguard the copyright. Francis Smith's later complaint that licensers kept booksellers waiting until their market was gone may also explain why few shorter,
topical pamphlets were entered, although it is not wholly borne out, for L'Estrange could be prompt. An account of a trial on 4 April was licensed and entered by 9 April, and the dates of licensing, registration and dedications for several other books are also very close. Indeed, sometimes speed may have led to
very cursory reading. *A Free Conference* was duly licensed on 11 February by Joseph
Williamson by appointment of Lord Arlington. Two weeks later the *Gazette*, with
impotent speed, published an official *mea culpa*, for the book contained 'indecent
expressions, and reflections upon the Most Christian King, . . . ; it must be acknowledged that the said Expressions and Reflections unhappily escaped the
View of the Peruser, and that nothing of that Nature ought to be justified,
whereof Order is given that signification be hereby made.' The *Gazette*, incidentally, is the most blatant case of post-publication registration: 40 issues for October to March were entered on 24 April.

It is clear that licensing and registration were sometimes confused, usually by
intent, and that external political pressures, often unconnected with the censor-
ing function, supplanted trade controls. Conversely, the Company could police
its commercial copyrights while ostensibly searching for unlicensed books. So
booksellers, having procured another man's copy, had it licensed in their own
name: in this way L'Estrange deprived Dover of his rights on one occasion,
Thomas Grigg aided and abetted Samuel Speed on another (although when advised of the consequence he revoked the licence). More seriously, Clavell's rights
in the *Term Catalogues* were protected by Arlington and L'Estrange although Starkey
registered his copies and Clavell did not. When conflict arose between Cornelius
Bee and Matthew Poole over Poole's plan to epitomise Bee's 9-volume collection of biblical commentaries, it was not the Company that adjudicated but
L'Estrange and the Secretaries. Just as Clavell's use of the Post Office parallels that
of Cave 60 years later, so is Bee's complaint about synopses revived in the 1730's
and charged against the monthly magazines.

L'Estrange had complained that the Company frustrated his efforts, and to
procure its cooperation the King had Norton, Mearne and Roycroft made members of its Court and told the Company that it was henceforth accountable for the
scandalous abuses of the Press. Mearne searched for, seized, and sold the books
himself, and then restored the equipment to its owners. When the Master of the
Company wrote of the imminent prosecution of three unlicensed printers he
said that although convicted 'they will retain their printing implements' and

suggests that the Company buy them off. L'Estrange was right when he spoke of the Company's indulgence of unlicensed printing and of its great concern for copyright infringements.

The details of searches by L'Estrange and the Company illumine the conditions of work and the methods of distribution; but I must pass over the long watches, back-alley probing, informers reports, warrants for arrest, questioning of hawkers, the imprisonment of Darby, Elizabeth Calvert, Elizabeth Poole, Anne Brewster and James Cottrell, the hunting down of Wallis for *The Cobbler of Gloucester*, of Wilson for *Nehushtan*. There are other details too that it would be interesting to dwell on: the importation of 5000 copies of a Dutch-printed book, dispersed through Gospright in London, Burton in Yarmouth, and others at Hull and in Scotland; the mercury sellers like Old Cornelius, Scotch George, Old Fox and, despite her name, Lame Cassie; the part-publication and monthly delivery of *Catechetical-Preaching-Exercises* to each house as the weekly bills of mortality are left, with prices and delivery charges; Robert Young's part-publications because 'many peny-Books, will sell for one or two pence or three pence price'; the advertisements which reveal what stock escaped the fire or which prove that title pages often lie; the vertical short-titles on an outer page; the self-consciousness about preserving Scottish words and idioms exactly in an English book, or publishing a medical book in English instead of Latin.

Instead, there are two general inferences which I wish to draw, arising from censorship and copyright, and one combined effect that I should like to note.

First, we can see in the series of broadsides a trend that I have already noted— and it occurs a century before John Wilkes—the use of obscenity as a political weapon. The series began with *The Humble Petition of the Undone Company of poore Distressed Whores*, dated Lady Day 1668, and addressed to the Catholic Lady Castlemaine. There was a further petition to the apprentices, the apprentices' answer, the poor whores' reply, the citizens' reply, and finally *The Gracious Answer of the Most Illustrious Lady of Pleasure the Countess Castlem*. This was virulent anti-Catholic propaganda at a time when the King was anxious to show sympathy. An informer advised that they were printed by Darby, that Anne Brewster and her son supplied 6 quires of them, and that a clockmaker sold two; but L'Estrange had to confess 'I can fasten nothing on *The Poor Whores' Petition* that a jury will take notice of.' The stratagem, that is, hit a middle ground where it was free from political attack and where moral objections against the obscenity had not yet been formulated.

My second inference relates to copyright. The two trade conflicts I have already mentioned—those between Poole and Bee, and Clavell and Starkey—were resolved from outside the Company by politically imposed compromises. That for Clavell and Starkey was short-lived, but Poole and Bee joined forces on the Synopsis and published it jointly. Of course there were piracies. Brooks' *String of Pearles* was one of which 'some dishonest booksellers, called Land-Pirates, who make it their practice to steal Impressions of other men's Copies . . . have lately printed a false and imperfect Impression . . . false printing many words, and leaving out all the Table of the Chief Heads, and of a bad paper and print, and crammed into eight Sheets, without Rules . . .'. Sawbridge complains of a piracy of *The Knowledge of Things Unknown*, authenticating his copies with John Stafford's device. Anne Seile warned against a reprint of Heylyn's *Cosmographie* without the addition she offers. Playfere claimed his edition of *The Visions* as the true one licensed according to order; but it is a meaner version of Herringman's which was translated by L'Estrange and bore a dated licence.

Nevertheless, the larger tendency to be noted is the bifold one of combination. It limited investment risks and piracy. Current work on 18th-century trade sale catalogues will come closer than any other study to revealing the intricate relationships between booksellers, but even in 1668 something of the kind is on its way. So far as possible, conflict was resolved by partnership, and imprints may not always reveal it. Bee, for example, had a half-share in his *Critici Sacri*, the remaining half being borne by five others. Barton's *Psalms* were entered without his consent to Parkhurst and Eglesfield; he objected, asking that Tyton and Pulleyn be substituted. They were added, but only Parkhurst's name is in the imprint. John Place had a fourth share in Wentworth's *Office and Duty of Executors* but the imprint lists only the printers as assigns of R. & E. Atkyns. Meriton's *Touchstone of Wills*, although entered only to Thomas Dring and John Place, was printed for 10 booksellers, Rolle's *Abridgement* for 13. These are clearly different from books like the fourth issue of *Paradise Lost* which lists 4 booksellers by whom the book is sold, or Prynne's *Third Tome*, printed for the author and sold by 5 booksellers, or Heylyn's *Cosmographie*, printed for Anne Seile and sold by 5 others. But the broader inference I wish to draw is that trade combinations, in their pursuit of non-political commercial interest, their resolution of conflict by cooperation, and the restricted commitment to any one book in the spread of investment to several, are economically stabilising, politically neutralising, and culturally distancing agents. It is no accident that the period of their fullest development coincides with one of economic expansion, political consolidation, and a broader philosophy of the rationality of order.

Again there were obvious exceptions to this image of a commercially self-preoccupied trade, but this growth in economic self-regulation was not wholly unconnected with that in morality and religion. In 1673, for example, the Quakers instituted their Morning Meeting to which all Quaker pamphlets were submitted for approval. In this, we see the formal institution of a system of self-censorship. Under these conditions (the expression of contradictions implicit in the trade in 1668) externally applied censorship gradually became unnecessary. At one level, I have suggested, this was in the economic interests of those engaged in trade; and within the Stationers' Company one can see the gradual emergence of shared rather than competitive interests, at first in the Company's own concern to police its members and control the dissidents, both in their political and commercially piratical activities, and then later in trade associations. On the religious side, one can see it occurring in the Friends' practice of reading and correcting MSS. before sending them to press.

The line of obscenity continues in political criticism as in 'polite' literature, but by the end of the century the society has found ways of formulating moral objections to it, outside the law, but shared by the Court, especially under Anne. At that point, the élitist groups within the trade develop their own reasons for self-imposed censorship, evident in Tonson's cleaning up of Rochester and in Congreve's bowdlerisation of his own texts.

III

With two exceptions there is little evidence of any sympathetic understanding by the trade of authorial intention. Indeed its commercial dominance over authors is manifest in the growth of the Grub-street race. Nor is there any concern to use typography to mediate knowledge and literary experience in any but the crudest way. But against the larger pattern of unrefined and uncomprehending commercial interest in 1668 we can set the books of Margaret Cavendish, Duchess of Newcastle, and John Ogilby. Neither one was, in the ordinary sense, a bookseller's client.

Margaret Cavendish's books are interesting for their surface tone—they're sumptuous, lavishly spaced, highly decorated folios printed in Great Primer or Double Pica on good paper. But they are vacuously over-blown, accepting convention and mistaking mere size for dignity. Ogilby's editions of Virgil, Aesop and the *Aesopics* in this year were far more sophisticated and it may be that in his work we see the beginning of a bifurcation of interest and endeavour of great significance. The main effect of his innovations was to extend the tonal range and expressive means of the book beyond the total abstraction of crowded, black, letter-symbols on an off-white page. In this he was, probably unconsciously, reviving the tradition of the emblem book and finding a form of image-making acceptable at a time when images were still under attack. More specifically, the high quality of the engravings he included, their size and profusion, but especially the attempt to relate them intimately to the narrative which he himself translated, made him a more self-conscious book-*maker* than anyone else at this time. He was, as he said, the designer of his *own* Fables, described by Pepys as 'very fine and satirical.' He created a luxury object, a cultural artifact, and catered for élitist tastes in an age of exceptionally poor printing, but the intelligence which informs his work, the dimension of his thought, gave it a life beyond itself. There are links with Tonson who used the plates of Ogilby's edition for Dryden's *Virgil*, albeit politicised by retouching. Pope recalled Ogilby's *Homer*: 'It was that great edition with pictures. I was then about 8 years old.'

Equally original and independent of the trade was Ogilby's method of sale by lottery. His second lottery was advertised for May 1668 but postponed because the adventures came in so fast that they could not be methodically registered. Ogilby's books were a portent in yet another way. The French paper on which they were printed was exceptionally large and we may see in it the beginning of a more general use throughout the trade of larger sheets. Margaret Cavendish's books confirm the trend. Mr Pollard has traced this development, as he has that of binding styles, but the reduction in formats which the larger sheet made possible, like the multi-volume binding which was its necessary corollary, came after 1668. What we see in that year, along with Ogilby's purposeful expansion of the concept of the book, are the germinal stages of a later flowering in which literary values, intelligent embellishment and convenient format are at best statements of one another. At this point the inquiry assumes a new significance for textual bibliography.

I have already intruded the names of Tonson, Congreve and Pope, and I must now bring my larger argument full circle, making 1668 a point of departure.

One of the few men in the trade itself who saw the advantages of catering for a cultured audience was Tonson. He dignified his authors, establishing their taste and superiority by styling their books, as Ogilby had done, in ways that contrasted with those of the trade at large. He was trapped by convention, so that even his books in the 1690's follow well-worn paths, but he reached his prime just as the trade experienced the liberating effects of the settlement of 1688 and just as a new wave of continental influence reached London. He had new resources, and he had a conception of the dignity of his trade. It was he who launched the new Cambridge Press on its quarto classics with their engravings by Gribelin. It was he who brought the Shakespeare folio down to size and had it cleansed of error. It was he who not only published Congreve but who presented him with a copy of the 1664 Rouen edition of the works of Corneille. He was the perfect instrument for giving public form to Congreve's intentions. It is on these that I wish to conclude.

I have said that few writers in the 17th century were conscious of the uses to which printing could be put in mediating their fullest textual intentions, but two stand out. One was Ben Jonson; the other was Congreve. Both were dramatists. Both therefore had an interest in presenting their texts in a form which mediated the dramatic experience, and to do this both adopted the French style of neo-classical scene division. Again, referring to 1668, it is evident from the plays printed in that year that they still unthinkingly reflect the conventions imposed by the trade without regard to dramatic form: they express, not any idea of the play as play, but merely the disparate and conflicting concerns of theatre and printing house. So do those of the 1690's. Q1 of *The Way of the World*, for example, (actually 1700), runs Act I, scene i; II.i; III.i; IV.i; V.i. The forms, that is, have no meaning. Congreve accepted them, yet even in the 1690's, as other evidence makes clear, he thought of his plays as having scenes in the neo-classical sense.

In his *Works* of 1710 he had at last available to him a range of resources and a sense of his own identity that permitted him to shape the book as a definition of himself and his creation. The *Works* are in 3 volumes, octavo, and the title page of the central volume emblematically states the comprehensive achievement:

The MOURNING BRIDE.	Tragedy.
The WAY of the WORLD.	Comedy.
The Judgment of PARIS.	Masque.
SEMELE.	Opera.

These were his finest works, flanked in the first volume by his three early plays, in his third by the poems upon several occasions. The format is unusual for collected works, especially plays. When Dryden's collected plays appeared in 1701, they were in folio, like Jonson's of 1692. Congreve's were influenced not so much by Rowe's Shakespeare, which preceded him, but by the belated impact of French and Dutch printing, the adoption of the larger sheet, and the change in binding styles. More significantly, he adopted throughout the neo-classical scene division favoured by French critical theory and characteristic of the printed texts of Corneille, Racine, Molière and Scarron. Tonson's printer could now draw on a greater range of decorative material which is deployed so as to emphasise scene groupings, not entries and exits. In this it reflects its age and its author in focussing on the stable group, the hard-won, contained poise, not the disturbing change. The point is that Congreve, his own best editor, is trying to convey to the reader a fuller sense of the stage experience. I can perhaps suggest it a little by citing two examples from *The Way of the World*: First Act II, sc. vi. and vii. Millamant exits with 'and when you have done thinking of that, think of me.' The new scene establishes clearly Mirabell's solitary wonder: 'I have something more—Gone—Think of you! To think of a Whirlwind in a Whirlwind etc . . .'. That 'I have something more—Gone! . . .'—just like Millamant's parting line, is a superb handling of the technique of scene change in a neo-classical sense. It has both continuity and distinction, and the reader is helped to realise the stage picture by its typographical isolation.

Conversely, Mirabell's later entry, and not only Congreve's but his *character's* ability to unite division—at Act IV, sc. v—is elaborately prepared. Poor Sir Wilful in the preceding scene can only demonstrate his boorishness when Millamant—to make the point—invites him to cap her quotation from Suckling, suggesting that to be a lover he should employ his 'power and art.' Sir Wilful is disgraced and on his bashful exit, Millamant sends him off with a laugh and one more line to end the scene:

> Aye, aye; ha, ha, ha!
> Like Phoebus sung the no less amorous boy.

New man, new scene, established with typographical flourish: enter Mirabell to complete the couplet, and the coupling—since he must complete Millamant's love:

> Like Daphne she, as lovely and as coy.

Finally, however, we must note Congreve's self-censoring bowdlerisation of his texts. The process began after *Love for Love* in 1695 so that Collier's attacks in 1698 were almost superfluous; but by 1710, in deference to the Queen, in defence of his actors, in the interests of preserving playhouses from threatened closure, and doubtless also because his own tastes had become more refined with age, Congreve was more than ready to follow Nahum Tate's advice that 'all Plays (capable of being reform'd) be rectify'd by their Authors if Living . . .'.

Textual bibliography as currently practised would have regard to none of these factors. Largely insensitive to book form, it would edit from the earliest version, placing a high premium on collation for minor press-variants. By adopting those texts, it would avoid the problem of bowdlerisation, the larger one of conflation if the 1710 *Works* are followed but the earlier readings restored, and therefore of course the critical implications of distinguishing between literary as distinct from moral revisions. It would ignore developments in the trade so positively applied by Congreve to mediate a *dramatic* experience to a *reading* audience through the *form* of the book.

Mr Ian Willison once remarked of the interdependence of authors, printers, publishers and public, that 'the true phases in the movement of printing history can only be established according to the succession of such complicities of interest.' I envy him that last phrase, for it suggests so succinctly the kinds of relationship I have had in mind, the need for us to recognise and describe those stages at which a new equilibrium of forces is struck, the need perhaps to see, from time to time, that enumerative, historical, analytical and textual bibliography, like the elements of Congreve's *Works*, are but statements of one another.

5

The London Book Trade in 1644

First published in 1992, this is the text of a lecture McKenzie delivered in 1988 on receiving the Marc Fitch Prize for Bibliography. Developing the preoccupations of his earlier study of the book trade in 1668, he again bases his arguments on a comprehensive investigation of the total output of London printing houses in a single year. He employs this labor-intensive but enormously productive methodology to reach significant revisionist conclusions in four main areas: bibliography, politics, and cultural and literary history.

First, he challenges the accuracy of conclusions drawn from the catalogue of "Thomason tracts," the "main source of evidence used by historians for the scale of publication in the years from 1641 to 1660"; revealing its incompleteness, he argues that "Thomason may give us less than half the story." At the same time, he tenders a number of observations about the general patterns of the seventeenth-century book trade to explain various problematic features of the contemporary bibliographical record. Second, he disproves the long-accepted understanding of censorship in seventeenth-century England promulgated by such notable historians as Christopher Hill and Keith Thomas. In opposition to their exclusively political readings, in which heroic printers nobly fought against oppressive state censors, McKenzie offers a less dramatic but more complex analysis, highlighting the "relative inefficiency of control," the policing role of the Stationers' Company itself, and the importance of commercial considerations in compromising censorship's effectiveness. Third, adducing a variety of examples from printed texts, he points to the problems of demarcating too precisely the boundaries between orality and the world of print. The culture of English letters in 1644 was alive, he demonstrates, both to "the anxieties created by print" and to "the possibilities opened up by it." Finally, he provides a new context for understanding the publication of *Areopagitica* (1644), Milton's celebrated anti-censorship tract.

In all these areas, McKenzie insists that we countenance a variety of determinants—ranging from the courage of writers and printers to the material and economic conditions of book production—that shaped the historical realities of seventeenth-century English culture. In so doing, he establishes enumerative bibliography as an indispensable tool for historical analysis.

I WAS INTRIGUED to note at a recent seminar that a minor typing error in the programme had transformed the distinguished Institute of Bibliography and Textual Criticism here at Leeds into one of Bibliography and Textual 'Cohesion.' And of course, like many misreadings, it is not quite so absurd as one might think. For a decade in which the key critical term has been 'deconstruction,' it might indeed be time to bring things together, to build a new synthesis, and to proclaim as our motto, like Adam Overdo at the end of Jonson's *Bartholomew Fair*, '*Ad correctionem, non ad destructionem; ad aedificandum, non ad diruendum.*'

If the challenge is to create a new synthesis, to trace relationships between the disciplines, to complement the deficiencies of one by the strengths of another, then it happens to be a challenge which bibliography is exceptionally well-placed to serve. Traditionally, the discipline of English studies has always defined its terms by creating, and from time to time adjusting, a literary canon, and where it *has* invoked the help of bibliography and textual criticism, it has been to correct and enhance the authority of a particular version of a relatively few canonical texts. And of course the vermiculate scholarship of that activity has its own fascination and commands our respect.

But bibliography itself knows no canon. Its terms of reference as a discipline are the whole archive of recorded texts, their production, re-production, dissemination, and their inter-textual relations. Our short-title catalogues are the tribute we pay to our society's perennial interest in its past. But they are also the most valuable resource we have for the comprehensive reconstruction of our own culture. If we see them in that way, then all past losses reduce our hope of fuller knowledge. By the same token, any prior selection of what it is acceptable or expedient to retain as the nation's archive can only in time distort our understanding of the past and pervert its application in the present. To make that point more precisely: historians and critics who now wish to resurrect marginal texts and their makers (the documents and writers who have always been excluded from the merely literary canon), have their greatest ally in bibliography. If a document was printed, and survives, we can in most cases recover it from Pollard and Redgrave, from Wing, and in due course from the eighteenth- and nineteenth-century short-title catalogues. These will in time become a single archive, searchable throughout at speed and low cost for author, subject, different editions, chronology, and location. When we have such a unified record, it will transform the study of our history, and in particular thereby the study of all who were kept from the centres of power by reason of their sex, race, religion, and their provincial or colonial status. It will enrich the study of any text in its full inter-textual setting, and the study of all versions of that text as new responses to social change. As Nestor says in Shakespeare's *Troilus and Cressida*:

> in such indexes, although small prickes
> To their subsequent volumes, there is seen
> The baby figure of the giant mass
> Of things to come at large.

What we cannot easily do at the moment, however, is construct a model to show the full complexity of text production at any one time. It is simple enough to take a single text and to document its metamorphoses. One might do the same for an author, a bookseller, or a printing house, again with relative ease. The real difficulty lies in reporting on those more limited products and processes in the rich diversity

of their relationships one to another, to offer in short a synchronic, not to say 'cohesive,' account. Almost all texts of any consequence are the product of the concurrent inter-action of ideologies and institutions, of writers, publishers, printers,
binders, wholesalers, travellers, retailers, as well as of the material sources (and
their makers and suppliers) of type, paper, cord, and all the appurtenances of a
printing house. We, like their writers, habitually think of texts as literary, and therefore either as discrete, as an oeuvre, or as a canon. Most booksellers in the seventeenth century, by contrast, would have thought of their stocks as a range of investments, or as a list of artifacts for sale. A printer almost certainly valued his
books and ephemera only as a succession of income-earning jobs. Where the main
participants themselves each posited a different interest in the product, and where
their labour to produce it was so differently organised by each of them, the
achievement of any synthesis true to all may prove to be an impossible ideal.

Still, if we posit as the point of our inquiry the creation of a model, however
imperfect, then we might at least begin by recording all we can know of a year, a
month, a week, a natural day, so that we can start exploring not just the products
themselves but the full dynamics of their production and reception in their human and institutional relations.

With that aim in mind, I chose to focus on one year—1644. In a sense, the
date was quite arbitrary, and for purposes of the exercise it would not really matter which year one took. Nevertheless, it is not without a certain felicity. Mr
William Sessions reminds me that, as the year of Marston Moor, 1644 was a crucial one for the history of printing in York. First, the royalist printer Stephen
Bulkley, who had left London hurriedly in 1642 to overlap briefly with the king
and his official travelling printers in York, stopped printing there with the
Marston Moor defeat. Second, by autumn 1644, the London-trained parliamentary printer Thomas Broad had arrived in York to begin a business which continued through his widow for over twenty years. In that way, and in microcosm
as it were, York provides an image of a time of transition, of the passage from
one dispensation to another. But 1644 was also the year in which Milton published, on 5 June, his letter 'Of Education' to Samuel Hartlib, and, on 23 November, *Areopagitica*, his plea for the liberty of unlicensed printing.

My remarks on this occasion, however, are not limited to 1644 but address a
range of interests which bear, I think, on several problems in literary and historical research. The topics I have in mind are the scale of text production; the economics of trade; attitudes to print; and the realities of censorship. I shall keep returning to 1644, but I shall also, for comparative purposes, refer to examples
from other years.

I begin with statistics. These are boring in their detail but fascinating in their
implications. The detail, with the qualifications there noted, is given in the Appendix. It does, I think, require us to modify the inferences drawn by some historians of the period, and suggests in particular the limitations of the Thomason
collection as their primary source. Dr Christopher Hill, for example, illustrates

as follows an increase in the number of books published in the 1640s: 'Milton's friend the bookseller George Thomason tried to buy a copy of every book and pamphlet published during these exciting times. In 1640 he purchased twenty-two titles; in 1642, one thousand nine hundred and sixty-six. This rate of publication was maintained for the next decade.'[1] As it happens, Dr Hill's equation of a rate of publication with one of acquisition, states my own ideal of copyright deposit; but it was certainly not achieved by Thomason. The wording of the third sentence is also curiously ambiguous. (I assume it does not mean that such a *rate of increase* was maintained for the next decade: a growth from twenty-two to one thousand nine hundred and sixty-six in three years would give an output in 1652 of something like three and a half billion titles.) But even accepting the probable meaning—that publication continued for the next decade at the high level set in 1642—it would still not be true. Excluding serials, the number of titles extant for 1642 is not one thousand nine hundred and sixty-six but actually about two thousand nine hundred and sixty-eight; it drops to half that for the next year; even lower for 1644; it is under a thousand for 1645; and only once again before 1685 (in 1660) does it even touch two thousand.

Because of its chronological arrangement, the Thomason catalogue, not Wing, is the main source of evidence used by historians for the scale of publication in the years from 1641 to 1660. Yet for all its splendid detail, it is no guide to total production. In 1644, for example, Thomason collected only six hundred and ninety-nine, or about sixty-three percent, of the one thousand one hundred and thirteen tracts known to be still extant. But even the total number of titles derived from Wing for that one year gives us only the minimum level of production. Excluding serials, but including later editions of the same title, Wing has about seventy thousand entries in all for the years 1641 to 1700. We can only guess the proportion that represents of the total output of the trade, but I suspect that it is not even sixty to seventy percent of the titles and editions actually published. And if production *was* thirty to forty percent higher than the entries in Wing suggest, then Thomason may give us less than half the story.

Again, however, evidence is elusive. We find the odd reference to books which seem not to have survived, and there are some lists by authors of the books they say they printed and published but which are unknown to Wing. A collection of some one thousand five hundred pamphlets recently acquired by Cambridge University Library and all dated between 1660 and 1695, includes some two hundred not traced in Wing. Title-page edition statements are notoriously unreliable, but they too tell us something of what we have lost. Michael Sparke's *Crums of Comfort* survives in only seven of the twenty editions published up to 1635; as Wing lists only the forty-first and forty-second editions, another twenty have disappeared without trace.

[1] 'Censorship and English Literature,' in *The Collected Essays of Christopher Hill*, 2 vols (Brighton: Harvester Press, 1985), I, p. 40.

So, when we come back to 1644, and any other year for which figures are given, we need to acknowledge the partial nature of the extant archive and be particularly cautious in attributing causes to the patterns of production throughout the century.

Sir Keith Thomas puts, I believe, a point of view commonly accepted by historians when he writes: 'In the 1640s, with the Civil War, all controls seemed to have lapsed altogether and the result was an extraordinary output of heterodox ideas of a kind which would not have been allowed before or afterwards. But normally the system of state licensing, which lasted until the end of the seventeenth century, had a deeply inhibiting effect on publication.'[2]

No one, I think it is fair to say, yet knows if that was so. In fact, it is impossible yet to say if the volume of production actually rose—as measured, for example, by the number of sheets in each book and the number of copies printed of each. At a guess, for my survey is not complete, perhaps half the items printed in 1644 were only single sheets, and at least as many again of those must have been lost, for as a class of ephemera they were the most vulnerable to extinction. Certainly there were more brief pamphlets and fewer substantial books. And although it is true that the number of extant titles rises sharply in 1642, witnessing to an increase in the reporting and exchange of opinions in print, one result of a systematic survey is to suggest that few in relation to the whole were heterodox. Indeed, many of the effects claimed for the lapse of licensing in 1641 are largely illusory; but this is a point to which I shall return.

In at least two other ways, the kind of annual surveys of book production I have suggested may help to refine our knowledge of the trade, and therefore of the past. One is better knowledge of the incidence of anonymous publication, as measured by the absence of the name or initials of an author, printer or bookseller. The other is printing for the author. Their attendant bibliographical signs are often read as evidence of the influence of censorship. Yet they may be read more correctly, I think, as a normal expression of the general pattern of trade.

The extent to which authors concealed their identity—or simply failed to mention their names in print—is not easy to assess, mainly because we are dependent, at least to begin with, on the form of the Wing attributions and the often ambiguous use of square brackets when authorship is only inferred. Nor does Wing always allow for internal declarations of authorship as distinct from title-page statements. I can say something, however, of the pattern shown by books published in 1644 and, for comparison, 1688. In each case, I assume that the presence of an author's, printer's or bookseller's initials in a work is a declaration of identity. I.M. or J.M., for example, can scarcely be read in the 1640s or the 1660s as a serious attempt by Milton to conceal his authorship. One might

---

[2] 'The Meaning of Literacy in Early Modern England,' in *The Written Word: Literacy in Transition*, edited by Gerd Baumann (Oxford: The Clarendon Press, 1986), p. 120.

have been tempted to think that the title page of one of the 1644 divorce tracts, *The Judgement of Martin Bucer*, had been set in code, for the 'I' and the 'M' of 'IVDGE-MENT' are much larger and stand out from the other letters; but Milton gives his full name on B4v. So too the 1644 edition of *The Doctrine and Discipline of Divorce* gives only J.M. on the title page but John Milton in full on A4v.

Again excluding serials, and any work in which we find either an author's name or initials, it is clear that anonymity is far more frequent than not. In 1644, authorship is acknowledged in only four hundred and thirty-six—or forty per-cent—of the one thousand one hundred and thirteen items now extant. The figure for 1688 is remarkably consistent at forty-three percent. Since very few of them could possibly have been influenced by censorship, what we have here is simply the perpetuation of a long-established convention of authors taking a low profile in making their thoughts public. Even as late as 1699, Dryden could write of a revival of Congreve's *Double Dealer* that 'the printing an Authors name, in a Play bill, is a new manner of proceeding, at least in England.'

The convention of anonymity for authors extends to printers, and—more surprisingly—even to booksellers. In 1644, only forty-six percent of the items published carry a printer's name; and only thirty-two percent a booksellers' name. For 1688, the figures are thirty-one percent for printers and thirty-nine percent for booksellers. Again, it is initially tempting to think that such anonymity in the trade betrays a wish to avoid detection. Did Samuel Simmons leave his name off the first two issues of *Paradise Lost* because of his fear of author-ity? I think not. If we look at the range of books involved, very few had any rea-son to conceal their origins. That applies even to those books which give neither a printer nor a bookseller: some twenty-two percent of the 1644 items, and thirty percent of those for 1688.

There is nothing sinister in any of this. Nor is there, I think, in the low inci-dence of entries in the Stationers' Register, notwithstanding the legal obligation to make them. In 1644, only twenty percent of the books and pamphlets were entered; in 1688, only seven percent. That decline by 1688 reflects changes in the way booksellers had come to hold and to share their copyrights. The entries for 1644 tell a different story, and again the explanation is more likely to be eco-nomic than political: a function of the increase in the number of titles published and a reduction in their length. Very few were likely to be pirated or run to a sec-ond edition. Spending 6d. to establish copyright by entry would not therefore have bought any protection worth paying for.

Those comments suggest how events now read as political may actually express straightforward conditions of trade. So too, in many cases, not the threat of re-prisal but the costs of printing, inhibited some authors from venturing into print and left them content to circulate their work in manuscript. Richard Williams did not print his book, 'A poore mans pittance,' consisting of tracts on Essex and the Gunpowder plot: 'I did pretende to haue put the same in printe and had gotten it lycensed accordinge to order. But a printer asked me a some of moneye for the impression whiche I was not able to paye and so I kepte it privatt.'[3]

When, by contrast, the printer Samuel Simmons agreed to make Milton three successive payments for *Paradise Lost*, Milton may well have been more fortunate than we are accustomed to think. The commoner situation mid-century for many classes of text, including poetry, was more like that of Richard Williams. Were we to know more about the extent of printing at the author's expense, we should be better able to judge why some works never reached print and why those that did may often be found with such bare imprints as 'Printed in the Year 1644.' The eccentric Lady Eleanor Audeley, or Davies, or Douglas—the same woman: she was much married—has sixty-one items in STC and Wing, but all except two are devoid of any mention of a bookseller or printer. Of the fifty-eight Wing items attributed to her, twenty-seven are anonymous. What we have here is almost certainly a case of books printed for the author: she bore all the costs, and neither printer nor bookseller (if there was one) saw any reason to be named. But, again, there was nothing sinister in their absence from such an imprint.

That solution was also, for some authors, a preferred alternative to the forms of aristocratic patronage common both earlier and later in the century. In 1644 the very idea of patronage was anathema to many. One can see something of feelings on the matter in comments that year by Richard Vines and Francis Quarles. In his book, *The Impostures of Seducing Teachers Discovered*, Vines writes, for example, *'AN Epistle Dedicatory usually bespeakes a Patron, and then the Reader is epistled afterward. I intreat Readers only and Patrons no further than the Truth may challenge them . . .'*. When Cornelius Burges was attacked for dedicating a book to the Earl of Pembroke, a practice described by his critic as *'a meer Popish Ceremony,'* Quarles came to his defence in *The Whipper Whipt* with an etymological argument that no subservience was implied by a 'dedication' but only a free act of presentation.[4]

But for many in the 1640s the very acceptance of print as a medium still remained problematic. Writing of literacy in early modern England, Sir Keith Thomas remarked that 'Early modern England . . . was not an oral society. But neither was it a fully literate one . . . it is the interaction between contrasting forms of culture, literate and illiterate, oral and written, which gives this period its particular fascination.'[5]

The reminder is timely, for a phrase like 'the impact of print'—however carefully it is qualified—cannot help but imply a major displacement of writing. In the same way, too great a preoccupation with writing and printing (as the technologies of literacy) may lead us to forget the superior virtues of speech.

As we know, an important difference between talking and writing is what is now called 'presence.' The spoken text can be more sharply defined, and its authority enhanced, by the speaker's control of tone, nuance, gesture, and respon-

---

[3] British Library MS Arundel 418, f. 24ʳ. I am grateful to Dr J. K. Moore for this reference.
[4] For Richard Vines, see Wing V557; for Francis Quarles, Wing Q121.
[5] 'The Meaning of Literacy in Early Modern England,' p. 98.

siveness to an audience. Hence for many, happier in the one medium, the dual pressure to speak *and* to publish or to listen *and* to read created problems of choice and adjustment.

Looking for first-hand evidence of those problems, we find it in the ephemeral world of seventeenth-century sermons, topical pamphlets, and serials. It is there that we get our clearest view both of the anxieties created by print and of the possibilities opened up by it. Almost every printed sermon in the first half of the century has something to say by way of apology for the loss of the preacher's presence. 'I know well that *the same* Sermon, *as to the life of it,* is scarcely *the same* in *the hearing, and in the reading . . .*', wrote John Ward in 1645. So too, in 1644, Peter Smith had feared that his printed sermon would '*want that little life it seem'd to have when it was utter'd* viva voce, *and entertained with your chearfull and religious attention.*' But these reluctant writers also had to acknowledge some advantages. So again Peter Smith, after quoting Romans to the effect that faith comes by preaching, nevertheless concedes that '*memory is frail; and to reflect again, by reading, upon that wch we have heard, may conduce much unto the improvement of your knowledge.*' Christopher Tesdale, also in 1644, says to his readers: '*I shall bee your remembrancer by restoring the losse of the eare to the eye: Words, we say, are wind, and unless they be taken upon the wing, even while they are flying, and brought to the Presse, they are gone and lost.*'[6]

Others express their concern with the psychology of knowledge in relation to the forms in which it is communicated: '*What the Pulpit sent to some of your eares, the Presse now sends to some of your eyes; the good God send it into every one of your hearts, into your hands, and lives; the Argument is worthy of your eares, eyes, hearts, and hands . . .*', wrote Edmund Staunton in 1644, self-conscious still about turning speech into print and doubtful of its ability to enter the heart. Dr John Strickland, the same year: the words '*have been already in your eares, they are now before your eyes, the Lord write them into our hearts, that we may be doers of the word, and not hearers onely . . .*'.[7] What is revealing about these unprofound comments is their frequency, their self-consciousness, and their still tentative, uncertain quality.

Concern and regret, if not quite the same anxiety, may also be found at the gradual shift from oral to written pleading in the law courts. Under the system of oral pleading, the forms were settled only after exhaustive debate in court, with all the opportunities it provided for clarification and correction. Then, when the pleadings were enrolled, they were accurate. By contrast, written pleadings, whose terms were settled by the parties out of court, were open to error. Hale, for example, in his *History of the Common Law Pleas of the Crown,* thought the oral evidence at common law far superior to the written evidence in courts of equity, because it is delivered 'personally, and not in writing; [in writing] often time, yea too often, a crafty clerk, commissioner or examiner, will make a witness speak what he truly never meant by dressing it up in his own terms, phrase

---

[6] For Peter Smith, see Wing S4142; for Christopher Tesdale, Wing T792; for John Ward, Wing W773.
[7] For Edmund Staunton, see Wing S5342; for John Strickland, Wing S5969.

and expressions. Whereas on the other hand, many times the very manner of delivering testimony, will give a probable indication, whether the witness speaks truly or falsely. And by this means also he has an opportunity to correct, amend or explain his testimony, upon further questioning with him; which he can never have, after a deposition is set down in writing.'[8] That is a good description of the virtues of speech as presence. The paradox of writing—that what seems exact when first written can be torn a thousand ways by critical reading—led Francis Bacon to resist the reduction of common law to statute form. As he said in 1616, 'there are more doubts that arise upon our statutes, which are a text law, than upon the common law, which is no text law.'[9] To bring words on a page up to date, we must either strain their meaning, or revise and reprint them.

The powerful myth of the permanence of print—the art that preserves all arts—is only part of the story. What we need equally to stress, I think, is the ephemerality of much that is printed. To do so would at least help us to see more readily certain affinities it still had, in the minds of many at this time, with speech.

When we look at the books themselves, we can see writers and printers seeking to limit the difference of print by devising ways to suggest its affinities with speaking and writing. It is most notable of course in forms of address and of dialogue; and it is one of the important uses of marginal notes.

So, Milton would speak in print: 'They who, to States and Governors of the Commonwealth direct their *Speech*, High Court of Parliament, or wanting such access in a private condition, write that which they forsee may advance the public good . . .'. As a rhetorical strategy, *Areopagitica, a Speech . . . To the Parliament of England*, assumes an oral condition. By adopting such a form, Milton becomes present to the Commons. And yet his pamphlet is clearly written to be read, not heard. The amphibolous state of that 'speech' or 'pamphlet' is shared in part by Milton's other addresses to Parliament at that time printed in *The Doctrine and Discipline of Divorce* and *Tetrachordon*. And when we come to the letter (or should it be tract?), 'Of Education,' we see Milton exploiting yet another interstitial space. Is this a private letter made public print ('Thus Master *Hartlib*, you have a generall view in writing of that which I had severall times discourst with you . . .'); or is it really conceived as a text to be printed which merely exploits the fiction of being a private communication? Milton moves easily and positively into the double role of speaker and writer; yet his fluency in speech, manuscript and print is not just a mark of his peculiar genius but a skill demanded by his times if he was to reach all members of his commonwealth. Writing of toleration in 1673, in his little tract *Of True Religion*, he holds that Protestants should be able 'on all occasions to give account of their Faith . . . by Arguing, Preaching in their several Assemblies, Publick writing, and the freedom of Printing.' In other words, in each and every mode.

---

[8] Sir Matthew Hale, *History of the Common Law* (1713), second edition corrected (1716), cited by W. S. Holdsworth, *A History of English Law*, 16 vols (1922–66), VI, p. 592.

[9] Cited by J. H. Baker, *An Introduction to English Legal History*, second edition (London: Butterworths, 1979), p. 189.

The development in print of different registers to signal that variety of forms is one of the fascinating features of the book trade at this time. Milton's words 'Publick writing' are exactly right for his own sense of address. This practice of using print more generally as if it *were* a public speaking and writing is found at its most efficient in the informal genres of ephemera, the small pamphlet, and the printed speech. There is a form of communicative interchange here, the extent of which would, I think, be hard to parallel in the years immediately before or after the seventeenth century.

It is quite remarkable, for example, how many texts imply some kind of direct address or dialogue. Milton's *Colasterion* is 'A reply to a nameless answer against . . .' *The Doctrine and Discipline of Divorce*. Wing lists four hundred and twenty-four titles which begin in the form 'An Answer to.' Another five hundred and sixty-two begin as titles of address in the form 'To the . . .'. 'Humble' addresses, desires, hints, petitions, propositions, remonstrances, representations, requests, supplications, and so on, account for another three hundred and twenty-seven. Petitions, proposals and propositions (the ones which do not begin as 'Humble') number three hundred and seventeen. 'His Majesty' answers, declares or sends messages to another thirty. Titles beginning with the words Animadversion, Answer, Antidote, Confutation, Dialogue (one hundred and fifty-three of those), Reflection, Refutation, Remarks, Reply, Response, Vindication, Voice and Vox, altogether number six hundred and eighty-two. 'A Letter' or 'Letters to' account for eight hundred and two items. The round total they make is at least three thousand one hundred and forty-four. That figure, moreover, excludes all separate-issues and re-issues and reprintings, and (with the sole exception of His Majesty) it also excludes every comparable item entered under or cross-referenced to an author's name. A quick test of how many more might be involved were we to include those classes may be made by taking the title entries for 'Vindication.' Only seventy-eight were included in the above calculations, but there are in fact one hundred and ninety-nine such entries, or two and a half times as many again. This interchange of highly topical texts, of short pamphlets with short lives, helped to break down the anxiety-provoking distinctions between speech, manuscript and print, and to confirm the use of printing in its ephemeral uses.

Printing is of course much inferior to speech when it comes to conveying the spatial dynamics of speaker and audience, but what is fascinating to observe in the 1644 books is the skill with which printers tried to 'set forth' in their own terms at least something of the social space of dialogue. Where the extensions of dialogue are most notable is in the inter-textual levels so many pamphlets present. This may be done by the alternation of texts and counter-texts. So Quarles, in his defence of Cornelius Burges, adopts a kind of typographic drama: the biblical David presents the text of Burges; Calumniator, son of Nimshi (a great worshipper of calves), speaks the text of Burges's critics; and Quarles's own text is given to Jonathan as The Replyer. Paragraph by paragraph throughout the book they take their turn in the debate.[10] In Cheynell's attack on Chillingworth, the questions are set up in italic, Chillingworth's answers in black letter, and Cheynell's comments in roman.[11] In *A Vindication of Episcopacie*, the pamphlet under attack is reprinted and then demolished, a paragraph at a time, for the entire book. We find the same thing in *The Cavaliers New Common-prayer Booke Vnclasp't*, first printed at York in 1644. This too is entirely reprinted in London 'with some brief and necessary *Observations*, to refute the Lyes and Scandalls that are contained in it.' These observations are interposed in smaller type between the paragraphs. When they fail to serve, qualifications, assertions, rebuttals, imputed meanings, all set in italic and put in square brackets, invade the main text itself. One of the neatest pieces of inter-textual presentation in the period is *A Solemn League and Covenant*, both as it was agreed at Westminster and then as modified in Edinburgh. It gives the Westminster text, but as one edition notes: '*The several additions to the Scottish forme are here printed in a different letter*' [namely, italics within square brackets] and '*The omissions and other alterations are noted in the margent.*'[12]

Marginal notes are one of the best pointers there are to the nature of textual exchange. In their citation of sources, they have an intertextual function. Milton, of course, could afford to be scathing about any marginal display of erudition. When he was abroad, as he records in *Church Government* (1641), he had 'to club quotations with men whose learning and belief lies in marginal stuffings . . . and horse-loads of citations.' Others, less confident than he, felt they had to make their excuses if their margins were bare. 'If it trouble thee (Good Reader) to see so bare a margin, so few Authors cited, or this Sermon come abroad in so homely and plaine a dresse . . .', wrote John Shaw in *Brittains Remembrancer*, it is all because his books and papers were plundered a year before; that copies of his sermons were demanded within three days of preaching it; and that '*I had only time to write it once over, so as the Printer got it from me by pieces of sheets, as it was written (which makes it somewhat more confused) . . .*'. Thomas Blake, in *The birth-privilege*, fears that '*Some will complain of a naked Margin, to which much might be said, The Author was with books when it was compiled for the Pulpit, but taken from them when it was fitted for the Presse. So that use of Marginal References must have put upon him the borrowed copies of others, and a new paines for the quotation of Chapter & Page.*' Even more pertinently, however, he argues that '*the quotations desired must either have been friends, and so their Evidence would be challenged; or else Adversaries, which perhaps might provoke some personall offences and distaste, which the Authour studiously professeth to avoid.*'[13] Challenge and provocation, so natural in oral debate but so hard to convey in print, are there seen as a function of the marginal note. Under those continuing conditions of uncertainty about the precise status of speech and print, it is not surprising to note the relatively late de-

[10] *The Whipper Whipt* (1644), Wing Q121.

[11] Francis Cheynell, *Chillingworthi novissima* (1644), Wing C3810.

[12] For *A Vindication of Episcopacie*, see Wing V477; for *The Cavaliers New Common-prayer Booke Vnclasp't*, Wing C1578; and for the *Solemn League and Covenant*, see, for example, *A Copie of the Covenant* (1644), Wing C6210.

[13] For John Shaw, see Wing S3023A; for Thomas Blake, Wing B3142.

velopment (in 1668) of the now familiar distinction between slander and libel.[14] In the 1640s, publishing a libel need not have involved printing it. Consequently the forms of suppression and censure were themselves less straightforward, as well as less severe, than some historians and critics have assumed.

Dr Christopher Hill and Professor Annabel Patterson, for example, have each argued that the censorship seriously inhibited writers, at worst silencing them and at best driving them into a rhetoric of obliquity. We are therefore enjoined, in effect, to study not only the texts that *were* written, but the unwritten ones too: 'certain words, certain ideas, that could not be printed.' As Dr Hill puts it, 'Historians looking only at the words on the page risk entering into an unwritten conspiracy with seventeenth-century censors.'[15] Of course, since such readings depend crucially upon a knowledge of the events and opinions that were suppressed and their relation to the words of the texts as we actually have them, they are not without their risks.

The problem is not just an academic one. Let me enforce the point by telling a slightly chilling story. The two editors of a recent joint edition of the letters of a major writer agreed to divide their labours. One dealt with letters before, the other with letters after, a certain date. Unbeknown to each other, they each edited the same undated letter and supplied it with a convincing set of notes to date it and to explain the allusions. Each 'edition' was in itself highly plausible, but of course the two were mutually exclusive. Happily, an alert copy-editor averted any public embarrassment. But one can easily see how the nature of language, which leaves a text open, and the density of history, which compels selection, can make for some intoxicating recipes.

There is not space to pursue at proper length on this occasion the topic of censorship, but since one of the most impressive books to appear in 1644 was Milton's *Areopagitica* it demands at least brief comment. One of the things I would wish to stress, by contrast with Dr Hill and Professor Patterson, is the relative inefficiency of control, and to affirm the courage of the writers, printers and booksellers who wrote, printed and dispersed the multitude of unlicensed texts.

The fullest recent discussion I know of seditious libel in the period is that by Philip Hamburger who makes it abundantly clear that 'most so-called seditious libel trials before 1696 were not for the common law offence of libel but . . . for violations of specific licensing statutes . . . or the royal prerogative to license printed books'.[16] Of the options open to government—such as prosecutions for treason, scandalum magnatum, and heresy, all of which carried heavy penalties—the simplest to execute was a system of licensing. When, in 1642, new legislation was

---

[14] The essential change may be charted in King v. Lake (1668); see A. Kiralfy, *A Source Book of English Law* (London: Sweet and Maxwell, 1957), pp. 154–63; Baker, op. cit., p. 374; and Holdsworth, op. cit., V, pp. 346–47, 360–61, 364–65.

[15] Christopher Hill, 'Censorship and English Literature,' pp. 32, 50; and Annabel Patterson, *Censorship and Interpretation* (Madison: University of Wisconsin Press, 1984), passim.

[16] Philip Hamburger, 'The Development of the Law of Seditious Libel and the Control of the Press,' *Stanford Law Journal*, 37 (1984–5), pp. 661–765, esp. p. 674.

being considered to control the press, the judges reported to the Lords that the mere printing of libels was a publication of them, since their printing implied distribution. But the law of libel was thought much more difficult to apply than pre-publication censorship, and when the Order of June 1643 came to be drafted, it therefore settled for licensing as the simpler means of control.

This almost uniform policy of all governments throughout the century to employ licensing laws to prosecute the press is of greatest importance in deciding the extent and seriousness of any infringements. To begin with, all punishments under the Star Chamber decrees of 1586 and 1637 were less severe than those prescribed by other laws. Only at times of greatest danger (1588, 1601, the 1630s, 1649, immediately after the Restoration, and in the 1680s) did government proceed under legislation which allowed the harsher penalties of death or mutilation. Indeed, in the absence of press laws, there was no lesser course open. It may seem a paradox, but the effect of the licensing laws, when they were in force, was to mitigate the crime. Lilburne's trial in 1638, just after the 1637 decree, was for violating its licensing provisions. Even when the charge *was* treason, it was rarely the testimony of a text which determined the verdict.

Nor did any government find it at all easy to restrain the press. In fact, as Hamburger says, 'the legal and political restraints on [its] ability to deal effectively with the press frequently left the Crown in very straitened legal circumstances.' Finally, 'it had a continual struggle to maintain a legal basis for prosecution [and was] obliged to abandon one law after another as those in use became inadequate, defunct, or otherwise obsolete.'[17] Against Dr Hill's view that 'The ending of ecclesiastical control seems to me the most significant event in the history of seventeenth-century English literature,'[18] one must stress Hamburger's view that control by licensing was virtually continuous, and only fitfully efficient, and Holdsworth's successive demonstrations that the abolition of Star Chamber in 1641 changed little.[19]

Indeed, the Star Chamber decrees of 1586 and 1637, like the order of June 1643 and the post-Restoration licensing acts, combined to serve the interests both of government and the book trade. They prescribed the licensing of books to be printed, they ordered the registration of copies, and they gave the Stationers' Company a role in enforcing the provisions. It is important to realise that those provisions were actively sought by the Company as a means of restraining competition, of ensuring (at least in principle) equitable conditions for members of the Company, and to secure the privilege of self-regulation. Licensing was a condition of the registration of copyright, and registration was some defence against piracy. The regulations limiting the number of master printers, presses, apprentices, and the size of editions, like the restriction of printing to London, Oxford and Cambridge, helped to minimise unemployment. The pow-

[17] Ibid., pp. 760–61.
[18] Christopher Hill, 'Censorship and English Literature,' p. 40.
[19] Holdsworth, op. cit., V, pp. 336, 338–40, 342, 360–61; VIII, pp. 406–07.

ers of search and seizure conferred upon the Company were economic powers, used as much to stamp out irregular and competitive printing as to serve government interests in the detection of seditious literature. The lapse of licensing provisions in 1641–42 removed the Company members' legal protection, and they were reduced to the informal acknowledgement of custom and precedent. There were, for example, no common law rights in copyright. To resecure its ancient rights, and later to have its charter renewed, it was formally requisite for the Company to add its voice to the frequent proclamations against scandalous pamphlets and their dispersers; and yet it was privately possible for any member of the Company to print and disperse such texts if it was in their commercial, personal or ideological interests to do so. Time and again, commerce compromised censorship. While members of the Company may have worked to discover scandalous printing, they also worked to conceal it. So long as the texts involved did not infringe other members' copyrights, or did not figure in the more general trade rivalries between patentees and splinter groups within the Company, there was little reason to fear exposure.

That complicity of the government's interests and those of the trade in the construction of a licensing system, ensured a certain level of routine efficiency, but it also involved some important tolerances. For example, it did not touch manuscripts. It substituted a less serious and often merely technical offence for those previously charged. As a corollary, it displaced harsher penalties by milder ones. As the normal condition of control, it reduced the incidence of more serious charges. When more serious charges were intermittently brought—for treason, scandalum magnatum, or seditious libel—it was less a question of censorship than one of acute political crisis and overt danger to the State. In its routine operations, licensing worked most efficiently for the least contentious texts. Conversely, its irrelevance to uncontentious texts bred a contempt for its procedures. That contempt is also revealed in the enormous output of radically subversive literature under conditions of ostensibly strict control, and the failure of authority to punish those responsible. The Journals of the Lords and Commons, and the State Papers (Domestic), are full of allusions to such unlicensed texts, and to those who wrote, printed or dispersed them—I have extracted all there are for the years 1641 to 1700—but proof of the offence, and evidence of arrest and punishment, are much more difficult to discover. Where one can find it, there is also enough evidence of mild fines, remission of penalties, merciful release, pardon granted for kneeling at the bar of the House—and sheer recidivism—to suggest that, for all the officially declared concern, infringements of the licensing laws were normally not harshly punished. It is called 'keeping up appearances.'

It is difficult to know what to make of Dr Hill's arguments for the savagery of the Laudian censorship following the decree of 1637, when the claim is also made that 'Apparently 65% of books published in 1640 were unlicensed.'[20] So,

---

[20] Christopher Hill, 'Censorship and English Literature,' p. 49.

the statement that 'The number of authorised printers in London was cut to twenty' is formally true (but several appealed to and were helped by Laud to continue); 'unlicensed printers were to be pilloried and whipped' (but they were not); 'corporal penalties were imposed on those who offended against these decrees, regardless of rank' (but those who offended by not printing the imprimatur went unpunished).[21] Greg has estimated that about one-third of all books published up to 1640 were never entered in the Stationers' Register, and yet that persistent offence against the decrees also went unpunished; and most of the few recorded whippings, brandings, ear-croppings and nose-slittings listed as proof of the harshness of the censorship were for greater and long-established crimes, not for offences against the 1637 or earlier decrees as such.

In 1644 *Areopagitica* was not, I believe, provoked by indignation at the penalties which might be imposed on any who transgressed, nor was it an instant and outraged response to the Order of 1643. What goaded Milton into writing was the irritant of harassment. The new licensing order against which he writes was published on 14 June 1643. Why did *Areopagitica* not appear until as late as 23 November 1644 (seventeen months later)? Was Milton at a loss for words?

The printers most closely associated with Milton throughout his life, from his earliest prose pamphlets to *Paradise Lost* itself, were Matthew Simmons, his wife Mary, and their son Samuel. Matthew Simmons and Thomas Paine were two printers who, it was said in 1641, 'have continually printed libels, are known to all the stationers, and have their press in Red cross Street.'[22] The words 'their press' tell us they ran a single shop in partnership, an association that had its origins in the time they spent together as apprentices in the printing house of John Dawson. Matthew's imprints are among the commonest in 1644 and his involvement with Milton, in particular, was not without excitement.

On 10 July 1644, the Stationers' Company reported two sellers of imported bibles to the Lords; and on 26 August, they petitioned the Commons about the deleterious effects on their own trade of the bible patentees (Matthew Simmons was one of those who signed the petition). But, seeking its quid pro quo, the very same day the Commons asked the Stationers 'diligently to inquire out the Authors, Printers, and Publishers, of the Pamphlet . . . concerning Divorce.'[23] This was almost certainly *The Judgement of Martin Bucer* that Simmons had just printed. It had been licensed and entered at Stationers' Hall on 15 July, well before printing; it was addressed directly to 'The Parlament' by Milton himself (his name is on B4v); it bore Simmons's imprint; and it was in Thomason's hands by 6 August.

It is ironic that it was the reception of this 1644 pamphlet, one that obeyed all the rules for publication, that provoked the writing of *Areopagitica*. Given the delay between the revival of pre-publication licensing in June 1643 and the publication of *Areopagitica* only in November 1644, we must, I think, see its writing as Milton's deeply personal reaction to criticism of his divorce tracts. This came from, among others, Thomas Hill and Herbert Palmer in August 1644 and coincided with the intervention of the Stationers' Company on the same theme at the same time. Milton matched the direct addresses to Parliament by his critics and the Stationers (Hill's and Palmer's were made by sermon, the Stationers' by petition) with a speech of his own. By contrast with that compelling pattern of events, there is simply no sign, in June 1643, of Milton's principled concern, as a writer, at the reimposition of pre-publication censorship.

Two weeks after *Areopagitica* appeared, the Lords asked the Stationers to find out the printer of a 'Libel against the Peerage of this Realm.' They reported back on 28 December that, despite 'their best Endeavours,' they had failed to 'make any discovery therefore, the Letter being so common a Letter.' But, needing the Lords' support, they took the chance to complain 'of the frequent Printing of scandalous Books by divers, as *Hezechia Woodward* and *Jo. Milton.*'[24] As a result, the Lords immediately ordered the examination of Woodward and Milton, and any others the Stationers reported. Simmons and Paine had printed both authors. But Simmons went on to produce, initially with Paine, within only a few weeks of the Lords' demand, a further edition of *The Doctrine and Discipline of Divorce*, and then first editions of Milton's *Colasterion* and the *Tetrachordon*, and almost certainly further books by Hezechiah Woodward.

It all points to a strange mix of irritating but impotent interventions by government and a sturdy refusal by writers and printers to be cowed. A telling example from 1644 of one licenser's attitudes to the system is Charles Herle's comments on Thomas Fuller's *Sermon: Of Reformation*. It was examined and censored by Saltmarsh, and then licensed by Herle in that form. Herle's answer to Fuller's complaint when he discovered the changes nicely reveals how the rules might be bent for the right person. But it is also interesting for what it implies about meaning.

> . . . I must confesse, had I knowne you to have been the Author [wrote Herle] I should have endeavoured to have satisfied M. Saltmarsh of your good meaning therein, before I had set my hand to his Examinations of it. Your other Books made me conceive the Authour some other of your name.

Then he added:

> [But the sermon] is not in itselfe so free from some passages that may admit of an ill meaning (at least, had the Authour been such as was reported) . . . My licensing the Examination of some passages of your Sermon, was (at most) but on supposition their meaning had been such as some conceited them, and suppositions are no accusations: you know the rule *nihil ponunt ni re*, they affirme nothing; nor (had they been accusations) is it but the rule of Parliamentary Iustice, to have heard the Authours sense of his own words, before it condemned him to a prison.

[24] LJ, VII, p. 116.

Those remarks preface the text of a book by Herle himself. He concludes by hoping that none will construe the references to King Ahab and Jezebel in his sermon as referring in any way to the Sovereign and his Consort![25]

Fuller, like Milton and Simmons, was one worthy to be Sealed of the Tribe of Ben. In his poem of that name, Jonson wrote:

> Men that are safe, and sure, in all they doe,
> Care not what trials they are put unto;
> They meet the fire, the Test, as Martyrs would;
> And though Opinion stampe them not, are gold.

It may have been a self-protective strategy for its printer to suppress his name from *Areopagitica*, but Milton had no qualms about boldly declaring his authorship on its title page and daring the Commons to strike back.

The politics of language, the power of texts, the impositions and subversions of authority in every communicative mode, have recently—and I think properly—become a dominant concern of those interested in literature, history and politics. But most of the inquiries into such questions are so focussed on the minutiae of verbal language, or are built on such shaky historical assumptions, that they seriously underestimate, not only the courage of writers, but the material conditions of production, the varieties of labour, the economics of trade, and their dominance in text production. These are conditions of such variety and complexity that no single historical explanation, like censorship, can be seen as so fully determinative. However sympathetic one must be to those oppressed at any time by censorship, and however disposed—as I am myself—to resent its revival in our own society, we cannot, as bibliographers, historians or critics, altogether free ourselves from certain laws of evidence, certain historical constraints on interpretation. To do otherwise, is to risk creating false assumptions about past writers' attitudes to, for example, print and censorship, and about their forms of response.

I have tried to sketch some of the material and other conditions which affected the ways in which texts were produced and disseminated in the mid-1640s. My evidence has been drawn almost entirely from the book trade and may be broadly described as bibliographical. To return to my opening remarks: if we are to move forward '*Ad correctionem*' and '*ad aedificandum*,' whether as literary, political, or social historians, we shall do so the more certainly, I venture to suggest, if we also recognise the importance of historical bibliography as the foundation of our enterprise.

[25] Wing H1551.

APPENDIX

Wing Statistics for Calendar Years 1644 and 1688

Books, etc.

			1644		1688
Total items so dated or attributed by Wing to those years (excludes serials)			1113		1519
London-printed:	named printers	324		347	
	no printer named	533	857	945	1292
Non-London-printed:	named printers	175		115	
	no printer named	66	241	74	189
Foreign-printed:	named printers	10		15	
	no printer named	5	15	23	38
All areas:	no printer or bookseller named	247		455	
Total items:	named printers	509		477	
	no printer named	604		1042	

Serials

		1644		1688
Number of titles (Nelson and Seccombe)		37		23
Number of issues		684		445+
Thomason Tracts		699		—
Term Catalogues		—		242
Stationers' Regr Entries—Books	231			101
Serials	417	648		—
Printing for Parliament—Extant	155			
(Lambert) Not found	53	208		

Wing items for 1641–9 (calendar years) as listed in Lambert, *Printing for Parliament, 1641–1700*. Those for 1649–84 are for old-style years (1649/50–1684/5) and are rounded to the nearest 25 from the graph given by Mason, *The Library* (June 1974). The figures exclude serials.

1641	1642	1643	1644	1645	1646	1647	1648	1649
1850	2968	1495	1020	978	1049	1488	1826	1250

1650	1651	1652	1653	1654	1655	1656	1657	1658
1025	875	925	1075	925	1000	975	950	975

1659	1660	1661	1662	1663	1664	1665	1666	1667
1725	2175	1250	1125	800	675	725	475	525

1668	1669	1670	1671	1672	1673	1674	1675	1676
625	600	850	700	850	825	875	1000	900

1677	1678	1679	1680	1681	1682	1683	1684	
800	950	1350	1775	1575	1475	1425	1425	

6

Trading Places? England 1689—France 1789

1998

This essay, based on materials McKenzie first used in his Lyell Lectures delivered at Oxford University in 1984, examines relations between the book trade and revolutionary change. Taking a pivotal moment in English history—the flight of the Roman Catholic King James II, and his replacement on the throne by the Protestant William III and Mary II—McKenzie considers the "subtle reciprocities" between textual forms and the political and publishing contexts in which they were produced. His study offers an impressive survey of the diverse printed archive for the year 1688–89, including political works that had previously circulated only in manuscript, the new vogue for translations of classical poetry into English, the advent of periodical literature aimed at women, and the emergence of the London periodical press in general. McKenzie also considers the relevance of censorship, the influence of the Stationers' Company, the growth of book auctions, and the unauthorized distribution of print.

As its playful title intimates, the essay complements Robert Darnton's influential explorations of book history during the era of the French Revolution. Both in its preoccupations and its scholarly methods, it reveals the productive traffic in ideas between McKenzie's revisionist bibliography—what he termed the "sociology of texts"—and the new French *histoire du livre*, best known in the work of Roger Chartier and Darnton himself. The essay first appeared in *The Darnton Debate: Books and Revolution in the Eighteenth Century* (1998).

THE NEW FORMS we give to texts in the acts of adapting, printing and publishing them constitute the most basic and ubiquitous evidence we have for a history of writing and a history of meanings. Every extant artifact tells a tale which we can read historically and which, by virtue of the *edition* (multiple copies of the same forms widely dispersed, successively altered, and variously directed), supports a high level of historical generalisation. By contrast, personal reports of reading, however revealing they are of the experience of discrete individuals, are fortuitous and singular survivals, idiosyncratic, anecdotal, and by definition subjective and mutable—but therein immensely generative of new meanings in new contexts. It has been one of Robert Darnton's great achievements to bring those distinct forms of historical evidence together in a series of absorbing narratives of the conception, expression, dispersal and reception of ideas as functions of the *trade* in books.

In casting so much new light on the movement of ideas in pre-revolutionary France in particular, his work has brought about a new appreciation of the dependence of political thought on *genres* as a whole series of quite diverse

144

publishers' categories, each with its distinctive market of buyers and readers. Ultimately reliant though they were upon essentially stable structures of production and distribution, under conditions of economic and political constraint they were also remarkably resourceful in their strategies of evasion.

Those tensions between material forms and their variously inferred meanings, between economics and ideology, and between the practices of conformity and subversion, mark crucial points of inquiry in Darnton's work as an exponent of *histoire du livre*. The present paper is not a direct commentary upon that work so much as a tribute to the nature of his evidence and the fertility of his ideas in their clear application to another country facing a quite different revolution a century earlier than that of the French in 1789.[1]

In its successive but fitful moves towards a revolutionary transformation of the structures of power, England in the earlier seventeenth century offers several significant precedents for the study of the relationships between a trade in the production of texts and their roles in resisting or promoting change. In many ways, speech was still the preferred mode for the direct control it permitted of its immediate auditors and the escape it could still offer from the embarrassingly fixed forms of print. In its most influential fictive form, the drama, its role was gradually usurped by the journalist, the newsbook and the pamphlet. But it was a time, too, when the publication and circulation of texts in manuscript could still rival the newer technologies of print, whether for their restriction to coterie readerships, their easier evasion of censorship, or simply because they were cheaper. For under a hundred copies the unit cost was likely to be lower, and until the end of the century, scriveners and scriptoria were still numerous enough to sustain a significant manuscript trade in parallel with that in printed books, promiscuously meeting a demand that ranged from political satire to student texts.

Indeed, there is little evidence of an unsatisfied demand for more printed books. Restrictive trade practices in London printing and publishing, it is true, nominally affected printers' productivity in the limitation of presses and apprenticeships, in copyrights and grants of patents, in the enforcement of licensing, and in the control of imports. But the increase in the output of print which is often related to political events of the 1640s was less an absolute increase in the volume of sheets printed than a nominal one, literally so in the increased number of titles, signifying a new form of dialogue by pamphlet, usually anonymous, but now pitched firmly in the Areopagus. It could be said to have extended readership by diversifying it, but not to have increased production in the rapid expansion of the trades of printing or bookselling. The profitable patents were in bibles, prayerbooks, primers, almanacs and law books, and the legal constraints

---

[1] The connection is by no means new of course. As Dr C. Y. Ferdinand informs me, it can be found along a spectrum ranging from the provincial English press of 1788 (*The Salisbury Journal*, 28 April) to a talk given in post-revolutionary America the same year and printed by Richard Price in his *Discourse on the love of our country* (London 1789).

upon making and selling them functioned only to limit competition not production. There was still no economically significant demand for other texts
which, if only it could have expanded freely, the trade might have met with
profitable editions in literature, the classics, politics, divinity, or even political
satire. For most such works printing at the author's expense was still the rule, and
the reason for the non-publication of many texts was much more likely to be
economic than political. There is also another explanation: for many authors, the
choice of textual form, whether speech, manuscript, or print, was still not free
from anxieties about the speaker's or writer's public role. This was only rarely a
matter of playing safe with the censor, an explanation which ignores the continued force of older conventions of anonymity, and trivialises a profound shift in
the psychology of communication. It was a more complex problem of how any
individual, whether printer or preacher, might move towards the declaratory
freedoms of a post-revolutionary England.

Whereas study of the book trades in France, especially in the eighteenth century, is richly served by their archival records, there is nothing comparable for
seventeenth-century England. The great fire of London destroyed all the working records of the printers and booksellers clustered around St Paul's, and a fitful and inefficient censorship has left few telling accounts to enliven our reports
of those affected by it.

There are, however, two invaluable tools, the archives of the Stationers' Company and the English short-title catalogues.[2] These, in turn, have largely directed
the kind of inquiries it is most profitable to make. So, by giving unrivalled access
to the total *extant* printed archive, including serials, they not only enable any
number of selective accounts of the textual biographies of authors, printers and
booksellers, and even of genres and formats, but also make possible our comprehensive analysis of the trade as a whole and its complex 'communications cir-
cuits.' Their main limitations are uncertainty about survival rates, the anonymity
of many of the people involved, and an almost complete absence of firm details
of edition quantities.

Since we need a date, the shortest period for any such analysis is a year, a good
span, perhaps, in which to trace the normal operations of trade. But, for the
events of a year like 1689 or 1789, even a decade is scarcely enough to reveal the
subtle reciprocities of textual forms and the most significant political events.

With those cautions it is nevertheless revealing to look at the English scene in
1688–1689 and to see, too, how in a decade of great political unrest the trade
adapted to new conditions, how publishing patterns altered, how the press
served an extraordinary variety of interest groups, how it responded to crises,
how the Stationers conceded to pressure and yet re-secured, through a new
Charter and a renewed Licensing Act, their old powers, trading independence
and internal loyalties for continued economic advantage. But there were other

---

[2] For details, see the note on sources at the end of this essay.

implications which involved ideas of transformation, adaptation and exchange: the adaptation of older texts to new situations; the shifts in women's roles as actors, writers and readers; the new vogue for translations from the classics; and, of course, climactically, the role of the press in promoting, resisting, confirming, the trading of one king for another.[3]

Robert Filmer's *Patriarcha* (Wing F922–924) is a text from which it is easy to summarise some of the points I have mentioned, especially those relating to the circulation of manuscripts. It shows, too, the indiscriminate use of any one of them for printing, and the dominance then of the far more important textual principle and practice, not of recovering an 'original,' but of appropriating it in new forms to meet new needs.[4] Filmer's writings had all circulated in manuscript, including the earlier versions of the *Patriarcha: a defence of the natural power of kings against the unnatural liberty of the people*. He had completed it some time between 1638 and 1640. Richard Royston, the constant factor for all scandalous books and papers against the proceedings of Parliament, had published some of his papers in 1647 and 1648. But it was not until 1680 that *Patriarcha* was finally printed. Filmer owes his reputation entirely to the fortuitous circumstances of the time when his work was resuscitated. In January 1680, its argument had a quite unprecedented relevance. During the exclusion crisis, Charles II needed a case to vindicate legitimacy. In the autumn of 1679 England had come nearer than ever again to its condition in 1641. This was a point made at the time by Henry Nevile: 'We are this day tugging with the same difficulties, managing the same debates in parliament [. . .] which our ancestors did before the year 1640; whilst the king has been forced to apply the same remedy of dissolution to his first two parliaments, that his father used to his four first and King James to his last three.'

When *Patriarcha* came to be published, however, it was printed from a very imperfect manuscript. Words, sentences, paragraphs were missing, Filmer's quotations were seldom marked as such, and—most significantly—the text had been interfered with to conceal its date. A much more reliable manuscript, described as the 'Original' (but later than one in Filmer's hand now in the Cambridge University Library), was edited by Edmund Bohun and published by Chiswell and others in 1685 (Wing F924).

But there was nothing exceptional about *Patriarcha*. The political controversies

---

[3] For an excellent discussion of the trade in this revolutionary period, see Michael Treadwell, 'The English book trade', in *The Age of William III and Mary II: power, politics, and patronage 1688–1702. A reference encyclopaedia and exhibition catalogue*, ed. Robert P. McCubbin and Martha Hamilton-Phillips (Williamsburg, New York and Washington 1989), p. 358–65. Another significant feature of the time was the development of the trade publisher who handled the distribution of small pamphlets for largely anonymous authors. See Michael Treadwell, 'London trade publishers 1675–1750,' *The Library*, 6th ser., 4 (1982), p. 99–134.

[4] This is well illustrated in the practice of the Society of Friends: not only should new books be orthodox, but their own old books must be reformed. Reprints were truly new editions in which the text was renewed as an immediate and living truth. So when Isaac Pennington's works were being reprinted in 1680–1681, it was ordered that a number of underscored lines in the text 'be wholly left out of all Impressions: Ben Clarke to take Care therein.'

of the 1680s and 1690s called forth the reprinting, and in some cases, the first impression, of large numbers of works written for quite other purposes.[5]

When, in 1682, Starkey wished to reprint Nathaniel Bacon's *Discourse, of government* (printed in two parts, 1647, then 1651, and reprinted in 1672 but dated 1647 and 1651: Wing B348f.), it was said that he would 'possibly pretend it is only an old book reprinted and an historical discourse of past times without any application to the present, whereas it appears it was dedicated to the service of the rebellion.'[6] In the same month, L'Estrange also told secretary of state Jenkins that John Sadler's 'The Rights of the kingdom [Wing S279] passes for an old piece of one Sadler's in '49, but I have compared them a good way and find many omissions and alterations of very great moment [. . .] 'Tis the work of no common hand [. . .] There is treason in it abundantly and this new methodizing of it makes it a new book.'[7]

A trade in new heads for old also developed. When Tonson published Dryden's *Virgil* in 1697, he re-used the plates originally cut for Ogilby's edition, only changing Æneas's nose to make it look more hooked like King William's. But, to others, the parallels between William and Cromwell seemed more exact, as we find in one of the poems on affairs of state: 'On the late metamorphosis of an old picture of Oliver Cromwell's into a new picture of King William: The head changed, the hieroglyphics remaining.' This new portrait was probably by William Faithorne.[8]

> Whether the Graver did by this intend
> Oliver's Shape with William's Head to mend,
> Or Grace to William's Head with Cromwell's Body,
> If I can guess his meaning, I'm a Noddy . . .
> Perhaps the artist thinks to get a Name
> By showing us how two may be the same.
> If so, he's gained his point, for he's a witch
> That suddenly can tell one, which is which.

In May 1680, a 'sculpturer' was charged with having printed the picture of the duke of Monmouth on horseback with the inscription 'his Royal Highness.' He pleaded that it was ignorance, and said 'he was told of the mistake about two years ago, on which he altered his plate and produced several of his copies that were altered.'[9]

---

[5] This phenomenon has been more recently surveyed by N. von Maltzahn, 'Republication in the Restoration: some trimming pleas for limited monarchy, 1660/1680,' *The Huntington Library quarterly* (Summer 1993), p. 281–305. As Maltzahn rightly acknowledges, 'the classic study of a late seventeenth-century rehandling of a mid-century text' is Edmund Ludlow, *A voyce from the watchtower*, ed. A. B. Worden, Camden Society, 4th ser., 21 (1978), p. 1–80. See also Mark Goldie, 'The Revolution of 1689 and the structure of political argument,' *Bulletin of research in the humanities* 83 (1980), p. 473–564.

[6] *Calendar of State Papers Domestic*, Car. II (1682), 421, no. 171.

[7] *Calendar of State Papers Domestic*, Car. II (1682), 418, no. 33.

[8] The poem, which had circulated in a great many manuscript copies, is printed, together with the prints, in *Poems on affairs of state: Augustan satirical verse, 1660–1714*, vol. v: 1688–1697, ed. W. J. Cameron (New Haven 1971), p. 149–51.

[9] *Calendar of State Papers*, Car. II (1680), Admiralty, Greenwich Hospital, 1, no. 50.

Of less immediately obvious or direct political significance, but possibly of greater long-term importance, was translation of another kind. This was fostered by the bookseller Jacob Tonson, but with all of Dryden's energies behind him. When Tonson produced an edition of Ovid's *Epistles* (Wing O659), translated by several hands, in 1680, Dryden noted in his preface the 'little Praise, and so small Encouragement for so considerable a part of Learning'; but Tonson went ahead with his *Miscellany poems* (Wing D2314) of 1684, which was made up mainly of translations by Creech, Tate and Rymer as well as Dryden; the *Sylvae* of 1685 (Wing D2379) was mainly by Dryden. Dryden encouraged the young William Congreve to contribute translations of Horace and Juvenal to his miscellanies of the early 1690s; and Dryden himself, after he lost the laureateship in 1688, was freed from the need to write propaganda—even if, in turning to Homer, Chaucer, Boccaccio, Ovid, and then, most notably, to Virgil, he adapted them in ways which allowed him to reflect on peace, war and tyranny, and William's seizure of power.

It was this sudden vogue that provoked Matthew Prior's savagely witty 'A satyr on the modern translators,' a poem widely read in manuscript but not printed until the first volume of the collections of *Poems on affairs of state* was published in 1697 (Wing P2719). Prior is troubled by the literal infidelities any translation involves; but he has some interesting reflections on the market, for he seems concerned that the prevalence of translating might displace new writing in English; and he clearly, if unfairly, implies that the whole impetus towards translation is fundamentally economic. The presence in London of only one acting company, for example, had led to a decline in the number of new plays:

> Since the united cunning of the Stage,
> Has balk'd the hireling Drudges of the Age . . .
> Those who with nine months toil had spoil'd a Play,
> In hopes of Eating at a full Third day . . .
> Have left Stage-practice, chang'd their old Vocations,
> Atoning for bad Plays, with worse Translations.

He opens his attack with Dryden and his aristocratic collaborator, John Sheffield, later duke of Buckingham:

> But how could this learned brace employ their time?
> One construed sure, while th'other pump'd for Rhime.

He then moves on to the Latinless Aphra Behn, consequently dubbed 'our blind Translatress.' She had contributed a 'A paraphrase of Oenone to Paris' to the 1680 edition of Ovid's *Epistles* where Dryden's preface explicitly forestalled criticism by saying that her poem was the only one to follow the method of imitation: 'I was desir'd to say that the Author who is of the *Fair Sex*, understood not *Latine*.' He betrayed his anxieties by preceding her imitation with a translation proper in subsequent editions. In spite of these precautions, in one fell swoop, Prior cruelly condemns her learning, personal appearance, and morals; and yet he *would* have her write her own work:

> let her from the next inconstant Lover,
> Take a new Copy for a second Rover:
> Describe the cunning of a Jilting Whore,
> From the ill Arts her self has us'd before;
> Thus let her write, but Paraphrase no more.

As for Creech's rendering of part of Ovid's *Fasti* (the story of the rape of Lucretia):

> better have I heard my Nurse relate;
> The Matron suffers Violence again,
> Not *Tarquin's* Lust so vile as *Creech's* Pen.

In his peroration, Prior shows himself quite unable to accept the kinds of appropriation that translation involves:

> when we bind the Lyric up in rhime,
> And lose the Sense to make the Poem chime;
> When from their Flocks we force *Sicilian* Swains,
> To ravish Milk-maids in our *English* Plains . . .
> I'de bid th'importing Club their pains forbear,
> And traffick in our own, tho' homely ware.

Here he shows himself really concerned for the state of new writing; and although decorum forbids him to do it graciously in a satire, he asks that we support our own writers instead:

> Whilst from themselves the honest Vermin spin,
> I'de like the Texture, tho' the Web be thin;
> Nay, take *Crown's* plays, because his *own*, for wit;
> And praise what *D'urfy*, not translating, writ.

Prior's concern for the fate of original writing in the 1680s was not entirely without foundation; and Blackmore, in his *The Kit-cats: a poem* (1708), reflected later on William's scant encouragement of poets, praising not the Monarch but the Bookseller:

> But tho' the Muses and their tuneful Train
> In that great Monarch's Military Reign,
> Had of the Royal Favour little Share,
> Still, they were kinder [Tonson's] tender Care:
> He still caress'd the unregarded Tribe,
> And did to all their various Tasks prescribe;
> From whence to both great Acquisitions came,
> To him the Profit, and to them the Fame.

Tonson's brilliant exploitation of the market is seen in his development of subscription publishing, in his definition of quite new readerships, and in his creation of a canon of writers worthy to be read—for it was pre-eminently Tonson who made the classics English and the English classics.[10] Translation of the classics into the vernacular extended their potential audience and opened up a vast new literature which was still deeply influential in providing the formal structures and allusions in most current writing. This was a great service to women in particular, whose education had denied them the possibility of reading the Greek and Roman authors in their original languages. The sense of exhilaration a woman might feel when able to read more of the classics than Ovid and Homer, is well captured by Aphra Behn's poem on first looking into Mr Creech's Lucretius. In her poem to Creech 'on his Excellent Translation of Lucretius,' she praises him for opening up to her a whole area of philosophical speculation from which her sex had hitherto excluded her.[11]

> Till now, I curst my Birth, my Education,
> And more, the scanted Customes of the Nation:
> Permitting not the Female Sex to tread,
> The mighty Paths of Learned Heroes dead.
> The God-like *Virgil*, and great *Homers* Verse,
> Like Divine Mysteries are conceal'd from us.

Women are imprisoned in an inferior present because they lack the linguistic entrée to a superior, heroic past:

> No ravishing thoughts approach our Ear,
> The fulsome Gingle of the Times,
> Is all we're allow'd to understand or hear.

But modern languages, especially French, were another matter, and their competence in these tongues gave many women a role with which they could be modestly but justifiably pleased. To illustrate the point, we retreat some decades to Lady Elizabeth Cary's comments in 1630, prefacing her translation of Du Perron's reply to King James.[12] This massive work of over 400 pages, we are told, she translated within a month. Her remarks to the reader are interesting for their honesty and their refusal to adopt the usual cloak of female modesty.

She opens by implying that to translate a classical writer would be a better way to seek 'glory,' were that her wish. But 'To looke for glorie from *Translation* is *beneath* my intention, and if I had aimed at that, I would not have chosen so late a writer.' Unlike Aphra Behn, she expresses no regret for exclusion from the classics: her purpose is the service of a Catholic cause, and the expression of her integrity as a woman:

---

[10] This last point is made by Michael Treadwell, 'The English book trade,' p. 361. For Tonson's role as a subscription publisher, see John Barnard, 'Dryden, Tonson, and subscriptions for the 1697 Virgil,' *Papers of the Bibliographical Society of America* 57 (1963), p. 129–51.

[11] It was included in her *Poems upon several occasions* (Wing B1757), published by Tonson in 1684.

[12] The original work criticising Du Perron was written by Isaac Casaubon at the direction of James (see STC 4740), published in 1612, reprinted by James in 1619 (STC 14346). Elizabeth Cary, Viscountess Falkland's translation, *The Reply of the most illustrious cardinall of Perron to the answeare of the king of Great Britaine* (STC 6385), was published in Douai in 1630.

> I desire to haue noe more guest at of me, but that I am a CATHOLIQUE, and a
> Woman: the first serues for mine honor, and the second, for my excuse, since if the
> worke be but meanely done, it is noe wonder, for my sexe can raise no great expec-
> tation, of anie thing that shall come from me.

She is not, of course, apologising for her sex, but framing the expectations that
readers might bring to bear on the work of a woman, and out-facing them by
affirming her confidence in the quality of her work: 'yet were it a great follie in
me, if I would expose to the view of the world, a work of this kinde, except I
judged it, to want nothing fit, for a Translation. Therefore I will confesse, I think
it well done, and so had I confest sufficientlie in printing it.'

She goes on explicitly to dissociate herself from the conventional excuse of
women who did publish: 'I will not make vse of that worne-out forme of saying, I printed it against my will, mooued by the importunitie of Friends: I was
mooued to it by my beleefe, that it might make those English that vnderstand not
French, whereof there are manie, euen in our vniuersities, reade Perron.' There
is no false modesty here. She compounds her commitment as a woman doing a
first-rate job by dedicating her work to Henrietta Maria: 'And for the honor of
my Sexe, let me saie it, you are a woeman, though farre aboue other wemen,
therefore fittest to protect a womens worke, if a plaine translation wherein there
is nothing aimed at, but rightlie to express the Authors intention, may be called
a worke.' The question implied by that last comment—is translation really a
'work'?—was one answered in terms of gender by Florio, in 1603, in his translation of Montaigne's *Essays* (STC 18041). He refers there to his previous work, the
World of words (STC 11098), as 'my last Birth, which I held masculine (as are all
mens conceipts that are their owne, though but by their collecting . . .),' and
contrasts it with 'this defective edition (since all translations are reputed fe-
males), delivered at second hand.'

If women were, as we have seen in Aphra Behn's poem, an eager and recep-
tive audience for literature, they were also a market ripe for commercial exploitation. It is, perhaps, a little surprising that it was not until the end of the seventeenth century that any effort was made to provide them with periodical
literature written specifically for them. Dunton, in 1691, started using his *Athenian mercury* to cater for them, expressing the belief that they should indeed be educated to do more than 'distinguish between their *Husbands Breeches* and another
mans,' and set a flatteringly high value on their intellect, attributing to them 'a
finer Genius, and generally quicker Apprehensions' than men, and arguing that
'women had superior powers of memory, due to the moist constitution of their
brain, and that their sedentary and solitary life [reflecting perhaps increased
leisure for bourgeois women, as work moved out of the home] was further
favourable to study.' For all his flattery, however, the periodical which he initiated
in 1693, *The Ladies mercury*, ran to only four numbers.

About twenty-three serials were published in 1688, and, of those, the *London
gazette/Gazette de Londres* was the only one to appear regularly throughout the year.

It is familiar enough. Most of its news is dry and impersonal, but occasionally it covered more exciting foreign events like the Grand Revolution deposing Sultan Mahomet (a story that was sent from Constantinople on 9 November 1687 and published on 2 January 1688).

More interesting now, perhaps, is Henry Care's *Publick occurrences*, which he began publishing 'with allowance' on 21 February 1688. James Sutherland says that 'Its semi-official standing may reflect, in a time of increasing difficulty, a need felt by the King and his ministers for a more favourable interpretation of current events than it was fitting for the official *Gazette* to give.'[13] And the paper does seem to have been a genuine supplement to the *Gazette*, presenting fuller, more sympathetic discussions of various religious and political issues, such as the failure of James's Declaration for Liberty of Conscience to be read in all churches, and the wrongs committed against dissenters by misguided members of the established Church. One might think it possible to draw a distinction between pamphlets, which dealt in *ideology*, and newspapers, which covered *events*, but the two were persistently interfused. Henry Care's *Publick occurrences* self-consciously purported to be a *newspaper*, and neither he nor Settle, who succeeded him, was entirely comfortable in the dual role of government apologist and objective reporter. A note at the end of an essay on religious tolerance neatly catches their editorial ambivalence in the apologetic comment: 'But 'tis News you want' (*Publick occurrences*, 13 March 1688). Complaints of bias came from their readers. A manuscript note, for example, in the Nichols copy of *Publick occurrences* for 8 May says that 'This is called ye jesuites Pissepot thrown by Henry Care in ye church of England men's faces.' The editors tried to defend themselves from the 'incredible Spight and Venom [. . .] against *this poor Paper*', even to the extent of publishing on 7 August, the day before Henry Care died, a letter threatening both the editor and the paper's printer, George Larkin: '*IF there be no possibility of stopping* H. C.'*s Pen, there shall be care taken to stop his Tongue; and since the Printer is a co-partner with him, he shall be so, in what is design'd for him. I thought the menace of* Slitting his Nose, *might have been enough*[.]' Publication of the letter was probably intended to raise some sympathy for the dying editor as well as for his printer, newspaper and cause. And the letter was newsworthy in itself. But it is a pretty clear indication of the 'Spight and Venom' that the *Occurrences* inspired. Elkanah Settle directly addressed some of the problems:

> And here I would remove an Objection, that some may urge against the Usefulness of this Paper; viz. That the first Part of it is made up of Invectives against the Church of England; and the latter part of Old News, which all the Town knew before.
>
> As to the former, those Papers of this sort, which were written in Mr. *Cares* Life-time, are already Vindicated in the Paper, *Numb*. 26 [14 August, in which Care's death is reported]. And for the *New Occurrencer*, he is not only a Person, whose principles are against all Uncharitable and Corrosive Invectives; but has steered a healing Course directly Opposite thereto.

---

[13] James Sutherland, *The Restoration newspaper and its development* (Cambridge 1986), p. 22.

For the latter it must be considered, This is only a Weekly Paper, and if our *Athenian* Age will have fresh News every 24 Hours, yet this would be an Imperfect *Intelligence*, without *Method*, and unfit to be given House-room by Lovers of History and News, that shall fancy to know seven years hence, how Transactions hapened successively, during the time of the *Occurrences Observations*; If I should omit any Remarkable Passage, because some few very Inquisitive Persons have it at this Juncture fresh upon their Minds by Conversation: (Though possibly, and most probably, falsly Represented, and told Twenty several ways.) Or, should this Paper Publish'd on *Tuesdays*, leave out all remarkable Passages, but what happen the day or two before its Publication; How strangely imperfect would it render the Account of Publick *Occurrences*, which it pretends to Transmit Successively, and to State Truly?

It reminds us of the character in Shadwell's *Squire of Alsatia* (*Publick occurrences*, May 1688) who said he had taught his son history only to get the rejoinder: 'History! That's a pretty study indeed. How can there be a true history, when we see no man living is able to write truly the history of last week?'[14]

So, the newsbook *Modern history*, which ran for two years from October 1687, explained its policy as one of careful monthly reflection:

A thousand Fables, and Falsities are Impos'd upon the World: Matters of Moment, Promiscuously Confounded with Things of Little Worth: And for want Separating the True from the False, The Good from the Bad and Useful Notions or Curiosities from Matters Unprofitable, men are at a loss what to Take, and what to Leave.

Now for the Preventing of these Inconveniencies for the Future, there is Order taken for the Drawing of All *Memorable*, and *Notable Events* and *Relations* out of the several Fragments that have been Publish'd concerning them into *One Entire Collection*: That is to say, in the Regular Series of a *Monthly Account*.

The Reason for Publishing this Relation *Once*, and *but once a Month* (as That's the Course Resolv'd upon) is This; First, that the Notices of Things to be made Publique may be Carryed-on *Methodically* upon Equal Distances of Time, and without *Wracking* Peoples Expectations by any Longer Intervalls. 2ly, That Matters may be Deliver'd with as much *Caution* for the *Certain Truth* of Matters as such an Undertaking will bear[.]

It is no surprise to discover that many of the newspapers were established in mid-December 1688. Exploiting the new demand for instant news, the parvenu *London courant*, for example, declared on 12 December:

IT having been observed, that the greater the itch of curiosity after News hath been here of late, the less has the humour been gratified: Insomuch that a modest enquiry

---

[14] Shadwell's *Squire of Alsatia*, itself an adaptation of Terence's *Adelphi*, has many other resonances pertinent here. Sir Edward Belfond educated his son in the classics at Eton and Oxford, in natural philosophy so that he could reason closely, and in law at the Temple, plus modern languages, travel, two campaigns, and music: 'I have made him a complete gentleman, fit to serve his country in any capacity.' His contrasting brother, Sir William, explodes: 'Serve his country! Pox on his country! 'Tis a country of sueh knaves, 'tis not worth the serving: all those who pretend to serve it mean nothing but themselves.' These allusions I owe to Dr J. C. Ross, who has also pointed out to me how Shadwell catches the polarised nature of the decade in so contrasting the ideal of polite literature with the scurrilous products of political factions. So, too, does Aphra Behn, concluding her pithy verse morals to Aesop's fables in Francis Barlow's 1687 edition: 'Many pretend in war their King to aid / When they in blood for private interest trade.'

where His Majesty, or his Royal Highness the prince of Orange was, or what they were doing, could scarce be resolved, till the news had been exported and imported in a Foreign News-Letter.

The Orange gazette for 31 December also took Occasion by the forelock, to exploit what must have seemed like a lucratively emergent market beyond politics:

> This Paper (if it finds Acceptance) shall be publisht Twice every Week, as Matter shall occur, without restraining our selves to the Time; And it shall not in the least make any Repetition, as usual in other Prints: But what shall be inserted, shall be matter of Novelty to satisfie the Curious.

A similar policy had in fact been followed earlier in the year by the only unlicensed paper to appear before the December free-for-all. This was the innocuous Poor Robin's publick and private occurrences, which bore the subtitle: and remarks written for the sake of merriment, and harmless recreation. Its first number was published on 12 May 1688, with the author's notice that the reader should 'not Cudgle your Brains to find out the Intent or Purport of this Paper if you Consider the Title [. . . the author will] in no wise give Offence to any.' It could be thought of as a seventeenth-century version of The Sun, without the graphics but with date lines from 'Cullies Dale,' 'Barley Juice Hill,' and 'Love-Intreaguing-Street.' While Poor Robin's specialised in sex, A true and impartial account gave a lot of coverage to violent deaths. Both were directed at what is usually called the lower but more populous end of the reading market; yet Poor Robin's lasted for only eight numbers, and A true and impartial account for only eleven. The Orange gazette made only eighteen issues. All three, for their time, must have demanded a competent literacy, a fact which, despite their vulgar appeal, may well have been fatal to their commercial success. No print culture was ever established overnight.

One of the important functions of serials was to carry advertising, in particular, from the point of view of histoire du livre, the advertising of books.[15] It is important to ask how people knew books were available, and where to get them. The means certainly included word of mouth; references in one book to others; prospectuses; auction catalogues; accumulated lists of various kinds (thematic, imported, second-hand, manuscript); book fairs; street-sellers; and broadside advertisements, including the posting of title leaves. But of the serials which carried advertisements for them, the most important to the public at large was probably the London gazette, since it was the only newspaper to be issued regularly through the whole of 1688.

It was issued twice weekly for most of 1688, except for the brief period from 17 to 29 November, when, 'For the Preventing of False News and Reports, it is thought Necessary, that the Gazette shall, for the future, be published Three times a Week' (London gazette, 17 November). In the case of the Gazette, book-trade advertisements (including books, book auctions, pamphlets and map advertise-

---

[15] For much of what follows I am indebted to the kindness of Dr C. Y. Ferdinand, who passed on to me the results of her own analysis of serial publication and book-trade advertising in this period.

ments) were usually listed before the others and were signalled by a hand with pointing index finger, or digit. Of the 695 advertisements in the London gazette for 1688, 162 of them (about 23 per cent) were for books and book-related items.

The main concern of those who advertised books in the *Gazette* was to give accurate notice of the title and to say where it could be bought. So, the title given in the advertisement usually follows closely the one in the book itself, or in the related entries in the Stationers' Company Registers and in the Term Catalogues. It is also made very clear exactly where orders for books should be directed. Of the 92 straightforward book advertisements in the 1688 *Gazette*, 86 included a 'sold by' statement in one form or another.

Books in the *Gazette* were generally more substantial and upmarket than those advertised in Henry Care's *Publick occurrences*, the only other newspaper during the period that regularly carried such advertisements. It may be significant that the *Gazette* rarely gives the price, or anything much beyond author, title and point of sale (a price is given for only fifteen books, and some of those are subscription titles where it is important that the terms of the subscriber's commitment are clear). By contrast, advertisements in *Publick occurrences* almost always give prices, and these are usually low, and usually for pamphlets.

It is well known that posting advertisements in public places was another means of bringing a book or pamphlet to a buyer's attention. It was not a practice wholly free from risk to the person, as an account in the *Impartial Protestant mercury* in 1682 reveals:

> It being usual and long-accustomed for Book-binders Servants on Saturday-nights, to Post up the Titles of such Books as their Masters have to Bind, and which are to be Publisht in the beginning of the week following: Two Apprentices the other Night having been doing the same, in their Return homewards, about One of the Clock, in Ludgate-street, one Tallman, a Surgeon, coming by, ask'd, What they were doing? And reading the Title, which was—Right, of the Kingdom, or Customs of our Ancestors, &c. Tore it down, and flung it in one of their Faces, and (as they say) struck one of them[.]

In *Publick occurrences* there is an example of a newspaper advertising another periodical, possibly one distributed nationwide with the newspaper. It is worth quoting for its description of the service it offered (17 July 1688).

> There hath been for several Years, and still is Weekly Printed every Monday, that most useful Half-Sheet, call'd, the Merchants Weekly Remembrancer, of the Present Money-prices of their Goods ashore in London [. . .] whereby the greatest and ablest Merchants may be, and oft are Advantaged: And smaller dealers, together with most sorts of Travellers, Shopkeepers (though never so ignorant) very much Assisted, by being inform'd of the true Rates of the Goods they either have to Buy or Sell, and when to make their Market, &c. Printed and Sold by the Author James Whiston, Moderator to Merchants, in Water-Lane, by the Custom-House, London; who for 20s. per year, sends them wheresoever Desired.

The Term Catalogues, by contrast, were 'Printed for the Booksellers of London,' and were, therefore, the main medium by which booksellers advertised their

books to the trade. Early in 1669, Robert Clavell had described his terms, pro-
posing then:

> for a reasonable Compensation for my Trouble in Collecting the said Catalogue, and
> dispersing 400 and upwards to as many particular Persons [namely booksellers, as
> an earlier document makes clear] in the three Kingdoms, I do expect for every Book
> inserted in my Catalogue of above 8 shillings, one Book in Quires, if under 8 Shillings
> to 2 Shillings, two Books, if under 2 Shillings, three Books in Quires. And that no
> stitcht Book shall be inserted in the said Catalogue under the price of 1 shilling, or
> any Books Printed a longer distance of time than from one Term to another.

Fewer than half of the books advertised in the *Gazette* (42 of 93) were also in the
Term Catalogues. And in *Publick occurrences*, with its cheap pamphlets and books,
the overlap was even smaller.

We discover a little more about the costs of advertising from the *City mercury*,
in which Robert Everingham began publishing 'A WEEKLY Advertisement of
Books,' in 1680. An advertisement of 11 November in particular emphasizes the
role of the book trade:

> IT is not unknown to Booksellers, that there are Two Papers of this nature Weekly
> published, which for general satisfaction we shall distinguish [necessary because
> both were called *City Mercury* and both were issued on Thursdays]. That printed by
> Tho. James, is published by Mr. Vile, only for the lucre of 12d. per Book. This
> printed by Rob. Everingham, is published by several Booksellers, who do more eye
> the Service of the Trade, in making all Books as publick as may be, than the profit of
> Insertions. All men are therefore left to judge who is most likely to prosecute these
> Ends effectually, whether a Person that is no Bookseller, nor hath any relation to that
> Trade, or those who have equal Ends with all others of the Trade, in dispersing the
> said Papers both in City and Country.

That appeal to trade solidarity may give a hint of other trade associations soon
to develop. Firm evidence of the practices carried on by the later congers does
not emerge until the early eighteenth century, but even in the 1680s a need for
something of the kind had begun to show itself. The registration of copies at Stationers' Hall was by then a practice honoured mainly in the breach, and the
Company's determination to keep alive the Licensing Act probably had more to
do with protection of its rights in the books of its English stock than in those held
by individual members of the Company.

On the lapse of the Licensing Act in 1679, and Parliament's persistent deferral
of its renewal, the Company tried every means to have it renewed. Richard
Chiswell made a good debating point on behalf of the Company in January
1684, when explaining his part in 'the business of Julian'. 'The law directs us to
no guides as in the time of licensing,' he said.[16] The Stationers led the cry against
scandalous pamphlets, unlicensed 'Hawkers and Bawlers,' and foreign booksellers. In many ways, this was just their old cry at any hint that they might

[16] *Calendar of State Papers Domestic*, Car. II (1684), 436, no. 41.

themselves lose control of their monopoly in printing and distribution, to which the structures of censorship and the trade's responsibility for a degree of self-regulation were still perceived as vital. Back in 1663, L'Estrange, in his *Considerations and proposals in order to the regulation of the press*, had made it very clear how complex the network was:

> Next to Printing, follows Publishing or Dispersing, which, in and about the Town, is commonly the work of *Printers, Stitchers, Binders, Stationers, Mercury-women, Hawkers, Pedlars,* and *Ballad Singers* [. . .] The most dangerous People of all are the *Confederate Stationers,* and the breaking of That Knot would do the work alone. For the *Closer* Carriage of their business they have here in the Town, Their Private Ware-Houses, and Receivers.[17]

Though in the 1680s the Stationers' workmen also joined in with a self-interested petition, they also made the point that the chief men of the Company, L'Estrange's 'Confederate Stationers,' were among the offenders who employed non-union labour. Indeed, they were never less than venal. In August 1683, L'Estrange complained that libels seized by them were commonly carried to Stationers' Hall, 'which I know by experience to have been none of the most effectual ways for suppressing them, and it may prove only the removing them from one warehouse to another.'[18] Janeway, answering charges by the Company in 1682 that he had printed seditious books, promptly listed them and the names of members of the Company for whom he had printed them. Benjamin Harris took the same line in 1685.[19]

As part of Charles's campaign to pack Parliament with those favourable to him, he instituted *quo warranto* proceedings in March and April 1684, and all the City Companies then surrendered their charters and petitioned for new grants. The Stationers responded at once—on 17 March. They had drawn up a list of 'loyal' Assistants by 7 April, and their new Charter was approved by 22 May. To secure it, they had apologised for the 'evill members of this Company,' a 'restless and perverse faction' among them, whose 'Presumption' the king had baffled; they promised to tighten control of the press and, of course, after all that—and much more to the point—they asked to be allowed to continue their precious copy-rights in certain books.

With the accession of James in February 1685, the Court of Aldermen ordered that a new list of Assistants be made 'of persons of approved & unquestionable Loyalty.' These were chosen by May, and a fully reconstituted livery established by August. But in October 1687, James ordered another reshuffle in which many

---

[17] *Considerations and proposals in order to the regulation of the press*, 3 June 1663 (Wing L1229). At the trial of Dover, Brewster and Brooks in 1664, the booksellers confessed that they might play safe by having politically sensitive pamphlets stitched in blue paper, so that (said Lord Chief Justice Hide to Mortlock) 'They might have been the *Devil of Edmonton*, for ought you knew.' See *An exact narrative of the tryal and condemnation of John Twyn* (Wing E3668).

[18] *Calendar of State Papers Domestic, Car.* II (1683), 431, no. 47.

[19] For Janeway, see Stationers' Company Court-book E, f.146r, 158r–159r; and for Harris, Stationers' Company Court-book F, f.45r, 47v.

of those ejected in 1684 were restored. The Stationers sent the Crown an address in which the king was asked to 'vouchsafe to pardon our honest Ambition to throw our selves downe at your sacred feet.' Yet, six months later, the Assistants were shifting places again, new officials were elected, and the Company started reshaping its old policies to meet changes in higher places.

Secure for a time in their new Charter and affiliations, the Stationers took their usual line in reinforcing their control. For example, they at once tried to stop non-members of the Company dealing in books, especially hawkers. As Blagden records, in 1687, by which time the Licensing Act had been renewed, ten chief booksellers even paid William Latham 10s. each a year (with the Company also bound to put up £20 a year) 'to Suppress [. . .] such as wander up and down Citty and Cuntry Selling or dispersing Books contrary to Act of Parliament.'[20]

Dispersal beyond London was a more difficult problem for them, and if the literature was non-conformist, it might involve very special arrangements, as it did for the Friends. In 1682, L'Estrange had said:

> Of my experience of the Stationers' ways and confederacies for dispersing libels, I am more and more confirmed that the certain ways of tracing and detecting them must begin from the country, for their course is this. The first thing they do on the printing of any remarkable pamphlet is to furnish the kingdom up and down with an impression or two, before they offer at the dispersing of any here[.][21]

That L'Estrange is completely right about the initial distribution of books to the country is made clear by an entry in the minutes of the Friends' Yearly Meeting for 1673: the printer of Friends' books is ordered to send them out to the counties before any be sent abroad in London.

One further development which put the Stationers' retail trade at risk was the growth of auction sales, as they were not slow to point out:

> We doe likewise tender to yor consideration the excessive losse and prejudice which the whole Company of Booksellers (except some few persons) have laine under and doe now suffer by the many and frequent Auctions of Bookes which are dayly and have beene for some yeares last past exposed to sale that way.[22]

One of those who had stayed in place throughout the troublesome years of 1679 to 1688 was old Henry Hills, John Field's partner in bible printing in the 1660s and one of the printers to Cromwell. It was said of him that he had 'ever made it his business to be of the rising side; let what Card would turn up Trump, he would follow Suit.'[23] He had been favoured by Cromwell, played the loyal Church of England man in 1684, turned Catholic under James, and as a reward for such a timely expression of his new loyalty, was given, on 3 March 1686, a

[20] Cyprian Blagden, *The Stationers' Company: a history, 1403–1959* (London 1960), p. 170.

[21] *Calendar of State Papers Domestic, Car. II* (1682), 421, no. 115.

[22] Printed by S. Hodgson, 'Papers and documents recently found at Stationers' Hall,' *The Library*, 4th ser. (June–September 1944), p. 27.

[23] Blagden, *The Stationers' Company*, p. 168.

special privilege to print missals—up to 5000 a year. Yet even his day was to come, and doubtless when it did, just after William's arrival, he was one sacrifice the Company, helped by a mob, was happy to make. On 12 December 1688, the mob attacked his printing house in Blackfriars, 'spoiled his Formes, Letters, &c, and burnt 200 or 300 reams of paper printed and unprinted.' Since he had himself dealt out similar treatment to his competitor in the bible trade, William Bentley, thirty-three years before, we might think that he received his just deserts after all. Hills crossed the Channel into a short-lived exile, his will being proved only six weeks later.[24]

There are many other questions which, in default of space to explore them more fully here, ought at least to be raised. How self-conscious were those who lived through them of the political and cultural changes that we now discern as historically significant? How urgent did writers then regard the redefinition of the Civil War, the execution of Charles I, the Restoration, the events of 1688–1689? The Whig rewriting of that history is one of the most successful and sustained publishing ventures of the next decade. How literary—in the more limited sense—are revolutions? As a matter of intellectual and publishing history, as Robert Darnton has so pertinently asked, are we looking for great books that changed the world, although (or because) they addressed an elite, or for a critical mass of texts that less perceptibly swayed popular opinion?

One quick way of indicating the relative poverty of the literary response at the time would be to cite the congratulatory poems written to either James or William. Very early in 1689 (she died in April), Aphra Behn, for example, wrote 'A Pindaric poem to the reverend Doctor Burnet on the honour he did me of enquiring after me and my Muse.' Burnet had asked her if she would write a welcome for William. Committed as she was in loyalty to the Catholic James, her response is a beautifully ironic and gracefully disdainful refusal. Burnet had just republished many of the papers he had written during 1688, in particular one that justified the rebellion. Behn would not stoop to that servility, in the way that Burnet had done. In satiric praise of his writings, she raises the whole question of what it is to be a writer and so prostitute one's talents:

> 'Tis to your Pen, Great Sir, the Nation owes
> For all the Good this Mighty Change has wrought;
> 'Twas that the wondrous Method did dispose,
> Ere the vast Work was to Perfection brought.
> Oh Strange effect of a Seraphick Quill!
> That can by unperceptible degrees
> Change every Notion, every Principle
> To any Form, its Great Dictator please:
> The Sword a feeble Pow'r, compared to That,
> And to the Nobler Pen subordinate . . .

---

[24] A broadside of 1681 gives *A view of many traiterous, disloyal, and turn-about actions of H. H. Senior* (Wing V363A).

And she concludes:

> 'Tis you that to Posterity shall give
> This Age's Wonders, and its History.
> And Great NASSAU shall in your Annals live
> To all Futurity.
> Your Pen shall more Immortalize his Name,
> Than even his Own Renown'd and Celebrated Fame.

As she writes here *against* the pressures to conform, she gives a superbly sharp edge to her lines.

Yet when, as Catholic writers, she and Dryden serve their own cause, we drop to bathos. For example, the son born to James and Mary on 10 June 1688 was instantly burdened with an insupportable weight of poetic prophecy. So again Aphra Behn:

> [Too] Full of JOY, no LINES Correct can write,
> My *Pleasure's* too Extream for *Thought* or *Wit*.
>
> Methinks I hear the *Belgick* LION Roar,
> And Lash his *Angry Tail* against the Shore,
> Inrag'd to hear a PRINCE OF WALES is Born:
> Whose BROWS his *Boasted Laurels* shall Adorn.
> Whose *Angel* FACE already does express
> His *Foreign* CONQUESTS, and *Domestick* PEACE.
> While in his *Awful little* EYES we Fin'd
> He's of the *Brave*, and the *Forgiving* KIND.

Dryden, in his *Britannia rediviva*, is not much better in failing to prophesy the form of things to come:

> When humbly on the Royal Babe we gaze,
> The Manly Lines of a Majestick face
> Give awful joy: 'Tis Paradise to look
> On the fair Frontispiece of Nature's Book;
> If the first opening Page so charms the sight,
> Think how th'unfolded Volume will delight!

The impercipience of this 'literary' writing and the inability of Behn, or Dryden, to accept the new dispensation, then only a few months away, suggests that the truly influential texts belonged to another genre.

Aphra Behn might see in Burnet's versions of his times a great act of misrepresentation, yet she is not guiltless of approving an equally partial account. Her poem to the Licenser of the Press, now Sir Roger L'Estrange, on the third part of his *Brief history of the times*, was licensed on 22 April 1688. In it she asks,

> In what loud Songs of everlasting *Fame*,
> Shall we adore the great *L'Estrange's Name*;
> Who like a pitying God, does *Truth* advance,
> Rescuing the *World* from stupid Ignorance.

Aphra Behn records her reluctance to accept Mary's role as queen:

> The Muses all upon this Theam Divine,
> Tun'd their best lays, the Muses all, but mine,
> Sullen with Stubborn Loyalty she lay,
> And saw the World its eager Homage pay . . .

But, as a woman, she found it impossible to resist:

> Even our Allegiance, here too feebly pleads;
> The Change—in so Divine a Form—perswades . . .

The rewriting of history in terms of the myth of an earlier Commonwealth was already well under way, and not just in the 'history' books. Drama and balladry were even more eloquent. In Crowne's *Darius, king of Persia* (1688), Nabarzanes concocts a plot which neatly catches the tune of the times. The plan is to support a ruined king in order to bring down his conqueror, and then destroy both in the interests of a republic:

> 'tis a brave design, to save one King
> And beat another; save a ruin'd King
> And beat his conqueror, then save the world
> From both, by liberty. It will be great,
> It will be *glorious* . . .

The grounds of such a liberty were to some extent recovered from the literature of the 1640s. When L'Estrange finally lost his office as Licenser of the Press in 1688 (after some twenty-seven years of power), he was replaced by James Fraser. Edmund Bohun's comment on Fraser, whom he himself later replaced, was that he allowed 'all the old trayterous books of 1640 [to be] reprinted to justifie our revolution [. . . Now] the old parliamentary rebels, and those that had been hottest for the exclusion and the Monmouth rebellion, were in greatest esteeme and authority, and employed in court, camp, and countrey; and all the rest represented as *Jacobites*; for now that word was invented.'

But one also finds in the common balladry of the time new myths being generated. So, *A new song of the misfortunes of an old whore and her brats* (Wing N767aA), written as an anti-Catholic sheet late in 1688, welcomed the prospective freedom under William, since until recently:

> If we open'd our Lips
> Wooden Peep-holes and Whips
> Was of late the mild Penance enjoyn'd us;
>   Now Truth's no more Treason,
>   We esteem it a season
> To be merry, and so you shall find us.
>
> Life-and-Fortune Addresses
> [Won't] wear out our Presses
> To flatter and sooth a Just Nero:

But loud Declarations
To secure the three Nations
From the French and from *Lilli-burlero*.

See how each Popish Gull
Does look silly and dull
O None! O None! all are Lamenting;
They've no Catholique Banter,
No wise *Hind* and *Panther*,
Nor anything else worth the Printing.

While we Hereticks do write,
Ay, and Print too in spite
Of the Devil, to revenge our late wrongs Sir;
And the Hawkers hoarse lungs
With our Lampoons and Songs
Make the Streets echo all the day long Sir.

In spite of ballads like this, there is something to be said for the view that the Glorious Revolution was less the expression of a democratic upsurge and the bloodless birth of modern liberty than a reversion to the state of affairs before James II. The repression of Catholics was the counterpart of the reaffirmation in 1688 of Britain as a Protestant state. When we come to licensing, never comprehensively effective, the non-renewal of the Act in 1695 had less to do with any principled argument for 'freedom' of the press than with changing conditions in a trade that could no longer be contained as a London monopoly, and with conditions of authorship which brought into question the old system of bookseller copyright. Philip Hamburger's account of its inefficiency, and his contention that Government was, in the end, prepared to let licensing go because it planned to use a new Treason Act to cover the most serious cases of seditious libel, is persuasive.[25] Happily, that policy failed, and the spread of trade simply re-enacted and extended the inevitable consequence of all printing—that the multiplication of copies and their widespread dispersal makes it tiresome and costly to seek them out again, and virtually impossible to suppress them. Those who produced seditious or blasphemous literature could still be prosecuted at common law.

In 1789 the French thought they were re-enacting the English experience of 1688–1689. Robert Darnton's reports on the French book trade before 1789—not only in his many publications, but also in numerous lectures, including

[25] In 'The development of the law of seditious libel and the control of the press,' *Stanford law journal* 37 (1984–1985), pp. 661–765, at p. 714f. Literary historians in particular have tended to give far too much credit to censors and too little, first, to the courage of authors, printers, and booksellers, and, second, to the general conditions of trade. The omission of printers' names from imprints, for example, had little to do with fear of identification: of the 1113 extant printed items (excluding serials) datable to 1644, over half (604) give no printer's name; in 1688, for which we have some 1519 extant datable items, the proportion is even higher: 1042 lack a printer's name. Since only about 1 percent of all items printed were ever the subject of inquiry, and the rest quite innocent of anything of interest to a censor, what we have here is evidence of a quite conventional anonymity in matters of trade.

those delivered as Lyell Reader at the University of Oxford in 1997, 'Policing literature in eighteenth-century Paris'—have stimulated a great many comparable
inquiries into the history of the British book trade. Indeed, the present essay
began in 1988 as an initial response to some lectures that Darnton had given in
Oxford in 1987, when he concluded by noting: the breakdown in France of the
crucial link between trade monopolies and police power; the declaration of the
Rights of Genius and the establishment de jure of author copyright; the end of
preventive censorship; the end of inspections of the book and Bastillement; the
shift from the book to the pamphlet, journalism and posters; an end to the du-
ality in the book trade between Paris and its provincial peripheries; and a general re-deployment of the trade. Those shifts from royal privilege to writers'
copyright, from monopoly to free trade, from corporate control by gilds to the
public and open exchange of opinion also, as it happens, mark the history of
the book in England a century before. It makes the point that, for all their differences, national histories which take the book as their subject have at base a common artefact, using comparable means of production and distribution to serve
comparable ends. In that sense, Robert Darnton's evocative but finely structured
studies, along with those of Henri-Jean Martin and Roger Chartier, have never
been merely about the French book trade, but have also made a massive contribution to establishing histoire du livre as a new and rewarding field of study
internationally.

Sources before 1700

Company Records

A transcript of the registers of the Worshipful Company of Stationers of London, 1554–1640, ed. Edward
    Arber (London and Birmingham 1875–1894).
A transcript of the registers of the Worshipful Company of Stationers, 1641–1708, ed. C. G. B. Eyre and
    C. B. Rivington (London 1913–1914).
Records of the Stationers' Company, 1576–1602, from register B, ed. W. W. Greg and E. Boswell (Lon-
    don, Bibliographical Society, 1930).
Records of the Court of the Stationers' Company, 1602–1640, ed. W. A. Jackson (London, Biblio-
    graphical Society, 1957).
Records of the Stationers' Company 1554–1920, ed. Robin Myers, 115 reels of microfilm with
    printed guide (Cambridge, Chadwyck-Healey, 1984–1987).
Stationers' Company apprentices, 1605–1640, ed. D. F. McKenzie (Charlottesville, Va: Biblio-
    graphical Society of Virginia, 1961).
Stationers' Company apprentices, 1641–1700 (Oxford, Oxford Bibliographical Society, 1974).

Short-Title Catalogues

A Short-title catalogue of books printed in England, Scotland, and Ireland and of English books printed abroad
    1475–1640, first compiled by A. W. Pollard and G. R. Redgrave; 2nd ed., revised and en-
    larged, begun by W. A. Jackson and F. S. Ferguson, completed by Katharine Panzer.

Vol. i, A–H; vol. ii, I–Z; vol. iii, Printers' and publishers' indexes; with a chronological index by Philip R. Rider (London, Bibliographical Society, 1976–1990).

Short-title catalogue of books printed in England, Scotland, Ireland, Wales, and British America and of English books printed in other countries 1641–1700, compiled by Donald Wing, Yale University Library; 2nd ed., revised and enlarged. Vol. i, A1–E2926; vol. ii, E2927–O1000; vol. iii, P1–Z28 (New York, Modern Language Association of America 1972–1988).

British newspapers and periodicals 1641–1700: a short-title catalogue of serials printed in England, Scotland, Ireland, and British America, compiled by Carolyn Nelson and Matthew Seccombe, with chronological, geographical, foreign language, subject, publisher, and editor indexes (New York, Modern Language Association of America 1988).

The Term catalogues, 1668–1709, ed. Edward Arber (London 1903). Reprints the lists produced each law term by Robert Clavell of books published that term. The entries often give information such as prices and names not found in the books themselves, as well as an approximate date of publication.

Most of the otherwise unsourced material given in this paper has been drawn from A chronology and calendar of documents relating to the London book trades, 1641–1700, ed. Maureen Bell and D. F. McKenzie (forthcoming, Oxford University Press). This work draws on book-related entries in the Journals of the House of Commons and the House of Lords, the State Papers (Domestic), the unpublished court records of the Stationers' Company, entries in the various reports of the Historical Manuscripts Commission, and printed proclamations and pamphlet literature.

Part Three
THE SOCIOLOGY OF TEXTS

7

"The Staple of News" and the Late Plays

1973

First printed in a volume of essays celebrating the 400th anniversary of Ben Jonson's birth—other contributors to the collection included Clifford Leech and L. C. Knights—this is McKenzie's only extended piece of published literary criticism. The essay offers a detailed analysis of Jonson's effective reappropriation of old theatrical forms to accomplish new dramatic ends, and it illuminates his changing attitudes to his medium and audience, most especially in *The Staple of News*, a late comedy originally performed in 1625 and printed in 1631. Characteristically, McKenzie focuses on Jonson's response to the advent of the "newspaper," which the playwright perceived as a threat to the institutional authority of the theater and the power of the stage to inform and shape public opinion. The play plots convoluted variations on the parable of the prodigal son, culminating in comic redemption and marriage. Yet, given his bibliographical and indeed political concerns, McKenzie directs his principal attention to Act 3, in which the prodigal, Pennyboy Junior, purchases a clerkship for his barber at the Staple (or "commercial center") of News, an office for the production of weekly "pamphlets of Newes . . . [with] no syllable of truth in them." Jonson's satiric excoriation of the printer-journalist Nathaniel Butter and his associates—who in 1622–23 virtually created the London press—prompts McKenzie's condemnation of the author's "failure to see the potentialities of an emergent medium" and the "thoroughly reactionary nature of Jonson's political idealism." For McKenzie, the development of a public press created the opportunity for ordinary readers to contribute more fully and responsibly to the commonweal. In marking "the end of theatre as the only secular mass medium, the end of the playhouse as the principal form of public debate," *The Staple of News* not only reflects Jonson's social prejudices and anxieties as a dramatist, but also captures a liminal moment in the history of English printing, reading, and politics.

O NE OF THE most rewarding, and worrying, things about Jonson is his accessibility to criticism. It is not that his works are so richly varied that they become an

> Ocean where each kind
> Does streight its own resemblance find . . .

giving the Critic as Narcissus a ready but watery reflection of himself. They are too firmly defined for that. Nor do I mean to suggest that they do not demand an analytical brilliance and fine sensibility to social conduct if Jonson's skills and the ethical concerns which they serve are to be realised with any truth. Indeed the erudition of his recent editors and interpreters, the

> Schollers, that can iudge and fair report
> The sense they heare, aboue the vulgar sort,
> [*The Staple of News*, Prologue for the Court]

is exemplary in the best Jonsonian manner. The remark by John Addington Symonds that Jonson 'put nothing into his plays which patient criticism may not extract' underestimates their subtlety of organisation as well as the problems of articulating their leading ideas in critical terms which test our own understanding of what society is and should be. And yet they *are* amenable to analysis and commentary which in a demonstrable and comprehensive way are capable of telling the truth about them, almost as if the criticism were a controlled projection from them. Because each play is itself a form of investigation, with its central idea and ingeniously elaborated structure, we sense immediately both the possibilities of and the real contribution offered in papers on the 'theme' or 'structure' of *Volpone*, *The Alchemist*, *Bartholomew Fair*. Art's hid causes *may* be found. Beyond that, there is clearly a sense in which Jonson criticism is cumulative and coherent, reflecting the works themselves, for each play adds to the œuvre, diversifying it but also advancing it; and when in a late play like *The Magnetic Lady*, 'finding himselfe now neare the close or shutting up of his Circle,' Jonson makes explicit both the continuities within his work and his pursuit of total form, we at once acknowledge this artistic and intellectual integrity. We may go even further, citing the poems as a complementary corpus positively affirming a civilised order subverted in the plays and harmoniously re-formed in the masques, so that taken together and cemented by the *Discoveries*, they embody the man himself in a way which transcends only in its extended unity the monumentally self-defining *Workes of Beniamin Jonson*. This idea of the man engaged in, indeed embodied by, the works, far from complicating their assessment by diluting criticism with psychology, has led to a fruitful branching of inquiry. The metamorphoses of the satirist figure, his gradual incorporation in the action, the dispersal of his functions through several characters, the tempering of judgment, serve our understanding of Jonson's personal development while imbuing the criticism with a self-endorsing moral seriousness. The relation of the poet to his society, his creations, and his customers, about which Jonson is so explicit, at one end of the scale opens out onto the real world of economic, religious, political, and social abuses and at the other brings them home to an actual flesh and blood audience whose immediate physical response in pleasured recognition, bemused stupidity, or aggressive rejection Jonson has somehow already made part of the drama. Even this compression of the spectrum, instead of confounding the categories, seems merely to yield a deeper truth—that history is aesthetics or, conversely and more conventionally, that criticism inevitably leads out towards history. But either way it is an enrichment of the possibilities for criticism. In between, while the characters beat out the forms of their creations in imaginative pursuit of some gilded nature or perfected justice, it is impossible to resist the analogies with Jonson's own role as dramatic artificer, so that affirming Jonson's craft of theatre is one with analysis of his characters' ingenuity in play-making, whether it is conceiving and directing an intrigue, enticing an audience, acting in disguise, setting a scene, finding a theatre, creating multiple perspectives on the action, distracting the eyes with gold, the nostrils with roast pig, the ears with ballads, or the mind with rhetoric. This deployment of the arts of theatre in an almost critically distanced way makes his plays a valuable source of identifiably theatrical forms. Since these further exemplify a sophisticated marriage of elements of old comedy, new comedy, native moralities, and popular 'shews,' each form demands its own scholarship; their structures, by relation to the past, assume a mythic depth or parodic surface; their integration frames Jonson's original response to change and signals his larger effort to inform the new order with values derived from the past adapted to the present. This same principle is at work in his translations and in the rich allusiveness of his poetry. Similarly, the linguistic variety of his plays, like their multiple plotting, offers the characteristic blend of local vigour and decorous relationship which makes commentary on it such a happy mixture of the particular and the general.

By now you will have discerned in this Jonsonian induction a familiar note of unease surfacing beside the slightly too insistent affirmations. You may even think that this attempt to say something about *The Staple of News* is perilously close to Jonson's later position of making, not plays, but models of plays. So let me be explicit.

My way into a judgment of the late plays, including *The Devil is an Ass*, is to see them simply as a reaction to the popular success of the middle comedies. They are a final attempt to come to terms with the problem of audience implication and to insist on the primacy of his judgment over theirs. The satirist's and teacher's dilemma, the impossibility of bringing to knowledge those too obtuse to see their folly, prompts Jonson to develop an impressive dramatic strategy for showing them—literally—what fools they are. But precisely because this formidable technique is so skilfully directed to taking in, framing, ridiculing, and then expelling his intractable audience, the plays themselves become inclusive, self-sufficient, and self-validating worlds. Endlessly and satisfyingly intricate in their internal relations, refined and deepened by selective use of the past and by plausible correspondences with the present, they create in turn a metaworld of criticism and scholarship whose terms of reference and content have been virtually predetermined by Jonson's forbiddingly intellectual effort of containment. Disengagement from their complete worlds, without being brutally destructive or broadly dismissive, is almost impossible. Jonson clings to his art in these plays, and so long as he stays within their magic circle his insights and the dependent criticism which notes them have an admirable density and cogency. But like Volpone, the moment he leaves his art-world and its controls to glory in the street, confusing the distinctive realities of art and nature, he loses his authority and falls prey to the real world. Whether it is a closed garden, a Bosch globe, or even a yellow submarine, the shutting up of the circle is not only an act of containment but an act of exclusion.

It is this exclusiveness of the later plays that worries me. It is not adequately explained as an 'artistic decline' or a failure to realise his designs in fully dramatic terms. The social conscience is as alert as ever, the fighting spirit as strong, the values he seeks to communicate are timeless, the literary traditions he draws on and works within, including parody of their degenerate forms, are indisputably the most fruitful way of defining and experiencing what we mean by civilisation, his innovative skill is everywhere evident. It is just that nobody any longer listens, because he himself has no ears for what we too are fraternally bound to call the new illiteracy. There are compelling analogies with critics and criticism in our own time, faced with the established press and its underground counterpart, with poster-theatre, and even with a political pornography that seems to make any civilised debate which is also fully democratic an impossible ideal. Jonson blames his audience for their failure to understand, but more significant than any self-exculpating pique is the prior distrust of their independent judgment which his dramatic structuring reveals. After *Bartholomew Fair* the reformation of society proceeds too literally by the purgation, segregation, or expulsion of its jeerers.

It is commonly agreed that Jonson was most at ease with his audience in *Bartholomew Fair*. His 'pretty gradation' from the everyday world to the theatre, the contract which binds audience and players in a common enterprise, the analogous entry of the visitors as audience to the fair with its company of stall-holders, their union in turn as a combined audience to the puppets, and even the invitation to supper, have one thing in common—a shared perspective. Everyone is looking the same way. The only difference is that the theatre audience sees most and therefore contains them all. There are of course many inner analogies, one of the finest of which is the purse-cutting scene, where the poetic text ('*Relent and repent, and amend and be sound*'), the moral stance and criminal act, have their own graduated scale of stage observers, from the absorbed Cokes to the all-seeing Quarlous and Winwife. But the puppets on whom this unified world of men and players fix their attention are also both an expression and a resolution of Jonson's own equivocal attitude to theatre. They confute Busy, and so even at its most vulgar and dehumanized, theatre has a function in transforming the images of wickedness with which men stock their minds. Like the mechanicals' play in *A Midsummer Night's Dream*, the puppet show reduces drama to its most fundamental form for the most simple-minded audience, and it works superbly. However sophisticated the frame and ironically allusive the myth, it is as primitive as street-theatre and shows a similar paradox in the insecure command of its own fantasies, for its actors naively move from play world to real world with a disturbing insouciance. The coarse and the fine, the verbal and visual, are one, and although there is no sentimental indulgence of folly and the admonition to go mend still stands, there is here a generous acknowledgment of the audience's basic humanity. It is a happy point of equilibrium which it took Jonson years to reach and which he was soon to lose.

If one thinks for a moment of the artist's predicament—where do I go from here?—and the difficulty of surpassing such a coherent play as *Batholomew Fair*, Jonson's conscious ingenuity in shaping a new drama with *The Devil is an Ass* must command our respect. Audience and players were one in watching the puppets, yet what did the puppets look out on but a mingled world of men and players in which the only distinguishing mark was the edge of the stage.

> They haue their Vices, *there*, most like to Vertues;
> You cannot know 'hem, apart, by any difference:
> They weare the same clothes, eate o'the same meate . . .
> [*The Devil is an Ass*, I.i. 121–3]

In *The Devil is an Ass* Jonson advances his stagecraft by turning the tables. He puts the old play-characters on the outside as observers of, or audience to, the natural human characters of the inner play. More specifically the world of dramatic art is now represented not by literal puppets but by the old morality stagers, Satan, Iniquity, and Pug, who, like pensioners at a matinée, come out of retirement to look at a new play in which a bunch of citizen-actors become independent of the poet, quit their seats, usurp the stage, parade their clothes and their rhetoric, and hatch hyper-diabolical intrigues. Their theatrical amateurism is one with their criminal skill or inherent folly, for they act viciousness and stupidity best in being themselves. Where in *Bartholomew Fair* all spoke prose except the puppets and songsters, the men and women, as becomes their role of players, now assume the artfully natural speech rhythms of the actors' verse along with their voices, leaving a superannuated Satan and Iniquity to swap the fourteeners of their heyday. Of course Jonson is saying that the devil is an ass, beaten at his own game by the ordinary people of this new age and rightly displaced by them; and of course this amounts to a manifesto claiming that the old theatre has been outstripped by life and that his own play is, and promotes, a new morality.

Fitzdottrell, however, is the only one who explicitly enacts the movement from audience to stage and thereby projects theatrically the audience's folly. His cloak, described as a stage garment, is probably a traditional Vice-costume. But folly is an epidemical disease, and his is a representative act which Jonson, by projecting and containing, theoretically distances and controls. For Fitzdottrell takes his world with him, a mirror image of the everyday, framed by the old morality. As those will who live in such a world, he makes plays, and in scenes like those between Wittipol and Mrs Fitzdottrell he re-enacts his role of audience breaking in upon the action to play the fool. The play which could not have succeeded in privately shaming his folly now publicly exposes it. The prologue expresses concern that public possession of the stage may make the actors impotent:

> Yet, Grandee's, would you were not come to grace
> Our matter, with allowing vs no place,
>   . . . This tract
> Will ne'er admit our vice, *because of yours* . . .
> We know not how to affect you.

Despite this confession of inadequacy, it is Jonson's greater achievement to prove
the superiority of his art to circumstance; and the fertility and vigour of Meer-
craft, together with the intrigues of Wittipol and Manly, make it a lively new play.
But the involuted cleverness is already an expression of his final solution. Like
Saturn, he begets children only to swallow them. For the organic unity of
Bartholomew Fair, which also expresses a fully communal spirit, he now offers a
structure which is intellectually ingenious and theatrically vivid but also divisive.
The projection and ridicule of his intrusive audience, though brilliantly com-
prehended by the play, even to the point where they make it, mark the beginning
of Jonson's movement into an art-world in which he can contain their independence, which he sees only as folly, and be entirely their master. The ending
of the play may seem indulgent:

> It is not manly to take ioy, or pride
> In humane errours (we doe all ill things . . .)

But its application is sadly limited, for most are barren and only

> The few that haue the seeds
> Of goodness left, will sooner make their way
> To a true life, by shame, then punishment.
>   [*The Devil is an Ass,* V.vii. 169–74]

Jonson creates an audience most literally in *The Staple of News.* The Prologue gets
out six words—'*For your owne sake, not ours*'—before Gossip Mirth, the spirit of
Comedy, who thinks it great fun, clambers on to the stage where she can see and
be seen, interrupting the Prologue and hardening Tattle's confidence with the
advice: '*be not asham'd.*' Set above the groundlings, that audience of 'graue' wits
who are not so much serious as dead, they call for stools and sit upon the play.
Judgment is physical, like the illumination. The tire-men mend their lights, and
with a principled demand for originality and a report on the poet, dead drunk
behind the scenes, silent in sack, his book torn, looking like a miserable emblem
of patience (in fact, the melancholic artist reduced to inactivity or self-
destruction from frustrated idealism), the hard labour ends and the man-
midwife-Prologue delivers the play.

   It is a vigorous opening which gives all the weight of exasperation to the Prologue's words when at last he is allowed to speak:

> For your owne sakes, not his, he bad me say
> Would you were come to heare, not see a Play.

One has to be careful in commenting on *The Staple of News* because Mirth has forestalled most critics. She is the dramatic theorist, literary historian, and sharp reviewer, one of a panel of speakers who pointed out long before Dryden that Jonson was a 'decay'd wit.' Expectation understands well enough that it is a prodigal play, and that a literal fool is unnecessary because they are all fools. They know their Jonson, recalling with affection Zeale-of-the-land Busy, keeping an eye out for the mad justice, and proving that they had taken the point of *The Devil is an Ass*, namely that Fitzdottrell was the devil and foolish enough to risk cuckoldry. Mirth extends the idea to the new play, identifying the Vices, although '*now they are attir'd like men and women o' the time.*' She not only calls Peni-boy Senior Old Covetousness but, like Canter, notes the link between money and sex by calling him Money-Bawd and Flesh-Bawd. Peni-Boy Junior of course she rightly calls Prodigality, and Pecunia, '*prank't vp like a prime Lady,*' is Mistress Money. She knows that the play is an allegory to be taken generally and refuses to allow any specific identifications. 'But the play is also a morality play on the value of money,' writes one of Jonson's finest critics.[1] What more do Pecunia's three names do, '*but expresse the property of Money, which is the daughter of earth, and drawne out of the Mines?,*' asks Mirth, giving the symbolism a bit more resonance. Having identified Peni-boy Junior and praised his lack of jealousy, she then shows her Aristotelian awareness that the Prodigal is more likely than the Miser to become 'communicative,' 'liberall,' and even 'magnificent'; but she also recognises that both urbanity and humanity would appear in the Miser '*an' hee were rightly distill'd.*' There is clearly a trained intelligence behind these comments and it is equally clear from her image of Jonson drunk backstage on royal sherry (the '*most miserable Embleme of patience*') that she is well acquainted with the emblem-books. She has a fashionably sharp eye for poet-presenters and sees that Peni-boy Canter is '*a kin to the Poet.*' Her capacity for discerning linguistic links and dramatic enactment shows not only in a readiness to see ironic point in the fact that Smug, who caught a dose of the staggers, was required by his part to be drunk, but in her hope that Jonson's play, although barrelled up so long, might prove true '*to the time of yeer, in Lent,*' and be '*delicate Almond butter,*' with its rich suggestion of a winter flowering. Her wit shows to comparable advantage when she anticipates, but puts more succinctly, Herford and Simpson's point, much repeated since their day, that Jonson's Staple, built upon money greed and 'held together' by the cash nexus . . . collapses upon the failure of funds.'[2] For when Expectation complains that the poet has let fall the Staple '*most abruptly,*' Mirth quickly adds 'Bankruptly, *indeede!*' This comment by Mirth, original with her, once more converts criticism to paraphrase. If, as many have claimed, the Staple itself is too fleetingly shown, it was Expectation who first said so, criticising both the delay in opening it and its

[1] L. C. Knights, *Drama and Society in the Age of Jonson* (London 1937), 220.
[2] *Ben Jonson*, ed. C. H. Herford and P. E. Simpson, 11 vols (Oxford 1925–52), IV, 178.

premature end. She was also quick to note in the consequential collapse of the Academy the loss of a new power in popular education and in particular the dashed hopes 'of so many towardly young spirits.' Or if Peni-boy Canter is too much of a direct moralizer and too little of a human being, Mirth and Tattle at least saw through his sham beggary and wished for a 'Court-Beggar in good clothes,' or 'a begging scholar in blacke, or one of these beggerly Poets,' or 'a thred-bare Doctor of Physicke, a poore Quacksaluer,' or 'a Sea-captaine, halfe steru'd.' These may be stereotypes but they meet late morality decorum. More important, they imply Jonson's failure to offer socially relevant comment on the genuine problem of enforced poverty.

These play-goers were also alert, like Jonson himself, to the seductive arts of theatre. Mistress Trouble Truth recoiled from *The Devil is an Ass*, believing that it taught wives how to cuckold their husbands; her frigid fears command no respect, but Mirth speaks of the risk with a hint of that richness of experience which informs the best criticism. She adds to her misgivings about theatre by pointing out, correctly, that the news offered in the play is 'monstrous! scuruy! and too exotick! ill cook'd! and ill dish'd!' Logically and responsibly she acts on her distrust and suggests that drama in schools should not be permitted to turn scholars into play-boys, or, to put it another way confirmed in the event, that *The Staple of News* is not really worth studying.

Jonson's projection of his audience of learned owls, wide-eyed but blind, is clearly not just a matter of having a bunch of women of fashion climb on to a stage to give their opinions. It is also a remarkably accurate forecast of subsequent interpretive comment and critical judgment, and a brilliant physical enactment of his deeper point that such intrusion need not be physical at all. There are more ways than one of getting between a play and its author.

> marke but his wayes,
> What flight he makes, how new; And then he sayes,
> If that not like you, that he sends tonight,
> 'Tis you haue left to iudge, not hee to write.
> [*The Staple of News*, Prologue for the Stage]

The play itself is properly larger than the Staple, for it is Jonson's own Staple of news. It is not synonymous with the city news office but is offered in serious public competition with it. Just as the gossips are part of our Jonson's play, so is the vice of interpretation part of its subject; and if such a literate audience is incapable of truly judging Jonson's carefully structured news, what hope has it, without the poet's help, of judging mere news, made like the time's news?

The play was long preparing, as we know from Jonson's use of similar material in *News from the New World* (1620), *Neptune's Triumph* (1624), and references to Butter, the Infanta, the coronation, and the destruction of some 'parcels of a Play' in his fire of 1623. It is not a sudden reversion after a decade of courtly distractions, but a deeply considered and carefully wrought statement, the comprehensive subject of which determines its fully public form. Its newness is that of a truth about the developing political and social pattern of England; and that sense of where the nation is going is more important than Charles, the Infanta or the news office. But Jonson is anxious to demonstrate how his new ways adapt the drama itself to new needs and thereby to show its continuing superiority as a medium of informed public comment.

The on-stage audience now makes literal and refines the analogies of *The Devil is an Ass*. It is part of a larger strategy of theatrical exposure in which appearance is a primary element. Unlike poets, although Jonson does so, actors must provide for their guests 'in the way of showes.' Hence it is a visionary theatre in which the traditional and easily recognised forms are preserved and adapted to the times. The play opens with a sit-in, moves on to costume scenes for young heirs, city liverymen, and academics, and later gives splendid opportunities for spectacle with Pecunia discovered in state, successive assemblies, the feast in Apollo, music and dancing, the beating up of Peni-boy Senior, a beggar unmasked, and the circus act of a mad justice and his performing dogs. It may seem to some that too often 'Jonson relies solely on symbolic action'[3] but this is a concomitant of his concern to thrust the audience into prominence, giving them drama apparently on their own terms, and focussing on their response. That their terms are not wholly his is obvious, which is only to say, as Jonson himself does in his figure of Expectation, that preconceptions are critically disabling and our judgment, unlike his, misguided.

Satan, Iniquity, and Pug disappear altogether and the Fitzdottrells, hardened into morality types, now sit as intrusive, prose-speaking spectators to yet another realistic play within, for it starts with a quite natural scene of Peni-boy Junior putting on his new clothes. With the poet silent and his book torn, this audience has to make its own play, but Mirth soon sees that Peni-boy Junior's situation and costume cast him in the old role of Prodigal; hence the play they are watching must be a morality. In fact, however, within the naturalistic family circle of the Peni-boys, it is Canter who sees the potential of drama in real life and puts the tradition to work in the old style by creating the play of the prodigal son. He, not Jonson, is also its enthusiastic presenter, another who forestalls the critics:

> See!
> The difference 'twixt the couetous, and the prodigall.
> 'The Couetous man neuer has money! and
> 'The Prodigall will haue none shortly!
>   [*The Staple of News*, I.iii. 38–41]
> Why, here's the *Prodigall* prostitutes his *Mistresse*!
>   [Ibid., IV.ii. 123]

But this inner world of ordinary people turned morality characters becomes audience to, indeed is dependently wedded to, another inner show, the Pecunia

---

[3] L. C. Knights, 222.

set, a group of figures, less realistic, more symbolic, whose life therefore is not innate but, being allegorical, exists only in our right perception and use of them, as of the drama itself. The morality characters and emblematical figures now combine as a further audience to see the real everyday world of London life, the Staple of News. But even this proves to be yet another construction, begotten and fairly helped into the world by Cymbal.

> You must be a Mid-wife Sir!
> Or els the sonne of a Mid-wife!
> [*The Staple of News*, I.v. 77–8]

In the range of its fictive characters and reported events, even in its further perspectives of outer and inner rooms, the Staple is a competing image of the theatre. In its linguistic variety it meets decorum by matching the style to the customers and their needs; for the unities of time, place, and action it has an efficient filing system and an extensive network which ensures the receipt and co-ordination of news from all four cardinal quarters of London—Court, Church, City, and Parliament—and with Tom the barber on its staff it can even cope with the arts. True to form, its leading actors 'sustaine their parts' in cloak and 'Staple gowne,' Picklock, like Mosca, declaring himself

> A true *Chamaelion*, I can colour for't.
> I moue vpon my axell, like a turne-pike,
> Fit my face to the parties, and become;
> Streight, one of them.
> [*The Staple of News*, III.i. 36–9]

So this play, in which 'Wit had married Order,' proves to be another morality and Peni-boy Junior, blinded by the expertise, plays Gossip to Cymbal's Staple of News. But this is far from being the innermost play of Jonson's calculatedly complex nest of successive audience-actor creations. Indeed, as if on some inflationary spiral, we go up the dramatic scale as we move towards its centre—from popular morality to court masque. It is now Peni-boy Junior's turn to move in on the act. The office is closed for lunch, and when we meet the group again they have been eating in the Apollo where, fittingly, they make a masque. It begins with an antimasque of jeering,

> A very wholesome exercise, and comely.
> Like lepers, shewing one another their scabs,
> Or flies feeding on vlcers.
> [*The Staple of News*, IV.i. 34–6]

But the real creator in this consumer society is Lickfinger. When he re-enters with the ladies the tone rises at once and we re-enact much of another banqueting-hall masque, *Neptune's Triumph*, which was also the cook's work. Lickfinger, who 'has *Nature* in a pot,' can cook, carve and colour it to a perfection which needs no mending by any toothpick art. It is his wisdom, more palatable than

Madrigal's, which leads to Peni-boy Junior's fruitfully witty praise of Pecunia as the light of the world. His eulogy is chorused by the others when, as Jonson's note says, 'They all beginne the encomium of Pecunia,' and this festive conjunction of minds transforms them into a community of kissing cousins. Madrigal, in perfect laureate verse, makes a poem in Pecunia's honour:

> The splendour of the wealthiest Mines!
> The stamp and strength of all imperiall lines,
> Both maiesty and beauty shines,
>   In her sweet face!

To this he adds words for a saraband, a slow Spanish dance befitting a projected marriage:

> According to Pecunia's Grace
> The Bride hath beauty, blood, and place,
> The Bridegroome vertue, valour, wit,
> And wisdome, as he stands for it.

The musicians arrive in Apollo too. The forceful precedent of Epicoene is invoked, as it is later confirmed in The New Inn, when words combine with music in the singing of Madrigal's poem. Harmony reigns. The audience is properly spellbound, for Jonson says, 'They are all Struck with admiration.' The revels begin and everyone dances except Peni-boy Canter, who has now lost control of his little play, and like a disaffected Jaques stands audience to the action, waving his finger and offering his own uncomprehending, puritanically dismissive commentary:

> Look, look, how all their eyes
> Dance i'their heads (obserue) scatter'd with lust!
> At sight o' their braue Idoll! how they are tickl'd,
> With a light ayre! the bawdy Saraband!
> They are a kinde of dancing engines all!
> And set, by nature, thus, to runne alone
> To euery sound! All things within, without 'hem,
> Moue, but their braine, and that stands still! mere monsters,
> Here, in a chamber, of most subtill feet!
> And make their legs in tune, passing the streetes!
> These are the gallant spirits o' the age!
> The miracles o' the time! that can cry vp
> And downe mens wits! and set what rate on things
> Their half-brain'd fancies please!
>   [The Staple of News, IV.ii. 130–43]

Like a good monarch, Peni-boy Junior praises his poet and offers him, as monarchs still do, sack and claret for his service. As in Neptune's Triumph, however, there is now a second antimasque, which is ushered in by Peni-boy Senior. Like Guyon in the Bower of Bliss he dashes the proffered cup, but he is more than matched by the virtuous Pecunia, who, once dull and tarnished from lack of air, now

celebrates her release from this malicious jailor who had kept her a 'close pris-
oner vnder twenty bolts.' He would have smothered her in a chest and strangled
her in leather; but sunlight and air, the liquidity of the dance, here imaged in the
masque, have restored her health. The antimasque ends with an excellent comedy of affliction in which the assembly spurns him and kicks him out while the
fiddlers drown his noise in music.

Nor is this the innermost play, for 'Spirits are not finely touched but to fine issues.' Prince Peni-boy now applies his new knowledge and prompted by dramatic example enters upon his own creation, one that will serve the professions,
knowledge, and society—the College of Canters. The coinage of his brain, a university, lies at the heart of this world made by the audience and players and completes its visionary order. At this point audience, gossips, and actors view the
central allegory in a perspective as formally unified as that in *Bartholomew Fair*; and
it is precisely at this point, following an immensely colourful, vibrantly alive,
and verbally witty masque, when spirits are riding high and a new vision is about
to be realised, that Peni-boy Canter plays Buzy to the puppets. Like an unruly and
destructive audience he breaks in upon these actors and ensures that their play is
still-born. '*It was spitefully done o' the Poet,*' says Censure, '*to make the Chuffe take him off
in his heighth, when he was going to doe all his braue deedes!*' Act IV is a tour de force of dramatic construction and ironic overlay and is integrally related to everything that
has gone before. The characters, closer to the several arts of theatre than they are
to real life, talk and act in accordance with their own understanding of dramatic
norms, from the outer morality to the inner masque, each of which has its successive presenters. It is on these planes and in contrivedly theatrical terms that
the degenerative actions are played out.

At the end of Act IV *The Staple of News* begins to unwind. The masque is ended,
Peni-boy Canter's abduction of Pecunia deprives the Staple-play of its life-force,
the gossips (although reluctant to leave) have abused and rejected the poet in
their 'mourniuall of protests,' and Canter's morality play, which has done its job
but is not adequate to a new threat, is superseded.

In a scene which re-enacts the opening of the prodigal play, Peni-boy Junior
appears in Canter's patched cloak; but it is also called a '*graue Robe*' and with it he
assumes his father's role as redeeming poet and playmaker. At first, like the poet
in the tiring house, he is sunk in lethargy, and being rejected thinks he has the
'*epidemicall* disease' upon him, but the collapse of the poet's competitor, the Staple
of News, arouses him. The last main action, in which he pits his clearer wits
against those of Picklock, is Junior's device, and by setting up his own little scene
and calling to witness an auditor who saw nothing but heard everything, he
strips the mask from Picklock, restores order to a corrupted community, and
both serves and rejoins his family. Peni-boy Senior will do so too, but not before
he has taught a lesson to Block and Lollard, his rebellious dogs, for jumping up
to, gnawing, and befouling his servants, instead of staying in their holes. The
dogs' names pair Wycliffe's 'idle babblers' with an image of execution. Even

their roles are taken over when like a latter-day Morose Peni-boy Senior suffers further vexatious baiting from the jeerers who burst in upon the trial scene.

Nevertheless, Jonson's play only contains all this; it is far from being one with it. In a sentence which he plants with a self-reflecting irony, he 'neuer did wrong, but with iust cause.' Even the prodigal theme is Canter's and the Gossips'. Jonson may seem to have altered the story, since it is the father who is thought to be dead, but of course that is not so: it is the son who was dead and by the end of the play is alive again. He may have seemed to depart from traditional forms ('That was the old way,' says Mirth), but the conventional wisdom of the parables is not outdated. Canter's stale sentences are news. Dramatically speaking, Jonson is not drawing farts out of dead bodies. Mirth may think that he has omitted beggarly heirs, poets, scholars, doctors, and sea captains, but Junior is a 'Begger in veluet' and Madrigal, Pied-mantle, Almanack, and Shunfield fit the others to perfection. For Jonson is a creator of a feigned commonwealth and its beggars are all there. When he says that the Staple of News is a place 'wherein the age may see her owne folly' he means the news office, his own play, and the succession of plays made within it where spectators take the stage and in affirming their independence are made to display the ignorance of their judgment and their betrayal of true theatre. His dramatic structure creates its own proof. If we see it at all, we may think that Act IV is a masque, but of course it is a fully-developed antimasque which must come to an end before the family reunion can take place in Act V. As Mr Orgel says, 'for Jonson it was the antimasque that served to give meaning to the masque, to explain it, to make the audience understand.'[4] The play ends only as Peni-boy Senior gives away the bride to his nephew and joins their hands. It is a cue for Canter to say:

> If the Spectators will joyne theirs, wee thanke 'hem.

and Junior to add:

> And wish they may, as I, enjoy *Pecunia*.

Paired with Junior and flanked by the brothers, Pecunia completes the tableau and both embodies and delivers its meaning.

The several levels of the action, like the receding planes of a toy theatre, also express with sharpening irony a hierarchy of values according to which the theatrical forms become more sophisticated and their substance more degenerate as we move in towards the masque. The apparent disparity between realistic and allegorical elements, like the varying density of the verse, is not a weakness but reflects with deliberate skill the several levels of apprehension appropriate to the forms. The true language of the play is in its powerfully co-ordinated structural statement, not in the odd speech. In this way too Jonson unites past and present theatre, and once we have seen that his ironic masque is a tissue of lies and his

---

[4] S. Orgel, *The Jonsonian Masque* (Cambridge, Mass. 1967), 93.

crude morality an instrument of truth, we then have to discount our conclusion, for Jonson's public play is larger than either the masque or the morality, and transcends both in the truth of its comment on the times.

These remarks about Jonson's organisation of the play in terms of dramatic depth and time should not obscure the more obvious surface unity, again consciously devised, of the Peni-boys, Pecunia, the Staplers, Jeerers, and nominees for the College of Canters. The links between the institutions have a basis in fact, but this is reinforced by ties of family and service, by the overlapping roles, especially those of Picklock, Cymbal, and Lickfinger, and by the actively integrative function of the news office in Act III. This jigsaw coherence is also expressed in the familiar Jonsonian construction of a representative world. The Staple itself is a comprehensive symbol for society, and, like the Stapler Cymbal, Jonson allots roles to his characters which, when related, account for most of its functions. Of course this reduction to type diminishes their humanity and credibility although this has been trebly justified. First, within the play their roles are self-created, even Canter's; second, they show the consequences of men abusing their own humanity (so Picklock, with forehead of steel and mouth of brass, is what he would be); third, where the characters constantly confuse art and reality and thereby lose the perspective necessary to knowledge, their very theatricality should prevent us from doing the same and ensure that we concentrate on the larger argument. The position is of course a Brechtian one, but the danger does not lie only in the audience's readiness to be distracted, for any actor would rather have the audience believe his character than view him as a mere contributor to an abstract design. Hence it is not surprising that several of Jonson's prefatory notes, especially that to *The New Inn*, suggest that he could do without actors.

Jonson's provision of a whole gallery of role-players is extended with perfect stylistic consistency to the staging itself. For *The Staple of News* is a play of shows. It works through costume, music, dance, display, and violent action, all of which call for brilliant visual staging. Its structure is ostensibly open and obvious and offers superb chances for ingenious use of stage space and lighting to express perspectives on the action and even audience-assault; it is an open invitation to a stage designer to display the symbolic characters literally larger than life, to show Pecunia as indeed a Venus of the time, with her banner-bearing prophets in their own poster-theatre act: *Pecunia omnia potest* and *Pecunia obediunt omnia*. Anyone who has been to recent Aldwych Theatre productions and experienced the auditorium lights going up during the act to force us on stage, or has seen the production by the same company of Genet's *The Balcony* with its outsize puppets, or had his hand shaken at the end of *A Midsummer Night's Dream*, can hardly doubt that *The Staple of News* is ripe for revival or that it would be brilliantly served by the Royal Shakespeare Company. Of course it would all be ironic, and Jonson would not thank one for defending his under-written characters by some formula which multiplied costume colour by length of stage exposure, but the irony would have a fine edge and one might be forgiven for suspecting that it was offered with both a genuine pride in the achievement of mounting such a show and disgust for the audience that enjoyed it.

I have scarcely touched on the thematic unity of the play, but in no other does Jonson offer to relate in such a penetrating and cohesive way economics and language as forces for binding or disrupting community. He had explored the relation of language to poetry in *The Poetaster* and that of language to government in *Cynthia's Revels*. In *Volpone* and *The Alchemist* he had exposed rhetoric as an index of diseased imagination and as a disguise for avarice, itself destructive of the true commonwealth. Only in *The Staple of News*, however, are the social uses of language fully explored. The consequences of man's readiness to pervert and exploit for gain his distinctive excellence are projected here in an impressively universal way in the Staple of News and the College of Canters as symbols of institutionalized corruption, and in the subversion of theatre as their victim in all its forms. The play itself, by contrast, sets out to show what drama can still do and how superior it is to the press as an instrument of political understanding.

In his epilogue Jonson expressed his hope that if the play should fail to please,

> It will not be imputed to his wit.
> A *Tree* so tri'd, and bent, as 'twill not start.
> Nor doth he often cracke a string of Art . . .

Recognition of the play's artifice and therefore of his artistry is essential to Jonson's self-esteem, and for us to see the pattern is at once a compliment to him and a recognition of our own responsibility to act on the knowledge conveyed. Jonson's subtlety is such that it is virtually impossible to fault him. There is no lack of skill in *The Staple of News* and he has effectively undercut any criteria we might use to say so.

How to say then that both *The Staple of News* and any critique of it were alike bound to fail? Perhaps it is simply that the ingenuity is after all just too self-satisfying, that the social problem of news, like the critical comments we offer, is too much of Jonson's own making. Perhaps the simplifications, however well-informed by respectably acceptable values, never wholly escape nor truly place the denser life they seek to contain and define. A theory of humours requires a matching concession of diminished responsibility. Reformation, we recognise, is not meant to be enacted in fully human terms on stage, for the characters have no life but what we give them, and the demonstration suffices if it speaks to our minds and changes us. But Jonson's conservatism runs deep and the way it pervades his dramatic form suggests that he has little faith in man's capacity even to see the light, let alone follow it. The anger which he shows for the Staple may seem to spring from a concern for the people, but its effect is to abuse them for visiting this 'house of fame'—

> Where both the curious, and the negligent;
> The scrupulous, and careless; wilde, and stay'd;
> The idle, and laborious; all doe meet,
> To tast the *Cornu copiae* of her rumors,
> Which she, the mother of sport, pleaseth to scatter
> Among the vulgar: Baites, Sir, for the people!
> And they will bite like fishes.
> [*The Staple of News*, III.ii. 115–22]

The moral earnestness comes close to the puritan intolerance he so berated in others. More seriously perhaps—and this gets close to the worrying problem of his artistic excellence—concern for his audience leads him into the devious ingenuity of the schizophrenic who plays off the real world with ironies, double-entendres, and situational games that permit him to keep his inner world intact while abusing his fellows with their forms. The late plays in particular become elaborate devices for proving the folly, irrelevant expectations, ignorant judgment, and false gratifications of his audiences. The final irony is that Peni-boy Canter *was* dead, and for all the brilliance of Jonson's redeeming arts, the theatre died with him. We return, past the irony of Expectation's words, to the simple truth that worried Jonson himself:

> Absurdity on him, for a huge ouergrowne *Play-maker!* why should he make him liue againe, when they, and we all thought him dead? If he had left him to his ragges, there had been an end of him.
> [*The Staple of News*, Fourth Intermean, 8–11]

The Staple of News is at once a supremely perceptive, intelligently argued, ingeniously structured comment on his times. In marking Jonson's return to the public stage it is also a courageous reaffirmation, deeply conservative but powerfully sanctioned, of the dramatic poet's public role as spokesman for his age, a role which the development of the press, with its unsifted reports and vulgarity of language, threatened to usurp. But for all its virtue, Jonson's response failed in one vital point: it shows no understanding at all of what a painful struggle it is for the ill-educated to learn a new language of conscience and independent political judgment. In deriding their attempts and shutting up his circle against them, Jonson sealed himself off from a world that was becoming uncomfortably intrusive, and in doing so he ceased to be a public poet.

It is only to be expected that the lover of true art and the enemies of all art, poet and puritan, will sometimes seem to speak with the same voice. Jonson's *Poetaster* and *Cynthia's Revels* make much of the paradox, and the false wit, empty rhetoric, parasitic acting, and visionary materialism of the middle plays are subtle variations on the same theme. But as a problem with both aesthetic and political implications it is most prominent in the period of Jonson's late plays.

The really trenchant expression of the puritan voice is Prynne's *Histrio-Mastix* of 1633, which had grown in bulk and vehemence in the three years it took to print. If Jonson was by then disenchanted with the court masque, his criticism was oblique and milky-hearted compared with that of Prynne, who took good example 'for all Pagan, all Christian Princes and Magistrates, to beware of being besotted with Plays, or Actors, as [one] prodigious Pagan Emperour & others were to their eternal infamy.' Nor did Prynne shrink from defining 'Women-Actors' as 'notorious whores' and from asking: 'dare then any Christian woman be so more than whorishly impudent, as to act, or speake publikely on a Stage . . . ?'[5]

The day after the queen had acted in a pastoral, Laud, soon to be archbishop, showed the book to the king and queen, who were duly enraged; but more seriously Prynne was charged not only with railing upon Stageplays but with writing 'diverse incitements, to stir up the People to discontent, as if there were just cause to lay violent hands upon their Prince.'

At the same time the king let it be known that he wanted the Inns of Court to supply, in Bulstrode Whitelock's words, 'the outward and splendid visible testimony of a Royal Masque in evidence of his subjects' love,' for 'it was hinted at in the Court that this action would manifest the difference of their opinion from Mr. Prynne's new learning, and serve to confute his *Histrio Mastix* against enterludes.'

Shirley's *The Triumph of Peace* began as a procession headed by twenty footmen, followed by marshalls and officers and one hundred gentlemen of the Inns of Court mounted on the best horses and making 'the most glorious and splendid shew that ever was beheld in *England*.' Then came the antimasquers, the first being cripples and beggars on horseback, 'the poorest and leanest Jades that could be gotten out of the Dirt-carts.' More horsemen and an antimasque of projectors followed, among them a 'Fellow with a bunch of Carrots upon his Head, and a Capon upon his Fist, describing a *Projector* who begg'd a Patent of *Monopoly*, as the first Inventor of the Art to feed Capons fat with Carrots . . .' And 'it pleased the Spectators the more, because by it an Information was covertly given to the King of the unfitness and ridiculousness of these Projects.' In the banqueting hall the masque was danced, played, sung, and spoken to perfection, and the queen and 'great Ladies were very free and civil in dancing with all the masquers.' They continued in their sports until it was almost morning, when there was a stately banquet; and thus, writes Whitelock, 'was this earthly Pomp and Glory, if not Vanity, soon past over and gone, as if it had never been.' The bill—over £21,000—was real enough, but the queen's preferred consolation was 'that she never saw any Masque more noble.'[6]

My point here is that an attack on the theatre had been construed as a political attack on the king. The king's answer was to command a theatrical parade of

[5] *Histrio-Mastix* (1633), 709 and index, art. 'Women-Actors.'
[6] Bulstrode Whitelock, *Memorials of the English Affairs* (1682), 18–21.

remarkably self-betraying inanity and extravagance to establish the political fact, as he saw it, of his subjects' love. Instead of answering Prynne it ironically proved him right; and since it could hardly have been better calculated as a final rebuff to Jonson, it thrust puritan and poet into a paradoxical alliance.

In their view of the relationship of stage and state, William Prynne and Ben Jonson are in this sense two faces of the same coin. The court was not to be improved by plays and Jonson, like Prynne, knew too well now how it could be corrupted by them.

> Playes in themselues have neither hopes, nor feares;
> Their fate is only in their hearers eares:
> [*The New Inn*, Epilogue]

Charles in any case had his own way of making men wise by their ears. While Prynne was pilloried, his ears sliced off, and his book burned—marking with a fine theatrical flare the innovation of a custom hitherto unknown in England—Jonson fiddled with *A Tale of a Tub*

> to shew what different things
> The *Cotes* of *Clownes*, are from the *Courts* of *Kings*.
> [*A Tale of a Tub*, Prologue]

The radical judgment on a corrupt state as imaged in its theatre is not Jonson's but Prynne's, as Laud and the king recognised. Jonson holds to his vision of an ordered society purged of folly and greed, and however bitter his resentment of failure or of 'Spectacles of State' supplanting his 'more remou'd *mysteries*,' he is inescapably committed to the court and is one with it in accepting its position of privileged exclusiveness and its policy of suppression in defiance of new voices. The imagery of his attack on Alexander Gill, who had dared to criticise *The Magnetic Lady*—

> A Rogue by Statute, censur'd to be whipt,
> Cropt, branded, slit, neck-stockt; go, you are stript.

—is less revealing for the indignation it expresses than for its endorsement of institutionalised barbarities. If Charles could fire the devil from Prynne's pages, Jonson was not above calling in Vulcan to second his execration of Jones:

> Lyue long the Feasting Roome. And ere thou burne
> Againe, thy Architect to ashes turne!
> Whom not ten fyres, nor a Parlyament can
> With all Remonstrance make an honest man.
> ['*An Expostulacion with Inigo Jones*,' 101–4]

Even conceding the impossibility of reforming this surveyor of the king's works and architect of the Banqueting Hall, there is little faith there in the efficacy of parliaments. Charles had ensured in March 1629 that his went into a long recess; in October 1632 'Stationers, Printers and Booke Sellers' were prohibited by a Star

Chamber decree from printing and publishing 'the ordinary Gazetts and Pamphletts of newes';[7] and in 1633 the Master of the Revels even required that old plays be recensored, 'since they may be full of offensive things against church and state, ye rather that in former time the poetts tooke greater liberty than is allowed them by mee.'[8]

Neither puritans, painters, parliamentarians, nor printers would have had much sympathy from Jonson, but neither was the court any longer one to shelter or respect him. It was futile to hope for reform from a mediocre monarch and since Jonson had no audience that he could respect it was equally futile to satirise the travesty of courtliness and good government that he observed. Like Ginsberg in his poem 'America', Jonson, when he would talk to his country, found that he was talking to himself.

The Staple of News is the hardening point of Jonson's isolation, and the wholly derisive view he presents of a stupid audience, gullible populace, and false educators, fed by a staple diet of Bourne and Butter, is logically climaxed by a symbolic act of suppression—which is only the mirror image of wishful thinking—in the destruction of the news office. His failure to see the potentialities for good of an emergent medium, in reflecting more fully than ever before the actual composition of the commonwealth in the very diversity of its opinion and the pressure of its barely articulated strivings, is not so much a failure of political awareness in itself as of artistic and human sympathy, and therefore of political awareness. Artistic because the society—the material, not the games he played with it—is more complex than he represents it to be, human because he cannot allow that a passionate sense of the self can be other than destructive. Humours are 'the root of all Schisme, and Faction, both in Church and Common-wealth,' says Probee in *The Magnetic Lady*.[9] Like an informant reporting in 1668, Jonson probably would have agreed that 'Conscience is made a cloak for ignorance, wilfulness and treachery. These people are children in understanding, but men in malice.'[10] By contrast, someone like William Prynne, despite the burning of his book about the theatre and the loss of his ears, knows of and speaks to a large class within a new and politically influential order, albeit, as his prosecutor affirmed, in 'all the vile Terms . . . of the Oyster women at Billingsgate, or at the Common Conduit.'[11]

I have said enough to show that Jonson did not let the sword sleep in his hand. His efforts to write a drama for his own times are clearly seen in his for-

[7] Folke Dahl, *A Bibliography of English Corantos and Periodical Newsbooks 1620–1642* (London 1952), 19.

[8] *The Dramatic Records of Sir Henry Herbert*, ed. J. Q. Adams (New Haven 1917), 21.

[9] Samuel Johnson: 'It is to be observed, that, among the Natives of England, is to be found a greater Variety of Humour, than in any other Country; and, doubtless, where every Man has a full Liberty to propagate his Conceptions, Variety of Humour must produce Variety of Writers; and, where the Number of Authors is so great, there cannot but be some worthy of Distinction.' *An Essay on the Origin and Importance of Small Tracts and Fugitive Pieces*, reprinted in *A Miscellany of Tracts and Pamphlets*, ed. A. C. Ward (Oxford 1927), 387.

[10] Public Record Office, London, *State Papers* (Domestic Series), 8 January 1668.

[11] J. Rushworth, *Historical Collections*, 7 vols (1650–1701), II, 220ff.

mal innovations and are explicit in the way he supersedes older theatrical forms in the very act of using them anew. But his movement is ineluctably elitist and escapist. The jeerers are expelled and the world of every day is left to Fly and his crew. As he moves towards pastoral he romanticises his lower characters and their rural settings, employs dialect and folk motifs, preluding his retreat in space and time to Sherwood Forest and a distant 'Landt-shape of Forrest, Hils, Vallies, Cottages, A Castle, A River, Pastures, Heards, Flocks, all full of Countrey simplicity': in the words of a great teacher of our own day, 'an organic community with the living culture it embodied' where one might find 'an art of life, a way of living, ordered and patterned, involving social arts, codes of intercourse and a responsive adjustment, growing out of immemorial experience to the natural environment and rhythm of the year';[12] where all evil is compressed at last, as at first in such a paradise, in a single figure outside the self, the witch Maudlin.

Failed by court or university, audience or students, Jonson evidences the same virtues and limitations of all whose passionate defence of minority culture is beyond criticism so long as it remains in a condition of high-minded self-abstraction from mass civilisation. However intemperate he might be, there is no questioning his integrity; as a teacher and dramatist he was courageous and ingenious in finding ways of mediating his values in forms all too capable of abuse by virtue of their public nature and in offering an imaginative reconstruction of British society which would make possible a life lived finely and responsibly. Neither the tone of the 'Ode to himself' and the 'Dedication, To the Reader' of The New Inn, nor his quarrel with Inigo Jones, should too easily divert us from the broader sympathy and generosity of spirit which the last plays show. They are not adequate to the problems he faces, his concern for people suffers from the artistic refinement which he so earnestly pursues, and his strategy of reformation is too cerebral to affect the court, too impersonal to strike the heart. But the concern goes deep and the skill to serve it is so seriously and dutifully offered that its rejection must have caused Jonson unimaginable pain.

> But doe him right
> He meant to please you: for he sent things fit,
> In all the numbers, both of sense and wit.
> [The New Inn, Epilogue]

And he never failed in intelligence:

> All that this faint and faltring tongue doth crave
> Is, that you not impute it to his braine,
> That's yet unhurt, although set round with paine,
> It cannot long hold out.
> [Ibid.]

---

[12] F. R. Leavis and Denys Thompson, Culture and Environment (London 1933), 150.

We should do him wrong to buttress our own cynicism or sociological self-righteousness by wrenching out of shape a fine play like The New Inn and converting it into a bitter attack on the false court or a parody of the absurdities of romantic comedy. It has such things in it, but it moves seriously and with deliberation towards a transformation scene which, in a most sophisticated act of theatre, offers to create within us an apprehension of the virtues that should inform our conduct and of the beauty which illumines the sensuous world that we inhabit. In this play Jonson creates a mode of discourse close to pastoral, and because he allows the relation between art and life, between literary experience and social action, to be less direct, more mysterious, he evades the test of literal truth.

> LOV. Is this a dreame now, after my first sleepe?
> Or are these phant'sies made i'the light Heart?
> And sold i'the new Inne? HOST. Best goe to bed,
> And dreame it ouer all.
>   [The New Inn, V.v.120–3]

The end of the play exists at the shadow-line of dream and waking, and when with the play behind them the characters 'goe out, with a Song' they invest the articulated vision of poetry with the even more comprehensive harmonies of a music heard but not seen.

> Where should this music be? i'the'air, or the'earth?

asked Shakespeare's Ferdinand. But Jonson's Lovel finds beauty in the palpable world of

> A skeine of silke, without a knot!
>   A faire march made without a halt!
>   A curious forme without a fault!
> A printed booke without a blot! . . .
>   [The New Inn, IV.iv.9–12]

and his poem sanctifies the most intimate union of sense and spirit when he offers it

> to light us all to bed, 'twill be instead
> Of ayring of the sheets with a sweet odour.
>   [Ibid., V.v.151–2]

There is nothing escapist about pastoral as such. At its best it places the feverish world of politics and restores a sense of the deeper rhythms of life which politics should serve. And in any case there is a toughness of experience in and beyond The New Inn which gives Jonson every right to his romantic close:

> I am he
> Have measur'd all the Shires of England over,
> Wales, and her mountaines, seene those wilder nations,
> Of people in the Peake, and Lancashire;

> Their Pipers, Fidlers, Rushers, Puppet-masters,
>   Iuglers and Gipseys, all the sorts of Canters,
>   And Colonies of Beggars, Tumblers, Ape-carriers;
>   For to these sauages I was addicted,
>   To search their natures, and make odde discoveries!
>   [*Ibid.*, V.v.92–100]

Of *The New Inn* Professor Bentley was probably right to say 'That the play deserved to fail in production can scarcely be doubted by any theatre-wise reader,'[13] for the art of theatre is rougher than sometimes, fondly, we imagine. Whatever the seriousness of Jonson's intention or the care he took to structure the event, it was no proof against drunken, tired, or disagreeable audiences, for which there is more evidence than for the intuition of solemn truths. And he felt himself triply betrayed this time for, if the king's subjects proved squeamish and censorious beholders, the King's Servants seemed also to have lost their integrity because *The New Inn* 'was neuer acted, but most negligently play'd,' and the court performance was cancelled.

The play is finer than much criticism or its all too brief theatrical history suggest, but the brute fact of its failure is proof of a kind that Jonson's dream of a degenerate monarchy transfigured, or of a factious and schismatic society reconciled, was incapable of realisation even as an image 'devis'd and play'd to take spectators.'

> It was a beauty that I saw,
>   So pure, so perfect, as the frame
>   Of all the universe was lame,
> To that one figure, could I draw,
> Or give least line of it a law!
>   [*The New Inn*, IV.iv.4–8]

There's a touching note of incomprehension there which is part of the mystery itself, but it is not far either from political bewilderment. Cruelly deceived in his hopes of a judicious hearing, Jonson turned again to his readers.

> How-so-ever, if thou canst but spell, and ioyne my sense, there is more hope of thee, than of a hundred fastidious *impertinents*, who were there present the first day . . .
>   [*The New Inn*, Dedication, To the Reader]

Plagued by illness and a dilatory and careless printer, Jonson was again to be disappointed. *The New Inn* appeared but his projected second folio collection of 1631 proved abortive, and his hopes of those who could but spell cannot have been profound. For in *The Staple of News* he had already diagnosed the ills of this society in terms of a populace seduced by its own curiosity into a dizzy search for novelty, dazzled and mesmerised by surface display in dress and theatre, betrayed of

---

[13] G. E. Bentley, *The Jacobean and Caroline Stage*, 7 vols (London 1941–6), IV, 623.

its birth-right by the economic exploitation of language in corrupting imitation of the public riot, and educated away from virtue and knowledge by an unholy alliance of business interests, professional ambitions, and colleges of higher learning. It sounds like a powerful and relevant indictment, and there is behind it a generalised concern for people that would save them from themselves.

> For your owne sakes, not his, he bad me say,
> Would you were come to heare, not see, a Play.
> [*The Staple of News*, Prologue for the Stage]

Modern instances seem only to confirm its truth:

> films, newspapers, publicity in all its forms, commercially-catered fiction—all offer satisfaction at the lowest level, and inculcate the choosing of the most immediate pleasures, got with the least effort.[14]

Like the theatre in Jonson's time, films

> provide now the main form of recreation in the civilised world; and they involve surrender under conditions of hypnotic receptivity, to the cheapest emotional appeals, appeals the more insidious because they are associated with compellingly vivid illusions of actual life.

Such a culture is disseminated by economic and literal mechanics and

> it is vain to resist the triumph of the machine. It is equally vain to console us with the promise of a 'mass culture' that shall be utterly new. It would, no doubt, be possible to agree that such a 'mass culture' might be better than the culture we are losing, but it would be futile: the 'utterly new' surrenders everything that can interest us.[15]

Jonson may cry 'Come, leave the loathed Stage,' but he finds no consolation outside in 'the more loathsome Age' where

> 'Twere simple fury, still thy selfe to wast
> On such as have no taste!
> ['*Ode to Himselfe*,' ll. 13–14]

Although he is aware from his own experience that no man is so lowly that he may not grow in both virtue and authority, Jonson adheres to court ideals and reverts to ridicule and sarcastic summation of this other England. But political ideas in their popular form will rarely be expressed initially through rational debate and any expectation he had of the conscious restoration of an ordered, equitable, and single-minded society in an atomistic England was a pathetic

---

[14] Leavis and Thompson, 3.

[15] F. R. Leavis, *Mass Civilisation and Minority Culture* (London 1930), 9–10, 30. The last sentiment is close to that of Henry James in a letter to William, who had recommended a 'Newspaporial' bearing: 'The multitude, I am more and more convinced, has absolutely no taste—none at least that a thinking man is bound to defer to.' See Leon Edel, *Henry James: The Conquest of London 1870–1883* (London 1962), 71.

illusion. He tried, with some success, to make his stage a speaking picture, but it went against the grain and he could never fully accept that demonstration was a dramatic language and therefore a political one too for those who had no other or for whom the existing one was obsolete. It is a truth that Shakespeare's Volumnia would have put to use:

> Action is eloquence, and the eyes of the ignorant
> More learned than the ears.
>
> [*Coriolanus*, III.ii.76–7]

But Jonson can ask nothing kindly of the crowd because he can only will its dissolution. It is no accident that in commenting on Shakespeare's mingled drama and saying that there is always an appeal open from criticism to nature, Jonson's namesake should observe that 'the high and the low co-operate in the general system by unavoidable concatenation.'

For if *The Staple of News* appears from one point of view to be an accurate forecast of a disastrous economic and cultural conspiracy, and singularly percipient in seeing an organised news network run for profit as the quite new phenomenon of a mass medium with comprehensive social and political consequences, from another point of view, like all the late plays, it too clearly shows the thoroughly reactionary nature of Jonson's political idealism. The voice that speaks truthfully both to its own times and to the embryonic future is that raised against the paternalistic spirit with its own limiting preconceptions:

> Nor is it to the common people less than a reproach; for if we be so jealous over them, as that we dare not trust them with an English pamphlet, what doe we but censure them for a giddy, vitious, and ungrounded people; in such a sick and weak estate of faith and discretion as to be able to take nothing down but through the pipe of a licencer. That this is care or love of them, we cannot pretend . . .
>
> [*Areopagitica* (1644), 23]

The pasteboard eloquence of the later masques was more self-revealing than even Jonson dared to believe. So too was the popular press. As an indicator of 'the body of the time, his form and pressure,' it mirrored more faithfully and in a richer dialectic than could Jonson's attenuated formalism and abstracted values the diversity of an England stirring at last to protest more openly against religious intolerance and political, social, and economic privilege, and struggling to define in a quite new way the nature of political responsibility. Jonson does not allow himself this density of material, nor therefore a corresponding complexity of analysis. Paradoxically, the deliberative ingenuity of his dramatic structure, instead of serving a deeper artistic compulsion, now inhibits it, as though the frame were more important than the mirror and order the one desperate necessity.

Truth's 'first appearance to our eyes bleared and dimmed with prejudice and custom is more unsightly and unplausible than many errors,' said Milton. The language of Jonson's jeerers is a crude caricature of an emergent dialogue by means of which the full range of the society, and the nature of the necessary accommodation, were at last knowable.[16]

In *News from the New World* Jonson had distinguished printer from factor. It was the latter who hoped

> to erect a Staple for newes ere long, whether all shall be brought and thence againe vented under the name of Staple-newes . . . [for] it is the Printing I am offended at, I would have no newes printed; for when they are printed they leave to bee newes; while they are written, though they be false, they remaine newes still.
>
> [II.45–7, 57–60]

The point is a neat way of relating news to opinion and rumour; it has its own predictive relevance to the ephemerality of some visual and aural media-content of our own time; and it is taken over into the later play. But the more important perception is Jonson's awareness of a development within the book trade separating artisan printers from entrepreneurial booksellers and an equation of freedom of the Company with investment in its stock, made up largely of textbook copyrights. When shareholders in the Staple combine in turn with the jeerers to staff the College of Canters, he completes with perfect consistency the link between economic freedom, capital investment, and education.

Just as the popular press was a reflection of an egalitarian movement, and immensely educative in forming a new language for talking about politics, so too developments in education outside the two universities and the Inns of Court were the natural expression of an independence of mind in religion and science for the forms of which Jonson had little sympathy. Lectureships in particular flourished in the 1620s. And Jonson's professional jeerers in their university of the air of 1626 are not far removed in time or style from the lecturers whom Charles called 'furious promoters of the most dangerous innovations' or those who, for Laud in 1629, 'by reason of their pay are the people's creatures and blow the bellows of their sedition.'[17]

More striking however is the parallel between the College of Canters and Gresham College, founded by a merchant, administered jointly by the City and the Mercers' Company, not by the Church, with lectures in English delivered 'In the most perspicuous method,' not as textual exegesis, and shaped with an absence of pedantry 'to the good liking and capacity of the hearers.'[18] There were seven

[16] Jonson and Milton both pay their tributes to Selden, but for Milton he is 'the chief of learned men reputed in this Land . . . whose volume of naturall & national laws proves, not only by great authorities brought together, but by exquisite reasons and theorems almost mathematically demonstrative, that all opinions, yea, errors, known, read, and collated, are of main service & assistance toward the speedy attainment of what is truest' (*Areopagitica*, 11).

[17] Christopher Hill, *The Century of Revolution 1603–1714* (London 1972), 83–5, 145.

[18] *An Account of the Rise, Foundation, Progress and Present State of Gresham College in London* (1707), passim. A convenient and informative discussion is that by Christopher Hill in *The Intellectual Origins of the English Revolution* (London 1972), 34–61. For Jonson's association with Gresham College see Herford and Simpson XI, 582–5, and C. J. Sisson, *Times Literary Supplement*, 21 September 1951. I am grateful to Professor L. A. Beaurline for suggesting the connection with *The Staple of News*.

professorships which, in their traditional number at least if not in all subjects, parallel those nominated for the College of Canters, as well as one moiety of the Staple parts.[19] Jonson's attitude to Gresham College must have been equivocal since many of his friends were associated with it and he himself may have lectured there on rhetoric in 1623. But it is hard to resist the conclusion that its religious affiliations, openness to practical learning and scientific demonstration, its economic auspices and popular pitch, were signs of a pragmatism too much at odds with his own vision of society for Jonson to tolerate.

These developments in news services and education that Jonson had seen fit to link dignified their audiences. By contrast, and fearful of popular influence on government, Jonson vilified them. But the culture needed to yield men of good judgment is not easily acquired and is scarcely available at all to most. To plead its necessity as a form of exclusion is a common strategy of established authority against aspirant power, perhaps simply of middle age against youth. The argument is sound in everything except a sympathetic sense of the pressures it excludes and can no longer quite control. Despite his formal innovations, what Jonson and perhaps criticism of him most lack here, in the moment of arguing for it, is a supple political language adequate to the times, and his conservative sympathies lead him away from its possibilities rather than towards them. Such a language was shaped in the years that followed, but it would be naive to think that its fine flowering in the writings of a Clarendon, Hobbes, Harrington, or Winstanley owed nothing to the developments in publishing and teaching which Jonson derides, for these were its undergrowth where the expression of particular conflicting needs, political, economic, and spiritual, sharpened moral awareness and created tensions which gave a fine edge to judgment.

Since Jonson insists on his function as teacher and on the relation between his feigned society and the real one, and since he exposes Nathaniel Butter to such heatedly withering ridicule that he ought simply to have melted away, it may not be such a naive question to ask whether that sounding brass, the press, symbol of mass ignorance, did anything but

> deride
> The wretched; or with *buffon* licence ieast
> At whatsoe'r is serious, if not sacred.
> [*The Staple of News*, V.vi.9–11]

---

[19] At I.v. 106–8 Cymbal says that he has 'the iust *moyetie*' for his part in the news office and that the other moiety is divided into seven parts. If, as Herford and Simpson suggest (II, 173–5), Cymbal is modelled on Captain Thomas Gainsford, this would leave the other moiety in the hands of the booksellers. Of the seven parts, six were full shares and one was divided into two half-shares. In the extant news pamphlets for the period 1622–6 six names, and only six names, frequently recur: those of Nathaniel Butter, Thomas Archer, Nicholas Bourne, William Sheffard, Bartholomew Downes, and Nathaniel Newbury. This actual syndicate corresponds very closely to the structure of Jonson's Staple. There could well have been a seventh part too, but its subdivision would have given the two shareholders only a small part in the venture and their names would be unlikely to appear in the imprints.

Leafing quickly through some news-sheets of early 1622, I came upon the following passage. It is not great and it has its point of view, but like that of many fine sermons in the period its focus is community, not conquest, and it would not disgrace the pages of our liberal press today in its concern to drive beyond partisan views to describe the ravages of war and the plight of those caught in it. The Dutch imprint on this news pamphlet is almost certainly spurious and it was probably printed by Edward Allde, one of several printers used by Bourne, Butter, and Archer to transmit such trifles through the barriers of censorship in order to satisfy the curiosity of their customers in 'a weekly cheat to draw mony.'

> By the occasion of these warres, and dilacerating the peace and plenty of Countries, this goodly Prouince of the Palatinate had come into the hands of cruell vsurpers, and vnnatural strangers, who haue respected nothing, but the present time, and supplying of wants, not caring what became of her hereafter, nor how deformed they made her for to welcome her owne parents: For they cut downe her Woods, even before Franckendale, and other places, to preuent annoyance from the Enemy, who kept in the same as vnder shelter, and from thence made many sallyes vpon the people, and lay as it were in Ambuscado to surprise the Souldiers: they ouertrampled her Vines, and made the hoofes of their Horses speake cruelly to the rootes: they digged up her fields for Trenches and Bulwarks: they pulled downe their houses round about their Townes to raise rauelings and counterscarps, they oppressed the people, suffering no man to enjoy his owne, nor to giue it away to whom they pleased: so that they which before in a manner liued securely without walls, and fortifications, are not now safe within walls, trenches, and the mounting of Cannons: and this is the misery of discention, and the rage of Princes, who will not be pacified without mischiefe and reuenge, as is apparant all ouer Bohemia and those Countries, where the Enemies haue come in with the sound of hostility.[20]

Again we might do worse than seek honest comment from Dr Johnson, who said that 'wit can stand its ground against truth only a little while,' and compound that remark with another in his *Essay on the Origin and Importance of Small Tracts and Fugitive Pieces* which recognised that 'In such writings may be seen how the mind has been opened by degrees . . .'[21]

Jonson is agile in self-defence and although he had to append a note to the readers of *The Staple of News* to insist on his allegory, he had already built in a defensive device in Canter's words:

> If thou had'st sought out good and vertuous persons
> Of these professions: I'had lou'd thee and them:
> For these shall neuer have that plea 'gainst me,
> Or colour of aduantage, that I hate
> Their callings, but their manners, and their vices.
> [*The Staple of News*, IV.iv. 135–9]

[20] *Newes from the Palatinate*, 'Printed at the Hage. 1622,' 10–11. There can be no doubt of course that the object of the news report was to inform and strengthen protestant opinion in England and to secure James's intervention in the Palatinate.

[21] Loc. cit., 388–9.

Canter's catalogue of professions makes no provision, however, for the role of the press as a public teacher, and in the note to the readers to which I have just referred Jonson makes clear his complete rejection of its right to any such function. The contrast he draws is not between a responsible and an irresponsible press, but between poets and news-vendors, ideal truth and that literal falsehood or competing fantasy of news made like

> the times *Newes*, (a weekly cheat to draw mony) and [it] could not be fitter reprehended, then in raising this ridiculous *Office* of the *Staple*, wherein the age may see her owne folly, or hunger and thirst after [*not righteousness, but*] publish'd pamphlets of *Newes*, set out euery Saturday, but made all at home, & no syllable of truth in them: then which there cannot be a greater disease in nature, or a fouler scorne put vpon the times. And so apprehending it, you shall doe the *Author*, and your owne iudgement a courtesie, and perceiue the tricke of alluring money to the *Office*, and there cooz'ning the people. If you haue the truth, rest quiet, and consider that
>   Ficta, voluptatis causa, sint proxima veris.

The sinister interpretation which Jonson was at pains to discount must have found parallels not only between 'Aurelia Clara Pecunia, the Infanta' and the Infanta of Spain, but between the prodigal Pennyboy Junior and Charles I, who assumed his full patrimony with his coronation robes on 2 February 1626, only a week or two before the play was performed. Given that, it is not at all difficult to spin a fanciful web in which the abortive Spanish match casts the glittering Buckingham as Cymbal in a group of Charles's false friends, the discord between Pennyboy Canter and Pennyboy Junior mirrors that between the late king and the prince, the abuse of Pecunia directly symbolises prostitution of the court masque (itself a measure of economic profligacy), Pennyboy Canter images the death and hopeful resurrection of James I in posthumous admonishment of his errant son, and even the dead Prince Henry, the elder brother of the parable, is present—by being absent.

> . . . though they are not truths, th'innocent *Muse*
> Hath made so like, as Phant'sie could them state,
> Or *Poetry*, without scandall, imitate.
>   [*The Staple of News*, Prologue for the Court]

Happily we have to reject these speculations: quite apart from Jonson's admonition and Mirth's salutary example, there is too little scholarly evidence and there are too many inconsistencies. Nevertheless they sharpen the platitude that Jonson saw his role as that of a serious public commentator observing quite concrete events whose underlying pattern it was his duty to discern, restructure, criticise, and realise in a public form.

> All that dable in the inke,
> And defile quills, are not those few, can thinke,
> Conceiue, expresse, and steere the soules of men,
> As with a rudder, round thus, with their pen.
>   [*The Staple of News*, Prologue for the Stage]

But those who dabbled in the ink were no longer simply poetasters like Madrigal, seeking a false reputation as artists by turning a vacuous lyric with merely technical skill. They were reporters of public events, and the conflicting information they offered, the variety of motive and opinion, shifted the burden of interpretation to the individual himself. Without the dramatist's powers of analysis and recreation he may have been most faint, but what strength he had *was* his own. The development of political responsibility in the seventeenth century, of which Jonson's audience games are a negative image, is inseparable from the growth of a new public function for the press and its writers. This is why the animus against mere news is central to Jonson's conception of the play and why it is not to be subordinated to some more abstracted, if formally unifying, theme. In a sense true of none of the other late plays, although they show its consequences, *The Staple of News* marks the end of theatre as the only secular mass medium, the end of the play-house as the principal forum of public debate, the end of the actors' popular function as the abstracts and brief chronicles of the time. The dramatic poet, as rhetor in the truest sense, had lost his vocation to a journalist.

8

Typography and Meaning:
The Case of William Congreve

(981)

First delivered at a symposium in Germany in 1977, this essay extends the argument of McKenzie's unpublished Sandars Lectures, "The London Book Trade in the Later Seventeenth Century," given at Cambridge a year earlier. Drawing on his extensive experience as an editor of Congreve, he challenges some of the established orthodoxies of textual editing which he found inadequate to cope with the historical realities confronting him in the 1710 three-volume octavo edition of Congreve's collected *Works*. In particular, W. W. Greg's seminal distinction between "substantives" and "accidentals," as commonly appropriated by scholarly editors, was, he found, too narrowly mechanical and historically unimaginative to do justice to the comprehensively expressive bibliographical form that the playwright had created in close collaboration with his publisher Jacob Tonson and the printer John Watts. Together they deployed a variety of typographical, bibliographical, and textual resources—many of them involving so-called accidentals—to bridge the gap between the ephemeral, three-dimensional stage and the enduring, two-dimensional page. Abandoning the generic form of the earlier quarto editions, which made no attempt to be expressive in this way, Congreve and his associates also conferred a more dignified cultural status on the text by adapting neoclassical conventions of formal presentation. Taking up a central theme of his "Printers of the Mind," McKenzie once again insists that the production of meaning and value is ineluctably collaborative. To produce the 1710 *Works*, Congreve needed Tonson, and Tonson needed his master printer, Watts.

As McKenzie affirms, the case of Congreve has larger methodological implications for textual studies. Adducing a wide range of references—he cites Stanley Fish, Hayden White, Frances Yates, speech-act theory, Chagall, and Picasso—he contends that "current theories of textual criticism" are "quite inadequate to cope" with the historical complexities of book production. A "new and comprehensive sociology of the text" should be developed if scholarly editing is to give proper weight to the intricacies of intention and the "architecture" and "visual language" of books. Although McKenzie never underestimates the importance of the author, he advocates an historically nuanced understanding of the political, economic, and social conditions of agents' intentions in every phase of the production process. As a consequence, in seeking to "marry the verbal preoccupations of literary and textual criticism, the material concerns of historical bibliography, and the economic and social dimensions of production and readership," he maintains that the text is best understood as "a complex structure of meanings which embraces every detail of its formal and physical presentation in a specific historical context." Accordingly, textual criticism needs to engage creatively with the history of the book.

198

C ONGREVE'S last play, *The Way of the World*, was performed early in March 1700, and although Dryden thought it had "but moderate success," Congreve himself was pleased enough. "That it succeeded upon the stage," he later wrote, "was almost beyond my Expectation; for but little of it was prepar'd for that general Taste which seems now to be predominant in the Pallats of our Audience."

The date, 1700, is a convenient one for our purposes; and Congreve's comment on the new tastes of those who patronized the theatre is a timely reminder that the ways of the world were changing as a new century was ushered in. Congreve, the practising playwright, belongs to the last decade of the 17th century; Congreve, the book maker, intimate friend of the great bookseller Jacob Tonson and sophisticated editor of his own *Works*, belongs indubitably to the 18th century. The movement from one century to the next, as mirrored in the differences between the quarto editions in which his plays were first published and the 3-volume octavo edition of *Works* 1710, is a most instructive one for the history of the book.

An explanation of the form of *Works* 1710 has its roots deep in the 17th century. I have tried elsewhere to trace some of them, but I must take a moment to recall in outline part of the larger argument I there used.[1] Briefly, the plays were printed and reprinted in quarto in a form which was probably fairly close to Congreve's autograph. In these editions the act and scene divisions, and the stage directions, follow the editorial and typographic conventions of the Elizabethan period. In his 3-volume octavo *Works* of 1710, Congreve revised the quarto texts, suppressed their indecent expressions, and adopted neoclassical scene division and character groupings. He saw this edition through the press himself, working in the closest possible collaboration with his bookseller and friend Jacob Tonson and with Tonson's printer John Watts. The authority of Congreve's preface, recommending that edition "as the least faulty Impression, which has yet been Printed," and noting the care he has taken "both to Revise the Press, and to Review and Correct many Passages in the Writing," command respect. Even more important perhaps is the very conception of *Works* as embodying a principle of self-esteem:

> It will hardly be deny'd, that it is both a Respect due to the Publick, and a Right which every Man owes to himself, to endeavour that what he has written may appear with as few Faults, as he is capable of avoiding. This consideration alone, were sufficient to have occasion'd this Edition.

The integrity of Congreve's collected *Works* in all its details is what we must first note. The author's preface, the readings of the text itself, its act and scene divisions after the neoclassical manner, its use of decorative head- and tail-pieces, the ornamental drop initials for each act, the type ornaments which separate the scenes, the size and styles of type, its capitalisation, punctuation, italicisation, its mise-en-

---

[1] *The London Book Trade in the Later Seventeenth Century*, being the Sandars Lectures for 1975–1976. The present paper extends the argument of the third lecture.

page, paper, the slighter bulk and lighter weight of its three-volume octavo format and the disposition of contents within and among those three volumes:—the highly conscious deployment of all these resources makes it quite impossible, in my view, to divorce the substance of the text on the one hand from the physical form of its presentation on the other. The book itself is an expressive means. To the eye its pages offer an aggregation of meanings both verbal and typographic for translation to the ear; but we must learn to see that its shape in the hand also speaks to us from the past. The full explication of those meanings, in all their contextual richness, is the prime textual function of historical bibliography. An edition of Congreve, for example, which failed to take account of the way in which the finest details of authorial intention were mediated by the trade to a preconceived and firmly defined readership, could not avoid gross textual error. Congreve, and indeed the 18th century, a period in which book form is an explicit and pervasive concern, is a useful point at which to marry the verbal preoccupations of literary and textual criticism, the material concerns of historical bibliography, and the economic and social dimensions of production and readership. The general theory which embraces them all, and would demonstrate their intimate relationship, is best described perhaps as "a sociology of the text."

The form of the quarto editions of Congreve's plays, on stage and in print, is intimately related to the theatrical tradition on the one hand and a set of publishing conventions for dramatic texts on the other. Throughout the 17th century, however, these two traditions had little in common. There is a professional disjunction of playwrights and printers. Before the ubiquity of newsbooks in the 1640's, the only secular mass medium was the stage. Its setting, the playhouse, was the principal secular forum of public debate. The writers who worked in it—Marlowe, Shakespeare, Jonson—were the news reporters of their day, analysts of personal and social action for a non-literate audience; their ethical duty as Jonson put it, was to

> speake of the intents,
> The councells, actions, orders, and events
> Of state, and censure them.

Its modes were oral and visual. The expressive instruments of its art were the voices and gestures of actors whose skilled articulacy in performance—when at its best—transformed the written word into a living experience which the audience thereby made its own. It was of course self-evident that print was not the proper medium for plays; most reached the printinghouse in a fortuitous and often surreptitious manner; and because the London book trade lacked any kind of literary idealism that acknowledged the popular drama as commanding typographic respect, few plays showed any intelligent and sustained editing for press. As a result, the textual models we have adopted for the drama reflect only the commercial opportunism of printers in the early 17th century, a time when the theatre was alive and confident of its own distinctively oral and visual mode. Later in the century we have only the ossified typography of a trade largely indifferent to the quite specific requirements, in book design, of dramatic texts. My point then is that the form of Congreve's quartos, in striking contrast to *Works*, is a direct expression of historical conditions quite unrelated to authorial intention and insensitive to the problems of mediating a theatrical experience in book form. Was there a moment in history when Congreve and Tonson, two intelligent, sensitive and original men, decided to make their pages speak, to edit and design their plays in a way which gave typography a voice in the hand-held theatre of the book?

I

I wish now to turn to certain theoretical considerations. It was, I believe, a recognition of historical conditions such as those I have mentioned that led the late Sir Walter Greg to develop his distinction between—and I quote—

> the significant, or as I shall call them "substantive", readings of the text, those namely that affect the author's meaning or the essence of his expression, and others, such in general as spelling, punctuation, word division, and the like, affecting mainly its formal presentation, which may be regarded as the accidents, or as I shall call them "accidentals", of the text.[2]

In a related footnote, he recognises of course that punctuation affects meaning but adds that "still it remains properly a matter of presentation, as spelling does in spite of its use in distinguishing homonyms. The distinction I am trying to draw is practical, not philosophic." That practical distinction, however, I need hardly remind you, has had a profound influence on editorial practice for the early 17th century drama, for that of the 18th century including my author Congreve, and for 19th century American writers. And current editorial practice based on that distinction has had the effect of inhibiting the development of a general theory of textual criticism which would embrace the history of the book. In its application by others, Greg's practical distinction has been utterly divisive, shattering any concept of the integrity of the book as an organic form, a material statement in which all its elements participate, a comprehensive rhetorical structure articulating an extremely complex set of relationships between author, bookseller, printer and reader in specific and definable historical contexts.

Greg's distinction of course, at least in others' use of it, has not been without its critics, but before turning to their objections I should like to isolate one other element in his statement. Greg's terms "substantive" and "accidental" are in fact translations; the first is a short-hand term for "the significant . . . readings . . . that affect the author's meaning or the essence of his expression"; the second is a matter of "its formal presentation." The first of these has hardened into a simple notion of authorial intention: one that underlies such definitions of textual criticism as "the establishment of a text as near as possible to that

---

[2] W. W. Greg, "The Rationale of Copy-Text," in *Collected Papers*, ed. J. C. Maxwell (Oxford, 1966), p. 376.

intended by the author." The words "author's meaning" and "essence of his expression" contribute the sense of an "ideal text." But this is contrasted with "its formal presentation," reinforcing what is almost a Platonic distinction between idea or essence on the one hand and its deforming, material embodiment on the other. Since I wish to suggest a line of argument which is almost exactly the reverse of this, one in which authorial control of the physical forms makes manifest the ideal, one in which the essence of a work's meaning is distilled in the detail of its formal presentation, I must offer some further comment on the theoretical implications of Greg's position.

It will be convenient to do so by considering three discussions by writers whose terms of reference are quite specifically biblio-textual. Each one rejects the idea of authorial intention as recoverable or constructable in an "ideal" or "definitive" edition. Each one would also reject as meaningful the distinction Greg drew between substantives and accidentals. So Morse Peckham, for example, in his "Reflections on the Foundations of Modern Textual Editing,"[3] states: "there is no 'definitive' version at which [an editor] must or can arrive. There is no one set of instructions which can mediate his behaviour to the exclusion of all other sets." For a moment he seems to admit some historical controls in the construction of certain versions of a work, insisting that "The analytical bibliographer is a historian, and he should not forget it for a moment," but this turns out to be a mere gesture, for he at once adds: "The object of his inquiry is not printed artifacts as physical objects but human behavior in the past, human behavior that no longer exists and *cannot now be examined*" (my italics). He later repeats the point: "situations are indefinable and an individual's perception and cognition of a situation are inaccessible as well as irrecoverable." In fact, he despairs of history and of the historical study of human behaviour. It was inevitable therefore that Peckham should also express dissatisfaction with the practical implications of Greg's "Rationale" and reject the distinction between substantives and accidentals: "The textual editor should do away with this theological terminology of accidentals and substantives, and talk simply and clearly about words, punctuation, spelling, capitalization, and whatever else he needs to talk about. These things are there, before our eyes; accidence and substance are not." The reminder is salutary, like much else in Peckham's article, but in default of an intelligent theory of history it leads nowhere. Few historians would thank him for the logic of his argument that authorial intention and reader response, since both are forms of human behaviour, cannot be examined let alone recovered. Although such a theoretical position allows one to present an eclectic text for any specified class of readers, it denies the possibility of access to, or the superior accuracy of, any edition which could represent the author's historic intention as embodied in his work for his contemporary readers.

---

[3] In *Proof* i (1971), 122–155, esp. 126, 131, 142, 155. Peckham properly emphasises Greg's restricted terms of reference: "Greg needed to make a distinction for a specific class of texts at a specific and limited period of dramatic history" (p. 124).

A much more carefully considered statement of dissent is Professor Hans Zeller's article "The Critical Constitution of Literary Texts."[4] He is particularly concerned with the problem of constructing a text from authoritative documents which differ because of authorial revision. In fact, he regards the problem as insoluble and is led to make two quite radical suggestions, each of which bears on Greg's "Rationale." The first involves rejection of the distinction between substantives and accidentals: "Should not the authority of a text be considered to extend equally to the texture of the text, to the relationship of its elements to one another and to the whole, and therefore to what constitutes a text as a text, to what makes it into a particular version?" "My conception rests on the linguistic idea of the text as a complex of elements which form a system of signs, both denoting (*signifiant*) and denoted (*signifié*). That it is a system means that a work consists not of its elements but of the relationships between them." This view of the text naturally leads to his second radical suggestion: that any textual change, however small, creates a distinct version because it modifies the interrelationship of elements which constitute the work. Again, then, there can be no question of an ideal, best or definitive edition, and no logical grounds for conflation. "Only the textual history is within the editor's reach: notes, extracts, drafts, when they have survived, and then the versions in chronological sequence, a diachronic succession of discrete semiotic systems." "As long as the editor sees his function as that of a historian, he has a wide range of freedom in the selection of the version for the edited text, but this version he must reproduce without contamination." Within each version "relationships exist not only between adjoining elements, but throughout the text on and between all levels, the phonological, metrical, rhythmical, symbolical, etc. . . . ."

Despite the lip service paid here to the editor as historian, to the historical status of the extant documents, and indeed to the historicity of each version as a distinct structure, Zeller's view of history, like Peckham's, is not good enough. Once more we are told that human behaviour in the past is much too complex for fruitful study:

> It is not possible (or only rarely, in exceptional cases), when a work is revised, to give a detailed account of the extent to which the reception of the first version, a change in society, a change in the author himself and in his relationship to his environment, a different incentive or purpose in publication, may be involved in the revision, and this holds the more true since right from the beginning, before he even thought of writing, the author was exposed to this play of forces from all sides. What is termed the intention of the author is an undetachable part of these forces, and therefore seems equally ill-suited as a criterion for editorial decisions or as a criterion for the evaluation of literary works.

Zeller's concept of structure, ostensibly the very basis of the theory of editing, is also critically and historically deficient. One might think that the concept of his-

---

[4] In *Studies in Bibliography* 28 (1975), 231–264, esp. 237, 240, 244, 256 n. 38.

torical relativity which confines authorial intention to a distinct version, and the concomitant insistence on the structural integrity of each version, would also open the way outwards to a *comprehensive* theory of textual criticism, one which would accommodate *every* possible historical relationship constituting the version. Since every structure implies reciprocal relationships, any authorial revision must imply an intention to modify those relationships. That intention, in turn, must a cause designed to create an effect. No theory of complex structure therefore can exclude inquiry into personal and social change, or into any aspect of that delicate network of inter-relationships which connects authorial intention and reader response. Professor Zeller's concept of structure, however, offers no such opening: ". . . for methodological reasons I find the idea perplexing" he writes, "that the editor should feel obliged not only to make inferences about the final intentions of an author, but also about the causes behind these intentions. I cannot regard the psyche of the author and its analysis as a substantial foundation for editing. All cases of actual and suspected self-censorship give rise to this kind of analysis."

Notwithstanding his gesture towards a complex theory of signs in his reference to "semiotic systems," Zeller's theory of versions implies an extremely limited structural field. It also forbids any concern for that extended structure constituted by the relationships between the discrete versions. Conflation, which as "contamination" is put quite beyond the pale, is simply an act of historical analysis and reconstruction within a more complex structural field. Zeller, frightened by his own logic, would leave that task to his readers, presenting them with the versions and bowing out before the delicate task of creating an historically accurate and complex structure of literary experience from them. Indeed, his description of the critical apparatus he proposes, with markings in the text and footnotes "to draw the attention of the reader to problems of textual criticism and to possible solutions while he is reading the text . . ." make quite transparent his indifference to a semiotic system which includes any historical sensitivity to book form. In my innocence as a pupil of Dr. F. R. Leavis at Cambridge, I was accustomed to think that the function of an edition of a literary work was to draw its readers into a literary experience and not to distract them into admiration of the editor's critical indecisiveness. Whatever an author intended in writing a work, it was not that a reader should study its genesis. But it is, alas, a fashionable idiocy, occasioned mainly by editors' widespread ignorance of the history of typography and book design.

The essential weakness in Zeller's response to Greg lies in his reluctance to accept the full implications of his definition of "version" as a structure which, even within a single work, extends far beyond the verbal limits he prescribes. In the case of Congreve, his theory would preclude conflation of the quarto editions with *Works* 1710. We could have one or the other, but not both since he admits no concept of the work as a reconstruction of the author's intention which is superior to that offered by any extant version. Such a theory, indifferent as it is to historical evidence of the kind I shall offer about the book trade in respect of Congreve's intentions, would leave us with a much impoverished "text" of that writer's "work."

The third critic I wish to cite is Tom Davis.[5] Referring to the implications of Greg's distinction for texts sponsored by the Centre for Editions of American Authors, he writes:

> The problem is of considerable importance to textual critics, since they propose to reproduce each and every sign that constitutes the work itself, but to omit or normalize all those that do not. If their distinction between the two classes is insufficiently clear, they may either omit whole areas of signification that do have relevant meaning . . . or pay excessive and obsessive regard to trivia.

That puts the problem well, but does little to resolve it. Davis acknowledges that "signs that do not usually affect meaning may very often do so, or be thought by authors to do so"; but the concessive way in which he makes the point, suggests an underlying scepticism. In one case where an author's quite explicit statement of intention survives (Harington's directions to Richard Field for the typographic arrangement of a section of his translation of the *Orlando Furioso*), Davis states that these intentions can be ignored since they "do not affect what *readers would declare* to constitute the work" (my italics). Here again we have the common failure of both critical and historical imagination. There is of course no single undifferentiated class of readers but only a great variety of individuals who bring different degrees of intelligence and sensitivity to their understanding of literature. The conditions of the best informed response to a printed text are the ones we must keep on trying to define. Davis points up the confusion at the heart of the CEAA editions:

> The most absurd consequence of excessively rigid, and erroneous, adherence to Greg's distinctions is that all CEAA editors are committed simultaneously to the dedicated pursuit of authorial spelling and punctuation, while being equally committed to the belief that these phenomena are meaningless.

But he consigns himself to the same pit when delivering his coup de grâce:

> The usual method of getting round this is to talk about the "texture of the accidentals," an inherently meaningless notion that has received its apotheosis in the suggestion that "questions about 'accidentals' . . . should lead us to think more about the function and meaning of an author's 'texture'—perhaps taking some lessons from the criticism of the graphic and plastic arts."[6]

---

[5] "The CEAA and Modern Textual Editing," *The Library* 5th ser. xxxii (1977), 61–74, esp. 64–65.

[6] Davis is here quoting Thomas L. McHaney, "The important questions are seldom raised," *Studies in the Novel* vii (1975), 400–401. Davis's comments on Harington's instructions to his printer and on "what readers would declare to constitute the work" are, as it happens, answered by Harington himself in his vitally important "Advertisement to the reader before he reade this poeme of some things to be observed as well in the substance of this worke as also in the setting forth thereof, with the use of the Pictures, Table, and annotations to the same indexed." Harington's advertisement is considered further below.

This dismissive derision about the language of visual display is characteristic of current practice in denying the relevance, the meaning, of typographic form. I shall suggest, by contrast, that the study of Congreve's scene divisions, which is essentially a matter of book design, typographic resources and the disposition of space, is quite fundamental to his dramatic intention and therefore to the meaning of his work.

If we are to develop a general theory which embraces book form, it is essential to resolve the confusions and contradictions which those responses to Greg betray and to find some way of controlling by historical methods our subjective perception of what might be quite arbitrary patterns. This was precisely what Greg attempted to do in respect of dramatic texts printed in the early 17th century. The completely unhistorical application of his comments to other texts of other times and the rash of pseudo-philosophising which he explicitly sought to prevent, would have struck him as acts of monumental irrelevance.

The two specifically textual points which have emerged so far are these: first, a deep scepticism about the possibility of establishing authorial intention, and hence a reluctance to conflate texts of independent authority in order to construct an eclectic, ideal form of the work; second, a refusal to accept a distinction between substance and accidence accompanied by an equal refusal to accept the corollary of that view, namely that *all* signs have meaning, that every element of the structure to which they contribute—I mean the book—is a proper concern of textual criticism. Some of those signs may be wholly ossified, mere skeletons of a typology that was once alive. Others may be significant innovations. But because signs change meaning in the minds of authors and readers and in the practice of designers and printers, their study is essentially *historical*.

But that brief survey of three characteristic discussions of current editorial principle and practice makes it quite clear to me that we have at present no body of critical theory that encourages us to bring together the discrete activities which constitute the history of the book. The idea of a *text* as a complex structure of meanings which embraces every detail of its formal and physical presentation in a specific historical context is quite remote from current practice. The idea of a *work* as an act of historical reconstruction, transcending the distinctive extant versions or texts, is also out of favour. The reluctance to establish with analytical rigour the motives which constitute authorial intention, or the historical contexts of printing house and market which affected the formal mediation of that intention, or the theories of reader response implied by *every* element of book form, implicitly denies the textual utility of historical analysis. Peckham, we recall, was quite explicit: such "human behaviour no longer exists and cannot now be examined."

From two points of view I believe that conclusion to be entirely misplaced. First, we must take account of developments in critical theory, closely related to the need to develop analytical techniques for the study of sociological phenomena. Second, we must look into the past, not only for the material evidence of printing-house documents, but for any references at all which express conceptions of the book or demand that its readers interpret its signs in particular ways.

To take critical theory first. The discussion ranges from authorial intention to reader response and is focussed on the question: is literary history possible? Our question is parallel: is bibliotextual history possible, as a fine conjunction of literary, cultural, social, economic, material and behavioural history expressed in the world of the book?

Addressing himself to the question of literary history, the Germanist J. P. Stern writes:

> every story, poem, and play was written in time, belongs to time, and *shows its time*, so that in some way or other (and not always in the same way) it is datable; . . . this dating is not a mere contingency of the text (like finding out about carbon 14), but is a function of some aspect of the work that matters. The datability, that is, the historicity of works of literature, is demonstrable and thus obvious, yet it is not exactly banal. It alone makes literary history possible; it is one of the conditions that enable history to contribute to our understanding of an era of literature, and literary history to our understanding of the past . . .[7]

Alastair Fowler affirms the importance of establishing an historic intention; claims that the assumption on which any literary history must rest is the significance of *original meaning and value*; and stresses the nature of literary works as "public semiological forms [shaped according to a] schematic rhetoric."[8] Fowler is exacting in his application of historical controls, but unfortunately he concedes too readily the problem of validating our subjective responses. A history of literature, he writes, and we might add a history of typology, "that depends on a non-existent history of sensibility and psychological event is not very practical." The problem is the absence of data: "the only reader responses we can know in detail are our own."

Despite his formal position then, that view allies even Fowler with the simple and somewhat defeatist pragmatism of Peckham and Zeller. Their sense of difficulty derives partly, I believe, from our commitment to inductive method and its use in the natural sciences. It is a method that tempts us to assume that the only evidence that counts is physical, not behavioural. Thus we are led to place undue emphasis on the symbolic images of manuscript or printed word-forms rather than on the interpretative act of responding to them. But of course every observed detail is itself the statement of an interpretative (and itself time-bound) act; and that body of evidence built up, like the generalisation it yields, cannot be independent of judgement, cannot be other than an interpretative model.

This recognition leads me to the point made by Göran Hermerén, that as recent work in philosophy assumes, the analysis of meaning needs to be connected with the use of language for the purposes of communication, yielding a theory

---

[7] "From Family Album to Literary History," *New Literary History* vii (1975), 113–133, esp. 115. The entire number is a useful source for focussing current concerns in literary history.

[8] "The Selection of Literary Constructs," *New Literary History* vii (1975), 39–55, esp. 41, 45.

of speech *acts* and making the text a form of social action.[9] In its most intimate form this action is located in the text as an embodiment of the author's primary intention and of the author's informed response *as his own reader* and representative of those like him to whom his work is addressed: "Hypocrite lecteur, mon semblable." The word "hypocrite" reminds us that the reader is an actor. This theory, I should perhaps say here, is fundamental to my understanding of Congreve's attitude to the typology of his works.

Instead of weakly accepting then the critical and historical nescience of the position taken by Peckham and Zeller, we may turn to an increasing body of work in literary criticism (including the history of reading), philosophy and sociolinguistics which is helping to make clear that intention—the key to understanding the meaning of a text or statement—must always be understood "against a background of human conventions, expectations, practices and procedures" and "in terms of the function it has by its conformation to that wider context."[10] The elucidation of intended meanings takes place in study of the "linguistic, stylistic and symbolic conventions . . . at the time and place where the work was created."[11] Language, and not merely verbal but visual language, is thus firmly placed in a context infinitely richer than any conceived by Peckham, Zeller, or Davis.

The next stage of my argument is offered by Stanley Fish in his work *Self-Consuming Artifacts*. For Fish, the entire culture is a text in which each element becomes active in the mind of the reader. His critical assumptions in general rest, as he says:

> on the belief that reading is an activity, and that meaning, insofar as it can be specified, is coextensive with that activity, and not, as some would hold, its product. For the questions "What is this work about?" and "what does it say?" I tend to substitute the question "what is happening?" and to answer it by tracing out the shape of the reading experience, that is by focussing on the mind in the act of making sense, rather than on the sense it finally (and often reductively) makes.[12]

Such a view transfers the pressure and attention "from the work to its effects, from what is happening on the page to what is happening in the reader." In directing us as it does to behaviour in the reader, this theory is one I find especially fruitful for the study of dramatic texts.

At the heart of the debate about intention are two radically divergent views. One would universalise response, especially to literary texts; it is expansive,

---

[9] "Intention, Communication, and Interpretation," *New Literary History* vii (1975), 57–82.

[10] Cited by Quentin Skinner in "Hermeneutics and the Role of History," *New Literary History* vii (1975), 217, from A. J. Close, "*Don Quixote* and the Intentionalist Fallacy," *British Journal of Aesthetics* 12 (1972), 321–330.

[11] Hermerén, loc. cit. 75–76.

[12] *Self-Consuming Artifacts: The Experiencing of Seventeenth-Century Literature* (Berkeley, 1972), pp. xi–xii; see also pp. 3–4.

mythologising a work to the point where meaning is what is irreducibly common. The other would intensify response, seeking an historic and contextual accuracy in the recovery of every possible element of meaning as intended by an author and perceived by an intelligent and sensitive reader of his time. Both formulations are subject to historical analysis since even general theories of value have a historicity which we must reconstruct because they affect our understanding of social change. So the transition from an oral to a literate culture, with all that that implies for book form, the relation of vocalisation to visual symbolization, and therefore the degrees of sensitivity shown historically to the typology of the book (including our own diminished sense of it) are here in question.

Hayden White, writing on the problem of change in literary history, notes that the main traditions of literary criticism direct us

> to the historical context, the audience, the artist, and the work itself as elements constituting the literary field. And thus, we might want to say that any comprehensive study of the changes occurring in the field would have to take account of transformations in the relationships obtaining among the elements thus differentiated. If we could agree that changes in any one of these elements must cause changes in the modes of relationships obtaining among all of them, we could conceive of a cognitively responsible *historical* analysis of the field in general . . . This would permit us to delineate the various phases through which the field, considered as a historical structure in a distinctive process of evolution, had passed in its development from its earliest to its most recent manifestations.[13]

White's comments are applicable to change as a dynamic of the book trade, but I am not aware that anyone has developed a general theory which would order our investigation of authorial intention, its mediation and reader response in a comprehensive disciplined way. Equally, however, textual criticism is entirely innocent of the implications of such questions. Its intellectual timidity and mechanical zeal, if they persist in the face of such advances in other fields, are a guarantee of imminent oblivion.

II

I turn now to that other line of inquiry, the historical study of conceptions of the book and of the material means deliberately chosen and disposed by authors, editors, printers and booksellers to mediate meaning and stimulate response. I can do no more of course than simply indicate the classes of evidence which need to be studied if we are to trace a tradition of consciousness of the book.

One of them is, quite simply, collected works. The highly idiosyncratic conditions that applied to the printing of dramatic texts in the early 17th century and our preoccupation with Shakespeare as the central problem and referent of

---

[13] "The Problem of Change in Literary History," *New Literary History* vii (1975), 97–111, esp. 97–98.

textual theory, have been responsible not only for the sterile debates over substantives and accidentals (and proof-correction); they have, more seriously, distracted us from proper consideration of the expectations of writers not committed to the ephemeral art of theatre. But even the Shakespeare first folio poses a
question of design which ought to have been tackled much more seriously than
it has. Had we asked with some persistence why *The Tempest*—Shakespeare's last
play—should head the *Works* of 1623, we might have been taught to show more
sensitivity to the concept of *Works* as something more than the sum of their parts.
Certainly we should have looked much more intensely at the construction of
other books. A recent study of Jonson's *Epigrammes* shows that they constitute a
carefully organised, microcosmic, social unity.[14] So too his *Forest* and *Underwoods*
are verse collections shaped by a concept of natural form. Does Jonson's folio of
1616, whose printing he took such a painstaking interest in, have a comparable
architecture?

In what sense do some authors conceive of the comprehensive design of their
Works as expressing a personal integrity of experience, a life lived creatively?
Montaigne, we recall, wrote of his *Essais*, "c'est moy que je peins . . . je suis moy-
mesmes la matière de mon livre [it is myself that I am painting . . . I am myself
the material of my book]" and we relish his comic exploitation of the book as
an expression of himself in a intimate relationship of part to part. Marvell too
came close to the same thought: "where yourself are the experiment, it is as if a
man should dissect his own body and read the Anatomy Lecture." The book as
an "anatomy" of both subject and man could hardly be more explicit than it is
in Burton's *Anatomy of Melancholy*. Was Jonson simply indulging a conceit (albeit
one delicately related to the physical placing of his poem in the prelims) when
he asked Shakespeare's readers to "looke, Not on his Picture, but his Booke" as
the man himself? The common use of the word "Remaines" as a term for
posthumous works ambiguously suggests both the items remaining to be published and, as the earthly relics of a departed soul, the close identity of a man's
body and his printed works. John Jewel's *Works*, as edited by Featley in 1606, gives
continued life to his mind by enacting the dialectic of his debates in a way which
exemplifies the original controversies in their historical setting. Walton's edition
of Donne's *LXXX Sermons* (1640) seems also to have a deliberately expressive design, shaped to give ordered definition to the works as a life. The author as frontispiece is an emblematic way of making this very point. The Festschrift is perhaps our closest equivalent.[15]

This identity of book and person, or rather the idea of the physical elements
of the book as an expressive medium, is vividly applied by Othello when he

---

[14] Edward B. Partridge, "Jonson's *Epigrammes*: The named and the nameless," *Studies in the Literary Imagination* vi (April 1973), 153–198.

[15] It is a further deficiency of Hans Zeller's argument that it leaves out of account that extended structure, the collected *Works*, an oeuvre greater than the parts which make it up and shaped over their lifetime
by many authors in an act of ultimate self-definition.

questions Desdemona: "Was this fair paper, this most goodly book,/ Made to write 'Whore' upon?" (IV.ii. 71–72). The conceit of the book as an expression of the soul is also common in Shakespeare. So Orsino: "I have unclasped/ To thee the book even of my secret soul" (12N I.iv. 13–14); or in the sonnets: "The vacant leaves thy mind's imprint will bear" (77) and "O, let my books be then the eloquence/ And dumb presagers of my speaking breast" (23). The sonnet *sequence* is certainly a clear example of the way in which books were seen to unify personal experience by giving it a physical order as well as an expressive power.

Because books persisted in defining and ordering what was otherwise transient, one could refer, locate and learn again. So Shakespeare's Richard II reads in "the very book indeed/ Where all my sins are writ, and that's myself" (IV.i. 274–275); for Hamlet the ghost's commandment will live in "the very book and volume of [his] brain" (I.v. 103). Even the predictive value of a title page as a statement of character receives its apt expression in the lines "This man's brow, like to a title-leaf,/ Foretells the nature of a tragic volume" (1H VI.i. 60–61).

This anthropomorphism is inextricably linked with the idea of a structured statement in Nestor's words:

> . . . in such indexes, although small pricks
> To their subsequent volumes, there is seen
> The baby figure of the giant mass
> Of things to come at large.
> (TC I.iii. 343–346)

A similar parallel is drawn by Volumnia of Coriolanus's son: "This is a poor epitome of yours,/ Which, by the interpretation of full time,/ May show like all yourself" (V.iii. 68–70). The book as child is mirrored in Paulina's comments on Perdita who, "Although the print be little," is "the whole matter/ And copy of the father" and in Leontes' words to Florizel, whose mother "did print your royal father off,/ Conceiving you" (WT II.iii. 97–98, V.i. 125–126).

Even when less directly equated with the inner experience of its author, the book stood as both a map to his created world and the *theatrum mundi* itself. Is it not useful to ask then, in Renaissance terms, whether writers and readers entertained concepts of the book not only as a mind, a body, a child, but as a memory system, a world, a well-ordered state, a garden, a theatre, a *Temple*? As George Herbert's editor remarks of Buck's 1633 edition,

> It was good fortune for *The Temple* to be first printed by Thomas Buck, the best printer that Cambridge had yet had. The lay-out was so obviously right that for the next fourteen editions, that is for seventy-six years, it was unchanged.[16]

The book as an instrument of *power*, which cannot therefore be arbitrary in its form, is perhaps the central image of Shakespeare's *The Tempest*. Godyere's *Mirror of Maiestie* (1618) pictures the prince of a well-ordered state. His left half is dressed

---

[16] *The Works of George Herbert*, ed. F. E. Hutchinson (Oxford, 1941, repr. 1964), p. lxxvi.

in academic gown and mortarboard, his right in armour. One hand holds a book, the other a lance.[17]

The idea that a book itself might be an expressive intellectual structure, in the way that a building directly manifests abstract architectural forms, is not easy to grasp. But books like Spenser's *The Faerie Queene*, at least in conception, aspired to an elaborate and harmonious structuring of the ethical and political virtues (even if it settled for seven days or seven sins). Bacon's *Essays or Counsels, Civil and Moral*, even his conception of Solomon's House and the College of Six Days, Du Bartas's very popular *Divine Weekes*, imply an ordered disposition of knowledge. Miss Frances Yates has written percipiently of the form of such books as Billingsley's translation of Euclid, printed by John Day in 1570, with its long preface by John Dee, and the several works of Robert Fludd which are notable for their attempt to translate his intellectual structures physically in book form.[18] Nicolas Barker has drawn our attention to a mid-17th century edition of Comenius, to its crude block-cutting and four-column, quadrilingual layout. Even more interesting than its surface arrangement is the conception of the book *as a whole*. The organisation of the *Orbis Pictus* exemplifies a belief in the unity of all human experience and a particular manner of interpreting the perceptual world. The relationship of words and images expresses for Comenius the dependence of the world of ideas on that of sensory experience; it is at once therefore a political, religious and educational statement. "It is a little book, as you see, of no great bulk, yet a brief of the whole world . . ." His *Janua Linguarum Reserata* of 1631, with its 98 topics, 100 sections, and 1000 sentences, did not reach those figures by chance. The impressive series of handbooks envisaged by Comenius—*Encyclopaedia sensualium; Panhistoria; Pansophiae opus*—all imply a comprehensive unity which their printed form would have been shaped to articulate. His *Opera didactica omnia* (1657) replaced the formal, logical patterning by a psychological arrangement drawn from knowledge of mental development.[19] To organise knowledge so that

---

[17] Cited by Robert J. Clements, *Picta Poesis* (Rome, 1960), p. 145.

[18] See, for example, *Theatre of the World* (London, 1969), pp. 42–59, 190–197, and *The Rosicrucian Enlightenment* (St Albans, 1975), pp. 103–114. *The Art of Memory* (London, 1966) also has its relevance to the general question of the schematic statement of mental structures.

[19] On Comenius, see Waldemar Voise, "Le Livre, 'instrument primaire de l'éducation' aux yeux des adeptes de Comenius," *Revue Française d'Histoire du Livre* v (1975), 221–227; and the introduction by James Bowen to his edition of the third London edition (1672) of *Orbus Sensualium Pictus* (Sydney, 1967). Charles Webster's *The Great Instauration* (London, 1975) offers an invaluable account of such mid-17th century schemes for the codification of knowledge and for popular instruction. The point has perhaps received most attention (with even more valuable work to come from the researches of Robert Darnton) in relation to the rise of systematic encyclopaedias, and Diderot's 1750 prospectus for the *Encyclopédie* as a "tableau général" of mankind's achievements. But the earlier stages of the book as compendium or thesaurus of the works of nature, most notably in a work like Burton's *An Anatomy of Melancholy*, also warrant independent study from this point of view.

A closely related question, and an excellent locus for discussion of reader perception in a specific historical context, is the attempt made by several other 17th century writers to bring language as close as possible to the natural phenomena it designated. See R. F. Jones, "Science and Language in England in the mid-Seventeenth Century," in *The Seventeenth Century* (Stanford, 1951; repr. 1969), 143–160. Of such writers,

people had ready access to it was the social ideal of his Pansophic College: how was that principle actively applied in the designing of his books to that same end?

One of the points that Miss Yates makes about John Dee is his deep understanding of the basic Renaissance principle of "design," and what Dee says of "the whole feate of Architecture in buildyng" applies equally to books. Dee himself depends extensively upon Vitruvius and Alberti. So does Geofroy Tory, whose *Champfleury* quite explicitly relates typography and architecture. Each art involves the exact placing of forms in space, and each judgement is informed by a profound respect for number and analogy. Durer on the "just shaping of letters" shares those assumptions and relates his letter proportions to those of the human body. Tory develops his own critique of Durer but in doing so expands on the idea of the 23 attic letters as representing the nine muses, seven liberal arts, four cardinal virtues and three graces. The letter "Y" is emblematic of Hercules at the crossroads, the foot of the "L" corresponds to the relation between a man's upright body and his shadow cast by the sun in Libra. Our "eyes this cunning want to grace their art." But although we may have lost the capacity for discerning such correspondences between inanimate forms and human values, we should not impute their absence in former times. Tory's plea should be sounding still in our ears: "Look to it well, therefore, O ye children, and leave not behind you the knowledge of well-made letters."

Similar preoccupations mark the work of typographers and book designers of our own day. Stanley Morison:

> . . . the form of symbols, principally those which are alphabetical, may signify to the bibliographer much whose relevance is not obvious to the historian . . . The bibliographer may be able, by his study of the physical form of an inscription, manuscript, book, newspaper, or other medium of record, to reveal considerations that appertain to something distinct from religion, politics, and literature, namely: the history of the use of the intellect.[20]

The whole of Morison's last great work, *Politics and Script*, would be salutary reading for many writers on "accidentals" and "substantives." So too would *The Fleuron Anthology*, a convenient collection of meditations by skilled designers and craftsmen, the true successors of men like Tory, who can speak without shame of the "spirit" of a book and the rules by which they seek to express it. As D. B. Updike remarks, although they "may seem insubstantial and difficult to convey in words, it is still true that they are seen and felt in the mind of the worker. They are illusive rules, and yet none the less a man works from them with as much

---

John Wilkins, and especially his *Essay towards a Real Character* (1668), would well repay study both for the theory of perception expressed in it and its typographic articulation of that theory. Another writer, William Petty, in his scheme for a "Dictionary of Sensible Words," would "translate all words used in Argument and Important matters into words that are *Signa Rerum* and *Motuum*. But the Treasury of *Sensata* are the main Miscelany papers of my Scripture, which I add and subtract, Compose and distribute as Printers do their letters."

[20] *Politics and Script*, ed. Nicolas Barker (Oxford, 1972), p. 1. Another work relevant to this part of the discussion is Nicolette Gray, *Lettering as Drawing* (Oxford, 1971).

certainty as if they were set down on paper." Simply to read Percy Smith on Tory's use of a stipple ground for a large initial to give even inking for both initial and text types, is a lesson in aesthetic sensibility, technically informed, serving the communication of meaning, the creation of the distinct experience of reading *that* work and no other. Again it is Percy Smith, the trained craftsman, who can say quite without the embarrassment of a Tom Davis on Thomas McHaney, that "Tory's success with his initials was probably due largely to the wide range of his understanding." He possessed "vision to see truly, and ability to use successfully, sufficient of the spiritual, intellectual and earthly material which was his environment."[21]

For an immediate historical, if also more literal, application of that spirit of inquiry, one could do no better than cite Miss Yates's discussion of the first English edition of Foxe's *Acts and Monuments* (1563) which draws a comparison between the reigns of Queen Elizabeth and the first Christian emperor, Constantine. The comparison implies the further identification of Foxe and Eusebius. The point is that the initial letter of the first word, Constantine, encloses a portrait of the queen, and the lower part of the letter is formed by the body of the Pope. In the 1570 edition, the first word of the new preface is Christ, the sentence is one affirming Elizabeth's divine role, and again the initial "C" enclosing her image is used. There is an interesting extension of the use of this initial "C" in Dee's *General and rare memorials pertayning to the Perfect Arte of Navigation* (1577), also printed by John Day. The idea of the work as a whole, says Miss Yates, was that it should be, in Dee's words, an "Hexameron or Plat Politicall of the Brytish Monarchie," and Dee's book of "Tables Gubernaticke" contains a Latin translation (beginning "Cum in navi gubernator") of Gemistus Pletho's advice to the last Greek emperor, here applied to Elizabeth. Not only does the initial "C" contain her image, as before, but the frontispiece "expands it to cover the theme of the book."[22]

One scholar who has made an excellent start on the theoretical implications of the study of such relationships between word and image is Alain-Marie Bassy.[23] I can only echo his hopes for a semiology which would recognise *all* the signs which have been chosen to convey information in printed form. As Bassy makes clear in seeking to define a particular historical moment (in 1668), words and visual images have not had the same relationship at all times, the balance changing between the merely aesthetic function of images and the merely intellectual function of words. When words cease to be vocalised in reading, they

---

[21] *The Fleuron Anthology*, ed. Francis Meynell (London, 1973). Updike's words are on p. 82, but note also his comment on p. 87 that "study of old models must be minute—not alone in the type used, but in all details of its management." For Smith, see p. 60.

[22] Frances A. Yates, *Astraea: The Imperial Theme in the Sixteenth Century* (London, 1977), 42–48. For an entertaining account of a 19th century example, see Joan Stevens, "Thackeray's Pictorial Capitals," *Costerus* ii n.s. (1974), 113–140.

[23] "Iconographie et littérature: essai de réflexion critique et méthodologique," *Revue Française d'Histoire du Livre* iii (1973), 4–33.

become images. In discussing the crisis of the illustrated book in 1660–1670, he suggests that this was born of the concurrence of the two means of communication in the same field of expression. Engravings show successive scenes on the same plate, thus becoming temporal; they become integral with the text in requiring to be *read* and applied at the direction of the text. The resolution of this crisis is attributed to the first six volumes of La Fontaine's *Fables* of 1668: the words cease to be so heavily and rhetorically moral and become more suggestive; pictures break with the intellectual tradition of emblematic images. In a remarkable confirmation of Stanley Fish's view of the reader's response in the act of reading, he writes of the illustrated book, not as an object (*objet*) but as *the place* (*le lieu*) *where the act of reading occurs.*

In England a comparable analysis might usefully take its origin in the Homily of 1563 on the Peril of Idolatry and superfluous Decking of Churches, the debates between More and Tyndale in 1529–1533, Ridley and Gardner in 1549, and Jewel and Harding in 1564–1568, which are all full of implications regarding the function of images in complex behavioural contexts.[24] For the Catholic apologists, the image leads directly to an apprehension of the divine; for the Protestant, only faith, doctrine—the book—and the works of God do so. The Catholic Sander prefers images, which speak directly to the mind; with words, he says, "I must have taken the pain to have changed the shape of the words into another forme and thereof to have formed a visible image." Understanding is thus linked, not with abstractions, but images of the material world. For the protestant, on the other hand, any visual intermediary, as the materialisation of a concept, must by definition falsify it. If imitation is at all in question, it lies in shaping the expressive force of an argument, or indeed a whole debate, by typographical means. In both cases, of course, the mediating agent is book form, whether emblematic or typographic, and the subtleties of each mode will be important to our understanding of the past. In many ways the debate simply reflects changing conditions of literacy, the Catholic view (like the mimetic and spoken forms of drama) assuming a largely illiterate populace. One strand of the Protestant attack reached its climax in the closing of the theatres in 1642, another with the publication of Milton's *Eikonoclastes*, the image-breaker, and the execution of the king in 1649. But the victory was no more absolute in book form than it was in politics or religion. As with La Fontaine's *Fables* of 1668, or Ogilby's books of the same date in England, word and image come to be seen as mutually supportive, reciprocally expressive, means. The point I am most anxious to make, however, is that the debates I have mentioned are centred on the book, and that they give access to distinct theories of perception and reader response in specific historical contexts. A book's total form is itself a significant historical statement.

The use of images to decorate or illustrate a text, whether finely integrated

---

[24] I am most grateful to my colleague Dr B. J. Opie for drawing my attention to this material and for giving me access to his paper on it. The substance of the argument at this point owes much to him, as do my references to Jewel's *Works* above and to Temple's *A logical analysis* below.

with it or merely in parallel, is perhaps the most obvious element in a book's design. But it prompts us to ask also about the expressive resources available to an author through his printer; it demands inquiry into their purpose and, as a criterion of significant function, the cost of fulfilling that purpose.[25]

The *Nuremberg Chronicle* is the best documented case of the elaborate preparation of design work on an early book, but its greatest value may be in compelling us to reconstitute that process for those books whose layout sketches have not survived.[26] We can do much inferentially. Bassy cites Trechsel's 1493 Strasburg *Terence* with its 150 illustrations intended to permit those unable to read to follow the action of the plays by looking at the pictures. (Indeed, this quality of mobility—the following of an action—is inherent in the movements of reading itself which, from line to line, page to page, animates the words.) In the 1496 Strasburg *Terence* each illustration is made up of some five pieces, three characters and two decors, arranged in different combinations for successive scenes. And so one could go on, extending the discussion through Durer's graphics, Holbein's title-page borders for Froben at Basle, Poussin's designs for the *Imprimerie Royale* at Paris, to the work of Matisse, Picasso, and Chagall in our own day. As Bassy says, the relationship between word and image changes: the poise of La Fontaine's *Fables* in 1668 gives way to the functional disintegration implied by the phrase, common in the 18th century, "adorned with elegant sculptures."[27] A significant act of reintegration occurs in Thackeray's illustrations of his own works; their exact alignment with the relevant text has a critical importance that his editors have only very recently discerned.[28] The immediate point to be made, however, is that the design and construction of books has always been a sophisticated activity, commanding great talents and expenditure of time and money. There is a growing scholarship of the illustrated book, but the present argument is directed more towards our need to understand the finer intentions which determined its very diverse forms. We ignore at our peril the historical importance of all that "design" implies about meaning, its mediation, and comprehension.

Writing in 1961, M. H. Black remarks that:

[25] Miss Yates makes this point well in discussing Robert Fludd's reasons for having his books printed abroad by De Bry, although Fludd's own comments bear more on the cost than on the poverty of English resources for diagram, hieroglyph and symbolic statement: "I sent them beyond the Seas, because our home-borne Printers demanded of me fiue hundred pounds to Print the first Volume, and to find the cuts in copper; but beyond the Seas it was printed at no cost of mine, and that as I would wish: And I had 16. coppies sent me ouer with 40. pounds in Gold, as an Vnexpected gratuitie for it."—*Doctor Fludds Answer vnto M. Foster* (1631), pp. 21–22.

[26] See Adrian Wilson, *The Making of the Nuremberg Chronicle* (Amsterdam, 1978).

[27] William Ivins, *Prints and Visual Communication* (Cambridge, Mass., 1969) also comments pertinently on this point. A comparable loss of poise is evident in the work of the younger Jacob Tonson in the 1720's. His books pursue a luxurious elegance at one extreme, at odds with the more central and habitual functions of a reader. The move from folio to quarto, octavo and comfortableness made by his uncle early in the century is reversed for the blowsy, over-blown effects of merely decorative display and all the false dignities of excessive space and size.

[28] See Joan Stevens, "'Woodcuts dropped into the Text': The illustrations in *The Old Curiosity Shop* and *Barnaby Rudge*," *Studies in Bibliography* 20 (1967), 113–134.

there have been few, if any, studies of the way the earlier printer set about turning manuscript into type, or the influences which affected his choice of convention. . . . no one has analysed these conventions of early design in detail, or followed their evolution over a number of years.

His own studies of the evolution of the form of the octavo bible from manuscript to the Geneva version and then of the folio bible to 1560 are most instructive in precisely this matter of the physical articulation of a text to handle every expressive need.[29] One immediate functional need for certain classes of book was portability. The Douai bible was proscribed, was therefore restricted to private use, and therefore perhaps regularly in quarto. The Geneva bible was also a companionable one and popular long into the 17th century for its size, the guidance given by its glosses, and its illustrations. Black's contributions have now been valuably matched for the manuscript book by M. B. Parkes in his recent study "The Influence of the Concepts of *Ordinatio* and *Compilatio* on the Development of the Book."[30] His discussion of the influences at work in shaping the *mise-en-page* of the manuscript book illustrates the same underlying principle of design as means to the finer articulation of the text. But simply because the process was an evolutionary one we are also made very aware of the specific historicity of any particular moment in it.

The printer-designer's own vocabulary developed into an extraordinarily flexible one of types in their different designs as well as different sizes of the same face, paper in diverse weights, colour, quality and size, ink weak and strong, red and black, format, title page, frontispiece, illustrations diagrammatic, hieroglyphic and figurative, bulk, the structural divisions of volumes, "books," sections, section titles, chapters, paragraphs, verses, verse numbering, line measure, columns, interlinear, marginal and footnotes, running titles, pagination roman and arabic, headings, initial letters, head- and tailpieces, braces, rules, indentations, fleurons, epitomes, indexes and, most important of all, blank white space.[31]

M.H. 36-0

[29] "The Evolution of a Book-Form: The Octavo Bible from Manuscript to the Geneva Version," *The Library* 5th ser. xvi (1961), 15–28, and "The Evolution of Book-Form: II. The Folio Bible to 1560," *The Library* 5th ser. xviii (1963), 191–203.

[30] In *Medieval Learning and Literature: Essays presented to R. W. Hunt*, ed. J. J. G. Alexander and M. T. Gibson (Oxford, 1976), pp. 115–141.

[31] The first codification of these elements appears to be Fertel's *La Science Pratique de l'Imprimerie* (St Omer, 1722) but I am not aware of any study of its underlying assumptions or of the sources of his models and examples. He admits that his style is simple, suitable to the contents ("Quant à mon stile, je sçai qu'il est simple, tel qu'il convient à la matière [Concerning my style, I know it is simple, as is appropriate given the material].") and he says that he has no other aim than to give instruction to those who wish to learn the science of printing and perfect themselves in it. But he is quite original in selecting, as Moxon does not, for example, a whole range of aesthetic concerns affecting choice of type size, capitalisation, italicisation, spacing, decoration, layouts for different kinds of book or printing job. He is extremely attentive to the anatomy of the book, especially in Part I. His own book is divided into four parts and each part is further subdivided into chapters. His separation of part from part, chapter from chapter, use of contrasting roman and italic, upper and lower case, indentation and so on betoken a highly sophisticated strategy. Although intended as a collection of models, how influential it was is another matter. Its immediate importance here is the evidence it shows of a highly developed consciousness of the elements, the language, of book production.

(Modern books by contrast are notorious for smoothing the text and dull our sensitivity to space as an instrument of order.)

William Temple's *A logicall analysis of twentie select Psalmes* of 1605 deliberately deploys all the devices of linear display, indenting, italics, numbering, and bracketed dichotomies, to offer his Ramist readings. In revealing typographically the logical structure in its "natural lineaments" each psalm becomes an attempt to persuade God according to reason by making clear to Him the rational order of the petitionary prayer; but the typography also makes that order instantly accessible to anyone who might take up the book, particularly a non-University readership lacking the esoteric literacy required to understand terms of formal logic.

One need not pursue here the whole question, initiated by W. J. Ong and taken up by Marshall McLuhan, of the shift from words as sounds to their visual form as items deployed in space.[32] It is a general theory well exemplified in books of Ramist logic, but even those did not subdue the writer's voice. As Temple's example would show, the reader's emotions were more finely shaped and more intensely expressed by the thoughtful rhetoric of print. Ong and McLuhan overstressed the connection between visualisation and quantification, leading to scientific discourse, a very narrowly defined function for "print," and a view of the book as a place for surface display and logical demonstration. Dialogue did not decay. Equally important is the relation between visualisation and performance, which has nothing to do with quantification or logic. This is particularly so in literature, where the spoken language is the very substance of poetry, drama and novel and almost demands vocalisation. It leads to a view of the book as a theatre in which a performance takes place. To Dr Johnson: "A play read affects the mind like a play acted."[33] The typographic vocabulary serves many ends.

Ong himself has come to realise the continuing importance of book forms throughout the past in mediating the author's voice to a listener, stressing that a word is not simply a sign of some "thing," but an enunciation, a speaking out, ultimately existential, a psychological event: that is why, in literature, "no typographic display can be merely formal, any more than it can be merely decorative."[34] The sermon, poetry and the drama all continued to exploit the fiction of a speaker and an audience. Milton's *Areopagitica: A Speech* . . . powerfully applies it;

---

[32] See W. J. Ong, *Ramus, Method, and the Decay of Dialogue* (New York, 1958), esp. section 8 of chapter 4; "System, Space, and Intellect in Renaissance Symbolism," *Bibliothèque d'Humanisme et Renaissance Travaux et Documents* xviii (1956), 222–239; and "Ramist Method and the Commercial Mind," in *Rhetoric, Romance and Technology* (Ithaca, 1971). For McLuhan, of course, the central book is *The Gutenberg Galaxy* (Toronto, 1962), a provocative work which ought by now to have stimulated more substantial refutations by historians of the book than it has.

[33] Drama, we might say, is a public reading by writer to reader. Jacques Schérer, *Le "Livre" de Mallarmé*, 6e éd. (Paris, 1957), p. 38, cites Mallarmé's praise of Zola for having "laissé parler le papier," and comments: "La recherche du Livre est donc aussi une recherche du Théatre."

[34] For his more recent emphasis on the book as a speech act, see "Media Transformation: The Talked Book," *College English* 34 (Dec. 1972), 405–410, in which he contrasts current trends in writing-as-edited-diction with past practice. However, in "The Writer's Audience is always a Fiction," *PMLA* xc (1975), 9–21, Ong comes full circle and, despite Ramus, recognises that authors have always spoken through print.

and the epistles dedicatory in 16th, 17th and 18th century books reveal an earnest attempt to secure the reader's personal sympathies. Indeed, Swift in *The Tale of a Tub* and Sterne in *Tristram Shandy* are historically interesting at least in part for what they imply about their readers' expectation of "address"—and they both exploit typography and book form as their essential means of attack. Irony can only work if there is a theory of response and an assumption in the reader himself of its sophisticated and knowing manipulation. The foundations of our amusement and instruction are psychological and aesthetic and they imply a rich context. Were it no so, *The Dunciad* would not exist.[35] An author like Spenser, who toyed with numerology, is unlikely to have been indifferent to the form in which his work was presented (literally so perhaps to the Queen); but in default of an examination of the physical disposition of Books I–III of *The Faerie Queene* as printed, we can note his skilled deployment of poetic devices which create an illusion of oral narrative within the symbolic and emblematic forms of print.[36] "Books are not absolutely dead things . . . ," but they may, in diverse ways, speak in print.

Herbert's poem "The Collar" creates a highly dramatic tension between the speaking voice of the persona and the space which confines it. His hieroglyphs, and the baroque lyric generally, also exploit space as a shaping element in the experience of reading. But perhaps Traherne's "Thanksgivings for the Body" offers us the finest 17th century example of *poésie concrète*.[37] In it lists are metaphors for exploration and discovery; control of their logical linear relationship is secured by the placing of a single article or preposition or brace which commands the space and ensures that one explores the body by words not as a succession of elements but as a dynamic and organic unity. In this way all parts manifest the thing itself and conversely the Word is manifest in every word. The allusion to Psalm 139.16 ("in thy book all my members were written") is pertinent not only to this extract from Traherne's poem but to my whole argument:

> *Ps. 139. 16.   *Enshrined in thy Libraries,
> ⎧ The Amazement of the Learned,
> ⎪ The Admiration of Kings and Queens,
> Are ⎨ The Joy of Angels;
> ⎪ The Organs of my Soul,
> ⎩ The Wonder of Cherubims.
>
>   Those blinder parts of refined Earth,
>   Beneath my Skin;

---

[35] The investigation of reader response has been initiated by linguists and literary critics rather than by editors and textual critics, but their findings must be taken into account now in any general theory of editing. Historians of the book, whose scholarship lies in the very materials which articulated meaning and guided response, have an obligation to contribute to the study of the history of reading. Apart from Stanley Fish's *Self-Consuming Artifacts* (see above, n. 12), other works relevant to this question are Wolfgang Iser, *The Implied Reader* (Baltimore, 1974), and Umberto Eco's *Opera Aperta* (Milan, 1962).

[36] See John Webster, "Oral Form and Written Craft in Spenser's *Faerie Queene*," *Studies in English Literature* 16 (1976), 75–93; and for the persistence of the custom of reading aloud (and being read to), see William Nelson, "From 'Listen, Lordings' to 'Dear Reader'," *University of Toronto Quarterly* xlvi (1976–1977), 110–124.

[37] I am most grateful to my colleague Dr A. F. Bellette for providing this example.

Are full of thy Depths,

For {   Many thousand Uses,
      Hidden Operations,
      Unsearchable Offices.

But for the diviner Treasures wherewith thou hast endowed

My Brains,   Mine Eyes,
My Heart,   Mine Ears,
My Tongue,   My Hands,

O what Praises are due unto thee,
Who hast made me
A living Inhabitant
Of the great World.

And the Centre of it!
A sphere of Sense,
And a mine of Riches,
Which when Bodies are dissected fly away.

From the sophistication of that example in which the book as words in the mind creates through spatial forms an experience of the body as spirit, we might move to the simple notion of the book as printed paper, mere bulk, tactile and of a certain weight. The extreme form is to be found in the salesman's dummy which is nothing but bulk. That point made, however, the mean of portability, and size of type and format in relation to price and literacy, might well be illustrated by a book like Bunyan's *The Pilgrim's Progress* (1678). No scholarly edition that I know has thought fit to re-present with any fidelity the physical form of that book as first published. It was a duodecimo, set in pica roman, to a measure of only 14 ems. The principle of the short prose line is one which popular newspapers still treasure as an aid to their less literate readers. So too the shoulder notes, keyed to the text, like cross-heads in a news column, ensure that the simple reader is "edified by the margent": they apply the lesson and locate the biblical text.[38] The paraphernalia of modern literary and textual scholarship may be so much lumber if it obscures such obvious formal characteristics of the original, allowing the measure to lengthen, the marginal notes to intrude on text, the format and bulk of the book to outgrow the hand and pocket.

Defining a public is, for a serious author, a social and cultural act; for the bookseller it may be primarily a commercial one. But the decisions they take, or impose on one another, in selecting paper, type, layout, illustration, decoration, and printer are unlikely to be arbitrary. The edition quantity and the speed with which a book is produced are, at base, decisions about the relatively volatile or

---

[38] A comparable work, written by an experienced bookseller for a specific public, is Michael Sparkes's *Crums of Comfort, a little book of prayers*. As his address to the reader suggests, the title and manner of the book are one, its size and its typography designed for modest and easy reading. First published probably in 1623 it went through at least some 42 editions.

stable nature of the reading and/or buying public (running the gamut from news sheet to classical text). Concepts of the public good in proselytising author or bookseller, whether political, religious or cultural, will affect decisions about number and price, just as estimates of the relative literacy and mode of reading (aloud?) determined the shape, layout and typographic texture of *The Pilgrim's Progress*. One looks forward to the publication of David Foxon's Lyell Lectures on Pope and the 18th century book trade for the demonstration which will henceforth make such factors central to textual criticism.

Happily, the Shakespearian "norm" of indifference to the fine details of print (at least for the text of his plays if not of his earliest poems) is beginning to fade as more attention is paid to other writers in other genres.[39] Those like Herbert and Milton, not caught by that unhappy disjunction between theatre and printing, must also be gathered up into any general editorial theory which makes assumptions about authorial intention and printing-house practice. We have already noted the accuracy of Buck's first edition of *The Temple*, but his subsequent editions for this (dead) author are equally remarkable for their "vigilant correction of any remaining defects in punctuation, spacing, and italicising" as well as substitution of "v" for consonantal "u" and a consistent distinction between "of" and "off."[40] Concept and care for its realisation in every step to the Temple are both acknowledged. Although her own and Milton's example have had no significant role in editorial theory, we should at least recall Helen Darbishire's comments on *Paradise Lost*: "Since to [Milton] every sound and syllable mattered, every pause or silence between sounds, he came to use spelling and punctuation deliberately to convey the sound, movement and meaning of his lines." And of Milton's detailed direction of his readers' responses, she writes: "In his art Milton aimed at perfection, and he tried to help his readers to read his lines as he meant them to be read."[41]

[39] It is ironic that Percy Simpson's *Shakespearian Punctuation* (Oxford, 1911) should have pursued subtleties of expressive pointing in those printed texts which were least likely to have them; but the same exercise proved to be most rewarding when applied to Jonson's texts. For a revealing sampling, see his comments on *Sejanus* in *Ben Jonson*, ed. C. H. Herford and P. Simpson, 11 vols. (Oxford, 1925–1954), iv. 338–344.

[40] *Works*, ed. Hutchinson, p. lxxvi. A French example of some importance (since Tonson presented a copy to Congreve) is the 1664 Rouen-printed folio edition of Corneille. Corneille's prefatory comments on his innovations in orthography (distinctions of i, j, u, v) in relation to pronunciation and meaning, are especially pertinent. This fineness of concern at the point of print, he hopes, will render "vn petit seruice à nostre Langue & au Public."

[41] *The Poetical Works of John Milton*, ed. Helen Darbishire (London, 1958; repr. 1961), pp. iii, ix. John T. Shawcross, in "One aspect of Milton's spelling: Idle final 'E,'" *PMLA* lxviii (1963), 501–10, has seriously questioned, if not wholly refuted, Miss Darbishire's and others' assumption that Milton used emphatic spellings. A compositorial study of *Paradise Lost*, however, might well offer fresh evidence. Miss Darbishire's general observation is nevertheless utterly sound in the particular case of Milton's punctuation, as Mendele Treip has shown in *Milton's Punctuation* (London, 1970). Alastair Fowler, while rejecting emphatic spelling as a feature of *Paradise Lost*, is impressed by the possibilities of a line-count numerology in the poem; and of course that is again a matter intimately and deliberately related to the architecture of the separate "books," the comprehensive book which contains them, and the author's formal shaping of his readers' responses. See Fowler's edition of *Paradise Lost* (London, 1971), pp. 23–24.

That last comment is central to my whole argument. We are not necessarily talking about a writer's private autograph forms but about the shaping of every detail of his works for a public role.

May I for my last example in this section turn once more now to Sir John Harington's translation of Ariosto (1591) and in particular to his "Advertisement to the reader before he reade this poeme." As Mr Simon Cauchi has pointed out to me, it is a remarkably informative statement about the range of reader responses that Harington thinks to elicit: "(because all that may reade this booke are not of equall capacities) I will endevor to explane more plainely then for the learned sort had haply bene requisite." Harington notes the diverse functions of his marginal notes, from signalling "apt similitudes and pithie sentences or adages" to the selective reading of the different stories "worthie the twise reading." The arguments before each book not only permit the reader "to remember the storie the better" but "to understand the picture the perfecter." The pictures before each book "are all cut in brasse and most of them by the best workemen in that kinde that have bene in this land this manie yeares; yet I will not praise them too much, because I gave direction for their making." He comments on other illustrated books but adds, "except it were in a treatise set foorth by that profound man, maister Broughton, the last yeare, upon the Revelation," most other English books have all their figures "cut in wood and none in metall, and in that respect inferior to these, at least (by the old proverbe) the more cost, the more worship." Further:

> The use of the picture is evident, which is that (having read over the booke) you may reade it (as it were againe) in the very picture, and one thing is to be noted which every one (haply) will not observe, namely the perspective in every figure. For the personages of men, the shapes of horses, and such like, are made large at the bottome and lesser upward, as if you were to behold all the same in a plaine, that which is nearest seemes greatest and the fardest shewes smallest, which is the chiefe art in picture.

His "exact and necessarie table" locates people, places and things, and at the same time, by virtue of his indexing method, it summarizes the narratives in which "the principall persons" appear. The functions of "the Morall, the Historie, the Allegorie, and the Allusion," notes on each of which conclude every canto, are also carefully described. Harington adds a life of Ariosto, "A briefe and summarie allegorie," a list of "The principal tales . . . that may be read by themselves," and a "Note of the matters contained in this whole volume." This last itself adds a space between "The first xxiii Cantos" and "The other xxiii Cantos." In doing so it makes plain the climactic nature at that point of Orlando's madness and it thereby helps to explain why Harington directed his printer to provide "a spare leaf" at precisely that point in the narrative (where the reader, like Orlando, might also bend his eye on vacancy?).

But the most important point of all is the way in which Harington's "Advertisement to the reader before he reade this poeme" directs him to read it in any of at least three ways for its narrative (straight through, selectively, pictorially) and in each of four ways for its import (moral, history, allegory, allusion). It clearly demonstrates the finely planned and purposive nature of the typography. That, in turn, firmly secures and brings to fruition the literary and moral grounds upon which he offers his "Preface or rather, a briefe apologie of poetrie" and in which he justifies the whole work. Greg, in his famous article on "An Elizabethan Printer and his Copy," does not mention Harington's advertisement.

To recapitulate: Greg's distinction between accidentals and substantives (historically derived and accurate in *his* use) offers no basis for a general theory, and attempts to use it as such reflect that failure of historical imagination which has blighted most recent work in textual bibliography. The better assumption is the integrity of the text in all its details, including book form, with an extension of the meaning of "error" to include all defects. Any emphasis on the integrated structure of a text is therefore welcome; but it must be extended to include non-verbal forms, and it must admit the more complex structures implied by "work" (the edition as a conflation of radically different versions or "texts").[42] Finally, we must extend our understanding of those structures by defining, with greater historical accuracy, the behavioural acts of reading which they generated; in particular we must seek a fuller understanding of those historical decisions made by authors, designers and craftsmen in deploying the many visual and even tactile languages of book form to help direct their readers' responses to the verbal language of the text.

III

I suggested earlier that the quarto editions of Congreve's plays follow the late 17th century trade stereotype, reflecting the absence of any sympathetic relationships between writer (or theatre company), bookseller and printer; and that their perfunctory presentation disguises the structure of the plays. In the changes which Congreve adopts in 1710, there are two remarkable features. The first is Congreve's self-censorship. The second is the typographic styling which I have already mentioned briefly, but especially the adoption of neoclassical scene division. The guidance we need to handle both features is to be derived from a study of the social context, but particularly from Congreve's and his bookseller's

---

[42] The concept of a "work" referred to above (see n. 15) is also discussed by Roland Barthes; but, if I understand him correctly, he uses the word "work" for the more specific item, the word "text" for its extended significances, where in English the terms would be reversed. Thus: "the work is a fragment of substance, occupying a part of the space of books (in a library for example), the Text is a methodological field" and "Over against the traditional notion of the *Work*, for long—and still—conceived of in a, so to speak, Newtonian way, there is now the requirement of the new object, obtained by the sliding or overturning of former categories. That object is the *Text*." See his essay, "From Work to Text," in *Image-Music-Text*, trans. and ed. Stephen Heath (London, 1977), pp. 155–164. Jacques Schérer, in *Le "Livre" de Mallarmé*, is also concerned with the relation between discrete items, occasional by nature and circumstances, and the work or book as a metaphysical conception, transcending the physical limits of the book as artifact (but shaped by its material forms). For Mallarmé the book was a living quality, evolutionary rather than fixed.

sensitivity to that context. Congreve's conception of his readers, Tonson's definition of his market, informed by changing moral and aesthetic values, determined their choice of language, of typographical resources, and of the human skills necessary to deploy them effectively. Congreve and Tonson were at one in defining and serving a common goal: the evocation in their readers, through the arts of the book, of the finest qualities of Congreve's own art as a dramatist.

I shall look first at those verbal changes which resulted from a process of self-censorship, a case which Professor Zeller's principles would inhibit him from arguing. I shall then consider those non-verbal elements of stage groupings and dramatic action whose mediation seems to me to depend quite crucially on a sophisticated use of typographic display.

Whether Congreve acted freely of his own choice, or reluctantly under social constraints, we may at least begin by noting that his revisions delete so many words and expressions of a mildly vulgar kind that he took a lot of the life out of his two earlier plays, reducing their vitality at a point of experience fundamental to the comedy of the time. In fact, as early as The Double Dealer of 1694, a play printed by Tonson, Congreve had already begun to tone down his language. He was therefore surprised and disappointed by the play's harsh reception and wrote a defensive dedication in which he repudiates the suggestion that his language was gratuitously foul:

> I have heard some whispering, as if they intended to accuse this Play of Smuttiness and Bawdy: But I declare that I took a particular care to avoid it, and if they find any in it, it is of their own making, for I did not design it to be so understood.

Nevertheless, it still contains some words which he later thought it wiser to suppress.

There are in fact at least four reasons for this self-censorship. One is simply Congreve's own increasing fastidiousness and a wish to work with greater economy of means to subtler ends of character. A second reason has more to do with the structuring of the play itself, a concern for stability and regularity, in which a literary ideal of correctness marries a social ideal of order. There can be no doubt that the form of The Double Dealer owes a direct literary debt to Terence, and it is not surprising to find, in the dedication, Congreve stressing the play's regularity:

> I confess I design'd . . . to have written a true and regular Comedy . . . I made the Plot as strong as I could, because it was single, and I made it single, because I would avoid confusion, and was resolved to preserve the three Unities of the Drama, which I have visibly done to the utmost severity.

Congreve's explicit concern there is with the form of his play, but his intention goes well beyond that. It is almost as if unity of tone—a polite, or a least politic, voice—were a concomitant of the other three unities. I would stress both those words, polite and politic. The first is evidenced by the purity of Love for Love (1695) and The Way of the World (1700). In The Way of the World only two later omissions could possibly be thought of as bowdlerisations. Praising Terence there as "the most correct Writer in the World" and "the Purity of his Stile, the Delicacy of his Turns, and the Justness of the Characters," Congreve had deliberately sought and attained refinement and regularity.

But this development was also politic, which brings me to my third and most obvious reason: there were external pressures on him too. The Lord Chamberlain, in January 1696, ordered that all plays be licensed, and again in June 1697 that lewd expressions be omitted in performance. Doubtless responding to feeling at court, Congreve dedicated his *Mourning Bride* (1697) to Her Royal Highness, the Princess, saying:

> a Play may be with Industry so dispos'd (in spight of the licentious Practice of the Modern Theatre) as to become sometimes an innocent, and not unprofitable Entertainment . . .

It was a delicate move in defence of the drama.

Shortly after Anne came to the throne she issued a proclamation for the "Encouragement of Piety and Virtue," "particularly in such as are employed near our Royal Persons." Much of this of course is a familiar story, but it is one crucial for our treatment of Congreve's text because he must have come to feel such social pressures personally. With Vanbrugh, he had been licensed in December 1704 to establish a new company of comedians by Her Majesty's command, and a condition of the licence was that the company should be established "under stricter Government and Regulations than have been formerly." In deference to the Queen, in defence of his actors, in the interests of preserving his theatre itself from threat of closure, and doubtless also because his own tastes had become more refined as he grew older, Congreve followed the advice given by Nahum Tate that "all Plays (capable of being reform'd) be rectify'd by their Authors if Living—and proper Persons appointed to Alter and reform Those of Deceased Authors . . ."[43]

There was also, however, a fourth, quite different, source of pressure on Congreve. I refer to his close friend and bookseller, Jacob Tonson. We know that Congreve was living with Tonson in 1695, and that he had probably begun to do so as early as 1693.[44] Certainly by 1694, with *The Double Dealer*, Tonson began to secure the major publishing interest in Congreve's works. We also know that Tonson bowdlerised Rochester's poems in 1691. The fourth *Poetic Miscellany*, published by Tonson in 1694, is not free from coarse language, but the fifth and sixth of 1704 and 1709 involve extensive purification. We must also remember the Whig majority in Anne's third Parliament of 1708 and Tonson's aspirations to Government business in the period when *Works* 1710 was being edited for press.

---

[43] Joseph Wood Krutch, *Comedy and Conscience after the Restoration* (New York, 1961), pp. 177–178, 186. The whole of chapter 7, "The Reformation of Manners and the Stage," is most useful for setting the context within which Congreve and Tonson were working.

[44] J. M. Treadwell, "Congreve, Tonson and Rowe's 'Reconcilement'," *Notes and Queries* (June 1975), pp. 265–269.

Such conditions seem to me to put Congreve's suppressed readings into a very special category of authorial revision. They are confined effectively to *The Old Bachelor* and *The Double Dealer*; and he has clearly been constrained to make many of them. The problem is complicated, however, by evidence that even during the 1690's his own tastes were changing.

There is no escaping the fact that we are here students of human behaviour in the past and that such behaviour, in its sensitive response to social context, has textual consequences. An editor faced with such a range of variant readings cannot abdicate. Every variant must of course be scrutinized for what it adds or loses in vitality of character and acuity of language. So too every modification of the stage action must be critically assessed for its gain in economy or loss in expressiveness. In the interests both of his author and his own readers, he must seek to serve the play at its fullest and best by restoring a reading when he believes its suppression to reflect a narrow moral, rather than a literary, judgement on Congreve's part. The problem is not to be evaded, as Professor Zeller would have us do, by taking the quartos as one version and including the first readings, or by taking 1710 as a different version and excluding them. Conflation is inevitable. But it is also critically and historically responsible only in so far as the causes of the variant readings have been explained, in this case by that peculiar complex of attitudes—personal, social and trade—which obtained for Congreve and Tonson in the first decade of the 18th century.

I turn now to the non-verbal elements of stage groupings and dramatic action, essential constituents of the drama. How could such elusive features be mediated at all by book form? What evidence is there that Congreve, following Ben Jonson's example of 1616, made any attempt to bring out the quality of his works *as plays* when he prepared them for press in 1709–1710? Does the neoclassical scene division really have the function I have imputed to it and represent a deliberate and intelligent attempt by Congreve in *Works* 1710 to edit his plays in such a way that their typography, the mere disposition of space, might mediate his stage action and stage image—especially in scenic form—to those who, as readers, may only recreate it in the mind? Does his editing of his works for print enhance our sense of *theatre*? Did the book trade itself have the sophisticated consciousness of book form, the skills and resources, to regard such questions as even meaningful?

The most notable development in the London trade at the end of the 17th century is Jacob Tonson's brilliant definition and exploitation of the market for "polite" literature in the 1680's and 1690's. Tonson could hardly have begun business at a more propitious time. The emergence of the trade publisher of ephemera at precisely this time, the new commercial optimism which followed the settlement of 1688, the imminent lapse of the Licensing Act, even the growing recognition of author's copyright, were developments which Tonson turned to his advantage. He was the first to exploit subscription publishing for selling English literature when he used it for *Paradise Lost* in 1688. It was Tonson who

suggested that Dryden translate the *Aeneid*; and in publishing it, he was supporting the greatest living *English* writer.[45]

In the 1690's Tonson was developing friendships and a mode of business
which combined a successful personal career with an inestimable service to English literature. During these years, at least from 1693, he was intimate with Congreve, using him as legal adviser in matters of business and lodging him in his
own house. What Tonson did *not* have in the 1690's was a printer worthy of and
wholly committed to a partnership which gave technical excellence to his books.
Such a partnership came only when Tonson began to employ John Watts: and
its first real fruits are Rowe's *Shakespeare* of 1709 and, with that most appropriate
dramatic precedent, Congreve's *Works* of early 1710. In those works the resources
and conventions of print make conscious a concept of the reader and offer opportunities to direct his responses in ways that manuscript papers in this period
have no cause to do. Once an author has a sympathetic relationship with his
bookseller and printer, as in Congreve's case, it is possible to plan a book in all
its forms, with deliberation and judgement, in matters of cost, function and design. What we are dealing with here, in contra-distinction to the conditions for
dramatic publishing in Shakespeare's day, is a new and intimate form of team-
work between author or editor, bookseller and printer. Perhaps one other way of
indicating the significance of this moment would be simply to recall that the
"Act for the Encouragement of Learning by vesting the copies of Printed Books
in the Author" came into effect in April 1710, the very same month that Congreve's *Works* were published.

There is no obvious archetype for the detailed typography of *Works* 1710 or the
further 12° edition of 1719–1720. I have in mind Congreve's use of letter-spaced
roman capitals and small capitals for headlines and character groupings, the centred italic capitals for speakers' names in 1719, the engraved headpieces and ornamental drop initials for each act, and the use of ornaments to separate the
scenes. For reasons I have indicated, the normal run-of-the-mill English dramatic quarto throughout the century, Congreve's included, shows none of the
refinements introduced by Congreve in his *Works*.

Against such a background it is tempting to accept that his innovations are
simply in direct imitation of French printing practice. There is undoubtedly such
an influence, but we should not underestimate the force of the English neoclassical tradition with its origins in Ben Jonson's *Works* of 1616, the continuous line
through the 17th century of texts of the classical drama, of printed versions of
the English masque, and—at the century's end—of texts of dramatic operas performed in London. These examples demonstrate a mixed tradition rather than a
purely French or classical one. Editions of Terence, Plautus, Corneille, Racine and

---

[45] See John Barnard, "Dryden, Tonson, and Subscriptions for the 1697 *Virgil*," *Papers of the Bibliographical Society of America* lviii (1963), 129–151.

Molière, as well as of English dramatists, that Congreve had in his library, together show such a wide range of combinations as to frustrate the formulation of any precise rules. But the text itself shows some gallicising in revision (note the change from "*Lodgings*" to "*Apartment*" in illustrations 1A and 1B), and French precedent must have played a strong role in influencing both Congreve's and Tonson's views on typography, as well as in determining the kind of resources that Tonson made available to Watts about 1707. The Cambridge quarto classics with their engravings by Simon Gribelin, which Tonson commissioned in 1698 and to which Congreve subscribed, are significant both as evidence of a new wave in English typography and for their tactful reflection of French and Dutch precedent.

> Certainly by 1700, Tonson was beginning to think European in the style of his book production. He looked at the resources available to him, made a culturally informed decision that they were inadequate, made distinct acts of selection in acquiring new ones, and embarked on a programme of book design with the deliberate aim of making the *design* of his books a significant statement of their cultural importance and a fine articulation of their literary meaning. It was in 1700 that he, Congreve and Charles Mein together travelled to the Low Countries.[46]

The three volumes and octavo format of Congreve's *Works* were a much more direct manifestation of a new development in trade practice than of broader cultural influences. Quite simply, the size of the sheet increased. To begin with, folios got bigger and a quarto at the end of the century was not much smaller than Jonson's folio had been eighty-odd years before. By adopting a large quarto format instead of folio for the Cambridge classics of 1698–1702 Tonson was beginning to get things back into perspective; and in adopting smaller formats, booksellers like Tonson naturally found it convenient to introduce multi-volume sets.[47] In 1697, instead of appearing in one large volume, Rochester's *Letters* appeared in two smaller ones. But 1700–1701 were the watershed years. In 1700, Cowley's *Works* appeared in folio for the last time and in 1701 Dryden's *Plays*. The next time Cowley appeared (in 1707), he was in two volumes octavo. The model had been established. In 1708 Dryden's *Virgil* reappeared in three volumes octavo. If we count only the English dramatists, we find a remarkable sequence: not a fifth folio but Rowe's multi-volume illustrated octavo edition of Shakespeare (1709); Congreve in three volumes octavo (1710), Beaumont and Fletcher in seven volumes octavo (1712), Otway in two (1712), Jonson in six (1716), Dryden in six (1717), Vanbrugh in two "pocket" volumes (1719), Congreve again in two (1719–1720), and Shadwell in four (1720). English authors were once more in the hands of their readers.

Tonson's succession of English authors is remarkable by any standards. To the

---

[46] *William Congreve: Letters and Documents*, ed. John C. Hodges (London, 1964), pp. 13–18.

[47] Graham Pollard, "Notes on the Size of the Sheet," *The Library* 4th ser. xxii (1941–1942), 105–137, and "Changes in the Style of Bookbinding," *The Library* 5th ser. xi (1956), 71–94.

roll of dramatists we have just called, we should add Milton, Prior, Spenser, Pope, Gay, Addison, Cibber, all published in newly and responsibly edited texts in the case of the dead, and with the author to hand in the case of the living. And all done within little more than a decade of Rowe's *Shakespeare*. It is an object lesson for modern editorial projectors and, in format, in tasteful but uncluttered design, in sheer readability, it is also an object lesson for modern publishers. The CEAA should take note. Tonson's editions mark his intelligent response to trade developments in book format, and whatever he owed to the continent for his typographic materials and styling, he gave a new dignity and currency, not only to classical but to national literature.

For these reasons Tonson was the perfect instrument, sharpened by friendship, for giving public form to Congreve's authorial intentions. For his part, Congreve at last had available to him for his *Works* of 1710 a range of resources and a sense of his own identity as a poet and dramatist that permitted him to shape the book as a definition of himself and his creation. The *Works* are in three volumes octavo, and the title page of the central column emblematically states the comprehensive achievement:

The MOURNING BRIDE.	Tragedy.
The WAY *of the* WORLD.	Comedy.
The Judgment of PARIS.	Masque.
SEMELE. '	Opera.

There is an originality about this moment which we discern in the way the physical forms of the book translate Congreve's sense of self-esteem, his literary ideas, his commitment—as a neo-classical author—to the dramatic art of Plautus and Terence. At the same time, it also expresses, along with Rowe's *Shakespeare*, a completely new phase in the economics of the book trade and the cultural and social aspirations of its central figure, Tonson.

I now pass to the question of neo-classical scene division, for the immediate point is that Congreve could now, through Tonson's printer John Watts, draw on a greater range of decorative material with which to enhance his conception of a theatrical scene, to emphasise the scenic grouping of characters in their set social relationships, not their entries and exits. He thereby expresses a social attitude inseparable from his neoclassical principles of dramatic construction. I mean the importance of the stable group, the hard-won, contained poise, not disturbing change.

Congreve's commitment to a neoclassical structure is there from the beginning in his plays. One may attribute it to the influence of works like Hédelin, Abbé d'Aubignac's, *La pratique du théâtre,* of which Congreve had both the English and the French editions, Madame Dacier's comments on Terence, or simply Congreve's own admiration for and imitation of Terence, which is what his prefaces to *The Double Dealer* and *The Way of the World* really suggest. But one point of neoclassical theory which he observes with superbly skilled variety and almost absolute consistency is *liaison de scènes*. There is nearly always some intimation within the dialogue of imminent arrival or departure, so that staging is woven into the fabric of the play in a way which makes *stage directions* seem naive and certainly superfluous. The old typography concealed all this; the new lifts his art to the light. These felicities are pervasive. We move from something as elementary as the word-play on *heart* for linking the third and fourth scenes of Act I in *The Old Bachelor*:

> *Sharp*. And here comes one who swears
> as heartily he hates all the Sex.

> ******************

> SCENE IV.
> [*To them*] HARTWELL.
> *Bell*. WHO *Hartwell*! Ay, but he
> knows better things—How . . .

. . . we move from that to its elaborate and marvellously embroidered form in *The Way of the World*, where Mrs Fainall ends one scene with "Here's your Mistress." NEW SCENE, and Millamant enters the play with banners flying to Mirabell's "Here she comes i'faith full Sail, with her Fan spread and Streamers out, and a Shoal of Fools for Tenders . . . ," namely Witwoud and Mincing.

At the end of the next scene, Millamant leaves Mirabell with the words "and when you have done thinking of that, think of me." Compare, if you will, the typographic presentation of this moment in the quarto (illustration 8A) with that of *Works* (8B). In the latter the new scene establishes clearly Mirabell's solitary wonder as he stands alone on stage, his voice reaching back to the departing Millamant across the typographic divide which images the stage space. "I Have something more—Gone—[alone] Think of you!" Like Millamant's parting line, which emphasises their separation, this is a superb handling of the technique of scene change in a neoclassical sense. It has both continuity and distinction, and I believe the reader is helped to realise that dramatic experience by its typographical isolation.

Conversely, Mirabell's later entry, and not only Congreve's but his character's ability to unite division—Act IV, scene v—is elaborately prepared. Illustrations 9A and 9C show the 1700 quarto and 1719 duodecimo versions. Poor Sir Wilful in the preceding scene can only illustrate his boorishness when Millamant invites him to cap her quotation from a poem by Sir John Suckling. The poem suggests that if he is to be a lover, he must show his "*Power and Art*." Sir Wilful is disgraced and on his bashful exit, Millamant sends him off with a laugh and one more line to end the scene:

> Like *Phoebus* sung the no less am'rous Boy.

The new scene, and typographical flourish, heightens with art our sense of a new man and a new power. Enter Mirabell to complete the rhyming couplet, and also the coupling with Millamant—since he is the one with the power and the art to complete Millamant's love—

> Like Daphne *she, as Lovely and as Coy.*

It is a splendid criss-crossing, over the divide, of Millamant to Phoebus and Mirabell to Daphne.

For Congreve this commitment was long standing, fundamental to his very conception of stagecraft. If, as there are grounds for thinking, he actually conceived of his scenes in this form as he wrote them, even perhaps so divided and numbered them in his manuscripts, the early quarto versions must in fact be seen as *less* faithful to his intention in precisely this matter. In fact it is demonstrable that the unthinking imposition of the old, outmoded and always inappropriate typography used for run-of-the-mill dramatic texts has seriously obscured Congreve's intentions. In his *Amendments of Collier,* of 1698—that is, twelve years before *Works* 1710—Congreve refers to *The Old Bachelor,* his first play, in a way which shows that he counted the scenes in the neoclassical manner. He locates a citation as "From Scene 3. of the 4th Act" and another in "*Act 5. Scene 2.*" whereas in the quarto text both the fourth and the fifth acts have only one scene each. In a reference to *Love for Love* Congreve says:

> If the Reader pleases to consult the Fourth Act of that Comedy, he will there find a Scene, wherein *Valentine* counterfeits madness.

Again, no such "scene" is distinguished in the quarto. These references match up perfectly with one other piece of evidence, even earlier, in the dedication to *Love for Love* in 1695:

> Here are some Lines in the Print . . . that were omitted on the Stage, and particularly one whole Scene in the Third Act . . .

The scene in question is one whole neoclassical scene, almost certainly Act IV, scene xi as printed in *Works* 1710.[48] It is not distinguished in the quarto. So Congreve, as a working dramatist in mid-career, fifteen years before *Works* 1710 were printed, clearly shaped his plays with this, and no other, scene structure in mind.

I must also acknowledge, however, that in other cases Congreve's scenes present us with *des liaisons dangereuses,* and I therefore draw your attention to some of the less desirable consequences of his adoption of neoclassical scene division. Whether right or wrong—again the editor cannot avoid his responsibility to make critical choices—every instance demonstrates the quite extraordinary dramatic significance of the non-verbal elements of display.[49]

---

[48] Anthony Gosse, "The Omitted Scene in Congreve's *Love for Love,*" *Modern Philology* 61 (1963), 40–42, suggests Act IV, scene xi as the one concerned.

[49] For the comments in this section of the paper I am greatly indebted to Dr Peter Holland of Trinity Hall, Cambridge. He supplied several examples of Congreve's failure to account adequately for certain stage actions when formalising his scene divisions for *Works* and his own study of the relations between text and performance will help to clarify many otherwise obscure points of interpretation.

In 1A, for example, the quarto version of *The Old Bachelor*, Belinda's action in calling Betty, Betty's entry, and the point of her question are clear. In 1B, however, Congreve lists her at the scene head and thereby implies her presence throughout the scene. He deletes Belinda's call, together with the stage direction, "*Calls*," but in doing so he makes Betty's line "Did your Ladyship call, Madam?" unmotivated and virtually redundant. In 2B, Vainlove's line "Well, I'll leave you with your Engineer" demands the "Exit" given in 1A or else a new scene. In 3A, a comical stage action is perfectly timed as the would-be adulterer escapes into hiding just *before* the husband enters, whereas in *Works* (3B) Congreve implies that Bellmour does not hide until the end of the scene, and there is thus no delay before Laetitia opens the door to Fondlewife. In 4A, Heartwell's words "Leave me," and the boy's exit as marked, leave Heartwell in soliloquy. But *Works* (4B) oddly omits the words and the stage direction, thus implying that the boy remains on stage, despite Congreve's demand, in the preface to *The Double Dealer*, that in terms of vraisemblance an actor in soliloquy must believe himself to be alone: "For if he supposes any one to be by, it is monstrous and ridiculous to the last degree." In 5B, the omission of the stage direction "*Runs out*" leaves Lady Touchwood on stage for Lord Touchwood's comments on her. This completely alters our interpretation of her character and of his; for if she stays she endures a complete humiliation and her husband glories in a real victory over her. Congreve in 1710 also omits from the stage direction the phrase "*from the other side on the Stage*," a clear indication to us of a shift in attention for the audience from side to side as he despatches one part of the plot and drags in another. In 6A, *Love for Love*, there is a slight pause between the dashing and flirtatiously enticing exit of Miss Prue and Tattle's decisive and purposeful exit in pursuit of her. It is beautifully timed in a way obscured by *Works* (6B). And finally, in 7A, Sir Sampson's words and exit as given lead him to storm out in ferocious if barely articulate anger. In 7B he says less, seems merely to reflect sorrowfully on his own folly, and stays on stage; and if Congreve really means that to be so, it implies a very substantial change in his character and a significant change in the moral structure of the whole play.

In his earliest work of all, *Incognita*, Congreve expressed a strong commitment to dramatic experience. "Drama," he said, ". . . brings forth alive the Conceptions of the Brain. *Minerva* walks upon the Stage before us, and we are more assured of the real presence of Wit when it is delivered *viva voce* . . . ." And

> Since all Traditions must indisputably give place to the *Drama*, and since there is no possibility of giving that life to the Writing or Repetition of a Story which it has in the Action, I resolved in another beauty to imitate *Dramatick* Writing, namely, in the Design, Contexture and Result of the Plot.

Congreve claims some originality for infusing into the novel some qualities of the drama and adds: "I have not observed it before in a Novel." As a dramatic artist in his plays, Congreve not only shows his sense of design in his use of language and his command of structure, but with a fine sense of patterning in language, character, movement and typography, he makes reading a dramatic experience.

Ben Jonson before him had also tried to solve the problem that faces all authors, printer-designers, and editors of dramatic texts: how to make a three-dimensional action come alive for the reader of a two-dimensional page. This concern to express a quality of performance came out most directly in Jonson's editing of his masques:

> Such was the exquisit performance, as (beside the pompe, splendor, or what we may call apparelling of such Presentments) that alone (had all else beene absent) was of power to surprize with delight, and steale away the spectators from themselves. Nor was there wanting whatsoever might give to the furniture, or complement; either in riches, or strangenesse of the habites, delicacie of daunces, magnificence of the scene, or divine rapture of musique. Onely the envie was, that it lasted not still, or (now it is past) cannot by imagination, much lesse description, be recovered to a part of that spirit it had in the gliding by.
>
> Yet, that I may not utterly defraud the Reader of his hope, I am drawn to give it those briefe touches, which may leave behind some shadow of what it was . . . .[50]

In the plays "those briefe touches" also include the typographic pointers, the arrangement of the text, the division of scenes and the descriptive stage directions.

Jonson's editorial comments on Hymenaei, from which that quotation is taken, draw on the imagery of body and soul to distinguish between the action of a masque and its meaning. Printing involved a transmigration of soul: its new body was the book. By extension, the Works are the man. John Milton's imagery is likewise organic. Books are "borne to the World" and their "potencie of life" is "as active as that soule was whose progeny they are." When Milton said "as good almost kill a good Man as kill a good Book" and defined a good book as "the pretious life-blood of a master spirit, imbalm'd and treasur'd up on purpose to a life beyond life," his idea of the book as an embodiment of the man futher implied that the knowledge it bestowed had a living force, a life beyond life, fulfilled only in its acting out.

If we are accurately to reconstruct our literary past, we cannot be indifferent to the details of book form, in the contribution design makes to meaning, in mediating authorial intention and directing the responses of readers. The textual and theatrical, and therefore behavioural, complexities I have indicated were created almost solely by Congreve's adoption of a form of scene division which owed nothing to words as such—to what Greg would call substance—but everything to the "accidentals" (dare we still use the term?) of typographic display. Despite the faults I have noted in Works 1710, it is clear that there was a mind at work in the actual presentation of the text for readers. The design of the book was intended to give a fuller sense of Congreve's art by bridging the gap between

---

[50] Hymenaei, lines 567–582; Ben Jonson, ed. Herford and Simpson, vii. 229. My colleague Dr Peter Walls has drawn my attention to the significance of the present tense for what it tells of performance in certain of Jonson's masque texts.

①B

S C E N E III.

Araminta, Belinda, Betty waiting, in Araminta's Apartment.

Belin. Prithee tell it all the World, it's false.

Aram. Come then, kiss and Friends.

Belin. Pish.

Aram. Prithee don't be so Peevish.

Belin. Prithee don't be so Impertinent.

Betty.

Aram. Ha, ha, ha.

Betty. Did your Ladyship call, Madam?

②B

[*To them*] SETTER.

TRUSTY *Setter* what Tidings? How goes the Project?

Setter. As all lewd Projects do, Sir, where the Devil prevents our Endeavours with Success.

Bell. A good hearing, *Setter.*

Vain. Well, I'll leave you with your Engineer.

Bell. And hast thou provided Necessaries?

③B

Fond. Cocky, Cocky, open the Door.

Bell. Pox choak him, would his Horns were in his Throat. My Patch, my Patch. [*Looking about, and gathering up his Things.*

Let. My Jewel, art thou there? No matter for your Patch—You san't turn in, *Nykin*—Run into my Chamber, quickly, quickly. You san't turn in.

Fond. Nay, prithee, Dear, lifck I'm in haste.

Let. Then I'll let you in. [*Opens the Door.*

S C E N E XVI.

LETITIA, FONDLEWIFE *Sir* JOSEPH.

Fond. KISS, Dear—I met the Master of the Ship by the way—And if must have my Papers of Accounts out of your Cabinet.

Let. Oh, I'm undone! [*Aside.*

④B

S C E N E XII.

SCENE, *Sylvia's Lodgings.*

HEARTWELL *and* Boy.

Heart. GONE forth, say you, with her Maid!

Boy. There was a Man too that fetch'd 'em out—*Setter*, I think they call'd him.

Heart. So-h.— That precious Pimp too—Damn'd, damn'd Strumpet? Cou'd she not contain her self on her Wedding-Day! Not hold out till Night! O cursed State! How wide we err, when apprehensive of the Load of Life!

— *It's hope to find*
That Help which Nature meant in Wo-
man-kind,
To Man that Supplemental Self design'd;
But proves a burning Caustick when ap-
plyd,
And Adam, sure, cou'd with more Ease
abide
The Bone when broken, than when made
A Bride.

---

①A OB II.iii

SCENE *Changes to Lodgings.*

Enter Araminta, Belinda.

Belin. Prithee tell it all the World, it's false. *Berg.* (*Calls*

Aram. Come then, Kiss and Friends.

Belin. Pish.

Aram. Prithee don't be so Peevish.

Belin. Prithee don't be so Impertinent.

Aram. Ha, ha, ha.

Enter Betty.

Berg. Did your Lad, ship, call Madam?

②A OB III.iv

Enter Setter.

Trusty *Setter* what tidings? How goes the project?

Setter. As a lewd projects do Sir, where the Devil prevents our endeavours with Success.

Bell. A good hearing, *Setter.*

Vain. Well, I'll leave you with your Engineer. → *Exit.*

Bell. And hast thou provided necessaries?

③A OB IV.xv

Fondl. Cocky, Cocky, open the door.

Bell. Pox choak him, would his Horns were in his Throat. My Patch, my Patch. [*Looking about, and gathering up his things.*

Let. My Jewel, Art thou there? No matter for your Patch.—You san't turn in, *Nykin.*—Run into my Chamber, quickly, quickly. You san't turn in. → *Ed. go in.*

Fondl. Nay, prithee, Dear, lifck I'm in haste. [*Opens the Door.*

Let. Then, I'll let you in.

Enter Fondle-wife, and Sir Joseph.

Fond. Kiss, Dear,—I met the Master of the Ship by the way,—and I must have my Papers of Accounts out of your Cabinet. [*Aside.*

Let. Oh, I'm undone!

④A OB V.xii

SCENE *changes to Silvia's Lodgings.*

Enter Heartwell and Boy.

Heart. Gone forth, say you, with her Maid!

Boy. There was a Man too that fetch'd 'em out:— *Setter*, I think they call'd him.

Heart. So-h,—— That precious Pimp too.—Damn'd, damn'd Strumpet! Cou'd the not contain her self on her Wedding-Day! Nor hold out till Night! Leave me. [*Exit Boy.*

O cursed State! How wide we err, when apprehensive of the Load of Life!
— We hope to find

That Help which Nature meant in Woman-kind,
To Man that Supplemental Self design'd;
But proves a burning Caustick when applyd,
And Adam, sure, could with more Ease abide
The Bone when broken, than when made a Bride.

5A (DD V.XXiii)

L. Touch. Stand off, let me go, and Plagues, and Curfes feize you all. (Runs out.)
Ld. Touch. Go, and thy own Infamy purfue thee,—
you ftare as you were all amazed,—I don't wonder at it,—but too foon you'll know mine, and that Woman's fhame.
Enter Mellefont lugging in Maskwell from the other fide of the Stage, Mellefont like a Parfon.

5B

Ld. Touch. Stand off, let me go.
Ld. Touch. Go, and thy own Infamy purfue thee.—You ftare as you were all amazed,—I don't wonder at it,—but too foon you'll know mine, and that Wo-man's fhame.

SCENE The Laft.
Lord TOUCHWOOD, Lord FROTH, Lady FROTH, Lady PLYANT, Sir PAUL, CYNTHIA, MELLEFONT, MASKWELL; MELLEFONT difguifed in a Parfon's Habit and pulling in MASKWELL.

6A

Tatt. Then I'll make you cry out.
Mifs. Oh but you fha'nt, for I'll hold my Tongue.——→
Tatt. Oh my Dear, apt Scholar.
Mifs. Well, now I'll run and make more hafte than you. [Ex. Mifs.
Tatt. You fhall not fly fo faft, as I'll purfue. [Exit after Her.

The End of the Second Act.
(LL II.Xi)

6B

Tatt. Then I'll make you cry out.
Mifs. Oh but you fha'nt, for I'll hold my Tongue.——
Tatt. Oh my dear apt Scholar.
Mifs. Well, now I'll run and make more hafte than you.
Tatt. You fhall not fly fo faft, as I'll purfue.

End of the Second Act.

7A (LL V.Xii)

Sir Samp. Oons you're a Crocodile.
Forr. Really, Sir Sampfon, this is a fudden Eclipfe.——
Sir Samp. You're an illiterate Fool, and I'm another, and the Starsare Lyars; and if I had breath enough, I'd curfe them and you, my felf and every Body— Oons, Cully'd, Bubbl'd, Jilted, Woman-bobb'd at laft—I have not Patience.—→ [Exit Sir Samp.
Tatt. If the Gentleman is in this diforder for want of a Wife, I can fpare him mine.

7B

Sir Samp. Oons you're a Crocodile.
Forr. Really, Sir Sampfon, this is a fudden Eclipfe.
Sir Samp. You're an illiterate old Fool, and I'm another.
Tatt. If the Gentleman is in Diforder for want of a Wife, I can fpare him mine.

8A (WW II.Vi)

may have been, I will leave you to confider ; and when you have done thinking of that ; think of me.   [Exit.
Mira. I have fomething more——Gone——Think of you! To think of a Whirlwind, tho' 'twere in a Whirlwind, were a Cafe of more fteady Contemplation ; a very tranquility of Mind and Manfion. A Fellow that lives in a Windmill, has not a more whimfical Dwelling than the Heart of a Man that is lodg'd in a Woman. There is no Point of the Compafsto

8B

and when you have done thinking of that, think of me.

SCENE VI.
Mirabell alone.

8C

SCENE VI.
MIRABELL alone.

I Have fomething more—Gone—Think of you! To think of a Whirlwind, tho' 'twere in a Whirlwind, were a Cafe of more fteady Contemplation; a very Tranquility of Mind and Manfion. A Fellow that lives in a Windmill, has not a more whimfical Dwelling than the Heart of a Man that is lodg'd in a Woman. There is no Point of the Compafs to which they cannot turn, and by which they are not ruffl'd; and by one as well as another; for Motion, not Method is their Occupation. To know this, and yet continue to be in Love, is to be made wife from the force of Inftinct.—O here come my Pair of Turtles.—What, billing fo fweetly! Is not Valentine's Day over with you yet?

9A (WW IV.V)

Sir Will. Your Servant, then with your leave I'll return to my Company.   [Exit.
Mill. Ay, ay, ha, ha, ha.
Like Phoebus fung the no lefs am'rous Boy.

Enter Mirabell.

Mir. —— Like Daphne fhe as lovely and as Coy.

9C

Sir WILFULL.
Your Servant, then with your leave I'll return to my Company.
MILLAMANT.
Ay, ay, ha, ha.
Like Phœbus fung the no lefs am'rous Boy.

SCENE V.
MILLAMANT, MIRABELL.
MIRABELL.
Like Daphne fhe as lovely and as Coy.
Do you lock your Gift up from me, to make my Search more curious? Or is that pretty Artifice contriv'd,

the fleeting image on a stage and the printed words on a page. The different verbal readings between quartos and *Works*, interpreted in the context of book trade history, oblige one to conflate. Textual faults which derive entirely from the non-verbal elements of display in the disposition of space significantly affect the dramatic form of Congreve's works and demand critical assessment and emendation. Our increased awareness of the role of typographic display in mediating the form of stage groupings and dramatic action should also compel us to show far more sensitivity to the same elements in our own printed editions of the same works. But current theories of textual criticism, indifferent as they are to the history of the book, its architecture, and the visual language of typography, are quite inadequate to cope with such problems. Only a new and comprehensive sociology of the text can embrace them.[51]

[51] I trust that this paper will have indicated some of the ramifications of the phrase "sociology of the text." Writers in the *Revue Française d'Histoire du Livre* have expressed a need for some such comprehensive approach to book-trade history. So G. Parguez writes: "Tout livre est un intermédiaire matériel mettant à la disposition de certaines classes des faits de civilisation. Ce n'est donc pas un objet isolé, à considerer en soi, pas plus qu'il ne se résume dans le message qu'il porte. Ce qui fait son originalité, c'est la manière dont le support matériel traduit le contenu notionnel ou social, ou si l'on veut, la manière dont certaines idées, certaines préoccupations propres à tel individu ou tel groupe ont utilisé pour s'exprimer ce moyen bien défini que constitue le livre imprimé" [Any book is a material intermediary which makes culture (literally "the facts of civilisation") available to particular social classes. It is therefore neither an isolated object, to be considered by itself, nor can it be reduced to the message it carries. Its uniqueness lies in the way in which its material form translates the notional or social content, or, to put it another way, the way particular ideas, the concerns of a certain individual or group, are expressed in and through this well-defined tool, the printed book] (*Revue Française d'Histoire du Livre* I (1971), p. 55). "La sociologie de la lecture" is a phrase used by Roger Chartier (ibid. p. 77), although Dudley Wilson, misquoting it as "sociologie du livre" in a review in *The Library* (Dec. 1972, p. 352), found it pretentious. Similar concerns inform the contributions to *Livre et Société dans la France du XVIIIᵉ Siècle* II (Paris, 1970), and of course the monumental exposition of the method is Henri-Jean Martin, *Livre, Pouvoirs et Société à Paris au XVIIᵉ Siècle* (Geneva, 1961). Robert Estivals in his contribution, "Bibliologie et Prospective," to *Le Livre Français Hier Aujourd'hui Demain*, ed. Julien Cain (Paris, 1972), argues for "une sociologie historique du livre" [an historical sociology of the book] which will wholly renew "la conception de l'histoire du livre" [the conception of the history of the book] (p. 291). [Trans. ed.]

As I understand it, however, in all those cases "sociology" is only a kind of predictive econometrics. It offers models of the book trade as interesting examples of categorisation but has as yet found no place for the fine detail of textual criticism. Unless applied to the subtleties of *that* relationship between author and reader, the generalisations will remain banal, at least for textual and literary criticism. The phrase "sociology of the text" does not exclude those concerns but seeks, by contrast, to make them bear finally on the most important one of all—what, exactly, an author in his own age did say to his readers and how he and his printers directed them to respond.

9

Speech—Manuscript—Print

1990

(↳ 1998)

McKenzie not only analyzed the physical features of seventeenth-century books, he also read them. This essay, which ranges over a broad spectrum of texts—including sermons, legal arguments, satirical "libels," political pamphlets, poems, catechisms, commentaries, didactic and devotional works, and almanacs—documents the anxieties and opportunities engendered by the growth of print in seventeenth-century England. Amplifying some of his arguments from "The London Book Trade in 1644," McKenzie sets out to correct misconceptions about "the impact of print" and its supposed "major displacement" of oral and manuscript communication. Examining the relations between speech and print and between manuscript and print, he argues that texts, in all their various forms, "tend to work in complementary, not competitive, ways." His analysis of paratextual and rhetorical strategies in seventeenth-century books demonstrates the extraordinary degree to which printed texts attempted to emulate features of speech and even dialogue. He also emphasizes that the traffic in manuscripts functioned concurrently with the book trade (a point more comprehensively treated in Harold Love's *Scribal Publication in Seventeenth-Century England* [1993] and Arthur Marotti's *Manuscript, Print, and the English Renaissance Lyric* [1995]), and he challenges the "obsession with the permanence of print," stressing instead its "ephemerality." Despite "its mythology as the art that preserves all art," printing, as any scholarly editor will know, is no guarantor of textual stability. Using detailed historical and literary evidence, McKenzie makes a broad conceptual point: an appropriately nuanced and responsible understanding of textuality in this period must take into account the fluidity that exists between apparently distinct textual modes. This essay first appeared in *New Directions in Textual Studies* (1990), a volume produced by the Harry Ransom Humanities Research Center at the University of Texas at Austin.

I N A RECENT PAPER on literacy in early modern England, Sir Keith Thomas remarked that "Early modern England was not an oral society. But neither was it a fully literate one. . . . It is the interaction between contrasting forms of culture, literate and illiterate, oral and written, which gives this period its particular fascination."[1] Even the title of Jack Goody's recent book, *The Interface between the Written and the Oral*, makes the same point;[2] and I was pleased to see it restated in Ruth Finnegan's *Literacy and Orality*.[3] Finnegan writes that orality and literacy "take

[1] Sir Keith Thomas, "The Meaning of Literacy in Early Modern England," in *The Written Word: Literacy in Transition*, ed. Gerd Baumann (Oxford: The Clarendon Press, 1986), p. 98.
[2] Jack Goody, *The Interface between the Written and the Oral* (Cambridge: Cambridge University Press, 1988).
[3] Ruth Finnegan, *Literacy and Orality* (Oxford: Blackwell, 1988).

diverse forms in differing cultures and periods, are used differently in different social contexts, and insofar as they can be distinguished at all as separate modes rather than a continuum, they mutually interact and affect each other, and the relations between them are problematic rather than self-evident."[4] That was certainly my own conclusion in a study, some years back, of orality, literacy, and print in early New Zealand.[5]

These reminders are timely, for a phrase like "the impact of print"—however carefully it is qualified—cannot help but imply a major displacement of writing as a form of record. In the same way, too great a preoccupation with writing and printing (as the technologies of literacy) may lead us to forget the superior virtues of speech. After all, we did not stop speaking when we learned to write, nor writing when we learned to print, nor reading, writing or printing when we entered "the electronic age." For those who market texts in those forms, some of them may seem mutually exclusive (do we read the book, hear it on tape, or see the film?), but for the speaker, auditor, reader or viewer, the texts tend to work in complementary, not competitive, ways. None surrenders its place entirely; all undergo some adjustment as new forms arrive and new complicities of interest and function emerge.

In taking speech, manuscript, and print as complementary modes, I had it in mind to ask about the extent to which, in the seventeenth century, they were thought to relate to one another; what anxieties there were about these different ways of communicating; what adjustments were made; whether or not the physical form of the texts might be read as in part effecting the meanings they convey; and how some consideration of these questions might bear on recent critical and historical work on printed texts.

Thomas Hobbes may have been right in saying that neither printing nor letters but speech was "the most noble and profitable invention of all other," but it is also the one most difficult to call from the past and give in evidence.[6] What we can recall, however, are records of moments of anxiety and of hesitant adjustment.

> When the Sunne lightneth one *Hemisphere*, another *Hemisphere* is full of darkenesse: so it seems you would conclude [said the troubled parishioner to his preacher], that one congregation which heares Preaching shall be saued; and another congregation which heares Reading shall be damned. The light of the one belike, is the darkenesse of the other; and the saluation of the one, is the destruction of the other.

So, should we hear the word preached, or hear the word read?

---

[4] Ibid., p. 175.

[5] D. F. McKenzie, *Oral Culture, Literacy and Print in Early New Zealand: The Treaty of Waitangi* (Wellington: Victoria University Press, 1985). In that essay I was concerned to reveal the serious political implications of certain Eurocentric assumptions about literacy and printing when introduced into an oral society.

[6] Thomas Hobbes, *Leviathan Or the Matter, Forme, and Power of A Commonwealth Ecclesiasticall and Civile* (1651), part I, chapter 4, Wing H2246.

The opposition of wicked men, and of the Diuell in all ages of the world, against preaching, and his and their quiet allowance of reading, argueth the extreame euill of ignorance, and the destruction that comes without preaching.[7]

Behind all this, of course, lies an important theological debate but the problem is also, I think, a psychological one. Even we feel some reverse anxiety as we shift from pen and paper to our PC screens—the fear that, by the flick of a switch, or the touch of a key, our words in this new form may once more prove as evanescent as . . . speech. But we do, in time, adjust.

The problem of knowing how people spoke or responded to speech is rather like trying to find out how people read and what they made of their reading: it is exceedingly difficult to recover, as a matter of history, the quality of such ephemeral textual acts. But a good start in tackling both problems is to begin with our own social experience of each. We know, for example, that an important difference between talking and writing is what is now called "presence." The spoken text can be more sharply defined, and its authority enhanced, by the speaker's control of tone, nuance, gesture, and responsiveness to an audience. Or we may—as an audience—resent these rhetorical limits on the free play of meaning and reject the spurious authority of such personal appeal. In communities where oral and literate traditions are still felt to collide, as they do in some post-colonial countries, the mode of exchange one adopts (speech or writing, personal or remote) is crucially important. For those whose habitual mode is oral, the very effort to receive or record experience in unfamiliar ways entails significant questions of self-definition and social exchange.

We come close to that kind of experience, I think, in Shakespeare's *Troilus and Cressida*. It is that painful moment when Troilus must, but cannot, tell himself that Cressid is a whore. Resisting the experience of even his own eyes and ears, he refuses to believe what they tell him. Were he to publish an account of Cressid's conduct, it must be received as a lie. He has seen her with Diomed, and overheard her speak. Ulysses would draw him away, but Troilus pauses; Ulysses asks, "Why stay we then?," and Troilus, half speaking to himself, says:

> To make a recordation to my soule
> Of euery syllable that here was spoke:
> But if I tell how these two did coact;
> Shall I not lye, in publishing a truth?
> Sith yet there is a credence in my heart:
> An esperance so obstinately strong,
> That doth inuert that test of eyes and eares;
> As if those organs had deceptious functions,

---

[7] Edward Vaughan, *A plaine and perfect Method, for the easie understanding of the whole Bible: CONTAINING Seauen Obseruations, Dialoguewise, betweene the PARISHIONER, and the PASTOR* (1603), cited here from the reprint of 1617, STC 24600, pp. 32–3, 42.

> Created onely to calumniate.
> Was *Cressed* here?
> [Fl, V.ii. 113–23]

At such a moment we catch the agony of Troilus's resistance to Cressid's recital of her new love; and in this challenge to what he thought he knew by what he now sees and hears, and in his effort to articulate and inscribe his new knowledge—to make that "recordation" to his soul, and even to *publish* its truth—we see too something of a condition others felt in coping with how truths (initially seen and spoken) should be reported and received.

Shakespeare, of course, goes right to the heart of the matter. Yet even among lesser writers we find, if poorly expressed, a similar concern with the psychology of knowledge in relation to the forms in which it is communicated: "*What the Pulpit sent to some of your eares, the Presse now sends to some of your eyes; the good God send it into every one of your hearts, into your hands, and lives; the Argument is worthy of your eares, eyes, hearts, and hands. . . .*"[8] So wrote Edmund Staunton in 1644, self-conscious still about turning speech into print and suspicious of its ability to enter the heart. Or John Strickland, the same year: the words "*have been already in your eares, they are now before your eyes, the Lord write them into our hearts, that we may be doers of the word, and not hearers onely. . . .*"[9]

The problem is familiar to everyone who has pondered the relation between dramatic performances and printed play texts: John Marston, for one. In his address to the reader of *The Malcontent* in 1604, he says it is "*my custome to speake as I thinke, and to write as I speake.*" And so he complains that "*Scaenes invented, meerely to be spoken, should be inforcively published to be read,*" and asks "*that the vnhansome shape which this trifle in reading presents may be pardoned, for the pleasure it once afforded you, when it was presented with the soule of lively action.*"[10] So too Peter Smith, in 1644, laments the loss, in print, of both his own and his congregation's "lively action," for his printed sermon "*will now want that little life it seem'd to have when it was utter'd viva voce, and entertained with your chearfull and religious attention.*"[11]

John Marston thinks of his text as one to be spoken and heard, not printed and read; he laments the loss of "the soule of lively action"; and he thinks of the book as fixing his play in an "vnhansome shape." But Marston had at least a prewritten and memorized text whose translation to print was not impossible. We have only to think of other essentially theatrical places—the fairground and the market, for example—to recall that some oral modes are even less compatible with print. Fairground speech is a series of most remarkable oral performances, and yet the delivery of the words themselves is only one of a whole range of bodily skills, both audible and visible, we see deployed at fairs: gesture, movement, costume, and, as any good barrowman still shows, the skillful use of props.

---

[8] Edmund Staunton, *Rypes Israelis: The Rock of Israel*, Wing S5342.
[9] John Strickland, *A Discovery of Peace*, Wing S5969.
[10] John Marston, *The Malcontent*, STC 17481, sig. A2ʳ.
[11] Peter Smith, *A Sermon preach'd . . . May 29, 1644*, Wing S4142.

These are all—including speech—kinetic arts, flexibly inter-active with their spectators, ephemeral as the fair itself. And we can't write them down. There's no script. Their conversion to print is impossible.

To cite Sir Keith Thomas again:

> Oral communication remained central, whether as speeches in Parliament, pleadings in the lawcourts, teaching in the schools, or preaching and catechizing in church. Despite their reliance on the Bible and the Prayer Book, the clergy still expected their flock to learn their articles of belief by heart and to listen to spoken sermons.[12]

And yet that dual pressure to listen *and* to read created problems of choice and adjustment. Almost every printed sermon in the first half of the century has something to say by way of apology for the loss of the preacher's presence. "I know well that *the same Sermon, as to the life of it, is scarcely the same in the hearing, and in the reading*," wrote John Ward in 1645.[13] In 1617, in his new edition of *A Plaine and perfect Method, for the easie understanding of the whole Bible,* Edward Vaughan presented a pastor who urged his parishioners to "sequester your selues from your publike affaires, and sometimes from your most private occasions, for the orderly and thorow reading" of the Bible. The whole point of his book was to encourage *reading.* Yet the pastor also needs to exalt *preaching*:

> Our eares were specially giuen vnto vs, to be as messengers and true embassadours to the heart. . . . No man can haue Faith without the *hearing* of Gods word—[and] how can a man *hear* without a Preacher? . . . Take away the preacher take away the word, take away the word take away hearing, take away hearing take away Faith, take away Faith take away calling vpon God, take away calling vpon God take away salvation in Christ.

His parishioner sees at once the contradiction: ". . . In prouing that faithe comes by *hearing* the word preached, you goe also about to proue, that the word being *read* priuately at home, or publikely in Churches, availes nothing. . . ."[14] There is a compromise, of course, in the advice that home reading of scripture has a complementary if secondary role to play to the preacher's one of direct address.

Concern and regret, if not quite anxiety, may also be found with the gradual shift from oral to written pleading in the law courts. Under the system of oral pleading, the forms were settled only after exhaustive debate in court, with all the opportunities it provided for clarification and correction. Then, when the pleadings were enrolled, they were accurate. By contrast, written pleadings, whose terms were settled by the parties out of court, were open to error. Matthew Hale, for example, in his *History of the Common Law,* thought the oral

---

[12] Thomas, "The Meaning of Literacy," p. 113.
[13] John Ward, *God ivdging among the Gods,* Wing W773.
[14] Edward Vaughan, *A plaine and perfect Method,* pp. 25–6, 29–30, 32.

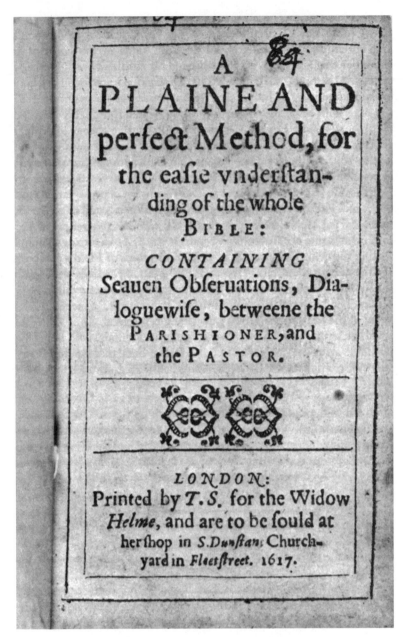

Title page from Edward Vaughan's *A Plaine and perfect Method, for the easie vnderstanding of the whole Bible* (London: T. S., 1617). HRHRC Collections.

evidence at common law far superior to the written evidence in courts of equity, because it is delivered

> personally, and not in Writing; [in writing] oftentimes, yea too often, a crafty Clerk, Commissioner or Examiner, will make a Witness speak what he truly never meant, by dressing of it up in his own Terms, Phrases, and Expressions; whereas on the other Hand, many Times the very Manner of a Witness's delivering his Testimony will give a probable indication whether he speaks truly or falsly; and by this Means also he has Opportunity to correct, amend, or explain his Testimony upon further questioning with him, which he can never have after a Deposition is set down in Writing.[15]

That is a good description of the virtues of speech as presence. Another legal example neatly shows how oral evidence may unwittingly outwit written proof. Francis North was trying an action brought by a cook for goods he had sold to a man who still owed him payment. The defendant produced a written receipt showing that the cook had been fully paid off to 1677.

> The cook started forth . . .; and, 'My Lord,' said he, very quick and earnest, 'I was paid but to 1676.' At that moment his lordship concluded the cook said true; for liars do not use to burst out in that unpremeditated manner. . . . Then his lordship . . . sitting under a window, turned round, and looked through the paper against the light; and so discovered plainly the last figure in the date of the year, was 6, in rasure; but was wrote 7 with ink.[16]

The paradox of writing—that what seems *exact* when first written can be torn a thousand ways by critical reading—led Francis Bacon to resist the reduction of common law to statute form. As he said in 1616, "there are more doubts that rise upon our statutes, which are a text law, than upon the common law, which is no text law."[17]

When William Laud delivered his last "Speech or His Funerall Sermon, Preacht by himself on the Scaffold . . . 10, of Ianuary, 1644[−5]," it was, we are assured by the title page of the printed text, "All faithfully Written by John Hinde, whom the Arch-bishop beseeched that he would not let any wrong be done him by any phrase in false Copies."[18] Laud had carefully written it out, not to read it but to speak it from memory, and then to leave a true manuscript record of his last words. But even these were edited, for his printed speech does not allow him to say, as a manuscript does, and as he did in person, that "as for this people They are this day miserably misled . . . , for at this day, The blinde lead the

---

[15] Sir Matthew Hale, *History of the Common Law* (1713), 2nd ed. corrected, cited by W. S. Holdsworth, *A History of English Law*, 16 vols. (London: J. Nutt, 1922–66): vi.592n.1.

[16] Holdsworth, *English Law*, vi. 389 n. 3. The story is told by Roger North: see *The Lives of . . . Francis North . . . Dudley North . . . and John North*, 3 vols. (1826), i. 234.

[17] *The Works of Francis Bacon*, ed. J. Spedding, 14 vols. (1857–74): xiii (*The Letters and Life*, vi. 67); cited by J. H. Baker, *An Introduction to English Legal History*, 2nd ed. (London: Butterworths, 1979), p. 189.

[18] For Laud's sermon, see Wing L599; the Bodleian pressmark for the annotated copy cited above ("Corrected from the Original") is : G. Pamph. 369 (16).

blinde. . . ."[19] Nor could he continue to say in print, as he did in person, "I am not only the first Archbishop, but the first man that ever dyed by an ordinance in Parliament in this way."[20] But the printed text of Laud's speech does catch a sentence in which we can see him more troubled by the transmission of his words in their perilous passage from manuscript back to memory, from memory to speech, and from speech to its printed memorial, than by his then more imminent journey. "I cannot say I have spoken every word as it is in my Paper, but I have gone very neere it, to help my memory as well as I could; but I beseech you, let me have no wrong done me . . . a phrase may doe me wrong."[21]

Laud's head was no sooner off than Henry Burton published an attack on him, accusing him of merely repeating by heart a lesson he had "writ out"—and as to his so-called "Sermon, *how it could be truely said to be preacht, when he read it verbatim, as also how he could properly be said to pray, what he read in his paper (for without his book he could neither preach nor pray) I leave it thy right judgement.*"[22] My own quotations from Laud's final speech come from a Bodleian copy of one of the printed versions altered in a contemporary hand after collation with what the annotator must have thought to be an authentic manuscript. But there must have been many other versions, for manuscripts were ubiquitous.

Just as some social functions could still only be performed orally, so too society could only be administered effectively at a distance by manuscript. Acts and proclamations might be printed and widely dispersed (though many orders and resolutions of Parliament were not—some were merely proclaimed), but most of the executive actions taken to implement them were initiated in writing. All government agencies, the church, law, education, and commerce were more dependent upon written records than printed ones. Scriveners drove a thriving trade in both the formal and informal production of texts; and for what we might think of as literary and political texts there was a well-organized manuscript trade, functioning concurrently with the one in printed books. Indeed, Dr. Harold Love has recently gone so far as to claim that "Scribal publication . . . [was] an accepted and important medium for the transmission of texts during the seventeenth century, quite equal in terms of status to transmission in printed form. . . ."[23] His findings chime perfectly with those of W. J. Cameron some twenty-five years ago.[24] When preparing his volume in the series of poems on affairs of state, Cameron discovered how many different manuscript collections

[19] Ibid.

[20] Ibid.

[21] Ibid.

[22] There were several attacks on Laud's sermon. For Henry Burton, see his (anonymous) *A Full and Satisfactorie Ansvvere*, Wing B6162A, and *The Grand Imposter vnmasked*, Wing B6163. See also William Starbucke, *A briefe Exposition . . . upon the Lord of Canterburies Sermon or Speech*, Wing S5266.

[23] Harold Love, "Scribal Publication in Seventeenth-century England," *Transactions of the Cambridge Bibliographical Society*, ix (1987): 147. This valuable essay has provided me with several examples pertinent to the argument of the present paper. His "Manuscript versus Print in the Transmission of English Literature 1600–1700," *BSANZ Bulletin* 9 (1985): 95–107, should also be consulted.

[24] W. J. Cameron, "A Late Seventeenth-century Scriptorium," *Renaissance and Modern Studies* 7 (1963): 25–52.

seemed, from their materials, contents, and scribal features, to come from a single source. His conclusion was that, far from disappearing with the advent of print, commercial scriptoria played a continuously active role in the publication of texts in manuscript copies right throughout the century. They were still highly productive even in the 1690s. In a 1662 "Project for Preventing Libells," we find the comment: "Of Libells some are only written, others printed; and those in Manuscript are commonly ye more seditious & scandalous of ye two; Besides that they are forty times as many, & by the help of Transcripts, well nigh as publick as the other."[25]

The fact that some scribal products were libels should not be allowed to distort the more important recognition of manuscript both as a normal form of personal record, and as a normal form of publication. Ordinary booksellers and stationers dealt in manuscripts, new and secondhand, as well as printed books. L'Estrange in 1675, though still obsessed with manuscript libels, said that "certain Stationers are supposed to bee the chiefe, and profest dealers in them, as having some Affinity with their Trade."[26] Law stationers, like Starkey and Collins, provided what was almost an instant service for students at the Inns of Court, supplying popular cribs quickly and (one supposes) cheaply. The last point is important. Manuscripts were economically competitive because printing requires high initial investment in typesetting and a low unit cost which is achieved only by having a large number of copies. Anything under a hundred is hardly economical. Manuscript production, however, like binding, was in part a bespoke trade: one-off or several copies could be done on demand; the market was almost self-defining; there was no problem of keeping type standing; and no problem of unsold stocks.

Robert Cotton, as Harold Love records, virtually confined himself to manuscript publication.[27] John Donne's verse, writes Mr. Peter Beal, "belonged essentially to a manuscript culture."[28] The copy for Selden's *Table Talk*, when printed in 1689, was simply one of several transcripts produced in a scriptorium. Again, as Harold Love reminds us, not only Donne, but King, Crashaw, Strode, Corbet, and Suckling all gained reputations as poets during their lifetimes "without ever issuing a printed collection of their verse."[29] One immediate, surprising, and textually challenging fact revealed by the relevant volume of *The Index of English Literary Manuscripts* is the existence of some 4,000 seventeenth-century manuscript copies of individual poems by Donne. Any single collection, of course, may contain up to a hundred; even so, to quote Mr. Beal, these "must be only a fraction

---

[25] The report was probably drawn up by Roger L'Estrange. He repeats parts of it in "Mr. L'Estraings Proposition concerning Libells, &c." of 11 November 1675: see H.M.C. 9th *Report*, Appendix, p. 66b. PRO SP29/51/10.1.

[26] "Mr. L'Estraings Proposition," p. 1, cited by Love, p. 142.

[27] Love, "Scribal Publication," p. 133.

[28] *Index of English Literary Manuscripts*, Volume 1, 1450–1625, compiled by Peter Beal (London: Mansel, 1980), p. 245.

[29] Love, "Scribal Publication," p. 131.

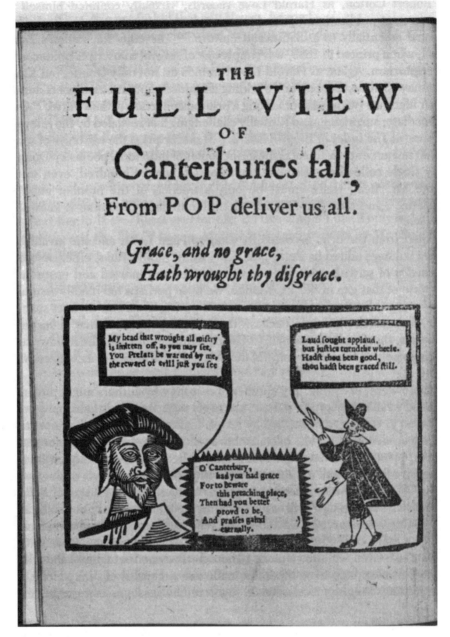

From William Starbucke's *A briefe Exposition, Paraphrase, or Interpretation, upon the Lord of Canterburies Sermon or Speech* (London, 1645), p. 14. HRHRC Collections.

of the number once in existence," and only one English poetical autograph of Donne is known to survive.[30]

Apart from the brief accounts by Cameron and Love, and the invaluable *Index* volumes edited by Peter Beal, the extent, implications, efficiency, and normalcy of scribal publication have remained unreported and unstudied. Because of that gap in our knowledge, we have perhaps too readily assumed the "non-publication" of texts (often also imputing irrelevant motives such as fear of censorship) simply because there is no printed edition. I suspect, however, that for all the normalcy of manuscript publication, the handwritten text also helped to assuage some of the psychological anxieties associated with print.

There were, of course, any number of reasons why authors might prefer to be read in manuscript. In part, it has to do with that question of presence (greatest in speech, still implied by script, least of all in print). Some writers were troubled by their loss of control over their texts; for them and for many others, printing was too impersonal, too public, too fixed, and often far too expensive for the small number of copies required.

Sir Thomas Browne, referring to the first unauthorized edition of *Religio Medici*, says any reader "will easily discerne the intention was not publik: and being a private exercise directed to my selfe, what is delivered therein was rather a memoriall unto me then an example or rule unto any other."[31] But private use often included a circle of friends. Browne lent it out—and it was copied. Subscription to a newsletter made one a member of such a circle. So Ben Jonson's *Staple of News* would report all the gossip in manuscript:

> FIT. O Sir! it is the printing we oppose.
> CYM. We not forbid that any *Newes*, be made,
> But that 't be printed; for when *Newes* is printed,
> It leaues Sir to be *Newes*. While 'tis but written—
> FIT. Though it be ne're so false, it runnes *Newes* still.
> P. IV. See divers mens opinions! unto some,
> The very printing of them, makes them *Newes*;
> That ha' not the heart to beleeue any thing,
> But what they see in print. FIT. I, that's an Error
> Ha's abus'd many; but we shall reforme it. . . .[32]

Donne had no intention of publishing his *Biothanatos*, so that its posthumous printing in 1646 is no evidence of some new liberal dispensation. As he wrote to Robert Ker in 1619: "Reserve it for me, if I live, and if I die, I only forbid it the Presse, and the fire."[33] In one of his Latin poems, cited by Mr. Beal in Edmund Blunden's translation, Donne writes:

---

[30] Beal, *English Literary Manuscripts*, p. 245.

[31] Sir Thomas Browne, *Religio Medici and Other Works*, ed. L. C. Martin (Oxford, 1964), p. 1.

[32] Ben Jonson, *Staple of News*, I.v.46–55, in *Ben Jonson*, ed. Herford and Simpson, 11 vols. (Oxford, 1925–52), vi.295. Jonson had used almost identical words in his masque *Newes from the New World*, first performed early in 1620: see Herford and Simpson, vii.515.

[33] John Donne, *Letters to Severall Persons of Honour* (1651), p. 22; cited by Love, p. 140.

What Printing-presses yield we think good store
But what is writ by hand we reverence more:
A book that with this printing-blood is dyed
On shelves for dust and moths is set aside,
But if 't be penned it wins a sacred grace
And with the ancient Fathers takes its place.[34]

For the reader of manuscripts, that association was less important perhaps than a sense of privilege at being close to the writer, at being one of a more select community than the amorphous readership of print. So Edward Coke of his reports: "As I never meant . . . to keep them so secret for my own private use as to deny the request of any friend to have either view or copy of any of them: so till of late I never could be persuaded . . . to commit them to print."[35] Edmund Plowden, writing of his law reports, says: "This work I originally entered upon with a view to my own private instruction only, without the least thought or intention of letting it appear in print. . . ."[36] Matthew Hale spent forty years collecting and ordering his manuscripts, but even in his will prohibited publication of anything he had not expressly approved as ready for press. He specifically enjoined Lincoln's Inn not to print them but to keep them as a consultable resource for law students: "I would have nothing of these books printed, but intirely preserved together for the use of the industrious learned members of that Society." They were, he said, "a treasure that are not fit for every man's view, nor is every man capable of making use of them."[37] Roger North's brother left him "all his draughts, such as he himself had corrected" and used as a working book of precedents.[38] Orlando Bridgman's reports were used in the same way by such authorities as Matthew Hale and John Holt, but they remained unprinted until 1823. Whether laziness or busyness was the reason, Egerton published nothing except his judgment in *Calvin's Case*; and this he says was only done at the King's command: "Thus I was put to an unexpected labour, to review my scribbled and broken papers."[39]

But papers like these were not all safe from the energy of copyists. According to the 1694 edition of Hale's *Pleas of the Crown*, he wrote it wholly for his own use, but an edition had been printed in 1678 "from a surreptitious and very faulty copy."[40] Plowden lent one "to a very few of my intimate friends" but "their clerks and others knowing thereof got the book into their hands, and made such expedition by writing day and night, that in a short time they had transcribed a great number of the cases. . . ."[41] Since they did it so badly, Plowden felt obliged

---

[34] Beal, *English Literary Manuscripts*, p. 245.
[35] Holdsworth, *History of Law*, v. 364 n. 3.
[36] Ibid., v. 364 n. 2.
[37] Ibid., vi. 583, 584 n. 1.
[38] Ibid., vi. 604 n. 7.
[39] Ibid., v. 234 n. 5.
[40] Hale, *Pleas of the Crown* (1694), cited by Holdsworth, *History of Law*, v. 366 n. 1.
[41] Holdsworth, *History of Law*, v. 366 n. 1.

to prepare it himself for press. Such explanations, or excuses, abound. In an oft-quoted passage, George Wither complained that if a bookseller "gett any Coppy into his powre, likely to be vendible, whether the Author be willing or no, he will publish it; And it shall be continued and named alsoe, according to his owne pleasure: which is the reason, so many good Bookes come forth imperfect, and with foolish titles."[42] Of the hundreds of seventeenth-century editions of law books, many are wrongly attributed and only a few have reliable texts (Humphrey Winch even records his own death). The main reason was the immense variety of manuscript sources, their wide textual divergence, and the reluctance of the best legal minds to accept that the law should be fixed in public print. On this last point, L. O. Pike says "the continual use of [manuscript records] must have rendered many obvious corrections in them a matter of comparative ease."[43] Manuscripts could be supplemented, shuffled, and re-ordered more easily than the folded and bound sheets of a book. But printers in time rose to the challenge. A favorite method of acquiring a practical knowledge of the law was to make up a commonplace book under alphabetical heads, and so, in 1680–81, Samuel Brewster produced an *Alphabetical Disposition of all the Heads necessary for a perfect Commonplace*. This was a printed book in which you could insert manuscript entries under any of 1,622 heads and sub-heads.

The law is a rich source of evidence on seventeenth-century textual practices and mal-practices—in oral, written, and printed forms. What the variety of legal texts makes vividly clear is the complementary nature of all three modes and yet the uneasiness many still felt about moving between them. Even lawyers show the signs of anxiety we have seen in playwrights and preachers.

The same is true of many poets. Some of course did print their work, though not without qualms. As Dr. John Pitcher has pointed out, citing the following example, Samuel Daniel seems to be a clear case of a writer troubled by the embarrassing permanence of print, its unrevisability, the unretractable nature of its statements.[44] In 1607, in a collected edition which he modestly called *Certaine Small Workes*, Daniel opens with a newly written poem addressed to the Reader. Would to God, he writes towards the end, that

> . . . [I] might revers
> The errors of my judgment passed here
> Or elswhere, in my bookes, and vnrehearce
> What I haue vainely said . . .
> I will aske nothing therein for my paine
> But onely to haue in mine owne againe.[45]

---

[42] George Wither, *The Schollers Purgatory, Discovered in the Stationers Commonwealth* (1617), p. 121; cited by Love, p. 141.

[43] Luke Owen Pike, *Yearbooks of the Reign of King Edward the Third*, vol. 12 (Condon: H. M. Stationery Office, 1883), p. 535.

[44] I am most grateful to Dr. Pitcher for bringing this example to my attention.

[45] Samuel Daniel, *Certaine Small Workes*, STC 6240.

The moments of self-definition offered by print and embraced so positively by Jonson, become for Daniel a prison in which he feels himself trapped. *Delia* may have been the perfect anagram of his *ideal*, but every attempt to capture her (or himself) in print proves in time to be imperfect, and so he pines for the less rigid modes of sight and sound, the tolerances of recall and revision. Yet, being printed, the earlier forms live on to testify against him. Anagrammatically, his "ideal" is never quite "a lie," but nor can it ever truly spell "Daniel."

This obsession with the permanence of print is a powerful element in its mythology as the art that preserves all arts. And yet it is only part of the story. What it fails to provide for is the problem that troubled Daniel and, later, Yeats and James: the impulse to qualify and revise. What needs, I think, to be equally stressed is the *ephemerality* of print. On any larger view, the book trade is economically dependent upon ideas wearing out—on the dynamics of change. Revised texts are a good excuse to go yet again to market; and, in the exchange of ideas, one book is never more than a thesis, or an antithesis, in an endless dialectic which is both intellectual and commercial.

That interplay is invariably occluded in the collected editions of single canonical authors, and yet we can recover it from the ephemeral world of seventeenth-century sermons, topical pamphlets, and serials, and it is here we get our clearest view of both the anxieties created by print and the possibilities it opened up.

Peter Smith, in 1644, after quoting Romans to the effect that faith comes by preaching, tentatively concedes that "*memory is frail; and to reflect again, by reading, upon that wch we have heard, may conduce much unto the improvement of your knowledge.*"[46] Christopher Tesdale, the same year, says to his readers: "*I shall bee your remembrancer by restoring the losse of the eare to the eye: Words, we say, are wind, and unless they be taken upon the wing, even while they are flying, and brought to the Presse, they are gone and lost.*"[47] John Brinsley modestly records that his sermon "not altogether *unsuccessefull* in the *hearing* [may be] not wholly *unusefull* in the *reading.*"[48] One can almost hear these writers sighing before conceding. Even Richard Baxter seems to suggest only that print is at least one way of making the best of a bad job: "When Vocal preaching faileth, and Preachers are ignorant, ungodly or dull," he wrote in 1673, printed sermons can help to supply those deficiencies.[49] And of course one can sometimes say

---

[46] Peter Smith, *A Sermon preach'd* . . . *May 29, 1644*, Wing S4142.

[47] Christopher Tesdale, *Hiervsalem*, Wing T792.

[48] John Brinsley, *The Saints solemne Covenant*, Wing B4728.

[49] For Richard Baxter, see *A Christian Directory* (1673), p. 60. The passage from Baxter is worth quoting more extensively: "Vocal preaching hath the preheminence in moving the affections, and being diversified according to the state of the Congregations which attend it: This way the Milk cometh warmest from the breast. But books have the advantage in many other respects: you may read an able Preacher when you have but a mean one to hear. Every *Congregation* cannot hear the most judicious or powerful Preachers: but every *single person* may *read* the *Books* of the most powerful and judicious; *Preachers* may be silenced or banished, when *Books* may be at hand: *Books* may be kept at a smaller charge than Preachers: We may choose Books which treat of that very subject which we desire to hear of; but we cannot choose what subject the Preacher shall treat of. Books we may have at hand every day and hour: when we can have Sermons but seldom, and at set times. If Sermons be forgotten, they are gone. But a Book we may read over and over til we remember it: and if we forget it, may again peruse it at our pleasure, or at our leisure."

more in print. Richard Vines, 1644, knew the brevity of an audience's patience: his sermon *The impostures of seducing teachers discovered* is presented "*to your hands and eyes, with some enlargements here and there, which the time denyed to your eares.*"[50] John Strickland says he was compelled to shorten his text of *Immanuel* when speaking it before the Lords in 1644, giving "the rest by pieces, . . . [but] Now the Presse hath given me leave a little better to gather the materialls, which then I scattered, and to couple all into some better proportion by the sinews of coherence, that I may present you with the intire (though yet unpolished) body of my Medita-tions. . . ."[51] What is revealing about these unprofound comments is their fre-quency, their self-consciousness, and their still tentative quality.

When we look at the books themselves, we can see writers and printers seek-ing to limit the difference of print by devising ways to suggest its affinities with speaking and writing. It is most notable of course in forms of address and of di-alogue; and it is there in the typography itself. So, as a rhetorical strategy, Mil-ton's *Areopagitica, a Speech . . . To the Parliament of England*, assumes an oral condition: "They who, to States and Governors of the Commonwealth direct their Speech, High Court of Parliament, or wanting such access in a private condition, write that which they foresee may advance the public good. . . ."[52] By adopting such a form, Milton becomes present to the Commons, and yet his pamphlet is clearly written to be read, not heard. The amphibolous state of that "speech" or "pam-phlet" is shared in part by the addresses to Parliament which precede *The Doctrine and Discipline of Divorce* and *Tetrachordon*. And when we come to the letter (or should it be tract), *Of Education*, we see Milton exploiting yet another interstitial space. Is this a private letter made public print ("Thus Master *Hartlib*, you have a generall view in writing of that which I had severall times discourst with you . . .");[53] or is it really conceived as a text to be printed which merely exploits the fiction of being a private communication? It seems to me that both texts (*Of Education* and *Areopagitica*) are genuinely ambiguous about their status, that Milton moves eas-ily and positively into their double roles, and that his fluency in speech, manu-script, and print is not simply a mark of his genius but one of the times. Writ-ing of toleration in 1673, in his little tract *Of True Religion*, Milton holds that Protestants should be able "on all occasions to give account of their Faith, . . . by Arguing, Preaching in their several Assemblies, Publick writing, and the free-dom of Printing."[54] In other words, in each and every mode.

The development in print of different registers to signal such a variety of forms is one of the fascinating features of the book trade at this time. Milton's "Publick writing" is a phrase exactly right for his own sense of address. This

---

[50] Richard Vines, Wing V557.

[51] John Strickland, Wing S5969.

[52] John Milton, *Areopagitica, a Speech . . . To the Parliament of England*, Wing M2092.

[53] John Milton, Of Education, Wing M2132.

[54] John Milton, Of True Religion, Haeresie, Schism, Toleration, and what best means may be us'd against the growth of Popery (1673), p. 8, Wing M2135.

practice of using print more generally as if it *were* a public speaking and writing is found at its most efficient in the informal genres of ephemera, the small pamphlet, and the printed speech. There is a form of communicative interchange here, the extent of which, as a proportion of the texts published, might be hard to parallel in the years immediately before or after the seventeenth century.

It is quite remarkable, for example, how many texts imply some kind of direct address or dialogue. Milton's *Colasterion* is "A reply to a nameless answer against . . ." *The Doctrine and Discipline of Divorce*.[55] His epigraph—"Answer a fool according to his folly, lest he be wise in his own conceit"—is a common imperative in the period.[56] Wing lists 424 titles which begin in the form "An answer to." Another 562 begin as titles of address in the form "To the . . ."; "Humble" addresses, desires, hints, petitions, propositions, remonstrances, representations, requests, supplications, and so on, account for another 327. Petitions, Proposals, and Propositions (ones which, not being "humble," are entered under "P") number 317. "His Majesty" answers, declares, or sends messages to another 30. Titles beginning with the words Animadversion, Answer, Antidote, Confutation, Dialogue (153 of this), Reflection, Refutation, Remarks, Reply, Response, Voice, and Vox, together number 604. "A Letter" or "Letters to" account for 802 items. The round total they make is at least 3,066—a figure which excludes all separate-issues and re-issues and reprintings, and (with the sole exception of His Majesty) every item (at least as many again) whose author is known to Wing and is therefore found under the author's name. This rapid interchange of highly topical texts, of short pamphlets with short lives, helped to break down the anxiety-provoking distinctions among speech, manuscript, and print.

Those features of social exchange are expressed also in the very form of many texts. We should not allow the almost uniformly poor execution of English printing in the seventeenth century to blind us to the virtues of its typographic display, or, in the phrase of the time, its "setting forth." The phrase is one we recall from the dedication to *Shake-speares Sonnets* (see facing page). This "setting forth" is both a financial venture and a careful display of the dedication and the text.[57] Marston in *The Malcontent* wrote: "*I have my selfe . . . set forth this Comedie.*"[58] Heminge and Condell wished that "the Author himself had liu'd to haue set forth, and ouerseen his owne writings."[59] Harington's 1591 *Orlando Furioso* has before it "AN ADVERTISEMENT TO THE READER BEFORE HE READE THIS POEM, OF SOME THINGS TO BE OBSERVED, *as well in the substance of this worke, as in the setting foorth thereof*. . . ."[60] That "setting foorth" is a highly intelligent disposition of all the book's communicative modes, not just to present a text for the reader, but to

---

[55] John Milton, *Colasterion*, Wing M2099.

[56] Ibid.

[57] *Shake-speares Sonnets* (1609), STC 22353, sig. A2ʳ.

[58] Marston, *The Malcontent*, STC 17481, sig. A2ʳ.

[59] *Mr. William Shakespeares Comedies, Histories, & Tragedies. Published according to the True Originall Copies* (1623), STC 22273, sig. A3ʳ.

[60] Ludovico Ariosto, *Orlando Furioso*, trans. Sir John Harington (London: Richard Field, 1591), STC 746.

TO.THE.ONLIE.BEGETTER.OF.
THESE.INSVING.SONNETS.
M⁅.W. H. ALL.HAPPINESSE.
AND.THAT.ETERNITIE.
PROMISED.

BY.

OVR.EVER-LIVING.POET.

WISHETH.

THE.WELL-WISHING.
ADVENTVRER.IN.
SETTING.
{FORTH.

T. T.

Dedication from *Shake-speares Sonnets. A Facsimile of the Earliest Editions,* published for the Elizabethan Club (New Haven and London: Yale University Press, 1964). *General Libraries.*

present a set of different texts for different readerships ("because all that may read this booke are not of equall capacities").[61]

Printing is much inferior to speech when it comes to conveying the spatial dynamics of speaker and audience. Even word spaces are not speech pauses. Yet space is one of the strongest weapons in a printer's arsenal. The multiplication of copies, portability, and permanence are all, in some way, time-space functions. On the other hand, printing is far superior to speech in the spaced presentation of forms that cannot be read aloud (lists, tables, branching and other graphic configurations), and with those skills at their fingertips, it is only to be expected that printers would try to "set forth" in their own terms at least something of the social space of dialogue.

The catechism is the commonest form in which we find speakers situated one to another in dialogue. Roger L'Estrange saw the appeal of the form as one that shared the qualities of speech and print. In his *The Observator. In Dialogue*, he writes of it "as a Method that is more *Familiar*, and *Entertaining*. Where you find Any thing in it, that pretends to *Salt*, or *Fooling*; you must Understand it as a kind of Composition betwixt Mee and the Multitude; For that which is *Serious*, and Necessary will not go down without it."[62] The title page of Edward Vaughan's *A plaine and perfect Method, for the easie vnderstanding of the whole Bible* (1617), continues: "CONTAINING *Seauen Obseruations, Dialoguewise, betweene the PARISHIONER, and the PASTOR*." The Parishioner discourses throughout in the increasingly demotic roman type and the Pastor in all the formal authority of black letter.

Where the extensions of dialogue are most notable is in the inter-textual levels we find within so many pamphlets. One common way of presenting them was for the writer to alternate his new counter-text with the excerpted, adapted, and re-structured texts of other writers. So Francis Quarles, in his defense of Cornelius Burges (1644), has the biblical David present the text of Burges; Calumniator, son of Nimshi (a great worshipper of calves), speaks the text of Burges's critics; and Quarles's own text is given to Jonathan as The Replyer.[63] Paragraph by paragraph throughout the book they take their turn in the debate. In Francis Cheynell's attack on William Chillingworth, the questions are set up in italic, Chillingworth's answers in black letter, and Cheynell's comments in roman.[64] In *A Vindication of Episcopacie or Animad-versions upon a late Pamphlet . . .* (1644), the pamphlet under attack is reprinted and then demolished a paragraph at a time for the entire book.[65] We find the same thing in *The Cavaliers new Common-prayer Booke Vnclasp't*, first printed at York (1644). This too is entirely reprinted in London "with some brief and necessary *Observations*, to refute the Lyes and Scandalls that are contained in it."[66] These

[61] Ibid.
[62] L'Estrange, *The Observator. In Dialogue*, 9 January 1683[-84].
[63] Quarles, *The Whipper Whipt*, Wing Q121.
[64] Francis Cheynell, *Chillingworthi Novissima*, Wing C3810.
[65] *A Vindication of Episcopacie*, Wing V477.
[66] *The Cavaliers new Common-prayer Booke Vnclasp't*, Wing C1578.

CHILLINGWORTHI NOVISSIMA.

OR, THE

Sickneſſe, Hereſy,

Death, and Buriall

OF

WILLIAM CHILLINGWORTH.

(In his own phraſe) *Clerk of Oxford*, and in the
conceit of his fellow Souldiers, the *Queens*
Arch-Engineer, and *Grand-Intelligencer.*

SET FORTH IN

A *Letter* to his Eminent and learned Friends,
a *Relation* of his Apprehenſion at *Arundell*, a
Diſcovery of his Errours in a *Briefe Cate-*
chiſm, and a ſhort *Oration* at the
Buriall of his Hereticall Book.

By FRANCIS CHEYNELL, late Fellow
of MERTON Colledge.

Publiſhed by Authority.

LONDON,

Printed for SAMUEL GELLIBRAND, at the Brazen
Serpent in Pauls Church-yard, 1644.

Title page from Francis Cheynell's *Chillingworthi Novissima. or, the Sicknesse, Heresy, Death, and Buriall of William Chillingworth* (London: Samuel Gellibrand, 1644). HRHRC Collections.

observations are interposed in smaller type between the paragraphs. When that fails to serve, qualifications, assertions, rebuttals, imputed meanings—all set in italic and put in square brackets—invade the main text itself. One of the neatest pieces of inter-textual presentation in the period is *A Solemn League and Covenant*, both as it was agreed at Westminster and then as modified in Edinburgh. It gives the Westminster text, but notes: "*the several additions to the Scottish forme are here printed in a different letter* [namely italics within square brackets]. . . . *The omissions and other alterations are noted in the margent.*"[67]

Printed marginal notes, like a reader's manuscript marginalia, are one of the best pointers to textual exchange. As in the last example, they have their inter-textual point. In citing sources, they split the text into its origins and by proliferating other authorities they enhance its own. Milton, of course, could afford to be scathing about any marginal display of erudition. When he was abroad, as he records in *Church Government* (1641–42), he had "to club quotations with men whose learning and belief lies in marginal stuffings . . . and horse-loads of citations."[68]

Others, less confident than he, felt they had to make their excuses if their margins were bare. "If it trouble thee (Good Reader) to see so bare a margin, so few Authors cited, or this Sermon come abroad in so homely and plaine a dresse . . . ," wrote John Shaw in *Brittains Remembrancer* (1644), it was all because his books and papers were plundered a year before; that copies of his sermon were demanded within three days of preaching it; and that "I had only time to write it once over, so as the Printer got it from me by pieces of sheets, as it was written (which makes it somewhat more confused). . . ."[69] Thomas Blake, in *The birth-privilege* (1644), has a different and rather lame excuse:

> Some will complain of a naked Margin, to which much might be said. The Author was with books when it was compiled for the *Pulpit*, but taken from them when it was fitted for the *Presse*. So that use of Marginal References must have put upon him the borrowed copies of others, and a new paines for the quotation of Chapter & Page. Besides the quotations desired must either have been *friends*, and so their Evidence would be challenged; or else *Adversaries*, which perhaps might provoke some personall offences and distaste, which the Authour studiously professeth to avoid.[70]

Challenge and provocation are here seen as functions of marginal notes, but they are effects the author ostensibly regrets and effectively forestalls. In this way, of course, he preserves the relative simplicity of the single voice, uncluttered and untrammelled by unspeakably radial marginalia.

The author of *Knaves and Fools in Folio* (1648), however, was quite convinced of the necessity of marginal notes: "*Good Reader, our earnest desire to give full satisfaction, hath inlarged the Margine, which I pray thee faile not to read, lest thou come short of our intention,—*

---

[67] For *A Solemn League and Covenant*, see for example *A copie of the Covenant*, Wing C6210.
[68] John Milton, *The Reason of Church Government* (1641–42), Book II, Wing M2175.
[69] John Shaw, *Brittains Remembrancer* (1644), Wing S3023A.
[70] Thomas Blake, *The birth-privilege* (1644), Wing B3142.

thine instruction. . . ."[71] And it is virtually impossible not to read them, since they run into, and sprawl across, the text in didactic over-kill. William Lilly's first almanac, *Merlinus Anglicus Junior* (1644), made a double entry into the market. The first edition went to press at the end of 1643, before it was really ready. Lilly continued working on it, finished his predictions on 6 January 1644, and then circulated several manuscript copies. Much later in the year, "fearing some Copy might be surreptitiously printed," he published a new edition.[72] By then of course many of his predictions had been fulfilled, and so (to prove his prescience) he pointed them all out in a series of marginal notes. It makes for a splendid piece of self-congratulation in a conversation among his past, present, and future selves. In the same year George Wharton reprinted, not his own text, but the whole of a tract by John Booker, keying into it his own vituperative marginal comments: "I send him his words againe. . . . Since you took my Dose, you have vomited filthy humours. I hope e're long to cure you."[73] He then appends to his puerile but savage construction his own full reply to Booker.

By contrast, Bunyan and Harington's use of the form seems highly civilized.[74] The first edition of *Pilgrim's Progress* (1678) is a beautifully designed pocket book, whose lines are set to a short measure for easy reading, with shoulder notes keyed to the text to apply the lesson and give the biblical reference. Harington's *Orlando* is more ambitiously and explicitly helpful. It's plain from his advertisement about its "setting foorth" that he knows his book will afford different meanings and different pleasures to its different readers, and he sensibly provides for them. They may read it in any of at least three ways for its narrative (straight through, selectively, pictorially), and in any or all of four ways for its import ("the Morall, the Historie, the Allegorie, and the Allusion"). Unlike the first edition of *Paradise Lost*, the *Orlando* puts an argument before each book, so that readers may "remember the storie better" and "understand the picture the perfecter."[75] And the use of the pictures before each book, he says, is "evident; which is that (having read over the booke) you may read it (as it were againe) in the very picture." Among the many other reader-friendly devices are a list of "The principall tales . . . that may be read by themselves"; and of course the marginal notes, which range in function from signally "apt similitudes and pithie sentences or adages" to the selective reading of the different stories "worthie the twise reading." As he says, "(because all that may reade this booke are

---

[71] S. H., *Knaves and Fools in Folio*, Wing H121.

[72] William Lilly, *Merlinus Anglicus Junior* (1644), Wing A1919 and A1919A.

[73] See George Wharton, *Mercurius Coelico mastix. Or an anti-Caveat*, Wing W1550, which he appends to his reprint of Booker's *Mercurius Coelicus*. Falconer Madan, *Oxford Books*, 3 vols. (Oxford: Clarendon Press, 1895–1931): ii. 317, details the exchanges between Booker and Wharton.

[74] See D. F. McKenzie, "Typography and Meaning: The Case of William Congreve," in *Buch und Buchhandel in Europa im achtzehnten Jahrhundert*, ed. Giles Barber and Bernhard Fabian, vol. 4 of *Wolfenbütteler Schriften zur Geschichte des Buchwesens* (Hamburg: Hauswedell, 1981), pp. 81–125, esp. pp. 103–105.

[75] Ariosto, *Orlando Furioso*, trans. Sir John Harington, advertisement.

not of equall capacities) I will endevor to explane [it all] more plainely then for the learned sort had haply bene requisite."

There is a refreshing common sense about all this which blows through a whole hay-wain of theory. There is no great anxiety here about print as a new medium: what we have is an exhilarating acknowledgment of its resources, a craftsmanly pleasure in the exploitation of their materiality, and the provision of a skilled service (in the words of a more famous book) "To the great Varietie of Readers."

It would be folly to write the mentality of a century into a marginal note, but the use writers and printers made of it, together with a whole range of other devices printers used to give voice to a text in its dialogic and inter-textual functions, was important and distinctive to the times. Dialogic and inter-textual functions seem to have been the dominant ones in the commonest forms of print; they are certainly the ones most evident in the pamphlets, and they are those that most approximate the element of presence in speech and writing as the more traditional discourse.

They also pose a challenge. Reporters and publishers, who have always known that there are lies, damned lies, and eye-witness accounts, share a natural impulse to report what people *said* as a means of enhancing their claims to accuracy. But in the report, say, of an exorcism, whose is the voice if "Satan" is "present" in the possessed? In the literature of revelation, whose is the stenographer's voice? And in death-bed confessions, how far can we trust the editor-confessor's published account of the words of the deceased?

A fuller knowledge of the range of seventeenth-century texts, and of the ways in which their forms gave presence, can only help to refine our interpretation of all such reports of "direct" speech. For the typographic disposition of text reveals a distinctive relation, in the seventeenth-century, between orality and print. Together with authors' and others' prefatory remarks, it reveals that some speakers and writers might happily use any or all of the modes of speech, manuscript, and print. It also shows that others were only made anxious by the problems posed by printing as the newest and least familiar form of communicating their views. In such a context, the reluctance of many to speak or write in type may well have been, not fear of the censor (as is too readily claimed), but a psychological response to technological change.[76] If they printed at all, however, they have left some typographic marks, genuine signs of the times. These are material to the text and indispensable evidence, along with the texts themselves, of the ways in which an age perceived and expressed its experience.

---

[76] Christopher Hill, for example: "So long as the censorship existed, authors had to take evasive action, and this has its bearing on literary forms and styles." See "Censorship and English Literature," in *The Collected Essays of Christopher Hill*, 2 vols. (Brighton: Harvester Press, 1985), i. 40.

10

"What's Past Is Prologue": The Bibliographical Society and History of the Book

---

Delivered as the Centenary Lecture before the Bibliographical Society in London, this essay was privately published by the Society in 1993, chiefly for circulation to its members. As a past President and recipient of the Society's Gold Medal for his outstanding contributions to the field, McKenzie's address carried particular authority. Firmly rejecting the rhetoric of self-congratulation, he used the occasion not only to assess the Society's scholarly achievements over the past hundred years, but also to raise challenging questions about its future. First, with an anecdotal reference to his own teaching practice—he loved to demonstrate the power of nonlinguistic signs by means of a blank book—McKenzie reestablishes a primary tenet of his revisionist bibliography: that every element of the physical book conveys meaning and thus contributes to our understanding of the work as a whole. Second, he reasserts the "unity of all bibliographical enterprise," surveys the considerable contribution of British bibliographers, and reflects on their methodological limitations. Troubled by their "resistance to abstraction" and by their "editorial and bibliophilic" preoccupations, he observes that they lacked the "conceptual framework" necessary to transform analytic bibliography into the more comprehensive "history of the book." Third, he considers the future of the Society's scholarly endeavors—and, by implication, of bibliography as a discipline. What, he asks, is the status of the book in the computer age? If the use of computers for text production, transmission, and storage necessarily undermines the "primacy of the physical artefact (and the evidence it bears of its own making) as the very basis of our historical knowledge," then bibliography must adapt accordingly. Drawing a loose analogy between the computer's "capacity for modelling" and the relationship of the dramatic text to its performances, he offers a tentative way into the complex problems for bibliography raised by the new technologies of the text.

I

ONE OF MY favourite teaching devices when talking with students about paper is to get them each to handle an utterly blank book: 'There's not even a "mark" in it,' I might say (begging the question of what a mark is), 'let alone words.' It's a bit like the blank books they sold in the 1960s to test a then fashionable theory among literary critics that, since it was *readers* who wrote texts, there was no need for an author. But this one has a precise history which I eventually reveal.

Well, the students seem only slightly hesitant to accept that it *is* (they suppose . . .) a *book*, but they're certainly agreed that it's not a text. Everyone feels the weight and texture of the paper and notes that it's folded and sewn in sections. They take it for granted that they *can* open it, flip the leaves back and forth, even mark two or three openings with their fingers. It's a good moment to stress the point that the codex can carry a phenomenal amount of information (in this case absent) in wafer-thin signs on each side of its leaves, and that (while it lets you read them *through*) it also breaks the linear tyranny of the scroll (whether manuscript, tape, film, or computerised database) and creates a far more open text. But that's just a bit of propaganda for the codex, a form I'm rather fond of; it isn't the real point of my present experiment. So we get back to the business of reading the signs. The students each hold the book and almost (as it were) dandle it to feel its bulk, put it under an arm to get a sense of its portability and conformability to the body, what we might call its *companionableness*. Again, for the benefit of sufferers from RSI or eye-strain from working at computers, I can't resist those tiny reminders of more comfortable, more human (indeed, more *humane*) textual forms. There are no boards and no jacket to supply any other clues.

Then, we play 20 questions. I ask the class to tell me what kind of text the blank book was designed for, and to date it. They invariably get it right, and yet there's not a word, a single linguistic sign, to guide them.

My questions are quite simple. 'Could the book be a manual of some kind?' ('No, the paper wouldn't stand up to a lot of handling, and a manual would need pictures.') 'Well, how can you tell it wouldn't have pictures?' ('The paper's too furry.') 'How about the type: would it be large or small?' ('More large than small: the paper isn't fine enough to take the detail of small print and still give a legible text.') They can see that the book's format is octavo and that it's about an inch-and-a-quarter thick (so they say, reverting unconsciously to another era and forgetting their metrics). I ask what they make of its bulk? ('Its *what*? Its bulk? Strange: it looks big, but it's actually quite light—sort of fluffed up.') 'Well, let's think again about the type and see if we can read between the (well, yes) non-existent lines of this non-existent text: if its type is something like pica,' a term they seem to know, 'would it be set solid or spaced out—given a bit of light and air by leading? And what about the margins? Do you think they'd be mean and narrow or comfortably generous?' ('No, it wouldn't seem to have been a very full or dense page: the kind of paper and the weight of the book both suggest a lightness or openness in the type—perhaps even in the text itself. You get the impression that it wants to ease the reader's passage through the text, not set obstacles in the form of small print or a dense page.')

Now it's getting to the point where I ask about the actual text itself; well, putatively actual. 'We know it's not a manual. Could it be a children's book?' ('Unlikely,' they say, 'unless for a teenager who could take a story without pictures.') 'Ah—you think the text might tell a story? Could it be an historical narrative, a learned book, a *critical* book?' ('Oh no,' they're quick to comment, 'critics take themselves much more seriously: the paper, type, and density of text-to-page wouldn't be right. It's much too open and light for a *critical* book.') 'No?' I ask. 'Something quite different then, something perhaps meant to give the reader *pleasure*?' ('Surely,' they say, 'being sort of light, open, and readable, isn't it more likely to have been a novel?') And of course they're right: it was. But now: 'What kind of novel?' It's worth asking at this point how expensive it might have been. ('It's obviously meant to have hard covers,' they say, 'but it's no luxury item: its size, paper, and bulk,' all of which we can see and feel, 'its typeface,' which we can only infer, 'and the probable absence of pictures, suggest something quite cheap in itself and yet calculated to give the impression of being a good read and value-for-money. Not, then, a dense novel to be read over several nights, but something you might buy to read on the plane,' they say.) 'Yes, or a train,' I say, hinting at its date, a distant era when you didn't need a whole travelling library to pass the time between leaving and arriving on British Rail. 'And what about that date? A decade will do: 1850, 1900, 1930, 1950?' They plump for the 1930s.

In fact it's a physical mock-up for an edition of a romantic novel by Frances Parkinson Keyes published in 1939. Since the students are therefore at least 30 years younger than the book, their experience of it is informed by its *difference* from the books they now know best. It's not a paperback, it's not perfect-bound, it's not economically—that is, meanly—designed. All of which, of course, makes it history. Yet more than that, they can read its period and its genre simply from its paper and its construction.

Finally, I ask why anyone should go to the trouble of making such a text-specific non-textual object. It's at this point they're usually foxed. There are of course two explanations.

The first is that, in this form, the book enables the publisher or printer to calculate (before they're printed) the number of sheets required for a certain edition quantity, given the choice of format, type size, line-length, and page depth. It's what—paradoxically—a conservator calls the text-block. Given the choice of paper and how it bulks, it also determines the width of the spine. This must be known before the binding cases can be made and the dust jacket designed. The width of the spine has its function in marking the book out from others at the point of sale on a bookseller's shelves.

The second explanation is even more directly related to marketing. Case-bound and jacketed but still wordless, the book then becomes the salesman's dummy. It's taken into bookshops and book clubs and orders received on the basis of its author's name, its pictorial dust jacket, its genre, and its bulk in relation to its price. The structures being all in place, its text has only to be melded into those predetermined and economically, generically, and socially understood forms to give it a local habitation and a name. But the forms themselves, having been conventionally established for the genre, will determine also its length, production costs, retail price, and readership—and therefore its vocabulary, narrative structure, and characters. The students I have mentioned discover (to their complete surprise) that the non-linguistic signs in a book they thought had no marks at all in it, have compelled them to discover its text—at least in the sense of establishing genre, readership, and date—solely from the evidence of the paper, which they'd thought to be an inert substance, a mere medium, signless and therefore nonsignifying.

In his early nineteenth-century French manual of typography, Marcellin-Aimé Brun notes that 'a knowledge of paper is very difficult to acquire. It takes a lot of study and experience to recognise at a glance its format when folded; the feel of a sheet, the weight of a ream; to know, by touch or the tip of your tongue, the quality and the amount of size used to give the sheets a smooth surface; its smell; whether it was made by grinding or pounding; whether it's naturally white or bleached with acid; the quality of the pulp; what its chain-lines and laid-lines reveal of its whole manufacture; which country it came from, even the mill it was made in. These details may seem tiny, but they're neither indifferent nor strange to those printers who have given us editions of the classics that no other nation has yet dared to imitate.' If you take the informed point of view of all those experienced in making textual artefacts, you quickly discover that every element signifies. As my old Cambridge mentor Bruce Dickins once said to me in the 1960s when I was callow enough to suggest that something was irrelevant: 'Nothing's irrelevant, my lad—if you know enough.' My students already knew more than they thought they did. One had only to make their knowledge conscious.

II

One of the points of all this is simply to convince students new to bibliography that every book tells a story quite apart from that recounted by its text. It's a simple matter to extend the argument to all recorded texts as collaborative creations—the product of social acts involving the complex interventions of human agency acting on material forms. Together with language itself, those forms and the information their signs encode are the most powerful tools we have with which to write a history of meanings.

It was only proper therefore that the history of books, if not 'history of the book,' should have been implicit in the work of the Bibliographical Society since it began. For the writing, replication, distribution, and reception of texts were always legitimate objects of inquiry and report, and their description, collection, and classification, as manuscripts or printed books, have drawn upon studies of the labour, materials, technologies, and processes used to make, sell, and house them.

Almost a quarter-century before the Society was founded, Edward Arber's *A transcript of the registers of the Company of Stationers of London* (1554–1640) had already begun to open up a treasury of evidence for contextual studies. Arber's work laid the foundations for the Society's *Century of the English book trade* by E. Gordon Duff, the handlists of printers which Duff also originated, H. R. Plomer's and others' dictionaries of printers, the lists of printers' and booksellers' wills and of alien members of the book trades, and the editions of further Stationers' Company and other records by W. W. Greg, Eleanor Boswell, and William A. Jackson. The work instrumental in placing the physical book and its production at the centre of literary studies, McKerrow's *Introduction to bibliography for literary students* (1927), began life in *The Library* in 1912–13.

Two concerns dominated the Society's first half-century: to create a systematic record of the extant printed books to the end of 1640, and to establish precisely how Britain's most important literary texts from the same period were transmitted from manuscript to print. Each of those concerns implied a history of the documents in their sequential relationships. Indeed, without such a basis no comprehensive history of books and their making, and no adequate account of the forms of texts and their influence, is possible.

Yet it remains true to say that such a concern for history was only implicit in the Society's aims. For the distinguished triumvirate who set its priorities in the earlier twentieth century—A. W. Pollard, R. B. McKerrow, and W. W. Greg—the rationale of bibliography lay rather in tracing the relations between the extant witnesses to the texts of a limited corpus of English classics and the even earlier versions, now lost, that their readings might be argued to imply. That enterprise and the specific bibliographical skills it calls for remain highly significant functions of the discipline. They contribute to and are informed by our understanding of the crucial historical roles of the book as such in general history. But in the Society's earlier years, those roles, let alone the relevance to them of the production of *all* texts in their great diversity of forms and functions, were not thought to be, strictly, a bibliographical matter.

For that extended interest in the book trade, we need to look instead to a distinct group of bibliographers brought into being by John Johnson, Printer to the University of Oxford. These were principally Johnson himself, Strickland Gibson, Stanley Morison, Theodore Besterman, and Graham Pollard, three at least of whom earned their living from the making or selling of books. Their story has been admirably told by Esther Potter. Johnson had long been collecting materials towards a history of printing and bookselling and by 1932 had begun to plan a collection of articles illustrative of trade practices. Within a month these had become, in prospect, a series of monographs. Percy Simpson was to write on proof-correction, Morison on the Fell types, Pollard on binding prices; Gibson, Besterman, Laurence Hanson, A. F. Johnson and Turner Berry were also recruited; and Johnson laid plans for Pollard to edit 'a modest chrestomathy of the principal documents' for the history of the book trade down to 1830. In the event, seven major works appeared, among them Simpson's *Proof-reading in the sixteenth, seventeenth and eighteenth centuries* (1935), Hanson's *Government and the press, 1695–1763* (1936), and Gibson's and Johnson's *Print and privilege at Oxford to the year 1700* (1946). Much of the interest aroused by Johnson continued to bear fruit in later years, as in Pollard's 1959 Sandars Lectures, *The English market for printed books*, Pollard's and Ehrman's *The distribution of books by catalogue from the invention of printing to 1800* (1965), and Morison's *John Fell, the University Press and the 'Fell' types* (1967).

Throughout that same period, however, from the early 1930s to the mid-1960s, and long before *histoire du livre* became a fashionable focus of enquiry, many other works contributed significantly to an understanding of the history of books and the role of the book in history. One thinks of Morison's *History of The Times* (1935–52), Marjorie Plant's *The English book trade: an economic history of the making and sale of books* (1939), Ellic Howe's *The London compositor: documents relating to wages, working conditions and customs of the London printing trade, 1785–1900* (1947), H. S. Bennett's *English books and readers* (1952–70), Cyprian Blagden's rich and intelligent forays into the history of the Stationers' Company, Allan Stevenson's, *The problem of the Missale speciale* (1967), Richard D. Altick's *The English common reader: a social history of the mass reading public, 1800–1900* (1957). There were many studies of publishers and their relations with authors, house histories of printing firms, and accounts of the more peripheral products of the press like ballads and chapbooks, children's books, maps, prints, and music.

The Society itself, as a distinctive and mutually supportive community of librarians, academics, collectors, and working members of the book trades, was ideally placed to demonstrate the unity of all bibliographical enterprise and the means by which it entered into the fabric of almost any historical enquiry, whether literary, religious, political, social, economic, or more broadly cultural. There was strong commitment to the principle of a national retrospective short-title catalogue for collection building. There was no lack of theory in textual criticism, and no lack of major historical studies. The record indeed is one of a remarkably diverse and sustained scholarship devoted to the historical study of the book trades in Britain, from at least Caxton to the mid-twentieth-century newspaper press. Thanks to the supplementary labours of Donald Wing, for the years up to 1700 we had unrivalled bibliographical control of the objects themselves—books as the products of trade—and of the record, by printer and publisher, of the contexts of their production. The Society had put Britain firmly ahead of any other country in the command of its printed past. While the full extension of that control into and beyond the eighteenth century had to await a new technology, not to mention the experience and energies of a Robin Alston, there were no conceptual doubts about the need. It would advance the frontier with every assurance that in the detail of such catalogues there also lay the evidence for a history of text production. Such is the testimony of David Foxon's second volume of indexes, especially the still under-exploited appendix of notabilia, in his magisterial *Catalogue of English printed verse, 1701–1750* (1975); and such also is the real significance of the third volume of the Society's *Short-title catalogue*.

What then was missing? Why should that larger enterprise—history of the book—seem to have been initiated, not in Britain but in France, with the publication in Paris in 1958 of *L'Apparition du livre* by Lucien Febvre and Henri-Jean

Martin? The fact is that if one were to seek, in the last few years of the Society's first half century and the early years of its next, any explicit claim for bibliography as a discipline defined by the full range of historical and analytical studies appearing at that time, one would seek it in vain.

The nearest we come to a conceptual framework of the kind offered by *histoire du livre* may be found perhaps in Pollard's earlier development of the book-trade sections of the *Cambridge bibliography of English literature* (1940) and his contributions to that work. In later years, as President of the Society, he sought to set up a publishing programme more sensitive to the primacy of trade documents as historical evidence. It would be wrong to rank his achievement higher than Greg's, for they were of quite different kinds, but it could be argued that Pollard's example spoke to the future in ways that Greg's then did not. It did so simply because he addressed more fundamental and more diversely complex conditions of text production, and a wider range of evidence (in its forms, dispersal, and chronology), than were entertained by those whose attention was confined to the early printed drama. Quite apart from the range of his learning, Pollard had an unrivalled ability to find the telling detail and then to extend it in a sketch of the broader patterns of production and distribution. Being concerned for the trade, he was unconstrained by canon and could range with ease from early to late, major to minor, manuscript to print. In those ways he surpassed the insights of *L'Apparition du livre* with what now must seem its misplaced emphasis on the event of printing.

But neither Pollard nor Greg quite perceived, or at least fully expressed, their common interest in the more comprehensively inclusive terms of general history. When, for example, in *An enquiry into the nature of certain nineteenth-century pamphlets* (1935), Pollard and Carter exposed the forgeries of Thomas J. Wise, sometime President of the Society, that work, informed though it was by the historical evidence of trade documents, paper technology, and type, was seen more as a triumph of analytical bibliography than as an exercise in book history. As the title implies, it reinforced an editorial and bibliophilic concern for authenticity. Much the same point might be made about a quite different work, the edition by Harry Carter and Herbert Davis of Moxon's 1683 *Mechanick exercises on the whole art of printing* (1958). However independently valuable the scholarship devoted to that edition (and it is massively so) the work itself spoke to what F. P. Wilson had called 'the new bibliography' and a then current concern to inform editors about the mechanics of the transmission of texts. Such was also the focus of the most magnificent product of the Society's publishing efforts in the 1950s, Sir Walter Greg's *Bibliography of the English printed drama to the Restoration* (1939–59). The record of British bibliography, pragmatic and (in John Feather's word) bibliocentric, reveals a deep resistance to abstraction. As Nicolas Barker notes in reference to *L'Apparition du livre*, 'Le Livre,' like the German *Buchwesen*, is an abstraction; 'It does not come naturally in English, which is equally insensitive to the definite article, or to its absence, as in Martin's later grand study of the press in seventeenth-century

France, *Livre, pouvoirs et société à Paris* (1969).' 'The Book' still has the ring of an imported phrase.

Paradoxically, a convergence of the various forms of British and North American bibliographical scholarship into a more unified historical discipline, and more abstractly describable one, might be said to date, not from *L'Apparition du livre* but from a new perception, in the 1960s, of the critical relevance of book-trade archives. Two important consequences were to follow.

First, the use of archival evidence to confute many ill-informed assumptions made by analytical bibliographers about the processes of book production, if initially disconcerting and subversive, was salutary in demonstrating the interdependent nature of text production in the printing house. This meant that the work of printing the sheets of one book (usually the sole concern of its later editor) entailed a complex series of relations with other jobs in concurrent production. These affected the division of labour, choice of materials, and the rate of progress on each book. But the more significant point was the clear necessity, in reconstructing those past events, of invoking the concept of a *network* and the roles within it of a great diversity of textual forms.

Second, the rich diversity of authors' manuscripts, proofs, revises, and successive revisions, which had to be confronted by the editors of nineteenth- and twentieth-century works, had a slow but cumulative effect in making untenable any idea of a single authoritative version of most literary texts. Their relation one to another came to be seen less in terms of their descent from a common archetype and more as differing responses, each with its own integrity, to distinct publishing contexts. Publishers' archives themselves, like those of printers, also revealed a complex matrix of conditions affecting by imputation the market for a work, the manner and range of its distribution, and the forms of its reception.

Both consequences bred an even sharper awareness of the value of short-title catalogues. Their prime role in organising and giving access to the extant national printed archive was unaffected, but they also came to be seen as an essential condition of our understanding the nature and scale of text production, whether by author (often anonymous, pseudonymous, and multiple), printer, bookseller, format, volume, place, and time, or in the dynamics of the relationships *between* texts in their successive metamorphoses from edition to edition, or as one work replied to, co-existed with, or generated others.

When the planning of an eighteenth-century short-title catalogue began in earnest in 1976, it was readily seen that such inquiries could be met by the new technology of computing: with its ability to search quickly on several fields, it transformed the nature of bibliographical and historical research. Once the catalogues to 1700 are also in machine-readable form they will make feasible far more complex analyses of the forms and uses of texts across three-and-a-half centuries of British history.

As the title of its centennial volume implies, however—*The book encompassed*—the Society's scholarship has always embraced the complete *world* of books. That range and the polyglot skills it demands are simply taken for granted in, for example, the study of incunables. It's not just a matter of knowing what copies are held in which countries, but of recognising the full implications of the fact that the international trade in books, and in the ideas they mediate, has always been such that we can only recover its history if all national archives of printed texts are brought up to comparable standards of cataloguing and complement one another. Used together, they can provide unprecedented access to evidence for documenting inter-textual relations between nations—whether by the direct import or export of textual artefacts, by translation, or in the dialectic of cultural influence and response. We can therefore note with unalloyed pleasure the initiative taken at a conference in Munich earlier this year on the retrospective cataloguing of all extant books printed in Europe from the 15th to the 19th centuries. Mr Michael Smethurst, Director General of the British Library, reports much good will for the project and a real prospect that a European Consortium of Research Libraries may, as he says, 'deliver the database we so urgently need if our libraries are to provide timely access to our European cultural heritage.' If, like the ESTC, the scale, cost, and complexity of such a project far exceed the Society's resources, it can take pride in the fact that its achievement in collaborative international scholarship, both in the expertise of its members and in creating and perfecting its own *Short-title catalogue*, continues to inform such new scholarship.

From the point of view of 'history of the book' the important thing about such catalogues is the changed perception of their use. Enumerative bibliography in Britain opened up riches unparalleled in other countries and well beyond the reach of descriptive and analytical bibliography. It has allowed us to resurrect the most marginal texts and their makers (the documents and writers who were always excluded from the merely literary canon), and thereby to study all who were kept from the centres of power by reason of their sex, race, religion, provincial or colonial status. With the completion of a comprehensive international retrospective catalogue of printed books, we can begin to contemplate a history of the book in the full mobility of its forms and ideas.

If those reflections suggest an explosion of bibliographical studies, a complementary implosion may be found in finer readings of the very physicality of the book. That relation between physical detail and intellectual history is the substance of Stanley Morison's argument in *Politics and script*:

> The bibliographer may be able, by the physical form of an inscription, manuscript, book, newspaper, or other medium of record, to reveal considerations that appertain to the history of something distinct from religion, politics, and literature, namely: the history of the use of the intellect.

The commonsense view is that the object 'book' is like any other discrete artefact, with a stable form whose detailed features can be traced back to an author and to the materials and processes of constructing its implied content or meaning. As such, its primary witness to the events which brought it into being as an object (the customary concern of analytical bibliography) presents indispensable evidence of its history. Yet Morison's point is also that the physical signs in a book only make sense in terms of our assumptions about the historical conditions and processes by which they were made. Meanings are not therefore inherent but are constructed by successive interpretative acts by those who write, design, and print books, and by those who buy and read them. For confirmation, we need only note as self-evident bibliographical and historical facts the diversity of a text's most obvious physical transformations when reprinted. Its presentation in different formats and typefaces, on different papers in different bindings, and its sale at different times, places, and prices imply distinct conditions and uses and must vary the meanings its readers make from it. In that sense, the text as an unstable physical form in its descent through successive versions is the more valuable in offering ubiquitous evidence for 'history of the book' as a study of the changing conditions of reading and the construction of meaning.

The last two decades have seen a remarkable expansion of studies devoted to the production and reception of texts, embracing not only the current preoccupation with writing and reading in critical theory but also the broader cultural implications of the forms in which texts are printed and marketed and the conditions of readership to which they're addressed. It has also come to be recognised that a distinctively Euro-centric notion of the book and its circulation cannot account for the role of such texts in other societies with different communicative traditions and widely varying standards of literacy.

It was against such a background of recent changes in the perception of our relationships with texts that the Cambridge University Press commissioned in 1989 a multivolume collaborative history of the book in Britain and vested responsibility for its preparation in three general editors (all long-standing members of the Society) whose own work has been more literary and bibliographical than conventionally historical. Such a history must be responsive to the wide range of interest in the ways in which all texts were made and used in the past, although (to achieve anything at all) it must also set limits. In defining those limits nationally (Britain) and formally (the book) it follows the example of the French *Histoire de l'édition française*, completed in four volumes in 1986.

Seven volumes are planned, the first six covering the history of the book in Britain from the time when Britain was part of the wider Latin culture of Europe, through to the invention of printing, the years of the Stationers' Company as arbiter of the book trade, to the coming of new technology and the effect of that up to 1914 in creating a massive expansion of printing and publishing for an industrialised, politically aware, increasingly literate and mobile society. The terms of reference for the seventh volume, 1914 to the present day, remain disturbingly imprecise, partly because the book shares its functions with other media with which it is complexly interdependent, partly because of the very richness of the archival resources, and partly because new technologies and multinational publishing challenge the very concept of a national history. Four research fellows funded by the Leverhulme Trust to work on projects related to the Cambridge history have already created substantial databases of new evidence relating to book ownership, membership of the book trade, book production, and printers' and publishers' archives.

Nor is Britain alone in following the French example. A six-volume history of the book in Germany over the past century has been launched and a history of the book in America is projected. Studies of the role of the book in the social histories of Australia and Canada are also under way.

III

Implicit in my remarks so far has been a tension between the primacy and relative stability of the kind of hard physical evidence we're used to calling 'bibliographical' and the unstable nature of texts themselves, whether because of the different media by which they're transmitted, the frequency and indeterminacy of their multiple metamorphoses, or the precise nature of their reception and interpretation. In this third and final section of the paper I'd like further to explore the implications of that second element in the tension, the indeterminacy of texts.

To acknowledge it is at once to recognise that histories of the book cannot tell the full story: they cannot fully account for our parallel use of manuscript even to the present day, the texts lost to history by their failure to survive, the import and export trade in books, the secondhand trade, the metatextual functions of libraries, the number and nature of successive readings and partial readings, the concurrent production and circulation of graphic images, and formal and informal oral texts—all these expose the limitations of any history of the book alone, complicating our reconstruction of how the great variety of texts were made and used, and of the people who read, viewed, spoke, or heard them. Even typewriters and computers could be said to be only chirographic aids, producing informal texts that escape cataloguing. And although by networking and the provision of multiple points of access, the computer screen is beginning to emulate the principle of replication fundamental to printing, fully efficient access to its texts, and systems to ensure their survival, are still in no way comparable to those developed for books.

'In the digital world, permanence is an illusion, a fantasy,' we are often told. Texts are too volatile; replications and their modifications are out of control; forms of access in terms of software and hardware, and conditions of access in terms of copyright and cost, still present insuperable problems. The proliferation of incomplete, unenterable, and technologically irrecoverable databases testifies to the trouble (if it's not sheer indifference) that this particular technology has in making history of and in itself. What's past in its brave new world is generally beyond recall. By contrast with the brief lives of computer-memory, whose function is still essentially referential and analytic, the analyses of human behaviour we have in the rhetorical structures of texts as the distinct artefacts we call books, constitute a stable resource from which we confirm the continuities of human experience and extend it in ways most congenial to ourselves. It's the *durability* of those textual forms that ultimately secures the continuing future of our past; it's the *evanescence* of the new ones that poses the most critical problem for bibliography and any further history dependent upon its scholarship.

Under such conditions the temptation is to retreat into defence of the traditional codex, seeking security in our familiarity with it and in the relevance of the expertise we've acquired applicable to it, whilst declining to confront the problems of recording, retention, and recovery—the traditional tasks of bibliographical control—of more recent and more volatile textual forms. Yet as the late Northrop Frye said, 'Society, like the individual, becomes senile in proportion as it loses its continuous memory,' and those texts are now part of that memory, significant products of our civilisation. If the challenge to take in such new forms is professionally and economically acute for national libraries, it's no less intellectually pressing for the Society: to what extent can it any longer limit the definition of its role to texts mediated by the codex? Is that an adequate response to the realities of the *past* century let alone to those of the next?

And what of the role of national libraries? Dr Terry Belanger has recently predicted the increasing disinclination of major research libraries in North America to maintain large permanent collections of paper-based books of any kind. Current stock, he foresees, will become gradually depleted and then destroyed. The economic pressures to contract are just too great to be resisted. In place of the books we know, libraries will keep banks of master-texts/master-negatives/master-disks from which temporary off-screen reading copies will be produced—'temporary physical manifestations of a permanent electronic ideal.' In the odd glass case you will be able to gaze at totemic books, icons of a culture with little more than the curiosity value most of us bring to a museum visit. Such fragments will we shore against the ruins. Dr Belanger's prediction begs a great many questions but I find it symptomatic that the director of one of the most successful rare books programmes in America should have mentally adjusted so rapidly to such a probable future. Yet when I asked him if the same arguments applied to *national* libraries and archives, he instantly conceded that their responsibilities were different. Not only is a national library professionally disciplined in its commitment to collect the fullest possible range of texts, as a publicly funded institution it must be politically sensitive to the needs of readers more numerous and more exacting than ever before. If, in the short term, their sheer number creates problems in the conservation and servicing of the collections, by the same token they represent an expanded role for our own discipline in meeting their needs. Yet even national libraries are being forced to develop defensive strategies of limitation, the first of them being a redefinition of the body of texts it's (as their managers must say) 'realistic' to collect. A *national* library itself already implies restriction by linguistic and territorial criteria. Other limits may be set by shifting the place of access, by reducing the hours of access, by imposing or raising a price of access, or (most critically of all for us) by changing the forms of the texts we're given by offering us surrogates.

There's nothing new in the idea of copying, and we all have reason to be grateful for the ubiquity of replicas. Potters and founders replicated pots and coins; print replicated written language; bronze and plaster casts, woodblocks, lithographs, photographs, sound recordings, all provide us with surrogates for 'the real thing.' Literature, especially the drama, has dealt in virtual realities for centuries. But with every replication we have to balance the immediate social gains of availability and utility against the loss of the historical evidence every original contains—and our natural instinct, given our training, is to resist and regret the new prohibition against reading books with our fingers. Once we accept the premise that the forms themselves encode the history of their production, it follows that to abstract what we're told is their 'verbal information content' by transferring it to another medium is to contradict the very assumption that the artefact is the product of a distinctive complex of materials, labour, and mentality. As we've seen, even *blank* books are far from uninformative. Any simulation (including re-presentation in a database—a copy of a copy) is an impoverishment, a theft of evidence, a denial of more exact and immediate visual and tactile ways of knowing, a destruction of their quiddity as collaborative products under the varying historical conditions of their successive realisations. In other words, there's an internal contradiction enforced by the very conditions of the medium used for the surrogate to simulate the very conditions to be examined. Traditional libraries (like museums and art galleries) have hitherto minimised the distortions inevitable with any *re*-production in a different medium—simply by giving us direct access to the artefacts themselves—encoded as they are with all the signs of their original production.

We shall of course have to deal more frequently in surrogate versions, restricting our consultation of the more fragile originals to very special purposes. But let's never forget what it is we lose in so doing. Thereby at least we pay respect to the richness of evidence *all* textual forms themselves contain, and to the skilled labour that went into the choice of their materials, design, and execution. The signs we read in the artefacts we keep tell us of lives lived by men and women who had identities just as distinct and valuable as our own.

The point I am making is fundamental to any history of the book which would seek to derive its primary evidence from original artefacts as products of distinctive contexts and yet also demonstrate their successive transformations in response to new needs. But let me take photography as a more succinct model of the problem, for it instantly poses the question of the relationship between the negative as a master-text and the print as a derivative which is almost infinitely variable by different agents—whether in size, selective detail, texture, colour, and any number of other qualities and features. Implicit in the problem is not only the accuracy and value of the product as historical evidence, but the question of *authority* in respect of any changes made.

The art photographer, Brett Weston, [recently] celebrated his 80th birthday with a deed that stunned collectors, shocked curators and historians, and upset his friends and family. Sitting by an open fire at his home in Carmel in California, Weston carefully burned all his negatives, thus sending a life's work up in flames.

'No regrets,' he said afterwards, explaining that it was all in the name of art. 'The prints are posterity, not the negs. This is not photo-journalism, or commercial portraiture, but my personal work. So I don't want anyone printing it, not students, not teachers, nobody. Nobody can print my photographs the way I do.'

With that, Weston departed for a holiday in Hawaii. . . .

Brett Weston's artistic arson was not an eccentricity but a new mark in a long debate among photographers about the primacy of negative or print. At one extreme is Henri Cartier-Bresson, who believes that a photographer's art is wholly in the negative and has always allowed his assistants to print them.

At the other extreme we may now place Brett Weston, [who] is renowned for the quality of his prints, in which the initially unpromising flat surfaces of engineering and steel construction appear sensuous or even mystical in his printed pictures. He believed that without the darkroom techniques he sees as part of the continuing process of a photographic work of art, the result is not what he intended and therefore inferior. . . .

[Ansel] Adams, peerless portrayer of California's most majestic scenery, also once toyed with destroying his negatives. He got a perforator banks use to cancel cheques and went to his basement to begin the grim work. But after he'd stamped some of his best-loved early negatives he couldn't stand it any more and gave up almost in tears.

[*The Guardian*, 2 January 1992]

The analogy with surrogates is not quite exact, but it's close enough to make my point, and the comparison with Cartier-Bresson neatly frames the problem. For Weston the prints were finite—no other product, no alternative versions, could possibly be generated from the master-negative. His prints alone carried within them the true signs of their construction. For Cartier-Bresson, the important point is the generative capacity of the master, beside which the multiple versions exemplified by prints are wholly acceptable but merely transitory expressions of the initial logic of the negative. It's this latter point I'd like now to address as an exemplum of the Society's dilemma.

The whole of my discussion so far has taken the Weston position in putting our classical argument that the physical evidence of books is the very basis of our discipline. Yet if it's one of the Society's continuing intellectual obligations to insist on that truth, it's equally part of its brief to account for the forms of communication currently evolving from the technologies of computing—forms which are essentially, I believe, expressions of the Cartier-Bresson position.

That obligation has acquired a new urgency with the arrival of computer-generated texts. The demands made of bibliography and textual criticism by the evolution of texts in such forms, the speed with which versions are displaced one by another, and the question of their authority, are no less compelling than those we accept for printed books. By the logic of our discipline, we're equally committed to acknowledge that these textual artefacts also embody the conditions of their construction. Devising means to describe, order, and conserve them, however, is by no means easy. It may indeed prove impossible.

While it was historically inevitable that *books* should have been the focus of the Society's attention in its first century, Greg recognised over eighty years ago that it was not logically compelling. In a paper he read to the Society on 19 February 1912, he remarked of our discipline:

> Thus it may be called bibliography, or it may be called by any other name you please, but what I want understood is that the characteristics of the science about which I am speaking cut far deeper than the distinction between writing and printing and apply to the transmission of all symbolic representation of speech or other ordered sound or even logical thought.

Only two years after the Society was founded, many thousands of miles away, an all-too-little-known New Zealand typographer, Robert Coupland Harding, foresaw, with remarkable prophetic insight, the world of the book in which we find ourselves:

> William Morris [Harding wrote in *Typo*, 27 January 1894] has predicted that typography will cease to exist during the next century, and he may be right in his forecast. I see it threatened by the camera, the etching fluid, and by the (at present) harmless and inoffensive 'typewriter,' in the keyboard of which lies the germ of something much greater in the future.

Harding's point about the generative power of the keyboard already implies a prodigality of texts escaping the definitive forms of print. Prediction is a fool's game, but we can, I think, build on those earlier comments by Greg and Harding, connect them with those of Cartier-Bresson, and suggest that the future of bibliography may come to be profoundly influenced, not by the *storage* capacity of computers, but by their capacity for *modelling*. One could take the well-known case of dramatic texts as models for performances which are really diverse exemplifications of a master text. Or we might develop an argument from the essentially generative function of musical scores. There may even be, in T. S. Eliot's concept of an objective correlative, a hint of the way in which bibliography could come to deal, less in specific manifestations of a work, than in the *formulæ for their realisation*. In 1919 Eliot wrote that

> the only way of expressing emotion in the form of art is by finding an 'objective correlative'; in other words, a set of objects, a chain of events which shall be the formula of that particular emotion; such that when the external facts, which must terminate in sensory experience, are given, the emotion is immediately evoked.

If the idea seems remote from our concerns or from my present argument, we've only to acknowledge the analogy between the examples I've given and computer *programming* to realise that our concept of ideal copy may need only slight modification to embrace the dynamics of the increasingly volatile texts of our new age.

If such are the ways in which bibliography now evolves it will represent a radical departure from the article of bibliographical faith which has informed the first part of this paper: namely, the primacy of the physical artefact (and the evidence it bears of its own making) as the very basis of our historical knowledge.

Yet such a new view of the world of knowledge would not be at all unprecedented. In our commitment to a cumulative, accretive model of learning, which a computer-memory might *contain* and to which each artefact *adds*, we've been infected perhaps (since about 1600) by the scientific belief in induction as a means to knowledge—since, logically, a truth arrived at by induction is always provisional, open to refutation by the contrary example for which we must never stop searching. Before the Renaissance that compulsion was not so fundamental to our culture—indeed more often than not it was severely criticised. Edmund Spenser describes the moral condition of such a mind in the figure of Tantalus:

> Deep was he drenchèd to the vtmost chin,
>   Yet gapèd still, as coueting to drinke
>   Of the cold liquor, which he waded in,
>   And stretching forth his hand, did often thinke
>   To reach the fruit which grew vpon the brincke:
>   But both the fruit from hand and floud from mouth
>   Did flie abacke, and made him vainly swinke:
>   The whiles he starued with hunger, and with drouth
> He daily dyed, yet never throughly dyen couth.

It's important to understand that Tantalus was said to be deeply learned, yet for all his intellectual acquisitiveness he remained as far as ever from the truth. When he pleaded with Sir Guyon to give him food and drink, the reprimand he received implied instead a superior form of knowledge:

> Nay, nay, thou greedie *Tantalus* (quoth he)
>   Abide the fortune of thy present fate,
>   And vnto all that live in high degree,
>   Ensample be of mind intemperate,
>   To teach them how to vse their present state.
>   [*Faerie Qveene* II. vii. 58, 59]

And when, later in his work, Spenser meditated the mutability of forms, he came to accept, like Prospero in *The Tempest*, that even we are such shapes as dreams are made on, that the permanence of the artefact, even when human, is to be located in a reality beyond its individual manifestations. In his Garden of Adonis,

> Infinite shapes of creatures there are bred,
>   And uncouth formes, which none yet ever knew . . .
>
> Daily they grow, and daily forth are sent
>   Into the world, it to replenish more;
>   Yet is the stock not lessen'd, nor spent,

But remains in everlasting store,
As it at first created was of yore.
[*Faerie Qveene* III. vi. 35, 36]

'The substance is eterne, and bideth so'—even when 'it changèd is, and altred to and fro.'

I need hardly, to conclude, spell out the analogy with computer-generated texts, nor the implication of my argument that what's past (our *last* century), upon which the Society can look back with considerable pride, is but prologue to a new dispensation, one in which the *programme* becomes the text, and *hard* bibliographical evidence is metamorphosed into *software*.

Greg's vision of a bibliography not limited to books but 'to the transmission of all symbolic representation of speech or other ordered sound or even logical thought' has already taken on substance and will in time demand an account of its history. Finding the terms in which it's to be written is an intellectual challenge of the highest order, demanding energy, foresight, and (most important of all) an imaginative hospitality to those new forms of texts. Only if the Society meets such a challenge will its role continue to be central to our understanding of the making and communication of meaning as the defining characteristic of human societies.

It was a signal honour to have been invited to give the Society's Centenary Lecture at the British Academy in July 1992, and a great sadness to me that illness prevented my delivering it personally. The further kindness of the Society's Council, however, in suggesting that it be published as a memento of the occasion, gives me the opportunity to record more publicly and permanently the depth of my indebtedness to Professor Peter Davison for agreeing to read it before members and friends of the Society and for having given them such pleasure in doing so.

11

Our Textual Definition of the Future: The New English Imperialism?

Given in 1988, this politically charged address, previously unpublished, was a response to an interim report on the British Library's internal review of acquisition and retention policies. An active member of the British Library Advisory Committee and an internationally renowned bibliographer, McKenzie sought to use his status to defend the principle of comprehensiveness—the project of acquiring, cataloguing, storing, and making accessible the nation's *entire* output of printed materials. While recognizing the financial costs and practical difficulties of such an enterprise, he believed this ought to be the primary mission of a publicly funded national library operating under a statute requiring "legal deposit" (although copyright legislation in the United Kingdom differs significantly from that in the United States, this statute puts the British Library in a position roughly comparable with that of the Library of Congress). He succinctly deploys a wide range of arguments focusing on the cultural costs of selective acquisition, raising issues as diverse as the shifting nature of canons; the representation of minority groups; revised conceptions of authorship, printing, and publishing history; and Britain's responsibility to English as a global language. Most important, he insists that selection in the present, however judiciously exercised, would inevitably impose undue constraints on the unforeseeable forms of historical inquiry carried out by future generations. McKenzie knew he was fighting a losing battle. His purpose, however, was to ensure that librarians affirmed a principled commitment to the future in all its unpredictability, even if this were to prove politically and fiscally problematic. Ultimate responsibility for any "dereliction from principle" had to rest with the elected government of the day. The final report on the British Library's future policies, *Selection for Survival* (1989), briefly acknowledged McKenzie's position but, as its title indicates, opted for pragmatism. This change of policy is still considered contentious, and its consequences continue to occasion regret (see John Ezard, "British Library Junks 80,000 Books," *Guardian*, 11 August 2000, 9h).

MY TITLE is perhaps a little provocative, but it's designed to high-light two points.

The first is the fact that by *any* act of selection now, we imply certain definitions of the future, impose a constraint upon its choices, and bias *its* interpretation of *us* as *its* past. Given the general futility of prediction and the fallibility of human judgement, the only principle we can safely espouse—as a *principle*—is that of comprehensive collection and comprehensive bibliographical control. I make that comment directly since, in another context in speaking to his report, Dr Enright has "suggested that the comprehensive approach would be self-defeating." The report we have, albeit only an interim one and despite its many qualifications, is I believe consistent with that view.

By contrast, I wish to argue a quite different set of attitudes, even if (in the event) the actions we find we *must* take are not very different from those envisaged by the report. My point is that no argument from expediency should be permitted to weaken the *principled* commitment to a comprehensive approach. It demands constant affirmation as an absolute, and it should be continually and positively invoked as a standard—from which we are obliged to depart—if we must—only by a superior political will, which is itself fallible and mutable. Happily perhaps, politicians decay even faster than books.

It then follows that we are not engaged in any redefinition of principles, nor of any reassessment of the essential aims of a national collection, but only in a strategic and one hopes temporary retreat from perfection. Our scholarship in the humanities rests on assuming the possibility of that perfection even when every act of research, every scholarly reading of the past, is necessarily an interpretation of incomplete evidence.

The rest of my title—"the new English imperialism"—draws attention to my second main point, and again its political implications, namely the obvious fact that English is the *lingua franca* of our times, a language with world-wide significance whose linguistic matrix is still primarily—so far as it can be *recovered* and researched—the printed texts of the mother culture. Important as the oral use of English is today in international diplomacy, commerce and travel, and however divergent the forms of English are elsewhere, the *fond*, the historically generative source, is the national printed archive here, in all its diversity. In such a context, the very comprehensiveness and therefore the indiscriminate variety, of the English language collections have a value-function far beyond immediate national interests. Because language knows no social or educational boundaries, but saturates society in all its complexity, it serves indifferently the canonical and the marginal, the classical and the vulgar, the serious and the trivial. No one of those categories, in each of those contrasting pairs, is self-evidently more valuable *linguistically* than any other. What is marginal, vulgar and trivial is ultimately a *political* judgement.

Let me now try briefly to explain why I believe the principle of comprehensiveness must not be surrendered as a *principle* governing research in the humanities. Underlying it is another, a concept of human communities in all their diversity, and the consequent complexity of their interactions.

I begin with some simple examples of bibliographical scholarship. One relates to canonical texts.

First, it's salutary to recall that these (shall we say, Shakespeare's?) have been selected—*not* by Shakespeare himself (who thought of his communicative mode, the theatre, as an oral and visual, not printed, one), nor by his contemporaries (who thought him marginal, not central to their religiously obsessed culture), but unpredictably by later generations. In their own time, plays (like

Thomason's tracts) were deemed at best emphemeral, at worst trivial—if not downright evil in their undermining of established moral norms. They contributed to an output of print already felt to be embarrassing in its volume compared with that of earlier productive means, and, in that fact alone, uncontrollably subversive of the economic and political structures set up—by Government, through the Stationers' Company—to confine it.

Second, literary and textual, if not historical, scholarship has until very recently worked with a canon. Attempts like that of Leavis to formulate Revaluations, or Eliot's to dislodge Milton, were met with great hostility. The canon was sacrosanct. It embodied a principle of economy in making it unnecessary to spend time and library resources on the uncanonical texts of our past. In textual bibliography, several generations have devoted their energies to establishing authoritative versions of canonical texts, giving highest priority to the versions most likely to have been approved by the author.

In three respects, that emphasis, and its corollary that secondary texts were relatively insignificant, has proved to be misplaced. First, no detailed analysis of the printing of any one text (like Hinman's of the first folio) can be complete (and therefore closer to the truth) unless it takes account of the practice of concurrent printing—the fact that printers worked on several jobs at a time, many of them quite trivial in canonical terms but absolutely essential in establishing production patterns and their effect on the other texts more central to our interests. If such subordinate texts are not available for study, the major enterprise is weakened. The principle is one of comprehensive analysis. Second, because of specific production conditions, copies from the same edition differ one from another. In the hand-press period, it is safer to assume that duplicates don't exist. That working assumption requires extensive collation of copies to reveal textual differences in the canonical text itself. The principle is one of comprehensive examination. Third, it's even more the case that subsequent editions—so-called reprints—are rarely replicas of an earlier edition. The principle of degressive bibliography—based in turn as it is on pragmatic economic assumptions—assumes the priority of (as it were) first editions, and the degenerative processes of all subsequent transmissional stages. But such primary physical evidence of change in later versions, whether verbal or presentational, is essential for the analysis of cultural change in its economic, technological, political and broadly educational dimensions. A comprehensive catalogue of reprints and translations is itself a telling form of historical analysis.

In all three cases, bibliographical analysis in the interests of establishing more accurate canonical texts as well as their historical significance at various times and places, requires the comprehensive approach. Then, when we think of how we must (as scholars) *annotate* the canonical texts, we're immediately plunged into a densely *inter*-textual world—not even the books that Milton owned, but all those he read, have significance. It's the central business of literary scholarship to establish the catholicity of any author's reading, its formative influence on new work, and to record specific debts. Given the variety of texts and of authors, any prior restriction of the texts to be considered is a prior enfeebling of the scholarship that should flow from such an inquiry. It demands the comprehensive approach. It's only the indiscriminate nature of bibliography as a comprehensive record that fully declares the possibilities of inter-textual relationships.

But the value of secondary texts is not merely relative to canonical ones. One has only to mention the word "marginal" to recall the struggle of all minority groups throughout the centuries to modify the established *central* power structures. Occasionally, but it's usually impossible to tell which, some of those groups themselves succeed to power. When they do, and we seek to chart their origins in the ephemeral texts of their beginnings, we find ourselves frustrated for want of textual records. In our own day, the most significant have been those at the geographical periphery, the former colonial territories, whose cultures have so often been supplanted by a text-led European imperialism. But here at home, within the immediate geographical nation, as distinct from the linguistically extended cultural one, or the imperially extended political one, feminists, and those who have suffered from discrimination on grounds of race, religion, and social status, are among the most obvious groups whose texts were marginalised by canonical assumptions, subordinated by administrative decisions about low-use materials, or even suppressed by direct political action. The recovery from the past of their human experience is one of the most significant developments in modern literary and historical scholarship. But it's a scholarship which faces extraordinary problems in even establishing the primary textual record. Such examples warn us again that our guiding *principle* must be one of comprehensive hospitality to the textual records of *all segments of society*, however disadvantaged.

That comment leads me to my next. Canonical assumptions elevate the individual *author* as the prime referent of research. Yet in critical theory that notion has been greatly weakened by demonstrations that all authors are themselves communal products, the agents of language as a communal possession, which functions in composition and in reading, by generating texts. In that sense, any linguistic community is a kind of supra-author, whose works are multi-form. How a community creates meanings, and therefore texts, whether as writers or readers, can only be usefully determined by the comprehensive study of the audible and visible texts it makes.

Here I'd wish to push the case for comprehensive acquisition even further. Texts are not confined to printed books. The renewed dominance of the visual image as a communal possession, the new icons of television and film, the renewed complementary role of sound as the commonest communal medium for imparting and receiving information, all demand recognition. None of those, let alone even the (by comparison) subordinate and more manageable media of microform and electronic texts, gets any recognition at all in existing legislation relating to legal deposit. Yet I have still to encounter a compelling argument that, in *principle*, such records of our own culture—these *other* English-language collections—should be excluded from the national archive of recorded texts. There are of course any number of arguments from expediency. But given that state of affairs, to pull back in any way from our principled commitment to creating and preserving the archive that is legislated for, would seem to me to be even more seriously reprehensible. We should rather be pressing for legislation to capture the texts in those new, non-book forms.

It may seem far-fetched to state so categorically as I shall that any act of selection—even on economic grounds—is an act of censorship, but it's worth recalling the historical connection between copyright legislation and government control of the press. In the 16th and 17th centuries, the provisions for licensing went hand in hand with an entry of copyright. The registration of an economic property in a text was a reward for submission to authority and making oneself accessible to government control. The deposit of copies, haphazardly selective as it was, only belatedly came to serve some concept of a national archive, the records of the cultural nation. When the overt concern for censorship vanished in 1695 with the lapse of the last of the licensing acts, effective control over the formation of an archive was exercised by a largely negligent (because economically self-interested) book trade. That self-interest still functions in respect of public access. When a book still in copyright goes out of print, and replication is forbidden on economic grounds, access to the text in a national collection is a further justification of comprehensive legal deposit. Without it, we're again subject to a censorship which is no less a censorship for being economic. Access to non-book texts is almost wholly dictated by economics—i.e., commercial—considerations.

Again, looking historically at copyright deposit, it's salutary to focus, not on the indubitable *strengths*, but on the *weaknesses* of Bodley and Cambridge—as institutions that have always acted selectively on their legal deposit privileges, especially as selection was influenced by then accepted notions of curriculum utility. Reconstructing the archive for the period up to 1640 has taken us well over a hundred years. Reconstructing it for the Wing period and the 18th century has taken millions of pounds. Reconstructing it in the future for the non-book texts we have failed to acquire, record and preserve will cost incalculable sums.

Contesting the negligence or economic self-interest of those who fail to deposit their publications, resisting any erosion of the *principle* of comprehensive record, extending it to include all the new text forms of our own time, and demanding the resources to do so seem to me incontestable obligations of those whose professional duty is to create, preserve and ensure access to the records of the cultural nation and to advise government as to their management.

I hope I'm mistaken in reading it there, but what disappoints me in the interim report is a certain defeatest tone. The penultimate paragraph (9.2) uses an alarmist rhetoric, the effect of which is almost to frighten one into abandoning principle. Much the same reading is possible on page 7, para iv. There's a big difference between frightening our masters and frightening ourselves, but if we're not firm on the principle we certainly risk doing the latter. When we read that the relationship between acquisition and retention can't be avoided/ignored "when even the state rigorously selects its own public records," we're invited to ignore the more important fact that "the state" is no more at any one time than the policies—enlightened or repressive—of a particular administration. It is particularly and nakedly repressive at the moment of many forms of non-book text production.

It will of course be argued that nothing so radical nor so harmful to the reiterated concept of "the national heritage" is envisaged by the working party. And of course there will be trade-offs in the ways listed for further discussion—decentralisation and shared responsibility, lighter cataloguing, selective retention of highly perishable categories, surrogate copies, and so on. It may well be that spreading resources by adopting any of those tactics would enable the Library to add significantly to the public good. As I've written elsewhere, we needn't argue for the British Library as a monolithic national institution which must alone bear the curatorial responsibility for all forms of texts, and every text published in those forms.

But it does need to be recognised as shared responsibility in a common enterprise, which must remain, in principle, the comprehensive acquisition and retention of all forms of texts. Affirming that principle nationally is a proper leadership role for the British Library. This is both an immediate organisational function, and a philosophical one. The appeal to other institutions that benefit from copyright deposit must be couched in terms of high principle: namely, a shared commitment to the continued creation and preservation of (at the very least) the total printed archive as still the most tangible embodiment of the nation's cultural (and not just high-cultural) heritage. Any strategy that appears to involve surrender of that principle on grounds of expediency can only beget the response that the British Library's problems are precisely that—the British Library's problems. The Universities are facing enough of their own, and from the same "unquestionable" state source.

Whatever the final report's recommendations, I hope they will be explicitly presented as a series of compromises enforced by a political will that professional librarians find inimical to the exercise of their responsibilities. We may be overruled, but the all-important principle should still be affirmed. Then at least the grounds of our dereliction from principle will be clear for all to see and ultimately to assess.

A Chronological Bibliography of McKenzie's Writings

"Richard van Bleeck's Portrait of William Congreve as Contemplative (1715)." *Review of English Studies* 51, no. 201 (2000): 41–61.

Bibliography and the Sociology of Texts. Cambridge: Cambridge University Press, 1999. 130 pp. Second edition of the Panizzi Lectures listed below (1986). It also incorporates (pp. 77–130) a revised version of "Oral Culture, Literacy, and Print in Early New Zealand: The Treaty of Waitangi" listed below (1985), together with a revised postscript to this essay.

Bibliografia e sociologia dei testi. Milano: Edizioni Sylvestre Bonnard, 1999. 136 pp. Includes accounts of the author by Renato Pasta ("Ciò che è passato è il prologo") and by Roger Chartier ("Testi, forme, interpretazioni"). [Italian version of *Bibliography and the Sociology of Texts* (as listed below, 1986). Initially published December 1998 (ISBN: 88-86842-04-X) but withdrawn for typographic reasons; line spacing reduced, and reprinted and republished January 1999 (ISBN: 88-86842-08-2).]

"Another Congreve Autograph Poem for the Bodleian." *Bodleian Library Record* 16, no. 5 (1999): 399–410.

"William Congreve in Dutch (1695) and His Travels Abroad (1700)." *The Library*, 6th ser., 21 (March 1999): 67–73.

"*Mea culpa*: Voltaire's Retraction of His Comments Critical of Congreve." *Review of English Studies*, n.s., 49 (November 1998): 461–65.

"Trading Places? England 1689—France 1789." In *The Darnton Debate: Books and Revolution in the Eighteenth Century*. Studies on Voltaire and the Eighteenth Century, vol. 359, ed. Haydn T. Mason, 1–24. Oxford: Voltaire Foundation, 1998. Republished in the Vif paperback series (Oxford: Voltaire Foundation, 1999, 1–24).

"Stationers' Company Liber A. An Apologia." In *The Stationers' Company and the Book Trade, 1550–1990*, ed. Robin Myers and Michael Harris, 35–63. Winchester: St. Paul's Bibliographies, 1997.

"Introduction." In *The British Book Trade and Its Customers, 1450–1900: Historical Essays for Robin Myers*, ed. Arnold Hunt, Giles Mandelbrote, and Alison Shell, 1–8. Winchester: St. Paul's Bibliographies, 1997.

"A New Congreve Literary Autograph." *Bodleian Library Record* 15, no. 4 (1996): 292–99.

"*What's Past Is Prologue*": *The Bibliographical Society and History of the Book*. The Bibliographical Society Centenary Lecture, 14 July 1992. Hearthstone Publications, 1993. 32 pp.

"Robert Coupland Harding, 1849–1916: Printer, Typographer, Journalist." In *The Dictionary of New Zealand Biography*. Vol. 2, 1870–1900, 194–95. Wellington: Bridget William Books, 1993.

"Re-covering the Past: Conservation and Scholarship," an address delivered as part of a seminar series, "Preserving Our Library Heritage," at Oxford University in May 1993; privately circulated.

"Congreve Cleans Up His Act." In *Of Pavlova, Poetry, and Paradigms: Essays in Honour of Harry Orsman*, ed. Laurie Bauer and Christine Franzen, 91–97. Wellington: Victoria University Press, 1993.

"Robert Coupland Harding on Design in Typography." In *An Index of Civilisation: Studies of Printing and Publishing History in Honour of Keith Maslen*, ed. R. Harvey, W. Kirsop, and B. J. McMullin, 187–205. Clayton: Centre for Bibliographical and Textual Studies, Monash University, 1993.

"History of the Book." In *The Book Encompassed*, ed. Peter Davison, 290–301. Cambridge: Cambridge University Press, 1992.

"The London Book Trade in 1644." In *Bibliographia: Lectures 1975–1988 by Recipients of the Marc Fitch Prize for Bibliography*, ed. John Horden, 131–52. Oxford: Leopard's Head Press, 1992.

"Éditorial" [on retrospective national and European bibliographical catalogues], *In Octavo*, no. 2 (1992): 1–16.

"The Economies of Print, 1550–1750: Scales of Production and Conditions of Constraint." In *Producione e Commercio della Carta e del Libro secc. XIII–XVIII*. Istituto Internazionale di Storia Economica 'F. Datini' Prato, Serie II—Atti delle 'Settimane di Studi' e altri Convegni 23, a cura di Simonetta Cavaciocchi, 389–425. Prato: Le Monnier, 1992. Cf. also "Dibattito," 1022–23.

La bibliographie et la sociologie des textes. Préface de Roger Chartier. Paris: Éditions du Cercle de la Librairie, 1991. 119 pp. French version of *Bibliography and the Sociology of Texts* as listed below, 1986.

"Computers and the Humanities: A Personal Synthesis of Conference Issues." In *Scholarship and Technology in the Humanities*, ed. May Katzen, 157–69. London: Bowker/Saur, 1991.

"J. C. T. Oates, 1912–1990." *Transactions of the Cambridge Bibliographical Society* 9 (1990): 401–8.

"Speech—Manuscript—Print." In *New Directions in Textual Studies*, ed. D. Oliphant and R. Bradford, 86–109. Austin: Harry Ransom Humanities Research Center, 1990. Also published as vol. 20, nos. 1/2 of the *Library Chronicle of the University of Texas at Austin*, 1990.

"Bibliography and History: Seventeenth-Century England." The Lyell Lectures, University of Oxford, May–June 1988. i. "Textual Evidence"; ii. "Speech—Manuscript—Print"; iii. "Censorship"; iv. "Simmons"; v. "Trading Places." Not yet published together.

"Poet as / Poet to / Printer: Letters from Denis Glover to John Johnson." In *Sinnlichkeit in Bild und Klang: Festschift für Paul Hoffman zum 70. Geburtstag*, ed. H. Delbrück, 26–54. Stuttgart: Hans-Dieter Heinz, 1987.

Bibliography and the Sociology of Texts. The Panizzi Lectures, 1985 (inaugural). London: British Library, 1986. 70 pp.

"'The Game of Quadrille. An Allegory': A Congreve Attribution." *Book Collector* 34 (Summer 1985): 209–13.

"On Scholars and Librarians, and Other Thoughts from New Zealand." In *Australian and New Zealand Studies*. British Library Occasional Papers 4, ed. Patricia MacLaren-Turner, 207–9. London: British Library, 1985.

"The Sociology of a Text: Orality, Literacy, and Print in Early New Zealand." *The Library*, 6th ser., 6 (December 1984): 333–65. Presidential address to the Bibliographical Society, London. Reprinted as *Oral Culture, Literacy, and Print in Early New Zealand* (Wellington: Victoria University Press, 1985). Reprinted in *The Social History of Language*, ed. Peter Burke and Roy Porter (Cambridge: Cambridge University Press, 1987),

161–97. Reprinted, with a postscript, in *Histoire du Livre: Nouvelles Orientations*, sous la direction de Hans Erich Bödeker (Paris: IMEC Éditions/Éditions de la Maison des Sciences de l'Homme, 1995), 349–82, 484–86.

"Six Variant Readings in a Recent Edition of Congreve's Comedies." *Notes and Queries* 31 (September 1984): 209–13.

"Stretching a Point: Or, The Case of the Spaced-out Comps." *Studies in Bibliography 37* (1984): 106–21.

"Universal Availability of Publications." In *Universal Availability of Publications*, 1–6. A Symposium. National Library Bulletin no. 18. Wellington, 1983.

"Type-Bound Topography." *Times Literary Supplement*, 17 December 1982, 1403.

"Printing in England from Caxton to Milton." In *The Age of Shakespeare: The New Pelican Guide to English Literature*, ed. B. Ford, 207–26. Harmondsworth: Penguin Books, 1982.

A Selection from "Typo," a New Zealand Typographic Journal, 1887–1897, edited by R. Coupland Harding. Wellington: Distributed by the Wai-te-ata Press, 1982. 169 pp.

"John Milton, Alexander Turnbull, and Kathleen Coleridge." *Turnbull Library Record 14, no. 2 (1981)*: 106–11.

"Typography and Meaning: The Case of William Congreve." In *Buch und Buchhandel in Europa im achtzehnten Jahrhundert*, ed. Giles Barber and Bernhard Fabian. Vol. 4 of *Wolfenbütteler Schriften zur Geschichte des Buchwesens*, 81–125. Hamburg: Hauswedell, 1981.

"'The History of Our National Debts and Taxes' (1751–53): Adam Smith's Copy." *BSANZ Bulletin* 4, no. 4 (1980): 289–90.

"Milton's Printers: Matthew, Mary, and Samuel Simmons." *Milton Quarterly* 14 (October 1980): 87–91.

"And Suddenly Last Summer: The Early Imprints Project in New Zealand." *New Zealand Libraries* 43, no. 2 (1980): 29–30.

"Dealers in Books outside the Stationers' Company circa 1685." *Factotum* 8 (April 1980): 12–13.

"Music from the Wai-te-ata Press." *Canzona* 1, no. 3 (1980): 71–72.

Printing, Bookselling, and Their Allied Trades in New Zealand circa 1900: Selections from "The Cyclopaedia of New Zealand." Ed. with K. Coleridge. Wellington: Distributed by the Wai-te-ata Press, 1980. 135 pp.

"When Congreve Made a Scene." *Transactions of the Cambridge Bibliographical Society* 7 (1979): 338–42. Journal presented to J. C. T. Oates.

Stationers' Company Apprentices, 1701–1800. Oxford: Oxford Bibliographical Society, 1978. xii + 514 pp.

"Richard Bentley's Design for the Cambridge University Press, c. 1696." *Transactions of the Cambridge Bibliographical Society* 6 (1976): 322–27.

"To Bishop the Balls." *Notes and Queries* 23 (March 1976): 107–8.

"The London Book Trade in the Later Seventeenth Century." Unpublished typescript of the Sandars Lectures for 1975–76. Distributed privately, but copies deposited in the British Library, the English Faculty Library, Oxford, and the University Library, Cambridge.

"Masters, Wardens, and Liverymen of the Stationers' Company, 1605–1800." 36 pp. Supplement to *Bibliographical Newsletter* 2, nos. 1–2 (1974).

"The London Book Trade in 1668." *WORDS: Wai-te-ata Studies in Literature* 4 (1974): 75–92.

Stationers' Company Apprentices, 1641–1700. Oxford: Oxford Bibliographical Society, 1974. 234 pp.

"The Staple of News and the Late Plays." In *A Celebration of Ben Jonson*, ed. William Blissett et al., 83–128. Toronto: University of Toronto Press, 1973.

Introduction to *A Guide to the Archives of the Cambridge University Press*, by E. S. Leedham-Green. Cambridge: Chadwyck-Healey, 1973.

"'Indenting the Stick' in the First Quarto of *King Lear* (1608)." *Papers of the Bibliographical Society of America*, 67.2 (1973): 125–30.

"Eight Quarto Proof Sheets of 1594 Set by Formes: A fruitfull commentarie." *The Library*, 5th ser., 18 (March 1973): 1–13.

"With Acknowledgements to McKerrow." *Times Literary Supplement*, 6 October 1972, 1024. Review of Philip Gaskell's *A New Introduction to Bibliography*.

"The Printer of the Third Volume of Jonson's *Workes* (1640)." *Studies in Bibliography* 25 (1972): 177–78.

The Hog Hath Lost His Pearle, by Robert Tailor. London, 1614. Edited for the Malone Society. Oxford: Malone Society, 1972. xvii + [64] pp.

"A Cambridge Playhouse of 1638." *Renaissance Drama*, n.s. 3 (1970): 263–72.

"The Genesis of the Cambridge University Press, 1695–6." *Transactions of the Cambridge Bibliographical Society* 5 (1969): 79.

"Printers of the Mind: Some Notes on Bibliographical Theories and Printing-House Practices." *Studies in Bibliography* 22 (1969): 1–75.

"Blake's *Poetical Sketches* (1783)." *Turnbull Library Record*, n.s., 1, no. 3 (1968): 4–8.

"William Allingham's Notebook of Poems by Blake." *Turnbull Library Record*, n.s., 1, no. 3 (1968): 9–11.

A Ledger of Charles Ackers, Printer of "The London Magazine." Co-edited with J. C. Ross. Oxford: Oxford Bibliographical Society, 1968. x + 331 pp.

"Hamlet." *Act*, no. 4 (1967): 11–20.

F. R. Leavis, 1924–1964: A Check-List. London: Chatto and Windus, 1966. 87 pp. Compiled jointly with Mrs. M. P. Allum.

The Cambridge University Press, 1696–1712: A Bibliographical Study. 2 vols. Cambridge: Cambridge University Press, 1966. xv + 432 pp.; ix + 381 pp.

An Early Printing House at Work: Some Notes for Bibliographers. Wellington: Wai-te-ata Press, 1965. 13 pp.

"Samuel Richardson, Mr W—, and Lady T—." *Notes and Queries* (August 1964): 299–300.

"[The Paintings of] Don Peebles." *Landfall* 70 (June 1964): 160–63.

"Shakespeare's Dream of Knowledge [on *A Midsummer Night's Dream*]." *Landfall* 69 (March 1964): 40–48.

Stationers' Company Apprentices, 1605–1640. Charlottesville: Bibliographical Society of the University of Virginia, 1961. 178 pp.

"Printers' Perks: Paper Windows and Copy Money." *The Library*, 5th ser., 15 (December 1960): 288–91.

"Two Bills for Printing, 1620–22." *The Library*, 5th ser., 15 (June 1960): 129–32.

"The Writings of Sir Walter Greg, 1945–59." *The Library*, 5th ser., 15 (March 1960): 42–46.

"A List of Printers' Apprentices, 1605–1640." *Studies in Bibliography* 13 (1960): 109–41.

"The Author of *Tables for Purchasing Leases*, Attributed to Sir Isaac Newton." *Transactions of the Cambridge Bibliographical Society* 3 (1960): 165–66.

"Press-Figures: A Case History of 1701–1703." *Transactions of the Cambridge Bibliographical Society* 3 (1960): 96–103.

"Notes on Printing at Cambridge, c. 1590." *Transactions of the Cambridge Bibliographical Society* 3 (1959): 96–103.

"Shakespearian Punctuation—a New Beginning?" *Review of English Studies*, n.s., 10 (November 1959): 361–70. Reprinted in *Reader in the Language of Shakespearean Drama*, ed. V. Salmon and E. Burness, 445–54. Amsterdam: John Benjamins, 1987.

"Compositor B's Role in *The Merchant of Venice* Q2 (1619)." *Studies in Bibliography* 12 (1959): 75–90.

"Apprenticeship in the Stationers' Company, 1555–1640." *The Library*, 5th ser., 13 (December 1958): 292–99.

"Men Made Free of the Stationer's Company, 1605–1640—Some Corrections to the List in Arber's Transcript." *Notes and Queries*, October 1958, 429–30.

Reviews (not listed): in *The Library*, *Times Literary Supplement*, *Notes and Queries*, *Book Collector*, *AUMLA*, *Cambridge Review*, *Landfall*, *Act*, *New Zealand Libraries*, and so on.

Edited, printed, and published: *WORDS: Wai-te-ata Studies in Literature*, nos. 1–4 ([appearing irregularly] 1965–74).